Electoral Reform
in the
United States

Electoral Reform
in the
United States

Proposals for Combating Polarization and Extremism

edited by
**Larry Diamond, Edward B. Foley,
and Richard H. Pildes**

LYNNE
RIENNER
PUBLISHERS

BOULDER
LONDON

Published in the United States of America in 2025 by
Lynne Rienner Publishers, Inc.
1800 30th Street, Suite 314, Boulder, Colorado 80301
www.rienner.com

Library of Congress Cataloging-in-Publication Data
Names: Diamond, Larry Jay, editor. | Foley, Edward B., editor. | Pildes,
    Richard H., editor.
Title: Electoral reform in the United States : proposals for combating
    polarization and extremism / edited by Larry Diamond, Edward B. Foley,
    and Richard H. Pildes.
Description: Boulder, Colorado : Lynne Rienner Publishers, Inc., 2025. |
    Includes bibliographical references and index. | Summary: "The result of
    a two-year bipartisan task force, presents practical ideas for reforms
    designed to counter the political polarization and extremism that has
    become part of the US electoral process"— Provided by publisher.
Identifiers: LCCN 2024044661 (print) | LCCN 2024044662 (ebook) | ISBN
    9781962551625 (hardcover) | ISBN 9781962551649 (paperback) | ISBN
    9781962551632 (ebook) | ISBN 9781962551656 (ebook other)
Subjects: LCSH: Elections—United States. | Voting—United States. |
    Polarization (Social sciences)—Political aspects—United States.
Classification: LCC JK1976 .E388 2025 (print) | LCC JK1976 (ebook) | DDC
    324.973—dc23/eng/20241030
LC record available at https://lccn.loc.gov/2024044661
LC ebook record available at https://lccn.loc.gov/2024044662

British Cataloguing in Publication Data
A Cataloguing in Publication record for this book
is available from the British Library.

Printed and bound in the United States of America

The paper used in this publication meets the requirements
of the American National Standard for Permanence of
Paper for Printed Library Materials Z39.48-1992.

5   4   3   2   1

Contents

Acknowledgments

The editors of this volume, in addition to thanking the chapter authors and the task force members for their contributions, wish to identify several individuals who made this work possible. The planning and operations of the task force were supervised by a steering committee that consisted of (besides the three editors) Didi Kuo, Ray La Raja, Frances Lee, and Charles Stewart. The steering committee met for untold hours to advance the task force's mission.

The task force was also supported by the superlative assistance of, first, Gillian Thomson and, later, Issrah Saleh, as well as others at the Ohio State University's Moritz College of Law, where administration of the task force was housed. Ty McCormick's expert editing helped to merge the separate chapters of this book into a coherent whole. Lynne Rienner and her team undertook extraordinary efforts to expedite the publication of the book so that its analysis could most benefit those engaged in on-the-ground efforts at electoral reform. The task force and publication of the book were generously funded by grants from Arnold Ventures, the Skoll Foundation, the NYU Law School Center on Democratic Governance, and Erica Lawson.

Task Force Members

Inclusion in this list does not necessarily entail agreement with the contents of the book, and institutional affiliations are included for identification only.

R. Michael Alvarez: Professor of Political and Computational Social Science, California Institute of Technology

Julia Azari: Professor of Political Science, Marquette University

Robert G. Boatright: Professor of Political Science, Clark University, and Director of Research, National Institute for Civil Discourse, University of Arizona

Brandice Canes-Wrone: Professor of Political Science and Maurice R. Greenberg Senior Fellow, Hoover Institution, Stanford University

Guy-Uriel Charles: Charles Ogletree Jr. Professor of Law and Director at the Charles Hamilton Institute for Race and Justice, Harvard Law School

Larry Diamond: Senior Fellow, Hoover Institution, and Mosbacher Senior Fellow, Freeman Spogli Institute for International Studies, Stanford University

Lee Drutman: Senior Fellow, New America

Edward B. Foley: Charles W. Ebersold and Florence Whitcomb Ebersold Chair in Constitutional Law and Director, Election Law, Moritz College of Law, Ohio State University

John Fortier: Senior Fellow, American Enterprise Institute

Erika Franklin Fowler: Professor of Government and Director, Wesleyan Media Project, Wesleyan University

William A. Galston: Ezra K. Zilkha Chair and Senior Fellow, Governance Studies, Brookings Institution

Jacob M. Grumbach: Associate Professor at the Goldman School of Public Policy, UC Berkeley

D. Sunshine Hillygus: Professor of Political Science and Professor in the Sanford School of Public Policy, Duke University

Elaine Kamarck: Director at the Center for Effective Public Management and Senior Fellow, Governance Studies, Brookings Institution

Michael S. Kang: Class of 1940 Professor of Law, Pritzker School of Law, Northwestern University

Rachel Kleinfeld: Senior Fellow, Democracy, Conflict, and Governance Program, Carnegie Endowment for International Peace

Didi Kuo: Associate Director of Research and Senior Research Scholar, Center on Democracy, Development and the Rule of Law, Stanford University

Ray La Raja: Professor of Political Science and Codirector of UMass Poll, University of Massachusetts Amherst

Frances Lee: Professor of Politics and Public Affairs, Department of Politics, Princeton University

Lisa Marshall Manheim: Charles I. Stone Professor of Law, University of Washington

Seth Masket: Professor of Political Science and Director of the Center on American Politics, University of Denver

Eric S. Maskin: Adams University Professor and Professor of Economics and Mathematics, Harvard University

Nolan McCarty: Susan Dod Brown Professor of Politics and Public Affairs and Director, Center for Data-Driven Social Science, Princeton University

Jennifer McCoy: Distinguished University Professor of Political Science, Georgia State University, and Nonresident Scholar in the Democracy, Conflict, and Governance Program, Carnegie Endowment for International Peace

Michael Morley: Sheila M. McDevitt Professor, Florida State University College of Law

Hans Noel: Associate Professor, Department of Government, Georgetown University

Richard H. Pildes: Sudler Family Professor of Constitutional Law, New York University School of Law

Lynda W. Powell: Professor Emeritus of Political Science, University of Rochester

Bradley A. Smith: Josiah H. Blackmore II/Shirley M. Nault Professor of Law, Capital University Law School

Charles Stewart III: Kenan Sahin Distinguished Professor of Political Science; Codirector, Caltech/MIT Voting Technology Project; and Director, MIT Election Data and Science Lab, Massachusetts Institute of Technology

Caroline J. Tolbert: Professor of Political Science and University Distinguished Chair, University of Iowa

1

The Election Reform Imperative

*Larry Diamond, Edward B. Foley,
and Richard H. Pildes*

Scholars, journalists, and the American people broadly agree that American democracy is in difficulty, if not grave danger. Recent surveys consistently find that 50 to 60 percent of Americans are not satisfied with the way democracy is working in the United States. And they think the problem is systemic.[1] In a 2021 Pew survey, a stunning 85 percent of Americans said the US political system either needs "major changes" or must be "completely reformed"; 58 percent of adults who reported wanting substantial reforms said "they are not confident the system *can* change."[2] These figures were among the highest of all advanced industrial democracies surveyed in 2021.[3] In 2022, Americans' confidence in their national government was the lowest among citizens of G7 democracies (31 percent),[4] about the level of Nigeria and Venezuela.[5] And early that same year, a Quinnipiac poll found that substantial majorities of both Democrats and Republicans believed "the nation's democracy is in danger of collapse."[6]

One result—or at least correlate—of declining public satisfaction with the way democracy is working in the United States is that Americans' support for the specific institutions and norms of democracy also is declining. Some studies find a generational erosion in support for democracy as a form of government, with "more supportive older generations being replaced by less supportive younger ones."[7] This pattern of erosion may have started decades ago, but it seems to have accelerated more recently. According to a recent survey of the Democracy Fund's Voter Study Group, comprised of scholars and analysts focused on public sentiment, few Americans show a consistent commitment to democracy.[8]

A major driver of America's democratic distemper is deepening partisan polarization. Over the past three decades, the American public and, even more so, the Congress have become increasingly polarized on partisan and ideological lines. Part of this stems from a political realignment that has sorted most right-of-center voters into the Republican camp and most left-of-center voters into the Democratic camp, with very little ideological overlap between them.[9] But the problem is not simply that Democrats and Republicans are further apart in their beliefs. It is that they are also much more likely to hold extremely unfavorable views of the other party and even to regard it as an existential threat to the country's well-being.[10] This is known as "affective polarization," which reflects "the extent to which citizens feel more negatively toward other parties than toward their own."[11] That emotional gap, as measured on a 100-point "thermometer" scale, has doubled over forty years—from 27 points in 1978 to 56 points in 2020.[12] Between 1994 and 2022, the share of Democrats with an unfavorable view of Republicans more than tripled (from 17 to 54 percent), as did the share of Republicans with an unfavorable view of Democrats (from 21 to 64 percent).[13] In recent years, this rise in partisan animosity has corresponded with a sharp increase in the percentage of voters who see members of the other party as immoral.[14]

One reason for this is that intense partisans of each party "hold major misbeliefs about the other party's preferences that lead them to think there is far less shared policy belief."[15] Some of these misperceptions no doubt reflect the exaggerated messaging and sense of fear and dread that are promoted daily on social media. But the polarization process has been going on at least since the mid-1990s, with the rise of "shock radio" and cable TV news. And while some other advanced industrial democracies have experienced a mounting emotive polarization of politics, the United States stands alone in the scale of impact. Among twelve advanced democracies (the United States, Canada, Australia, New Zealand, Japan, and seven European countries), "the U.S. experienced the most rapid growth in affective polarization" over the four decades ending in 2020.[16]

Americans are also reacting to the fact that the Congress has become increasingly polarized and dysfunctional. The voting patterns of the two major parties have become ever more ideologically polarized in both the House and Senate, a process that began around 1980 and has accelerated ever since. While part of this stems from the decampment of southern Democrats to the Republican Party, the biggest factor has been the growing shift to the right in average Republican voting patterns in

Congress.[17] There is now essentially no ideological overlap in voting patterns between the least conservative Republican and the least liberal Democrat in either house of Congress.

Intense polarization threatens democracy for several reasons. First, it makes governing more difficult. Particularly in a country with bicameralism and the separation of powers, it is harder to forge the minimum consensus needed to pass legislation and implement policies when representatives of the two parties—and behind them, their most vocal supporters—are so far apart in their views and policy preferences. A wide emotional gap between the parties—with each viewing the other as a mortal threat to the nation's future—makes cooperation more difficult still.

Second, intense polarization makes it more difficult to sustain policies over time. Even if a temporary majority can adopt a certain policy, the next administration or the next Congress may seek to repeal it. It is difficult to govern when policy lurches from one strongly defined position to another in a short period. Both markets and social actors need some degree of stability and predictability to function well.

Third, opposing political parties that take an extremely dim view of one another also harbor mutual distrust. And that may lead their partisans to reject the results of an election out of a belief—and an underlying readiness to believe, in a context where the opposition party is essentially seen as evil—that electoral defeat could only have been produced by fraud or manipulation of the rules.

Finally, if both parties view the other as an existential threat to their values, they will be more inclined to do whatever is necessary to keep that party from coming to power or from exercising power effectively. In such a scenario, adherence to the rules breaks down and politics becomes political warfare, a naked struggle for dominance. That, in turn, leads to the kind of violence and insurgency witnessed on January 6.

Political extremism is thus both a handmaiden and a key driver of political polarization. We use the word "extremism" here, and throughout this book, in two senses. As Seymour Martin Lipset and Earl Raab put it in their classic *The Politics of Unreason: Right-Wing Extremism in America, 1790–1977*, there is "extremism as a generalized measure of deviance from the political norm; and extremism as a specific tendency to violate democratic procedures."[18] In this volume, substantively and in the literal sense of the term, we use extremism to refer to political actors who are located at extreme ends of the ideological spectrum. Extremists are those whose ideologies and policy preferences place them on the far right or far left of the political continuum, making compromise with them difficult. But we also use extremism in a behavioral sense to refer to political actors who are willing to act in extreme, or what Lipset and Raab called "politically repressive," ways to acquire or wield political power. For political extremists, the outcome of political conflict is more important than adhering to democratic methods. That risks grave danger to democracy, of which the January 6 assault on the Capitol was one manifestation.

Dating all the way back to Aristotle, scholars of democracy have worried about the threat that extremism and polarization pose to democracy. This has led to a long-standing prominent scholarly and philosophical tradition arguing for the importance of a "culture of *moderation, accommodation, cooperation,* and *bargaining* among political elites," so that laws can be made, budgets passed, and governing done even when there are sharp differences among opposing parties.[19] These elements of political culture are necessary to solve a fundamental dilemma intrinsic to democracy. Democracy is about competition among parties, interests, and policy preferences. If there were no clear differences or competing interests expressed in politics, democracy would become unnecessary, vacuous, and lifeless. But if conflict becomes too intense and existential, it is difficult to contain within constitutional boundaries. Hence, for democracy to be sustainable over time, citizens must commit to pluralism by accepting the legitimacy of and need for "coexistence" among diverse "political entities, ethnic groups, [and] ideas."[20]

This commitment is bound up with other critical democratic norms: mutual trust, tolerance of opposing beliefs and positions, pragmatism, and a willingness to compromise—as well as an underlying commitment to democracy and its specific constitutional rules.[21] With mutual tolerance—the acceptance by competing parties of one another as "legitimate rivals"—must go "forbearance, or the idea that politicians should exercise restraint in deploying their institutional prerogatives," write Steven Levitsky and Daniel Ziblatt.[22] These two norms, they argue, have constituted "the guardrails of American democracy" for most of the twentieth century. But what happens when those guardrails weaken, as they have been doing in the twenty-first?

If major changes in underlying forces—in the economy, social relations, globalization, media, technology, and so forth—erode the cultural guardrails of democracy, then it falls to political institutions to fortify them. If norms are no longer sufficient to contain polarization and discourage extremism in politics, then we must examine whether and how institutional designs can generate incentives for moderation or at least a willingness to compromise—by making getting elected harder for factional candidates (who are more likely to be extremists, in both senses of the term) and easier for politicians whom a majority of the general electorate support. If the institutional arrangements of our democracy—for example, the way we elect our legislators and president—worked so well for so many decades, why do we need to change them now? The answer, many argue, and which we explore in this book, is that the old rules are operating in a new political and social context. What worked passably well for many decades, and indeed for most periods since the American founding, may no longer be suitable for our intensely polarizing times.

The Focus of This Book

This book is the product of a task force that was formed in the aftermath of the January 6, 2021, attack at the Capitol aimed at disrupting the counting of votes in the 2020 presidential election. The purpose of the task force was to consider possible institutional reforms to elections in the United States that would diminish extremism and polarization and hence the potential for future existential threats to American democracy. The guiding premise of the task force has been that the current institutional rules enable politically extreme actors to achieve electoral success to a greater degree than voters harbor extremist views. In other words, the current system enhances rather than reduces the voice and power of extreme candidates and factions. And this also makes our politics and governing institutions more polarized and less amenable to compromise. Our goal has been to identify reforms that could reverse the overrepresentation of extremists and ease polarization. The task force consisted of thirty-one political scientists, law professors, and other scholars, whose names are listed at the end of the acknowledgements.

Our focus in this book is on a limited set of potential reforms to several key elements of the democratic system of the United States: our method for electing representatives and state executive offices, the system of primary elections by which we choose candidates for the general election ballot, the presidential nominations process, and campaign finance.

First, we examine the way that legislators—principally, members of Congress and state legislatures—are elected in the United States. As we explain later in this chapter, the United States is now among a minority of democracies in the world that continue to use the simple plurality method of "first past the post" (FPTP), in which legislators are elected from single-member districts and (in most states) whoever gets the plurality of votes wins. Then we consider (in Chapters 2 and 3) two major alternatives to the current system of "first past the post": various forms of ranked-choice voting (RCV) that enable voters to indicate their preferences among candidates, with the victor required to win a majority of votes, and multimember districts using proportional representation (PR). Chapter 4 offers a skeptical view of PR, while Chapter 5 analyzes alternatives to the current system of nominating candidates in party primary elections, a system that has become popular in many democracies over the last century but which the United States has implemented to an unusual degree. Chapter 6 examines the unique system used in the United States to nominate major-party presidential candidates. And Chapter 7 takes up the issue that has most vexed American political reformers in recent decades: campaign finance.

We will return to these themes shortly, but first we want to address questions we anticipate many readers will have about what we left out. Initially, we had planned to examine the process of redrawing congressional and state legislative districts and the common historical practice of gerrymandering, in which state legislatures draw districts in such a manner as to maximize the number of seats their party can win (while also maximizing their own personal chances of reelection). Like most other scholars of democracy, the members of our task force generally consider gerrymandering to be a sordid practice that does not serve the interests of democracy. It is not so much the shape of the resulting districts (which can be shamelessly stretched and squeezed to meet political objectives) that reformers object to as it is the outcome, which often violates democratic principles in two senses. First, it artificially constrains competition by giving incumbents of the party controlling the process "safe" districts that the other party has little to no chance of winning. (Districts often lean heavily toward one party or the other for reasons of geographic sorting, but gerrymandering carries this natural bias to an extreme and, perversely, also gives the opposing party safe districts, since it packs as many of their supporters into as few districts as possible). And second, where one party is firmly in control of a state's redistricting process, it typically draws boundaries in a grossly unfair manner, so that it can expect to win a much larger share of seats (in the state legislature and for the state's congressional delegation) than its share of the vote.

Ultimately, however, we decided not to examine legislative districting because the process, which takes place at the start of each decade after the decennial census, was already nearing completion just as our task force was organizing its work. This meant that it would be eight years before our recommendations could inform the next round of redistricting. In addition, even if the problems of gerrymandering were solved, the problems of polarization and extremism would persist. Elections for statewide offices, such as governor and US senator, are not subject to redistricting and thus cannot be gerrymandered, and yet they too are afflicted by polarization and extremism. The US Senate, like the US House, has become noticeably more polarized in recent years. Especially among Republicans, less extreme incumbents (such as former Ohio senator Rob Portman) are being replaced by more extreme officeholders (such as J. D. Vance, who succeeded Portman in the Senate and at the time of this writing was former president Donald Trump's running mate), even when the seat is occupied by someone nominally of the same party. For these reasons, our task force embraced the goal of considering potential remedies for the increasing problem of extremism other than redistricting reform.

Readers may also have hoped we would address possible reforms to the Electoral College or the structure of the US Senate. Among the world's democracies with popularly elected executive presidents, the United States is utterly unique in its method of choosing the president not by a direct popular vote but through the indirect method of an electoral college. The Senate, meanwhile, is the most undemocratically structured legislative chamber of any among modern democracies. But given the constitutionally embedded nature of these institutions, we leave to others more extended critiques and analyses of them.

Reforming the Electoral System

All democracies face a systemic challenge: How do they translate votes for parties and candidates into the election of officeholders, including allocation of seats in a legislature? Americans take this challenge for granted because, from the beginning, members of Congress were chosen by the simple and intuitive method of "first past the post" in single-member districts, as legislators were in all former British colonies. In the classic British (and, for the most part, American) version of this method, whoever wins the most votes in a single-member district is elected, even if they fall short of a majority. Hence this system is known as the "single-member-district, plurality" (SMDP) method.

But this is just one of many potential ways of electing a legislature, and even a single seat (whether for the legislature or the executive) can be elected by methods other than a first-past-the-post plurality. Indeed, in some states at the time of the nation's founding (especially in New England), winning an election required a majority, not just a plurality, of votes and thus necessitated some sort of runoff procedure if no candidate received a majority. Moreover, the implications of this system for political polarization and extremism may change over time with social circumstances and with the method used by parties to nominate candidates for the general election. Thus, we give considerable attention in this volume to the interaction between general election systems and the structure of primary elections (the principal focus of Chapter 5). There is no one obvious and perfect answer to the question of which electoral system is best and, we would argue, no universal answer that is best for all societies. Indeed, as one of us (Edward B. Foley) argues in the next chapter, there is a strong case to be made for experimentation among US states to find the best methods for countering rising political extremism, given states' diverse political and social profiles. One of our purposes in this volume is to present a menu of reform options from which states might choose.

No electoral system translates the individual preferences of voters into a collective choice in a purely passive and neutral way,[23] although an electoral system can produce results more or less aligned with the collective preferences of the electorate.[24] Thus, it is necessary to consider what democratic aims or values an electoral system seeks to advance and to recognize the inevitable trade-offs involved. Prominent among the goals of any democratic electoral system is to enable an expression of the public will, in at least two senses. First, who should be given the responsibility for governing? And second, how can governing officials and legislative representatives be held accountable for their decisions and actions? Another consideration that has figured in debates over electoral system design is "governability"—what electoral system offers the best prospect of producing a government that can rule effectively, by virtue of enjoying broad majority support, political legitimacy, and durability (so it can survive until the next election). A principle strongly related to majority support is discouraging extremism, or extreme factionalism. This has been a core concern of our project. By this logic, a government can be more effective if it does not veer too far programmatically from the preferences of the median voter.

These principles of governability may complement or be in tension with the goal of fairness. To what extent does an electoral system produce outcomes that are viewed by citizens as a fair and accurate expression of the preferences they register at the ballot box? One measure of fairness is proportionality, for example, with regard to the representation of parties in parliament. If electoral districts are drawn in fair and neutral fashion, FPTP electoral systems may often give each political party a share of legislative seats reasonably close to its respective share of the vote. But this is not always the case. Distortions can arise in either direction, with parties winning a much smaller share of seats than their vote share, or vice versa. To the extent that proportionality is the value that system designers most wish to elevate, the natural method for doing so is proportional representation. PR systems are designed to give each party a share of seats in parliament proportional to their share of the vote (after they clear an electoral threshold at the district level, the national level, or both). But PR systems vary considerably in design and in their degree of proportionality, with significant implications for the competing values of electoral system design.

However, proportionality is only one metric of fairness. Within the context of a single-member-district system, some may view the paramount principle of fairness as electing the candidate who would defeat all others in head-to-head contests. As Foley explores in depth in the next chapter, this robust victor is known as the "Condorcet winner," named for French Enlightenment scholar the Marquis de Condorcet, who pioneered the idea. Not every single-mandate election among multiple candidates produces a "Condorcet winner," but most do, and even when they do not, systems can be designed to elect the candidate who comes closest to meeting that standard of victory. The Condorcet winner is the candidate who is most broadly acceptable to the electorate, or, put differently, the one who is least obnoxious to the largest number of voters. Thus, advocates of Condorcet-compliant systems argue they are most likely to make it difficult for extremists (by either definition of the term) to get elected.

Yet we can imagine a third principle of fairness that might be invoked: transparency. To what extent does the electoral system translate individual votes into a collective decision that voters can understand and accept? One value of SMDP is its utter simplicity—whoever gets the most votes wins—although this simplicity comes at the price of confusion, as most citizens mistakenly think that a majority (rather than a plurality) is necessary to win. As we add on layers of complexity, with ranked ballots, vote transfers, multiple seats in a district, multiple ballots cast by voters, or even multiple ways of voting for the same candidate (on different party lines, as with fusion voting), things get more complicated, and the system demands more of voters cognitively. It is not impossible for voters to learn and understand these more complex systems, but it requires time and educational effort.

And in highly polarized circumstances where trust in electoral administration may be in question, there is a price to be paid if the process by which a winner is determined cannot easily be explained to voters. This question of "accessibility" of the electoral method to the average voter is considered by Foley in the next chapter.

One need not tread far into the debate to see how different values may collide in the choice of electoral systems. To the extent that political accountability is a prime goal, this may be difficult to achieve in PR systems, because, as Richard Pildes notes in Chapter 4, PR systems give rise to multiple political parties (and the more proportional the system, the greater the number of parties it elects to a legislature). When multiple parties compete, it may be difficult to determine in advance how they will form governing coalitions after the election. Thus, even if a voter wants to punish one or more governing parties for poor performance by voting for an alternative, that alternative party may still form a coalition with the party the voter wishes to punish. The more proportional the system, and hence the higher the number of political parties, the more difficult electoral accountability may become, as the proliferation of parties makes predicting the precise shape of an alternative governing coalition harder and harder.

Geographical representation is a separate value that electoral systems may wish to elevate. Citizens want representation not only as members of a political party (or an identity group closely tied to a party) but as residents of a physical place that has distinctive needs and interests. The smaller the district in population size, the better the prospect that its residents can have their place-based interests represented and that they can hold their legislators accountable for the job they do in representing and protecting their constituents. Mathematically, this value is intrinsically at odds with the value of proportionality. The larger the district (up to the theoretical maximum of the entire country constituting a single electoral district, as in the Netherlands and Israel), the more proportional the system can be. But if legislators represent districts with many members (say, ten or more, or even half that), and hence a large population, their ties of accountability and access with citizens become diluted, and it may be very hard for constituents to identify a single legislator who specifically represents them. Even in a multimember district of three to five members, constituents will likely find it much more difficult and confusing to get their elected representatives to be accessible, supportive, responsive, and accountable than they would if their district were represented by a single member, as is now the case in the US House of Representatives and most state legislatures.

As Pildes notes in Chapter 4, the goal of proportionality is also in tension with that of government durability. PR tends to produce parliaments of multiple political parties; even "moderate" systems of PR (with design barriers to the proliferation of parties), such as Germany's system, may feature five or more parties with significant shares of parliamentary seats, and more proportional systems feature many more. Even though it is relatively small, with only 150 seats, the Dutch parliament now hosts fifteen parties, and the current coalition government is composed of four parties. In general, the more parties it takes to form a coalition government, the shorter its lifespan and the greater its difficulty in governing may be. That is not as serious a problem for a presidential system like the one in the United States, which gives a single executive the power to form a government for a fixed term, but some scholars worry about the possible difficulty of assembling legislative majorities in the House of Representatives if that body were composed, as it surely would be under a PR system, of multiple political parties.

However, advocates of PR for the United States argue, as Lee Drutman does in Chapter 3, that it has become increasingly difficult under the current highly polarized two-party system to legislate and govern when a single political party does not enjoy the "trifecta" of control of both houses of Congress and the White House. Perhaps counterintuitively, these advocates argue that PR would reduce political polarization in the United States via three mechanisms. First, they maintain that breaking up the polarized solidarities of the two existing political parties would free up moderates from both to join with other parties in new and shifting coalitions to pass legislation. Second, they envision that under a proportional system, different types of political issues would become salient. In other words, politics would become "multidimensional" rather than reducing everything to a single broad left-right dimension that always pits the same two parties against each other. Electing more parties to the House of Representatives would also, they argue, reduce affective polarization by unhitching American politics from its current "us-versus-them" bifurcation into Republicans and Democrats. With multiple political parties emphasizing different kinds of issues, the system would be less likely to reproduce the same level of animosity between parties. And third, they expect that PR would free extremists on the left and right to assemble into distinct (and smaller) parties, which could then more easily be marginalized from a role in governing. This "cordon sanitaire" approach would either leave these smaller extremist parties to complain on the sidelines or induce them to moderate as the price for participating in a legislative coalition.

As practiced in European parliamentary democracies, however, PR has had its share of difficulties, including protracted negotiations to form governments and rising support for extreme parties (as noted in Chapter 4). Moreover, PR has rarely been used to elect legislatures in presidential systems like the US system, and its record of performance in Brazil's presidential democracy does not offer compelling reassurance of its governing value. In cautioning against PR, Pildes maintains that with five or six ideologically diverse parties in the House, passing legislation would become even more difficult.

Reformers (and defenders of the current system) must ask the following core questions: What goals do we want to prioritize? What trade-offs are we willing to tolerate? And how do different elements of the electoral system interact with one another?

Although the first-past-the-post system still has strong defenders in the United States who tout it as simple, transparent, and familiar to all Americans, it has long ceased to be the global norm. With a long provenance in England, which has used the system to elect members to the House of Commons since the Middle Ages, it then spread to the British colonies: the United States, Canada, Australia, New Zealand, and many others that still use the method to elect their parliaments, including India, Jamaica, Kenya, and Nigeria.[25] Most European democracies use some form of PR, and some countries in the last century have either introduced a partial system of PR alongside single-member-district FPTP seats (creating a "mixed" or "two-tier" system) or switched entirely to PR. Australia uses ranked-choice voting (what it calls "preferential voting") to select its lower house of parliament. Some countries that elect presidents use FPTP for this purpose, but most presidential elections globally use a runoff system if no candidate wins a first-ballot majority, while Ireland uses RCV to choose its (largely ceremonial) president.

Among reformers today who seek to reduce political polarization and extremism in the United States, RCV is the most popular electoral reform that has been adopted so far. It has been implemented in its conventional form (instant-runoff voting [IRV]) in Maine and with the pairing of primary election reform in Alaska (the "top-four" model). The attraction of RCV for reformers is that it requires candidates to appeal more broadly to the entire electorate, because general election candidates must win a majority of the vote to be elected. But the efficacy of RCV in this respect is dependent on the particular form of RCV used as well as the degree to which the electorate is polarized. Under the most common rule for ranked elections, if no candidate wins a majority, the one with the lowest number of first-place votes is eliminated, and in an "instant runoff," those votes are rerouted to the second-choice candidate marked on the ballots that ranked the eliminated candidate first. The process of runoff and elimination continues until someone wins a majority of the vote.

There are strong intuitive grounds to expect that RCV will both make it more difficult for politically extreme candidates to win and reduce political polarization. Once voters are free to rank their preferences rather than vote for a single candidate, they can rank an independent or third-party candidate first without wasting their vote. Such a candidate (possibly coming from the middle of the political spectrum) might even be poised to win if one or both parties nominate extreme candidates. But Foley shows that if the electorate (in a state, for example) is largely "bimodally" distributed in its preferences (that is, mainly divided into two politically polarized camps), the final round of IRV is still likely to reduce to a bare-knuckles contest between the polarized options, leaving out the middle-of-the-road candidate. To better combat extremism and polarization, he argues in Chapter 2 for a counting rule that elects the Condorcet winner.

Foley's simulations offer a deep analytic dive into how RCV might work in different electoral contexts in the United States. In its two most high-profile applications, in Maine and Alaska, RCV worked about as intended by returning to office the two most moderate Republican senators, Susan Collins of Maine and Lisa Murkowski of Alaska, while also enabling (in its first application in 2018) a moderate Democratic challenger in Maine, Jared Golden, to defeat a Republican incumbent, Representative Bruce Poliquin, who was much further from the political center.[26]

Where elections are for inherently single-member seats—for state executive offices, such as governor or attorney general, or for the US Senate—the principal reform option is some form of ranked voting. But where the issue is the method for electing an entire state legislature (or city council or Congress), there is no inherent reason why elections must be in single-member districts, and indeed the Constitution is silent on the matter. In 1967, Congress banned multimember districts for the US House (to ensure that states would not use the method to create statewide at-large districts that would make it difficult for racial minorities to be elected). However, states and municipalities remain free to use PR in multimember districts to elect their assemblies, and Congress could pass a new law on elections for the House, either allowing states the option of using PR in multimember districts or mandating it. It is also possible to achieve a version of PR with single-member districts using a "self-districting" system, in which voters first choose which constituency they wish to join for electoral purposes and then elect a single representative for their self-selected constituency.[27]

A bill that has periodically been introduced in Congress by Representative Donald Beyer, the Fair Representation Act, would require that (1) all states with six or more House members establish multimember districts of three to five members; (2) states with two to five House members elect them at large in a single statewide district; and (3) states use a form of PR that builds on the ranked-choice model to elect these members. (The bill also mandates that states use RCV to elect their senators.)[28] As Drutman explores in Chapter 3, this is a "moderate" form of PR. The relatively small size of the electoral districts means that parties would have to win at least 17 percent of the vote to gain any seats; thus, extremely small splinter parties would not win enough votes to qualify for a seat in a five-member district.[29] This is appealing to many reformers because, by creating a multiparty system of something like five parties, it would break what Drutman calls the "doom loop" of polarization into two warring political camps. In the positive view of proponents, political parties would find new ways to pass legislation through shifting coalitions, and legislators who now fear defying rigid party orthodoxy would be free to join a different party and to cooperate and compromise more frequently. The House would be more reflective of American society because it would include moderate Democrats from very Republican states and moderate Republicans from very liberal states, perhaps grouped into new political parties. Another appealing feature of this system is that it would essentially end gerrymandering, because as districts become larger (even up to a few members), it becomes much harder to "game" redistricting for comparative advantage. And it would greatly reduce the unfairness of a party winning a much larger share of US House seats than its share of the popular vote.

But as Pildes and his colleagues argue in Chapter 4, there are serious possible downsides to this system that must be considered as well. We can do projections of what electoral outcomes might look like in different states if they were broken up into three-, five-, or even up to ten-member districts. But these are, of course, speculative. We cannot be sure what kinds of parties would form—and win—in such scenarios. We can speculate as to how the House of Representatives might function with five or six (or more) parties, but what if one or more of these parties were not just politically extreme but openly antidemocratic and obstructionist? Numerous reformers believe that extremism in this form has already overtaken one of the two political parties, and they favor PR in part for this reason. But the truth is that we do not know how the system would function and how a president would govern if his or her party controlled only 30 percent of the seats in the House.[30] These concerns lead some analysts (including a few who participated in the drafting of Chapter 3) to urge caution, recommending no more than gradual experimentation with PR at the state level. And they lead some members of our task force to worry that PR could make the US House *more* polarized as parties of the Far Left and Far Right seek to pull members and voters to the extremes in a dynamic of outbidding that Italian political scientist Giovanni Sartori termed "polarized pluralism."[31] In such a scenario—which would be plausible if PR did generate something like six parties in the House with enough members to figure in bargaining over coalitions—the danger is that extreme or antisystem parties might not be marginalized but might instead drive a process that Sartori called "the enfeeblement of the center, a persistent loss of votes to one of the extreme ends (or even to both)."[32]

Primary Elections

In the United States today, the system used to elect winning candidates in November interacts with the system that is used to nominate candidates in the months preceding the general election, the primary elections. In the nineteenth century, party machines nominated candidates through the opaque decisions of their bosses or through state or national conventions of party activists. During the twentieth century, this system was replaced with the state-mandated direct primary, in which voters chose the parties' nominees in primary elections. Opening up the party nomination process to the free competition of candidates in a primary election ostensibly represented a big breakthrough for democracy at the time. But increasingly critics have charged (and many politicians have privately lamented) that party primaries have imposed an ideological and partisan purity test that requires officeholders to vote and govern in a more ideologically polarized and politically uncompromising fashion than they would prefer. In other words, to appeal to the party faithful in primaries and to ward off challenges by more extreme candidates, politicians have been forced to become less moderate and flexible than they would otherwise be.

There are four potential responses to this dilemma. One is to do away with party primaries altogether and go back to nominating candidates in party conventions. But there is little popular support for this retreat from popular control of the nominations process. A second option is to hold "open primaries" in which any voter can choose to participate, regardless of party affiliation. In theory, this would enable more moderate voters to help more moderate, compromising candidates win their party's nomination. But there is little evidence that open primaries reduce partisan or ideological polarization,[33] perhaps because voter turnout remains quite low in primary elections, where the people who vote tend to be the ones with more intense partisan motivation. A third option is to convert the primary election from a series of *party* primaries (principally, Democrat and Republican) to a single, nonpartisan "all candidates primary," in which all candidates compete and then some number advance to the general election—the "top two" in California and Washington, the "top four" in Alaska, and, potentially, the "top five" in Nevada if it adopts a voter initiative to that effect in November 2024. Under this system, the top vote getters in the primary advance regardless of party, which creates two potential "pathways to moderation." In a "top-two" system, if two candidates of the same party contest in November, the more moderate (less extremely partisan) candidate may win by appealing more broadly to the electorate beyond his or her party. The "top-four" or "top-five" systems, by contrast, use RCV to determine the general election winner. Chapter 2 explains and analyzes these and other options for single-winner elections.

As Robert Boatright and his contributors to Chapter 5 make clear, the question of primary reform turns in part on the importance attached to political parties as institutions in a democracy. Many political scientists worry that as political parties in general have weakened, so has their capacity to aggregate interests—which renders them more vulnerable to capture by more extreme elements. Boatright and his colleagues therefore recommend a flexible approach to primary reform, encouraging experimentation with such alternatives as RCV in party primaries, open primaries, and nonpartisan primaries. They also recommend that parties assume a stronger "gatekeeping role" to discourage or winnow out "unfit and politically extreme candidates," through such mechanisms as preprimary conventions to vet candidates or even preprimary endorsements of candidates. At the same time, they recommend that candidates who are defeated in a party primary be allowed to gain access to the ballot in the general election by eliminating the "sore loser" rule that prevails in some form in forty-seven states.

Presidential Nominations

As Pildes and Frances Lee explain in Chapter 6, our current system for nominating presidential candidates embodies a profound irony. Over the last half century, it has become much more democratic by effectively giving voters in each party the power to nominate the presidential candidates through the vehicle of the party primary. But moving almost purely to this system of direct democracy for choosing major-party presidential nominees has removed the filters of elite judgment that might screen out extreme or demagogic candidates. Thus, the system has become more democratic in one sense but also more vulnerable to assaults on democracy. As Pildes and Lee explain, the United States is an outlier in using such a "plebiscitary" method for nominating candidates for executive office. In no other advanced liberal democracy is there so little in the way of "peer review" for a potential presidential nominee.

Pildes and Lee consider several possible reforms that might restore some prudential balance to the process. One possible route is to tilt the process in favor of contested conventions, by instituting a shorter primary calendar and awarding convention delegates in each primary election on a more proportional basis. The former change would make it easier for candidates to stay in the race until the end, and the latter would make it less likely that one candidate could amass a majority of convention delegates in advance. The goal would then be to encourage a more deliberative party convention that "could negotiate compromises, balance competing party constituencies, and perform the function of peer review." This would also require candidates (or parties) to choose more delegates with the experience and competence to play a deliberative role at the convention. In addition, the authors recommend the selection of "superdelegates" who would be able to vote on the first ballot of the nomination process without necessarily being committed in advance to a candidate. This would ensure more peer review and also reduce the chances of a first-ballot victory. Alternatively, party office-holders in Congress and the states could be given an opportunity to render an official judgment about the candidates ahead of the primaries, which could be prominently publicized. The authors also recommend that the national political parties take full and direct control of organizing and hosting the primary debates, including making decisions about which candidates are invited to participate and by what criteria.

As the 2024 presidential primaries demonstrated, however, even salutary reforms along these lines cannot guarantee the avoidance of extremist major-party nominees. Despite his role in attacking the outcome of the 2020 election, including his responsibility for what unfolded at the Capitol on January 6, 2021, Trump became the nominee of the Republican Party with the support of its transformed leadership.[34] As became increasingly evident during the course of the primary campaign, former South Carolina governor Nikki Haley was the insurgent candidate attempting to recapture the party for its recently dispossessed traditionalists. But to no avail. Moreover, as this book goes to press, there is the possibility that Trump will win the presidency again without a majority of votes—either nationally or in the states that provide an Electoral College victory—because of the "spoiler" effect of a third-party or independent candidate. Thus, insofar as the goal is to protect the United States from extremists who do not have majority support within the electorate, an important lesson of 2024 is that electoral reforms will need to extend beyond the process for nominating the two major-party candidates to encompass some mechanism for preventing the risk of a spoiler effect resulting in the election of an extremist. Determining exactly what institutional reform this should be we leave to future endeavors.

Campaign Finance

Reforming campaign finance poses vexing challenges as well. Among them are that the First Amendment, or at least the way the Supreme Court interprets it, makes it difficult for Congress to control the amount of money candidates spend on their campaigns, and reforms that would strengthen political parties and their ability to raise money for candidates are not very popular among voters.

In Chapter 7, Ray La Raja and his colleagues find that current patterns of campaign finance contribute to political extremism in the United States, in that they increasingly privilege financing from individual donors who are more ideological and politically extreme than institutional donors (such as traditional political action committees [PACs]) or party establishments, not to mention rank-and-file voters. Moreover, as political finance, even of statewide or congressional races, has become more and more nationalized, candidates for Congress have been incentivized to become more hyperpartisan and politically extreme. Independent political expenditure committees (which legally cannot coordinate with candidates' campaigns) also tend to favor more extreme candidates and to undermine transparency and accountability.

La Raja and his colleagues propose two reform strategies. One is to increase funding to candidates from more broadly representative sources, especially political parties (but also multicandidate PACs and even public subsidies). The other is to create incentives for political finance to run through transparent and accountable committees that disclose all their major donors and in general to strengthen disclosure for large donors. However, the authors of Chapter 7 would also like to make it easier for small donors to contribute privately so that they do not face social pressure or reprisals.

The problem is that these may not be the reforms voters want, particularly in an era when there is so much skepticism about political parties and government, which would be the source of public subsidies for campaign finance. And some reforms that appear to be popular with voters, such as lowering limits on campaign contributions, may make things worse by forcing candidates to rely on more ideologically extreme and hyperpartisan small donors and independent expenditure committees. Programs to match small political donations with public funds carry the same risk of reinforcing the power of more militant activists, but some types of subsidies for small donors merit continued experimentation at the local level.

What the People Think About Political Reform

Our study used expert political, legal, and historical analysis to consider what kinds of reforms might be most effective in restraining polarization and extremism. But we also had the opportunity to examine what the American people might think about many of these reforms through the unique method of a deliberative poll. In contrast to a regular public opinion poll, where voters are asked their opinions on issues about which they have relatively little knowledge or information, voters in a deliberative poll are surveyed twice. The first survey is a normal public opinion poll, with no effort made to educate the respondents. After that, a representative sample of the public is given a balanced briefing paper on the issues, which explains (in this instance) the various reform options and offers arguments for and against each proposal. The respondents are then brought together to deliberate in small groups of ten to twelve individuals and periodically in plenary sessions of the entire sample, where they hear experts with competing points of view answer questions that the small groups have agreed upon.[35]

In June 2023, Stanford's Deliberative Democracy Lab, in coordination with our task force, brought together a representative sample of over 500 Americans to deliberate on a number of democratic reform proposals. This was the third in a series of national deliberative polls termed "America in One Room," and like the second one, it was conducted on an online platform designed to encourage active and respectful participation.[36] The respondents deliberated and were surveyed on several of the proposals we discuss in this book: electoral reforms (in particular, ranked-choice voting and proportional representation), reform of party primaries, and campaign finance reform. We close this introduction by briefly summarizing those results.

Among the electoral reform options offered in the deliberative poll were various versions of ranked-choice voting. Participants were asked if they would oppose or favor RCV in six circumstances: in primary elections for local offices, state offices, and Congress and in general elections at the same three levels. The pattern was similar for each of these six options. Before deliberating, proportions of the sample ranging from 44 percent (for Congress) to 49 percent (for local elections) favored using RCV for primaries, whereas after deliberating, the share of support rose to majority levels (53 percent for Congress and 59 percent for state elections). Before deliberation, about 47 percent of respondents endorsed using RCV in general elections at each of these three levels. This support rose after deliberation to 52 percent for congressional elections and 57 percent for state elections (with local elections in between). Similarly, support for the Alaska-style "top-four" system of RCV with nonpartisan primaries rose from 44 percent before deliberations to 53 percent after. But these support levels were not evenly distributed across parties. Democrats (most of all) and Independents were much more supportive of RCV than Republicans, and they were also more likely to be persuaded to endorse it after deliberating. For example, Democratic support for RCV in state general elections increased from 62 to 70 percent, and Independent support increased from 41 to 65 percent, but Republican support only rose from 34 to 40 percent. Republicans warmed more to the "top-four" RCV system, increasing their support after deliberation from 32 to 43 percent (with Democrats' support rising only modestly from 59 to 63 percent and Independents' support increasing dramatically from 40 to 58 percent).

Crucially, it appears that the rise in support for RCV may have come in part from a better understanding of it through education and deliberation. The percentage of the sample agreeing that RCV "will better reflect the public's views on all the candidates" increased from 44 to

57 percent after deliberation. And the percentage *disagreeing* that RCV is "too complicated to use" increased from 41 to 51 percent.

Interestingly, while voters warmed somewhat to the idea of an "instant runoff" through some form of RCV, they did not much like the idea of having to come to the polls to vote again in a general election runoff if no candidate wins a majority of the vote. Support for this option declined after deliberation, from 43 to 40 percent, with each of the three groups of partisans declining in enthusiasm. Participants were much more skeptical of fusion voting (which allows multiple political parties to nominate the same candidate and counts all the votes for that candidate equally). Support for that option remained after deliberation firmly stuck at slightly less than 20 percent of the sample. That said, participants did clearly signal that they want a more competitive political system. Support for the principle of making it easier for third-party and independent candidates to appear on the ballot rose from 58 to 68 percent after deliberation and had majority support among Democrats, Independents, and Republicans.

Support also rose after deliberation for PR, but it began with a weaker base of support among each of the three partisan groups. Once again results were similar for elections at all three levels, with participants slightly more supportive of PR for state legislatures than for local councils or for Congress. Before deliberation, Democrats were more than twice as likely as Republicans to support PR (about 45 to 19 percent). They remained much more supportive after deliberation, but the difference narrowed. For state elections, overall support for PR increased from 30 to 46 percent, with support rising from 44 to 59 percent among Democrats, 22 to 35 percent among Independents, and 19 to 37 percent among Republicans. For Congress, each group was a few percentage points less supportive of PR (with 43 percent favoring this option after deliberation).

Participants were also surveyed about proposals to reform campaign finance and party conventions. The general finding here is that it is an uphill battle to persuade Americans to support reforms that would strengthen political parties, even though there was strong support for many of these proposals from within our task force. Should political party leaders be given a more important role in choosing their presidential nominees—for example, by setting aside something like a quarter of convention delegates for elected officeholders? Support for that was scant before deliberation and barely rose after, from 14 to 17 percent. Similarly, few participants endorsed the proposals of our campaign finance working group to strengthen the role of parties. Only about 15 percent before or after deliberation supported increasing the limits on individual donations to political parties, and support for increasing the amounts that parties can contribute to congressional candidates rose only slightly higher, from 15 to 19 percent. Our sample also did not like the idea of using public money to help fund political campaigns. Matching small donor contributions with larger amounts from public funds (which carries the risk of turbocharging more extreme partisans) began and finished the deliberation with less than 20 percent support. Giving all voters publicly funded democracy vouchers to support candidates of their choice also fell flat, with support increasingly only slightly to 24 percent after deliberation.

The one recommendation of our task force that the deliberating sample of American voters did endorse was transparency for major donors. Support for requiring PACs to disclose their top donors and officials rose from 69 to 79 percent after deliberation. But while our team of experts suggested giving smaller donors more privacy (by raising the threshold for reporting above the current $200 limit), that was opposed by two-thirds of our sample.

While this deliberating sample of the American public did not endorse all the reform proposals discussed in this book, they did firmly embrace our motivating principle. One of the goals that garnered the strongest support from the sample was "overcoming divisions in American society." The percentage identifying that as important rose from 70 to 83 percent after deliberation.

*　*　*

This report of our task force does not emerge from a vacuum. As we discuss briefly in our conclusion, reformers have been working at the state level for many years now to enact changes to reduce the polarizing divisiveness of our politics and improve the quality and governing capacity of our democracy. As we see in several of the chapters that follow, reform can have unintended consequences, producing dynamics very different from what its advocates sought. But the genius of the American system still partly lies in its federal character, which allows for the possibility of many experiments with reforms to electoral systems, primary elections, districting, and systems of campaign finance. As more states innovate with different ballot structures and variations of ranked-choice voting, new provisions for campaign finance, and other reforms, we will be able to evaluate the impact of these changes to see what works and why. In this respect, the analysis here should be viewed as preliminary, awaiting a greater range of experience. Despite their considerable differences in perspective, the members of our task force broadly agreed that the problems of political polarization and rising extremism in the United States are serious and in need of attention. We remain in the early days of reform thinking and advocacy, and it is not unreasonable to imagine that the United States will gradually find its way through an iterative process toward a more effective democracy, as it did during the era of democratic reform a century ago.

Notes

1. "How Americans See Their Country and Their Democracy," Pew Research Center, June 30, 2022.

2. "How Americans See Their Country and Their Democracy," Pew Research Center, June 30, 2022.

3. "Citizens in Advanced Economies Want Significant Changes to Their Political Systems," Pew Research Center, October 21, 2021.

4. "Confidence in Governments at Lowest Level," Gallup, July 24, 2023.

5. Dan Balz and Clara Ence Morse, "American Democracy Is Cracking. These Forces Help Explain Why," *Washington Post*, August 18, 2023.

6. "Political Instability Not U.S. Adversaries, Seen As Bigger Threat, Quinnipiac University National Poll Finds," Quinnipiac University Poll, January 12, 2022. https://poll.qu.edu/poll-release?releaseid=3831.

7. Christopher Claassen and Pedro C. Magalhães, "Public Support for Democracy in the United States Has Declined Generationally," *Public Opinion Quarterly* 87, no. 3 (fall 2023): 719–732. https://doi.org/10.1093/poq/nfad039.

8. Joe Goldman, Lee Drutman, and Oscar Pocasangre, "Democracy Hypocrisy: Examining America's Fragile Democratic Convictions," Democracy Fund, January 4, 2024.

9. "Political Polarization in the American Public," Pew Research Center, June 12, 2014.

10. "Political Polarization in the American Public," Pew Research Center, June 12, 2014.

11. Levi Boxell, Matthew Gentzkow, and Jesse M. Shapiro. "Cross-Country Trends in Affective Polarization," *Review of Economics and Statistics* 106, no. 2 (2024).

12. Levi Boxell, Matthew Gentzkow, and Jesse M. Shapiro, "Cross-Country Trends in Affective Polarization," *Review of Economics and Statistics* 106, no. 2 (2024).

13. "As Partisan Hostility Grows, Signs of Frustration with the Two-Party System," Pew Research Center, August 9, 2022.

14. "How Democrats and Republicans See Each Other," *The Economist*, August 17, 2022.

15. Rachel Kleinfeld, *Polarization, Democracy, and Political Violence in the United States: What the Research Says* (Washington, DC: Carnegie Endowment for International Peace, 2023).

16. Levi Boxell, Matthew Gentzkow, and Jesse M. Shapiro, "Cross-Country Trends in Affective Polarization," *Review of Economics and Statistics* 106, no. 2 (2024).

17. Nolan McCarty, "What We Know and Don't Know About Our Polarized Politics," *Washington Post*, January 8, 2014.

18. Seymour Martin Lipset and Earl Rabb, *The Politics of Unreason: Right-Wing Extremism in America, 1790–1977*, 2nd ed. (Chicago: University of Chicago Press, 1970), 4.

19. Larry Diamond, *Developing Democracy: Towards Consolidation* (Baltimore: Johns Hopkins University Press, 1999), 165.

20. Seymour Martin Lipset and Earl Rabb, *The Politics of Unreason: Right-Wing Extremism in America, 1790–1977*, 2nd ed. (Chicago: University of Chicago Press, 1970), 5.

21. For elaboration, see Seymour Martin Lipset, *Political Man: The Social Bases of Politics* (New York: Doubleday, 1960); Gabriel Almond and Sidney Verba, *The Civic Culture: Political Attitudes and Democracy in Five Nations* (Princeton, NJ: Princeton University Press, 1963); Robert A. Dahl, *Polyarchy: Participation and Opposition* (New Haven, CT: Yale University Press, 1971).

22. Steven Levitsky and Daniel Ziblatt, *How Democracies Die*, Reprint ed. (New York: Crown, 2018), 8–9.

23. Donald L. Horowitz, "Electoral Systems: A Primer for Decision Makers," *Journal of Democracy* 14 (October 2003): 115.

24. See Nicholas O. Stephanopoulos, *Aligning Election Law* (New York: Oxford University Press, 2024).

25. "First-Past-the-Post Voting," Wikipedia.

26. Poliquin challenged the constitutionality of the system in federal court because he led slightly in first-preference votes, but he lost in court and lost his seat.

27. Edward B. Foley, "Self-Districting: The Ultimate Antidote to Gerrymandering," *Kentucky Law Journal* 111 (2023): 693.

28. "H.R. 3863—Fair Representation Act, 117th Congress (2021–2022)," Congress .gov.

29. The minimum threshold for winning a seat in such a system is $1/M + 1$, $+ 1$, where M is the district magnitude—that is, the number of representatives to be elected from the district. In a single-member district, that is $1/2$ (or 50 percent) $+ 1$. In a two-member district, it is $1/3$ (about 33 percent) $+ 1$. In a five-member district, it's $1/6$ (or nearly 17 percent) $+ 1$. The larger the district, the smaller the threshold a party must meet to win a seat.

30. Of course, the Senate would in any case continue to be elected from single-member districts, making it likely that it would be mainly composed of members from the two largest parties.

31. Giovanni Sartori, *Parties and Party Systems: A Framework for Analysis* (Cambridge: Cambridge University Press, 1976), 132–140; Juan J. Linz, *The Breakdown of Democratic Regimes: Crisis, Breakdown, and Reequilibration* (Baltimore: Johns Hopkins University Press, 1978), 26–27.

32. Giovanni Sartori, *Parties and Party Systems: A Framework for Analysis* (Cambridge: Cambridge University Press, 1976), 136.

33. See Chapter 5 and Lee Drutman, "What We Know About Congressional Primaries and Congressional Primary Reform," *New America*, last updated July 1, 2021.

34. See Seth Masket, "The Surprising Takeaway from My Survey on How Trump Got a Grip on the GOP Grassroots," *Politico*, March 4, 2024.

35. For a detailed explanation of the method and the logic behind it, see James Fishkin, *Democracy When the People Are Thinking: Revitalizing Our Politics Through Public Deliberations* (Oxford: Oxford University Press, 2018).

36. For a more detailed description, see "Results of America in One Room: Democratic Reform," Stanford Deliberative Democracy Lab.

2

Ballot Structures

Edward B. Foley

To what extent do electoral institutions in the United States contribute to overrepresentation of political extremism among officeholders? And what institutional reforms might counteract this overrepresentation insofar as it exists? This chapter seeks to answer both questions,[1] posed in our task force's mission statement, by examining the traditional electoral system in the United States: partisan primaries followed by a general election in which voters cast ballots for a single candidate and the candidate with the most votes wins, whether or not they receive a majority. This system differs from other possible ways to structure a single-winner election, which this chapter explores. Chapters 3 and 4 consider the possibility of proportional representation (PR) for seats in a state legislature or the US House of Representatives, an option unavailable for any election for a single officeholder, such as a US senator or a state governor.

Focusing on the goal of constraining extremism, this chapter considers how the following alternatives compare to the current system:

1. The two-round system used in California and Washington, which hold nonpartisan "top-two" primaries that advance only two candidates to the general election. These two finalists can be from the same party or different ones, or they can be independents (since party affiliation is irrelevant for participation in the nonpartisan primary), and the winner of the general election is simply the finalist who receives more votes than the sole opponent (by definition, a majority of valid votes cast).[2]

2. The two-round system recently adopted in Alaska and provisionally adopted in Nevada (subject to a confirmation vote in November 2024). These states hold the same kind of nonpartisan primary as

California and Washington do, except that four (in Alaska) or five (in Nevada) candidates advance to a general election where ranked-choice voting (RCV) is used to determine a single winner. The type of RCV employed in these systems can be called lowest-plurality runoff (LPR), because it functions by sequentially eliminating the candidate with the fewest first-place votes until there is a single winner.

3. A system that makes a modest but significant modification to the Alaska-Nevada model, altering the tabulation method of RCV used to identify the winner from the four or five finalists in the general election. Instead of LPR, this system uses a sequential elimination procedure that guarantees the election of the candidate who is preferred over each of the other candidates; it can thus be called most-preferred voting (MPV).

4. A "top-three" variation on the nonpartisan primary used in California's "top-two" and Alaska's "top-four" systems. Under this version of MPV, the three-finalist general election is conducted with direct head-to-head choices between each pair of candidates rather than with RCV.

5. A partisan primary system such as Maine's that uses RCV, whether by LPR or MPV.

Comparing these different electoral systems, this chapter assesses their relative propensity to either cause or counteract the overrepresentation of political extremism among the winning candidates. A significant portion of the task force's deliberations concerned different possible definitions of political extremism. Broadly speaking, there are two main types. The first might be called "substantive" or "absolute" extremism because it is defined in terms of its content, which in the context of a democracy embraces antidemocratic stances. This kind of antidemocratic extremism can exist on the right or the left (for example, Nazism or Leninism). The second type of political extremism can be called "empirical" or "relative" because it is defined by its distance from the electorate's median voter: the further the winning candidate is from the electorate's median, the more extreme that candidate is. While this distance can be measured in terms of ideology, it can also be measured in terms of degree or intensity of partisanship—which can be a function of other factors besides ideology, including emotional loyalty or allegiance to the party.[3]

For the purposes of comparing and evaluating different electoral systems, this chapter employs the "empirical" or "relative" definition of extremism. That is because the choice of electoral procedures should be content neutral, both to align with First Amendment values and to advance related notions of "political liberalism" as the philosopher John

Rawls used the term: to convey the government's neutrality to all reasonable but divergent viewpoints.[4] But this chapter should also be useful to those concerned by the threat of political extremism defined substantively as antidemocratic postures, since substantive extremism also tends to be relatively extreme as measured by distance from the median voter.[5]

The type of relative extremism this chapter employs is *partisan* rather than *ideological* extremism. In doing so, this chapter does not take a position on the relationship between partisanship and ideology or the extent to which partisan polarization is or is not related to ideological polarization. Instead, this chapter rests on the commonplace observation that more and more Americans display a kind of tribal loyalty to their political party, with a corresponding hostility to the opposing party. This animosity is often called "negative" or "affective" polarization. But however partisan polarization is characterized, the important analytical point is that voters and candidates can be understood as varying in the degree or intensity of their partisanship.[6] The "overrepresentation" of extreme winners produced by an electoral system can be defined as the tendency of that system to produce winning candidates who on average are further from the electorate's median voter in terms of their degree of partisanship than the voters are on average themselves.[7]

For purposes of this analysis, the electorate can be either an entire state or a district within a state. In the latter case, the median voter may be much "redder" or "bluer" than the median voter in the state as a whole. (The Cook Partisan Voting Index is one well-known measure of how much redder or bluer a state or district is relative to the nation.[8]) An electoral system that aims to produce winners supported by the electorate's median voter—as any majoritarian electoral system does—will seek to elect candidates supported by a district's median voter if the electoral system operates at the district level. Thus, if this kind of electoral system is used for all the districts of a state's legislature, it will not endeavor to produce representatives who all correspond to the *statewide* median voter. Instead, it will aim to produce representatives who correspond to their district's median voter.[9] With respect to statewide elections—for governor or US senator, for instance—the goal will be to elect a candidate who reflects the choice of the statewide median voter in keeping with the principle of majority rule.

The overrepresentation of extreme winners can occur in highly competitive "swing" (or purple) electorates, either statewide or district specific, or in more lopsided (deep-red or deep-blue) ones. To illustrate how different electoral systems perform with respect to the problem of overrepresenting extreme winners, this chapter focuses mostly on highly competitive "swing" electorates. (The online appendix to this chapter contains a similar analysis for more lopsided districts.)[10]

This chapter concludes that the traditional system of partisan primaries followed by plurality-winner general elections is especially susceptible to overrepresentation of partisan extremism when the electorate itself is highly polarized and voters are relatively far from the electorate's median. The kind of system adopted in Alaska and provisionally in Nevada can help considerably to counteract the election of extreme winners. However, as polarization of the electorate intensifies, the ability of the form of RCV used in these states, LPR, to avoid the election of extremists is reduced dramatically, and the only effective method of substantial depolarization is to adopt some form of MPV.[11] This could be a modified version of the Alaska-Nevada RCV system or the kind of "top-three" system described in more detail below, in which voters directly mark their preference for each pair of candidates.

Moreover, if the goal is to counteract the overrepresentation of extremism, it is essential to replace partisan primaries with the kind of nonpartisan primary used in the Alaska-Nevada system or the "top-three" variation: combining RCV with partisan primaries, as Maine does, cannot counteract the election of extremists if the electorate itself is highly polarized—unless the tabulation method of RCV is MPV instead of LPR (and even then, partisan primaries are likely to disadvantage candidates for major-party nomination who are more "moderate" in that they are closer to the median voter in the state or district).

The Challenge of Partisan Polarization for an Electoral Democracy

Scholars of democracy have long understood that when a polity is evenly yet extremely divided—with almost half of voters at each polar opposite and very few voters in the middle—sustaining government through traditional electoral procedures becomes exceedingly difficult. Robert Dahl, perhaps the preeminent theorist of democracy in the United States during the second half of the twentieth century, made this point in *A Preface to Democratic Theory*, first published in 1956 and reissued fifty years later with additional reflections from the author. Figure 2.1 presents Dahl's visual representation of this situation.

Dahl was pessimistic about democracies' capacity to handle this type of division: "Where each side is large and each regards the victory of the other as a fundamental threat to some very high ranked values, it is rea-

Figure 2.1   Visual Representation of Extreme Political Polarization

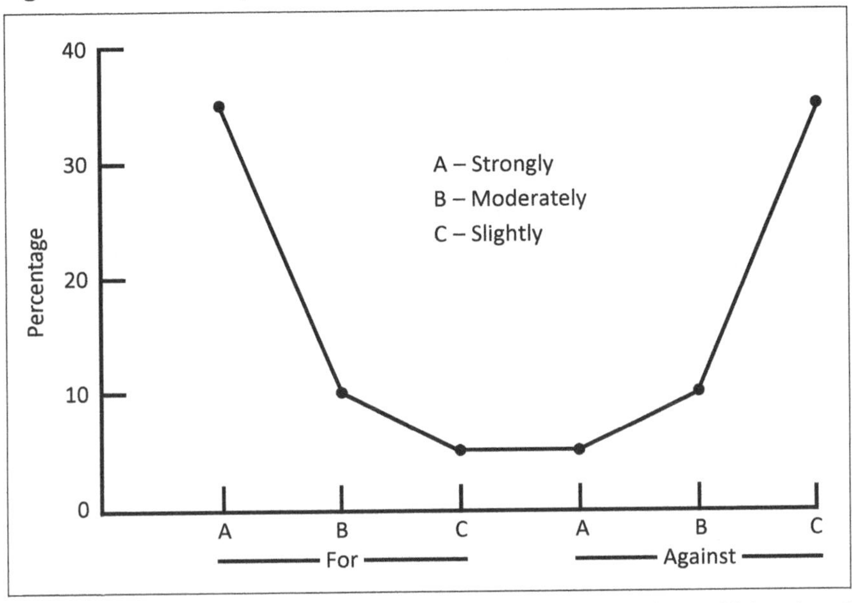

Source: Robert Dahl, *A Preface to Democratic Theory* (Chicago: University of Chicago Press, 2006).

sonable to expect serious difficulties in the continued operation of a [democratic] system," he wrote.[12] Dahl worried that this situation could lead to revolution, secession, or other disruptions negating the "legitimacy" of the existing regime—including in the United States, which is the country Dahl had primarily in mind. Viewing the American Civil War as an example of this circumstance, Dahl doubted that any "constitutional machinery" could cope with such a "profoundly rooted social conflict."[13]

A year after Dahl made that observation, Anthony Downs made a similar point in his seminal 1957 study, *An Economic Theory of Democracy*.[14] Downs was also pessimistic about the capacity of a conventional plurality-winner electoral system to remain intact when it has become so divided. "In a two-party system," he wrote, "whichever party wins will attempt to implement politics radically opposed to the other party's ideology, since the two are at opposite extremes." Thus, he continued, "government policy will be highly unstable and"—even worse—"democracy is likely to produce chaos." Like Dahl, Downs predicted that "this situation may lead to revolution."[15] Whether or not Downs was focused specifically on the US system (or instead thinking more about a parliamentary system such as Britain's), and whether or not he should be understood as exclusively describing a pattern of oscillating gyrations (rather than one also encompassing the kind of cataclysmic regime collapse that occurred during the American Civil War), it is clear that Downs, like Dahl, did not believe this kind of highly polarized bimodal distribution of the electorate was sustainable in a democracy.

With the sobering analysis of Dahl and Downs in mind, it is worth exploring whether there are forms of electoral innovation that might ameliorate or forestall a dire situation of this nature. Electoral institutions interact dynamically with the political culture in which they exist. Political scientists speak of electoral institutions having "centrifugal" or "centripetal" tendencies.[16] Centrifugal institutions pull people apart, exacerbating or accelerating polarization that already exists in society for cultural reasons. Centripetal institutions, by contrast, tend to depolarize society, pushing politics back toward the center. In fact, it is possible to develop a simple measure of an electoral system's centripetal, or depolarizing, tendency. We can call this measure an electoral system's *centripetal force*, or C-force for short, and define it as $1 - w/v$, where v is the average distance (as an absolute value) of each voter from an electorate's median voter, and w is the average distance (as an absolute value) of each winner from an electorate's median voter.[17] Where $w = v$, meaning that winners on average are no more or less extreme (distant from the median voter) than the voters themselves are on average, the C-force of the electoral system is zero. It has no positive tendency to yield winners less polarized than the electorate but also no negative tendency to yield winners more polarized than the voters themselves. By contrast, where $w < v$, meaning that winners on average are closer to the electorate's median voter than the voters themselves are on average, w/v is less than 1, and the electoral system has a positive C-force (greater than zero). The larger a system's C-force, the more depolarizing it is—producing winners closer to the electorate's median voter. If all the winners in an electoral system are exactly congruent with the electorate's median voter, then w/v is zero and the electoral system has a perfect C-force of 1. Conversely, if $w > v$, meaning that winners on average are further from the electorate's median voter than the voters themselves are on average, then w/v is greater than 1, and the electoral system has a negative C-force, indicating that it has a centrifugal (polarizing) effect. It "overrepresents" extremism, to invoke the terminology of the task force's mission statement.

Compared to mid-twentieth century, the United States today is experiencing much greater partisan polarization—a trend that has worsened from one decade to the next, to the point where American politics is increasingly characterized by the deep enmity that each side of the partisan divide has for the other.[18] Both sides view victory by the other as the kind of "existential threat" that Dahl feared. Although the fifty states vary in their degree of partisan polarization, as well as in their competitiveness (with some "purple" states evenly divided between "red" and "blue" and others leaning to varying degrees one way or the other), the overall character of national electoral competition is fierce, as it is in the most competitive states like Arizona, Wisconsin, or Pennsylvania. In these purple states, it would be a mistake to think that voters are all clumped in the middle—purple themselves, so to speak. Rather, they have drifted far apart in the degree of their partisan leanings, although they are not as polarized as their elected representatives. Consequently, in a 50–50 purple state, a slight shift can result in the election of candidates who are unacceptable to nearly half the electorate.[19] (Depending on its electoral system, an electorate that leans red or blue can end up lurching even further toward the extreme than the median voter in that electorate.[20]) In this context, considering whether a particular type of electoral system would have a centripetal tendency, producing an electoral system with a larger (and positive) C-force, is an undertaking of value.

This chapter specifically addresses elections for a single office. Some elections are necessarily of this nature, such as those for governor or other statewide executive offices, including secretary of state and attorney general. Each US senator is also elected this way. So too are members of the US House of Representatives, although—as considered in Chapters 3 and 4—it would be possible to introduce a system of proportional representation for elections to the House (except in states that have only a single member). Most elections for seats in state legislatures are also single district-by-district races,[21] although these too could move to a system of PR.

Therefore, the analysis in this chapter serves two functions. First, it explores possible electoral reforms to address partisan extremism in elections for which PR is not an option, such as those for governor or US senator. Second, it explores electoral reforms that might reduce the potency of partisan extremism for single-seat offices such as those in the US House of Representatives or state legislatures, in the event that PR is not a desired or achievable reform.

This chapter does not specifically address how partisan gerrymandering—or even the "natural" gerrymandering that occurs as a result of sharp political differences reflecting geography (urban, suburban, rural)—amplifies the problem of partisan extremism that can occur in single-seat elections.[22] Even in a purple state that is evenly split between Democrats and Republicans, such as Arizona, Georgia, or Wisconsin, some urban districts will be deep blue and some rural districts will be deep red.

In addition, primary elections in these "extreme" districts can accentuate extremism even further, since the general election will not be a competitive check on the outcome of the primary, as it would be in a purple district or a statewide election.[23] Chapter 5 specifically addresses the issues of primaries. Here, the main focus will be a statewide election that even in a 50–50 purple state can be susceptible to the problem of political extremism depending on the electoral system.[24] (The same analysis also holds for 50–50 purple districts, whether the state is purple, red, or blue.)

Introductory Background

Below are current partisan profiles of the electorates of several US states for illustrative purposes.[25] Arizona is a 50–50 purple state that is highly polarized, with many deep-blue and deep-red voters (those scoring near −0.4 or +0.4 on the partisanship scale), fewer moderately blue and red voters (those scoring near −0.2 or +0.2), and still fewer purely purple centrist voters (scoring near 0.0), as shown in Figure 2.2.

Pennsylvania is a highly polarized purple state with even fewer centrist voters (see Figure 2.3).

Georgia, Michigan, Nevada, and Wisconsin (the other proverbial battleground states in recent statewide and presidential races) are also polarized to varying degrees (see Figures 2.4 to 2.7).

Figure 2.2   Arizona Simulated Voter Population

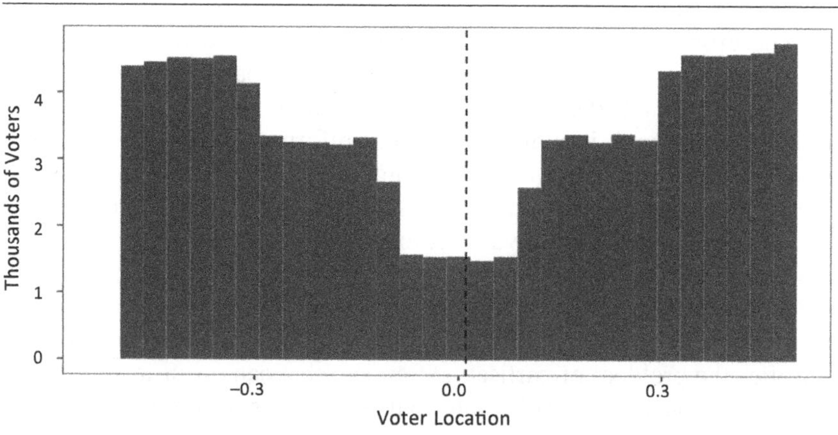

Other states have relatively high levels of partisan polarization but overall lean red or blue and are therefore not purple swing states. Examples of especially polarized red states are Mississippi and South Carolina (see Figures 2.8 and 2.9).

Polarized blue states include Delaware and Illinois (see Figures 2.10 and 2.11).

The simplest measure of partisan polarization for a state's electorate is the average distance of all its voters from its median voter. The larger

Figure 2.3   Pennsylvania Simulated Voter Population

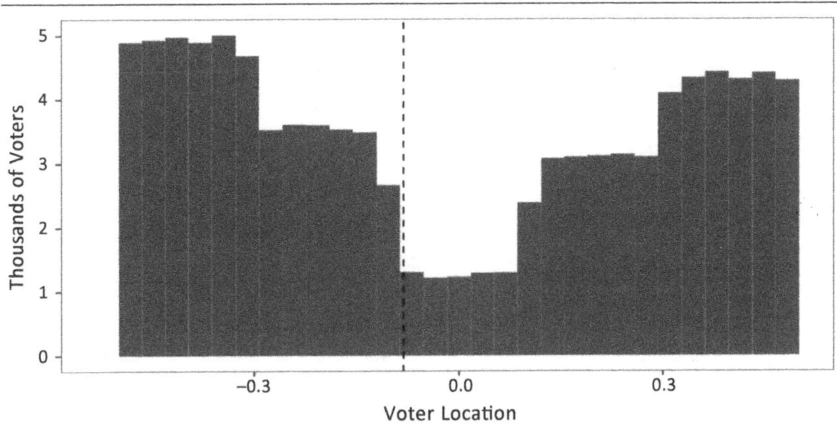

Figure 2.4   Georgia Simulated Voter Population

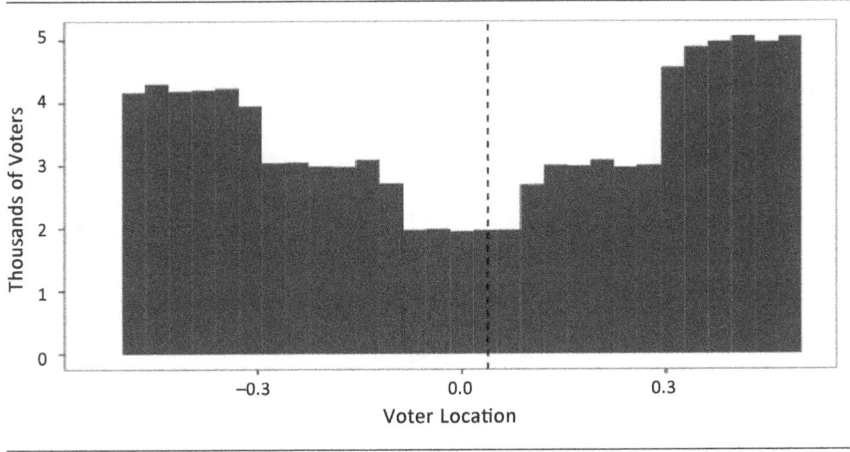

this average distance, the greater the polarization, and vice versa. States with the lowest levels of partisan polarization include Vermont and Hawaii, deep-blue states (see Figures 2.12 and 2.13), and Wyoming, a deep-red state (see Figure 2.14).

Given this partisanship data for all fifty states, we can imagine candidates occupying five different partisan positions, or "lanes," in an effort to appeal primarily to five different groups of voters or segments within the electorate:

Figure 2.5   Michigan Simulated Voter Population

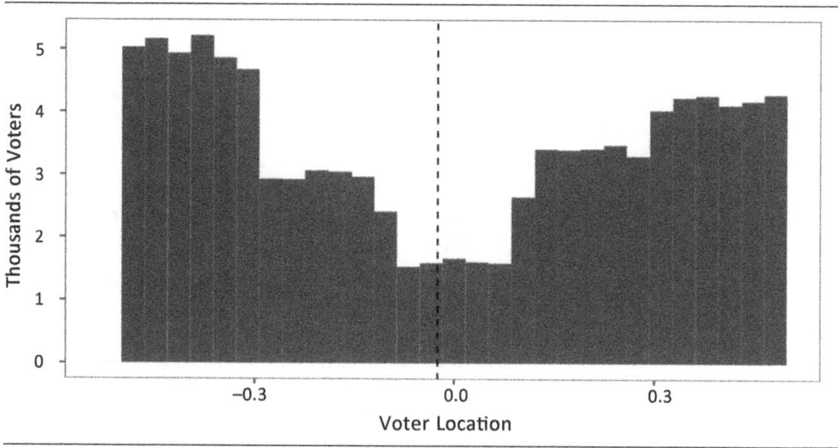

Figure 2.6   Nevada Simulated Voter Population

Ultramarine: intense Democratic partisanship (around −0.4)
Blue: average Democratic partisanship (around −0.2)
Purple: centrist independent (around 0.0)
Red: average Republican partisanship (around 0.2)
Scarlet: intense Republican partisanship (around 0.4)[26]

In addition to corresponding usefully to voter segments in state electorates, this breakdown of candidate "lanes" facilitates analysis of a

Figure 2.7   Wisconsin Simulated Voter Population

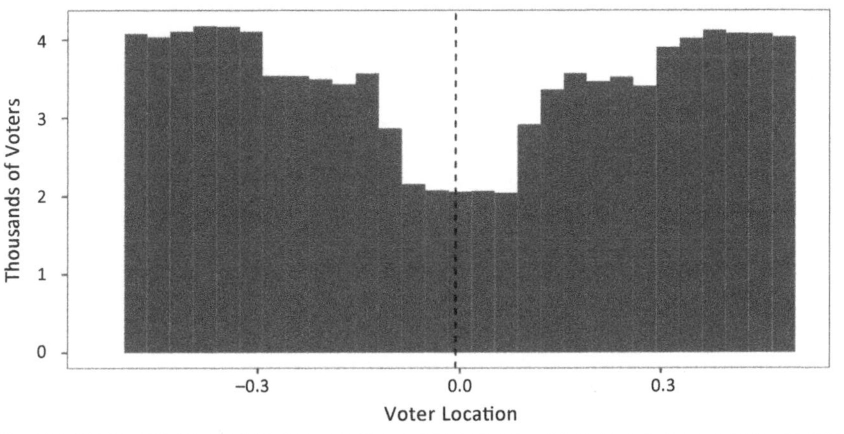

Figure 2.8   Mississippi Simulated Voter Population

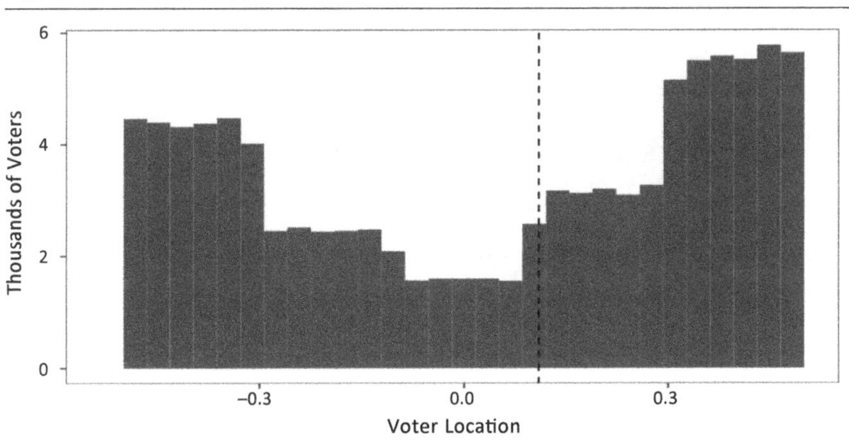

leading electoral-reform proposal: the "final-five" system currently under consideration in Nevada.[27] As noted above, if adopted in a second vote in November, Nevada's new system will use a nonpartisan primary in which the top five candidates advance to the general election, where the lowest-plurality runoff form of ranked-choice voting identifies the winner. We can thus consider how various alternatives based on Nevada's model would handle an election involving five candidates, one occupying each of these five partisan lanes, depending upon how polarized the electorate is.

Figure 2.9   South Carolina Simulated Voter Population

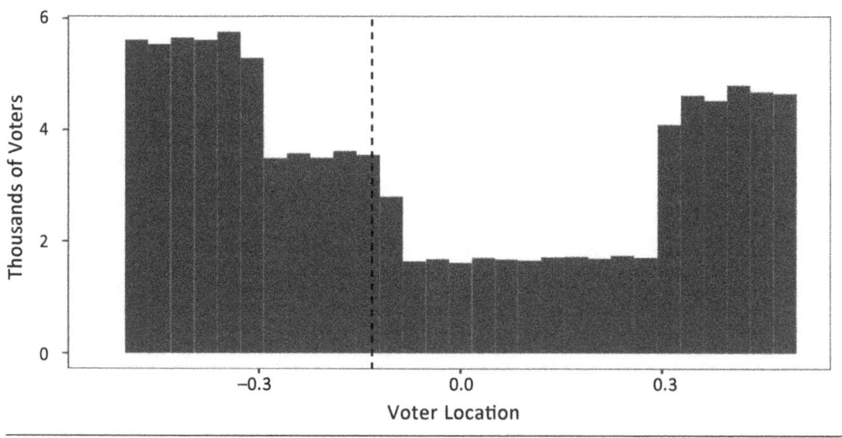

Figure 2.10   Delaware Simulated Voter Population

Before we undertake this comparison of alternative electoral methods based on Nevada's model, it is important to point out that the conditions of American electoral competition have not always been so polarized. The electoral system used in most states for decades—partisan primaries followed by plurality-winner general elections—worked successfully when partisan polarization was lower. That same electoral system, however, may not be capable of performing as well now that conditions have changed.

Figure 2.11   Illinois Simulated Voter Population

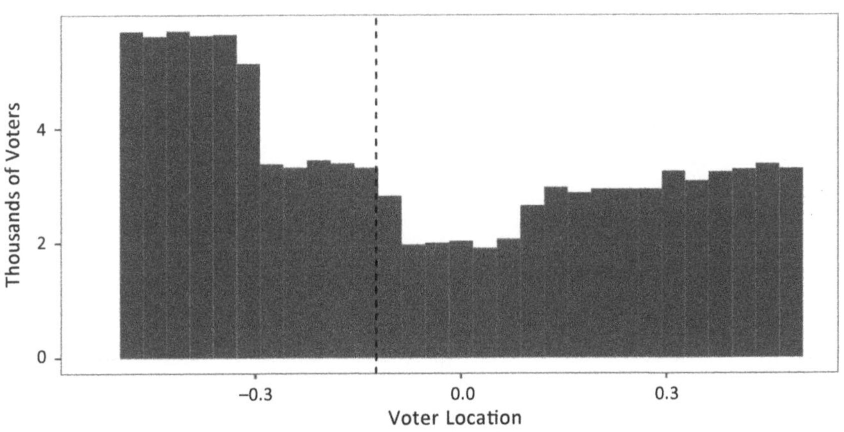

Figure 2.12   Vermont Simulated Voter Population

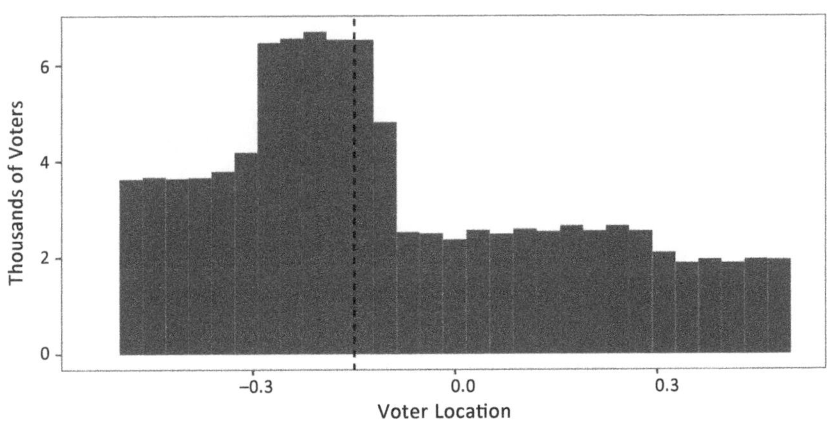

Historically, electoral competition in the United States has been between two of the five positions identified above: moderately blue Democrats and moderately red Republicans. Moreover, the gap between these two positions has been relatively narrow. To use an old football analogy, American politics is played between the forty-yard lines (or between −0.1 and +0.1 on the partisanship scale for each state's electorate profile).

When there is relatively little partisan distance between Democratic and Republican candidates and most voters view themselves as aligned

Figure 2.13   Hawaii Simulated Voter Population

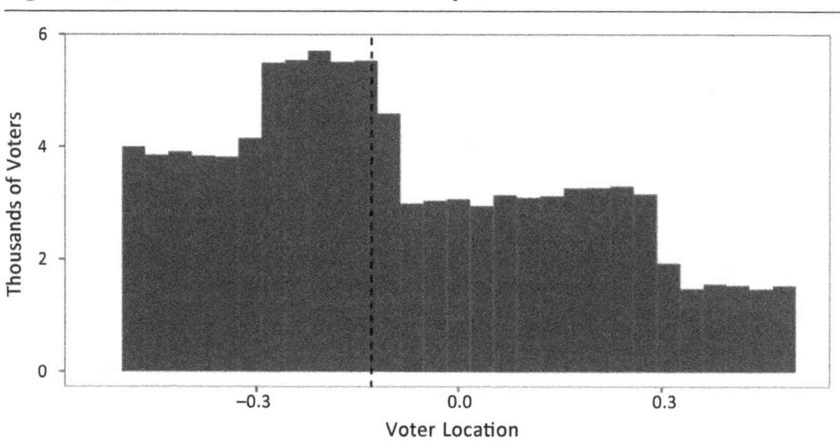

Figure 2.14   Wyoming Simulated Voter Population

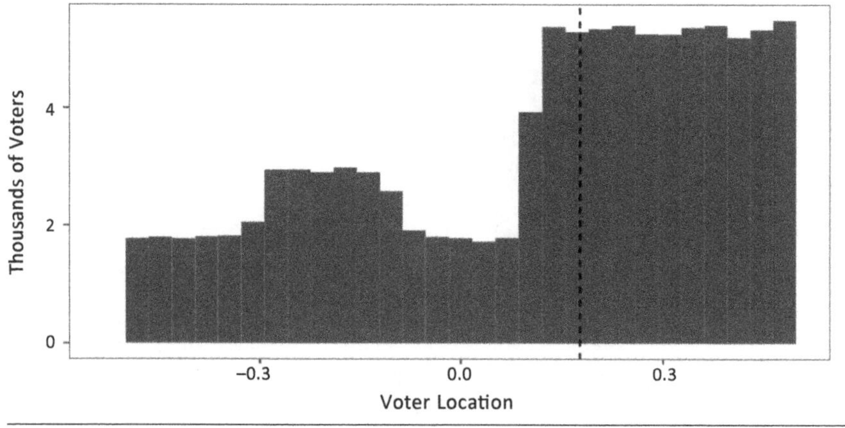

with one or the other (or relatively indifferent to both), then the traditional electoral system of partisan primaries followed by a plurality-winner general election works reasonably well to represent the collective preferences of voters fairly.[28] In this situation, if the state has a 50–50 purple electorate overall, the Democratic primary will nominate a moderately blue candidate not far from the purple center of the electorate, and the Republican primary will likewise nominate a moderately red candidate not far from the electorate's center. The winner of the general election will then be whichever of these two nominees can attract more votes from the truly centrist (purple) voters who are willing to go with one side or the other depending on the specific circumstances of the election.[29]

But regardless of which way the election goes, the winner will not be too far from voters on the losing side. A victory on one forty-yard line is always a mere twenty yards from the voters clumped together at the other forty-yard line. We can visualize this "low-polarization" scenario (see Figures 2.15 and 2.16), which prevailed in the United States for many decades after World War II, by simulating 100,000 elections conducted in the traditional method of a simple plurality-winner general election following two separate primaries for the two major parties.[30]

This visualization shows the winners staying within the proverbial forty-yard lines. In this case, the electoral system has a C-force of 0.374—meaning when the level of polarization in the electorate is relatively low, the traditional method of partisan primaries followed by a plurality-winner general election will have a moderating, "centripetal" effect. At least, it won't produce winners who on average are further from the median voter than the voters themselves are. Here, $w = 0.732$, while $v = 1.169$.

In this scenario, moreover, there are not enough pure centrists to form a third "Moderate" party to compete against the center-left Democrats and center-right Republicans. Instead, they must decide whether they wish to support one side or the other, with the understanding that they can always switch sides in the next election. We can illustrate this point with a simple example. Suppose 45 percent of the electorate aligns with the center-left Democrats (either as party members or simply in terms of their fairly consistent electoral preferences),[31] and suppose another 45 percent aligns with center-right Republicans (again, either as party members or in terms of stable electoral preferences), leaving only 10 percent as truly unaligned centrists. These pure middle-of-the-roaders might prefer to have their own candidate to support, rather than having to choose a center-left Democrat or a center-right Republican, but few would think the electoral system unfair insofar as it forces this 10 percent of the

Figure 2.15   Low-Polarization Swing Electorate

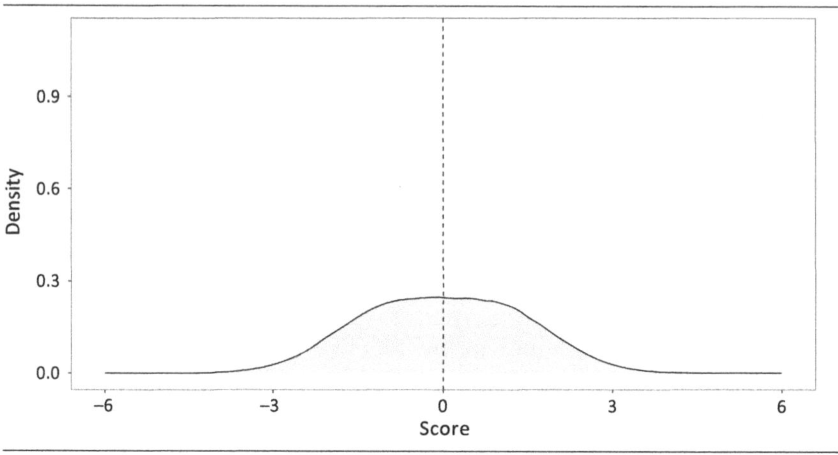

Figure 2.16   Plurality Winner Distribution, Low-Polarization Electorate

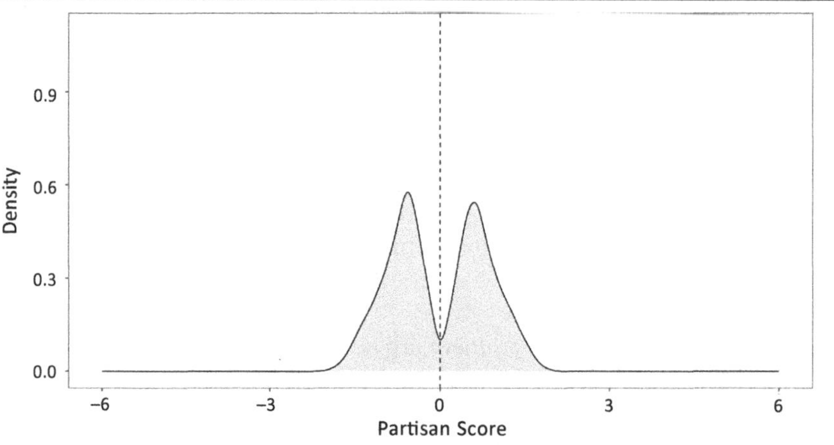

electorate to make a choice between candidates who represent the 45 percent on one side or the other.

Not all of this 10 percent will make the same choice. Some will go with the Democrats and some with the Republicans. In a very tight election, the split within the 10 percent may be close to 50–50, which in turn will make the overall electoral outcome close to 50–50. Moreover, if in one year the 10 percent splits 60–40 for the Democrats, then the Democrats will win 51–49; and if in the next election the 10 percent split 60–40 in the opposite direction, then the Republicans will win 51–49.

So long as the partisan distance between Democrats and Republicans is relatively narrow and politics is played between the forty-yard lines, then this pattern of alternating victories between the two parties is a sign of healthy electoral competition. The policy positions of elected representatives will not lurch wildly from one extreme to the other but rather tack back and forth in modest increments as the center of the electorate moves marginally to the left or right in response to changing conditions.

The Problem of Increasing Polarization

Such was the basic construct of American politics from mid-twentieth century until recently. The Democratic Party of Harry Truman and the Republican Party of Dwight Eisenhower were not so far apart. Indeed, the postwar period from 1945 to 1960 was the lowest point of partisan polarization in US history, at least since the end of Reconstruction (see Figure 2.17).[32]

In the Truman-Eisenhower era, there was no need, or even room, for a centrist party between the Democrats and Republicans. The same was true of the Democratic Party of John Kennedy and the Republican Party of Richard Nixon. Indeed, even as late as the presidential election of 2000, when Democrat Al Gore ran against Republican George W. Bush, the gap between the two major-party candidates was relatively narrow. Despite the so-called Reagan Revolution, which had moved the Republican Party to the right, and the perception prior to Bill Clinton's election that the Democratic Party had moved too far left, at the turn of the century electoral competition within the United States was still largely within the forty-yard lines.

Increasingly, however, this traditional construct is breaking down.[33] Polarization has pulled members of the two parties further and further apart to the point where each side sees the other as an "existential threat" to the nation.[34] This kind of "affective" polarization, or partisan "tribalism," means that members of Team Blue and Team Red often view team loyalty as more important than policy positions.

The partisan polarization of the electorate has been accompanied by an even greater partisan polarization among members of Congress. As the data and analysis that follow suggest, there is reason to believe that the existing electoral system—partisan primaries followed by

Figure 2.17   Party Polarization, 1879–2012

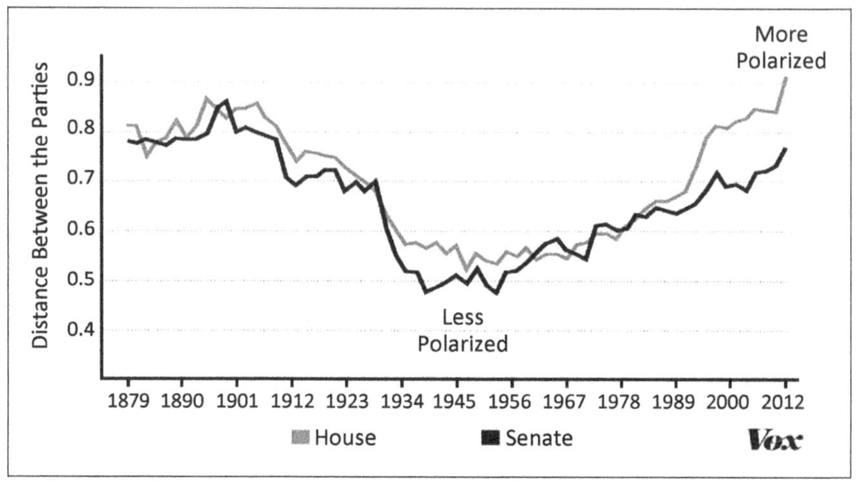

Sources: Vox; Voteview.com and DW-NOMINATE scores.
Note: Each line depicts the degree of polarization in each chamber of Congress over time.

plurality-winner general elections—is to blame for this trend.[35] More-over, one consequence of this magnified partisan polarization is that each side of the electorate fears that the other will gain power. Unlike in the past, when slight shifts within the electorate would lead to office-holders tacking incrementally in either direction—keeping government policy well within the forty-yard lines—in today's polarized environ-ment, a slight shift within the electorate in either direction can cause a pronounced swing from one partisan extreme to the other.

Who Represents the Middle if the Two Parties Have Polarized?

As the two parties have polarized, a gap has grown in the center. The election of members of Congress who are more intensely blue and, to an even greater extent, red than their constituents—more "ultramarine" and "scarlet"—has meant that more moderately blue and red voters have started to feel less represented (especially on the Republican side).[36] This creates an opening for a third "purplish" party to form between the Democrats and Republicans and attempt to capture these disaffected voters who see themselves as more moderate than what the two major parties have become.[37] Indeed, it is commonplace now to hear former Republicans talk of being politically homeless as a consequence of their former party moving sharply to the right. Correspondingly, there is increasing talk of the Republican Party becoming divided into its new MAGA and old GOP wings.[38]

Suppose that as a result of polarization, a 50–50 state has a choice of three candidates: an ultramarine Democrat, a scarlet Republican, and a purplish independent (or nominee of a new third party attempting to fill the gap that has grown between the two major parties). Let's imagine reliable polling shows that in this race, the ultramarine Democrat is the favorite of about 35 percent of the electorate, as is the scarlet Republican, with the purplish independent the first choice of a coalition of moderate Democrats, Republicans, and independent voters amounting to the remaining 30 percent of the electorate. We can envision the purplish independent candidate as drawing support from all the voters who remain within the proverbial forty-yard lines, while the ultramarine and scarlet candidates are backed by those voters who have moved further toward the partisan (or "tribal") end zones along with the nominees of their parties.[39]

Suppose the reliable polling also shows that, because of affective polarization and the tribalism of contemporary politics, the supporters of each major-party candidate strongly oppose the election of the opposing major-party candidate. Thus, the 35 percent of the electorate that wants the ultramarine Democrat to win also really doesn't want the scarlet Republican to win—and vice versa. This means, as the polling also reveals, that if the election were a one-on-one contest between the purplish independent and either of the two major-party nominees, the purplish independent would win decisively, by about 65 to 35 percent (or almost two-to-one). In other words, virtually all the voters who prefer the ultramarine Democrat would readily vote for the purplish independent over the scarlet Republican. Likewise, virtually all those who prefer the scarlet Republican would choose the purplish independent over the ultramarine Democrat.

Given this polling data—assuming it's reliable—which candidate should win the election? As discussed later in this chapter, it is possible to design a "top-three" electoral system that would permit voters to cast ballots expressing their preferences among each possible pair of these candidates: ultramarine Democrat versus scarlet Republican, ultramarine Democrat versus purplish independent, and scarlet Republican versus purplish independent. This system would declare as the winner the candidate who beats each of the other two in their one-on-one ballot match-ups.[40] As long as voters cast their ballots in line with the polling, the purplish independent would win in this case.

But that is not the result the existing electoral system would produce. Instead, either the ultramarine Democrat or the scarlet Republican would win, given the plurality-winner (often called "first-past-the-post") general election system in most states, depending on which of the two major-party candidates manages to finish slightly ahead of the other. As long as the purplish independent candidate has a ceiling of first-choice support of about 30 percent—because of tribal polarization—this candidate cannot win in a first-past-the-post system. Indeed, the purplish independent is likely to drop out of the race, or not even run in the first place, because of their inability to compete in the plurality-winner system. This is true even though the same candidate would easily clobber either of the other two in one-on-one contests.[41]

We can visualize this with a model of a highly polarized 50–50 electorate (see Figure 2.18) and the winners of 100,000 simulated elections using the existing plurality system (see Figure 2.19).

With relatively fewer voters in the middle, there are virtually no winners in the middle—and this is true even assuming that voters in each of the two major-party primaries perfectly mirror their half of the overall electorate. With this assumption, the plurality system has a C-force close to zero for this highly polarized electorate, 0.1060, meaning that the system has virtually no capacity to yield winning candidates closer to the center than the voters themselves. But if we assume instead that each of the two parties' primary voters are more partisan than their half of the overall electorate, then the C-force of the existing plurality system actually becomes negative: winners of the general election on average are more distant from the electorate's median voters than the voters themselves are.[42] In other words, if voters in the Democratic Party's primary are more ultramarine on average than the blue half of this 50–50 electorate, and likewise the Republican Party's primary voters are more scarlet than the red half of the electorate, then the general election's winners will tend to be more ultramarine or scarlet than the general election's voters. This negative C-force causes extremists to be overrepresented in office.

One implication of this analysis might be that it is necessary to reform major-party primaries to make them as congruent as possible with each half of the overall electorate. Considering potential reforms along these lines is the subject of Chapter 5. Here it is necessary to wrestle with a more basic question: Even if we could make the existing system have a C-force close to zero, as in the model case where the combined electorates of the two primaries matched exactly the electorate as a whole, would we still have a sound electoral system for a highly polarized electorate (as, even in this situation, depending on how polarized the electorate is, it will still produce winners who are further and further from the center)?

Figure 2.18   High-Polarization Swing Electorate

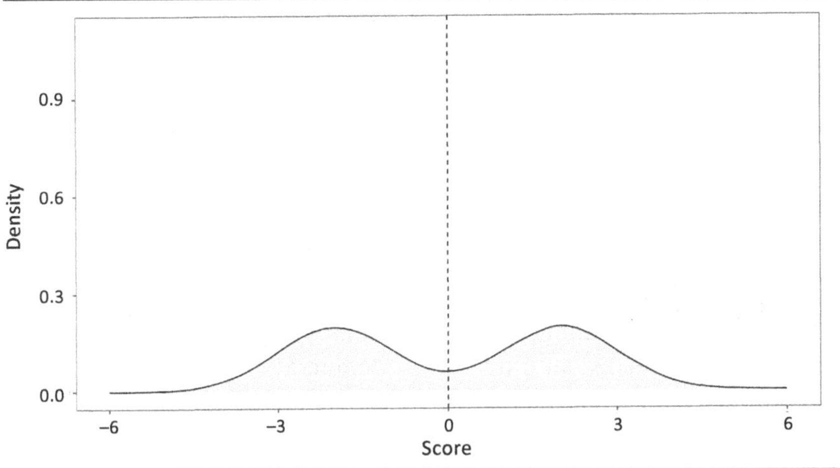

Figure 2.19   Plurality Winner Distribution, High-Polarization Swing Electorate

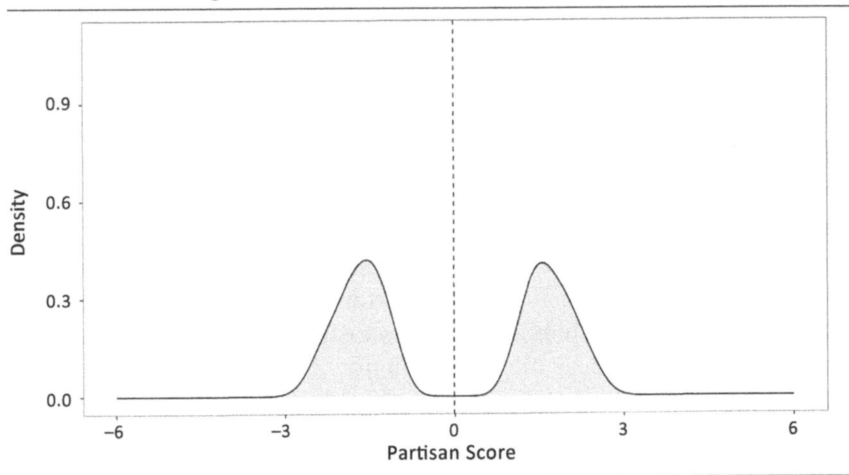

To return to the hypothetical three-candidate example, suppose that the 30 percent of voters who prefer the purplish independent see it as in their interest to vote in either the Democratic or Republican primary, since their favorite candidate can't win the first-past-the-post general election. Let's assume in this 50–50 state that half of these voters join one primary and half join the other. In this situation, the purplish independent would be unable to beat either the ultramarine Democrat or the scarlet Republican one-on-one in their party's primary. The 35 percent of the electorate whose favorite candidate is the ultramarine Democrat will crush the purplish independent in the Democratic primary. Likewise, the 35 percent of the electorate whose favorite candidate is the scarlet Republican will crush the purplish independent in the GOP primary. Indeed, even if all 30 percent of the electorate who prefer the purplish independent vote in either major party's primary, their candidate will not prevail, assuming that all 35 percent who support the ultramarine or scarlet candidate turn out to vote in their party's primary. In other words, even if the two major-party primaries work perfectly to represent each half of the overall electorate, under conditions of increasing partisan polarization, the prevailing electoral system will produce two polarized major-party nominees: an ultramarine Democrat and a scarlet Republican. This forces all voters to make a choice between these two more extreme alternatives, even though the electorate as a whole in the general election would much prefer a purplish independent over either of the two polarizing major-party nominees.

If PR were possible, each segment of the electorate could be given seats in the legislature in proportion to its share of votes. But in this chapter, we are considering those offices that cannot be elected on the basis of PR, such as US senator or governor. So, what would be the best way to elect the winner of a single statewide office in this circumstance?

Searching for a More Centripetal Electoral System

As we have seen, the conventional plurality-winner system will not elect a broadly acceptable compromise candidate under conditions of high polarization. In this system, moreover, it does no good to come in second. Even if a purplish independent or third-party candidate could manage to poll ahead of one of the major-party nominees, the result would be no different than finishing behind both of them. For example, imagine that in the hypothetical three-way race, the scarlet Republican finishes first with 35 percent, the purplish independent second with 34 percent, and the ultramarine Democrat third with 31 percent. In the plurality-winner system, the scarlet Republican wins regardless of which opponent comes in second.

In an alternative electoral system, however, a more broadly acceptable moderate could be elected if that candidate managed to come in second. One alternative is the "top-two" system used in California (which Georgia also uses for runoff elections if no general election candidate receives a majority of the vote).[43] In a situation such as the one described above where the scarlet Republican and purplish independent are the top two candidates, the purplish independent would prevail in the California general election or Georgia runoff by picking up second-choice support from the voters who preferred the ultramarine Democrat the most. (France's 2022 presidential election was almost a version of this. The top three candidates in the first round were centrist Emmanuel Macron with 28 percent, far-right Marine Le Pen with 23 percent, and socialist Jean-Luc Melenchon with 22 percent. In the final round, Macron picked up most of Melenchon's support, trouncing Le Pen 59 percent to 41 percent. Even if in the first round Macron had finished slightly behind Le Pen, he would have pulled ahead of her in the final round by picking up enough support from Melenchon's first-round voters.[44])

Similarly, the lowest-plurality runoff version of ranked-choice voting used in Alaska and Maine will elect a compromise moderate who has the second-highest number of supporters.[45] RCV permits voters to rank their preferences among all the candidates. Under the LPR system, if no candidate wins a majority of first-preference votes, the candidate with the fewest first-choice votes is eliminated, and the votes for that candidate are redistributed to their voters' second preferences. (LPR is sometimes called instant-runoff voting [IRV], even though the term "instant runoff" can be applied to other tabulation methods for the ranked-choice ballots, as discussed below.) As long as the moderate candidate is ranked at least second, he or she will prevail.

The 2022 Alaska state senate race involving Republican Cathy Giessel is a close approximation of this scenario. Giessel had lost her seat to further-right Roger Holland in the 2020 Republican primary election. Then in 2022, under the new "top-four" RCV system, she placed slightly ahead of Holland in first-preference votes, with the Democrat slightly trailing in third place. Even if she had finished behind Holland, however, she would have prevailed because of the second-choice support she received from the voters who ranked the Democrat first.[46]

Alaska's 2022 US Senate race also illustrated this basic point. Moderate Republican Lisa Murkowski finished slightly ahead of Kelly Tshibaka, who was endorsed by Donald Trump, in the first round of the state's new "instant-runoff" system: Murkowski had 43.4 percent, Tshibaka 42.6 percent, and the third-place Democrat 10.7 percent.[47] But even if Murkowski had finished slightly behind Tshibaka in the first round, Murkowski would have pulled ahead because she received the most second-choice votes from the Democrat's supporters.

The capacity of a second-place moderate to win in either the "top-two" or LPR systems is a reason to prefer these systems to the traditional plurality-winner system as a way to counteract extremist winners. Whereas the plurality-winner system will let a polarizing candidate on the far right or far left prevail as long as he or she finishes first (even with barely more than a third of the votes), the "top-two" and LPR systems will elect the more broadly acceptable moderate (so long as he or she has the second-most first-choice votes and can pick up enough second-choice voters who preferred the eliminated third-place candidate).

Recall the model case of an electorate with relatively low polarization. In this context, Alaska's new electoral system—a nonpartisan "top-four" primary with LPR in the general election—will tend to produce winners closer to the electorate's median voter than will a plurality-winner general election after partisan primaries (see Figures 2.20 and 2.21).

In 100,000 simulated elections with each of these two systems, the plurality-winner system (as mentioned above) yielded winners who on average had a distance from the median voter of 0.732. By contrast, Alaska's system yielded winners with an average distance from the median voter of 0.565—meaning that these winners tended to be closer to the center. This difference in the value of w, in turn, meant that the two electoral systems had a different C-force for the same electorate. Whereas the plurality-winner system had a C-force of 0.374 (assuming primary voters mirror exactly general election voters), Alaska's system had a higher C-force of 0.517.

These alternative electoral systems have a weakness, however. Neither the "top-two" system nor the LPR system will counteract severe polarization and avoid the election of an extreme candidate if the more moderate candidate finishes third, behind candidates on both the extreme right and extreme left, rather than second. In a highly polarized 50–50 electorate, with a bimodal distribution that has a hollowed-out center, this is very likely to be the case.[48] Indeed, Alaska's LPR system does no better than the plurality-winner system in elect-

Figure 2.20   Plurality Winner Distribution, Low-Polarization Electorate

Figure 2.21   LPR Winner Distribution, Low-Polarization Electorate

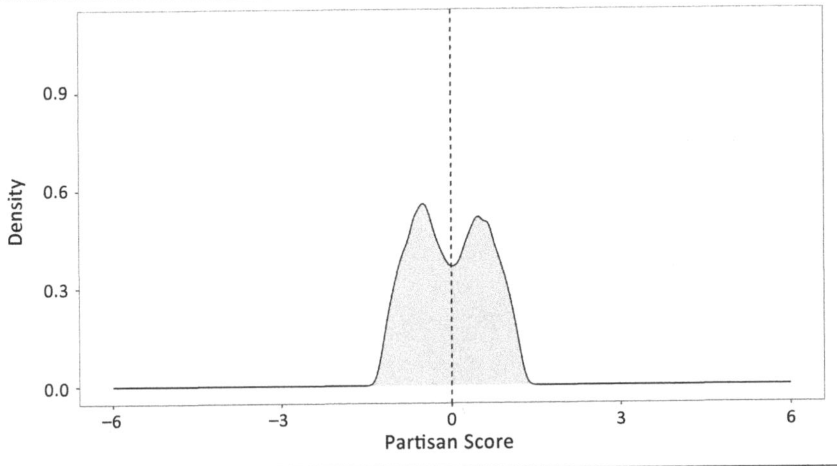

ing more centrist candidates when simulating 100,000 elections in a model highly polarized 50–50 electorate, as demonstrated in Figures 2.22 and 2.23.

As we have already seen, for this electorate, the plurality-winner system has a C-force close to zero (0.160) when voters in the two party primaries combined are identical to the voters in the general election. (The system's C-force, again, is negative if the voters in the

Figure 2.22   Plurality Winner Distribution, High-Polarization Electorate

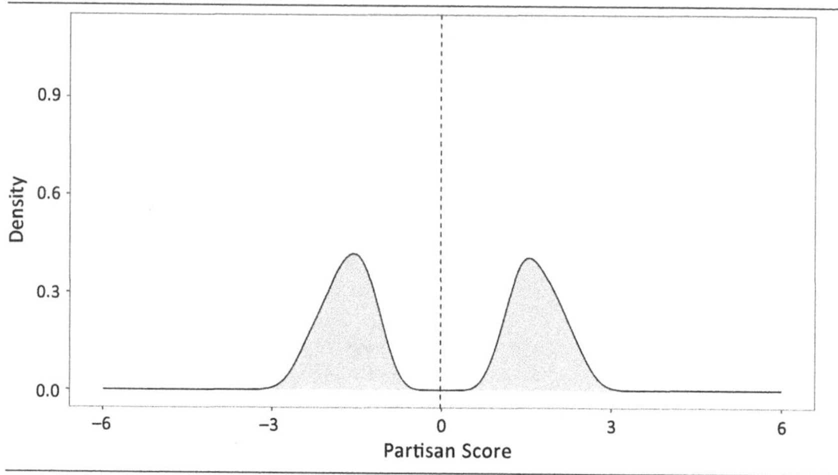

Figure 2.23   LPR Winner Distribution, High-Polarization Electorate

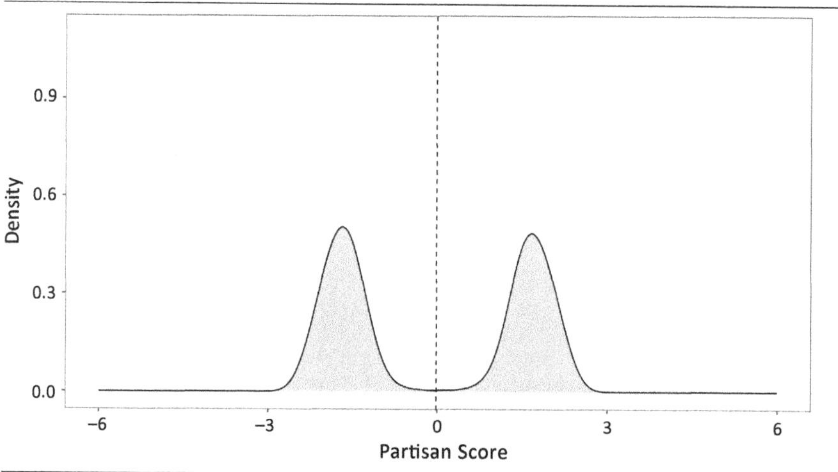

two primaries are more polarized than the general election voters.) Strikingly, the C-force of Alaska's LPR system is essentially the same: 0.163. In other words, using an "instant runoff" of this particular type—in which the candidate with fewest first-choice votes is eliminated—has no greater centripetal tendency in a highly polarized electorate than a plurality-winner general election as long as those voting in the primaries are not more polarized than each half of the overall electorate. Of course, the possibility that voters in partisan primaries are more extreme than voters in nonpartisan primaries is a reason to prefer Alaska's new electoral system even if its LPR method is not especially effective in counteracting extremism.

We can confirm this general point by returning to our initial three-candidate hypothetical example. In a race where an ultramarine Democrat and a scarlet Republican both have approximately 35 percent of the first-choice votes, while the purplish independent has only around 30 percent, the LPR method will eliminate the purplish independent first, making the "instant runoff" a choice between the two polarizing nominees of the major parties.

But there are multiple electoral systems that will elect a moderate compromise candidate instead of a more extreme candidate, even if the moderate is not the first choice of most voters who are evenly split between the two more extreme candidates. Most of these alternatives are variations of ranked-choice voting that differ from the LPR procedure (although the "top-three" system described below does not use ranked-choice ballots at all). It is worth considering several of these alternatives, as no single one is generally considered the absolute best in all circumstances, and different states suffering from hyperpolarization may find different systems better suited to their particular needs.

Survivor-Style RCV

The simplest of these alternatives to explain is the same as the LPR method, except conducted in reverse order. Instead of eliminating the candidate with the fewest first-place votes, this alternative eliminates the candidate with the most last-place votes. As with the LPR method, it looks to whichever candidate is ranked next on the ballots that ranked the eliminated candidate last; in this case, next means next-to-bottom rather than next-to-top. As with the LPR method, the elimination procedure repeats until one candidate remains as the top choice on a majority of ballots (or only one candidate remains after all others have been eliminated).

Labeled the "Coombs method" in the literature on electoral systems (after the scholar who first proposed it), this system can be more descriptively called "*Survivor*-style" RCV after the well-known TV show of that name.[49] In the show, contestants are voted off the island one at a time until only one contestant—the "sole survivor"—remains. By using ranked-choice ballots, rather than multiple rounds of separate ballots, the Coombs method is simply an instantaneous form of the *Survivor*-style elimination procedure.

Survivor-style RCV is well suited to redressing polarization when voters are motivated by a desire to prevent the election of candidates they strongly dislike and even fear.[50] This negative motivation—voting against, rather than for, a particular candidate—is almost as strong, and for many voters maybe even be stronger, than positive motivation in favor of a particular candidate. Think, for example, of all the voters whose main electoral motivation is to stop the election of Donald Trump rather than to elect any particular other candidate. *Survivor*-style RCV, because of how it structures instantaneous elimination, places special emphasis on these oppositional motivations of voters to defeat particular candidates.

We can see how *Survivor*-style RCV works with an illustration built on our previous example. Let's suppose the ranked-choice ballots are those listed in Table 2.1.

These ballots show that Purplish has 32 percent of first-choice votes, barely behind Ultramarine (with 33 percent), but still in third place. Thus, under the LPR method, Purplish would be eliminated; and because the second-choice votes of Purplish's supporters are split evenly between the two other candidates, Scarlet would win the "instant runoff" 51 to 49 percent.

Under *Survivor*-style RCV, by contrast, Ultramarine would be the first candidate eliminated based on having the largest number of last-choice votes. Ultramarine is the last choice of 51 percent of voters: the 35 percent who rank Scarlet first plus the 16 percent who rank Scarlet second after Purplish. Once Ultramarine is eliminated, Purplish wins the *Survivor*-style RCV election because he or she is now the top choice of the remaining candidates on 65 percent of ballots, which is more than the minimum majority necessary for election. (Also, after Purplish is eliminated, Scarlet is the remaining candidate with the highest number of last-choice votes—the same 65 percent.[51])

Table 2.1   Ranked-Choice Ballots to Illustrate *Survivor*-Style RCV

Percentage of Voters	First Choice	Second Choice	Third Choice
35	Scarlet	Purplish	Ultramarine
33	Ultramarine	Purplish	Scarlet
16	Purplish	Scarlet	Ultramarine
16	Purplish	Ultramarine	Scarlet

In this case, *Survivor*-style RCV thus yields a different winner than the LPR method, although the ranked-choice ballots are the same. Moreover, the *Survivor*-style method selects as the winner the moderate compromise candidate, whereas LPR selects a more extreme polarizing one. The difference in outcomes is a function of how the two methods order their similar elimination processes. By eliminating the most disliked candidate first, *Survivor*-style RCV knocks out highly polarizing politicians, narrowing the electoral competition to candidates with broader acceptability among all the voters. The LPR method keeps in contention highly polarizing politicians who have relatively strong first-choice support at their end of the ideological spectrum but provoke very strong opposition from the other end. This method is prone to eliminating compromise candidates who have relatively little first-choice support but also do not provoke widespread antipathy. Everyone's second choice but no one's first choice cannot survive an LPR election, whereas this kind of consensus figure would easily win a *Survivor*-style election.

These two electoral methods thus handle hyperpolarization in opposite ways. LPR produces results that replicate extreme polarization within the electorate. We see this quantified in the C-force of Alaska's LPR system, which measures 0.163 in a highly polarized electorate. By contrast, *Survivor*-style RCV counteracts extreme polarization by eliminating especially disliked candidates until a politician remains who commands majority support within the electorate. Because it is a "Condorcet-consistent" electoral method—meaning that it will elect a candidate whom a majority of voters prefer to each other candidate and thus will always elect whichever one is closest to the electorate's median voter—*Survivor*-style RCV has the same C-force as any other "Condorcet-consistent" method.[52]

In the model case of a highly polarized 50–50 electorate, any Condorcet-consistent method will have a C-force of 0.479, nearly three times that of the LPR method. Put differently, while LPR produces winners who on average have a distance from the median voter of 1.683, Condorcet-consistent methods produce winners with an average distance from the median voter of only 1.048, meaning that such methods have a greater capacity to yield less extreme winners even when the electorate is highly polarized. We can see this in visualizations of the winners of the two different systems applied to the same highly polarized electorate, as illustrated by Figures 2.23, shown previously, and 2.24.

Thus, a state with a highly polarized electorate could employ *Survivor*-style RCV in statewide elections, such as those for governor and US senator, to counteract political extremism.

Figure 2.24   Condorcet Winner Distribution, High-Polarization Electorate

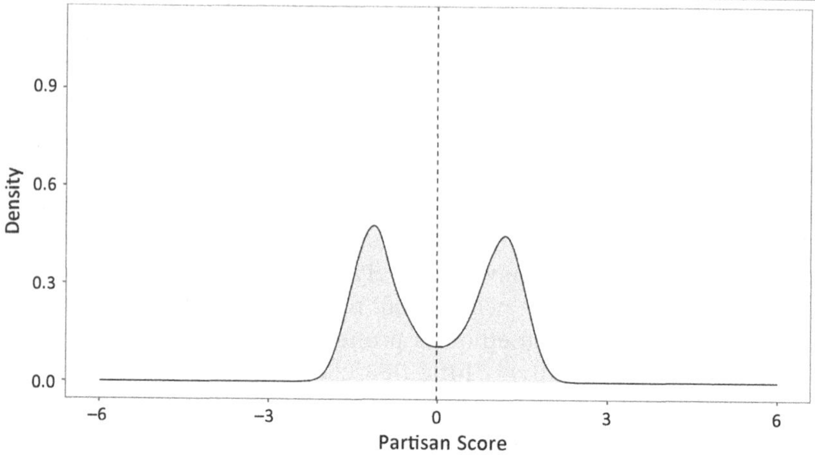

Density

0.9

0.6

0.3

0.0

−6   −3   0   3   6

Partisan Score

Bottom-Two Runoff

Another Condorcet-consistent version of ranked-choice voting will also tend to elect a compromise candidate under conditions of hyperpolarization. As a Condorcet-consistent method, it too would have a C-force of 0.479 in the model case of the highly polarized electorate. Called a bottom-two runoff (BTR), it is similar to the LPR method—except that, instead of eliminating the candidate with the fewest first-choice votes, it conducts a direct head-to-head face-off between the two candidates with the fewest first-choice votes and then eliminates whichever one is preferred by fewer voters overall.[53] Like the LPR method, BTR repeats its version of the elimination procedure until one remaining candidate is preferred by a majority of voters.

BTR is Condorcet-compliant because it will always elect the candidate who would prevail against every other candidate in direct head-to-head matchups, based on the preferences of all voters as indicated on their ranked-choice ballots. This is true even if that candidate has the fewest first-choice votes and thus was paired against the candidate with the next fewest first-choice votes in the initial face-off prescribed by the system. BTR will thus elect whichever candidate is least extreme and polarizing. To use the same illustration as above, Purplish and Ultramarine are the two candidates with the fewest first-choice votes: 32 and 33 percent, respectively, as in Table 2.2.

In a head-to-head matchup, Purplish prevails over Ultramarine 67–33 by picking up all the second-choice votes of those who ranked Scar-

Table 2.2   Ranked-Choice Ballots to Illustrate BTR Method

Percentage of Voters	First Choice	Second Choice	Third Choice
35	Scarlet	Purplish	Ultramarine
33	Ultramarine	Purplish	Scarlet
16	Purplish	Scarlet	Ultramarine
16	Purplish	Ultramarine	Scarlet

let first. Then, with Ultramarine eliminated, Purplish wins with 65 percent of votes to Scarlet's 35 percent by being ranked second by the voters who ranked Ultramarine first.

There is a fear, even among those who find the BTR method theoretically attractive for its propensity to elect compromise centrists, that it could be undermined through strategic manipulation.[54] Using the same example, suppose supporters of Scarlet rank Ultramarine second rather than Purplish, contrary to their true preferences. Then, Ultramarine would defeat Purplish in the first round of the BTR process, and Scarlet would defeat Ultramarine 51 to 49 percent (given the even split among Purplish's supporters in their second-choice preferences). In this way, insincere strategic voting by Scarlet supporters undermines BTR's capacity to elect compromise centrists and simply replicates the polarizing outcome that LPR produced: a narrow 51–49 victory by Scarlet.

The *Survivor*-style method is less susceptible to strategic manipulation. Suppose Scarlet's supporters try the same strategy of ranking Purplish last instead of Ultramarine. This strategy backfires under the *Survivor*-style method: instead of Ultramarine being the first candidate eliminated, as would occur if Scarlet's supporters ranked their ballots sincerely, Scarlet is eliminated. To see this, let's review the ballots cast assuming this insincere strategy (see Table 2.3).

Now, Scarlet has the most last-choice votes with 49 percent. Once Scarlet is eliminated, Ultramarine prevails against Purplish 68 to 32 percent. This result is the worst outcome based on the true preferences of Scarlet's supporters, thus confirming the counterproductive nature of this strategy.

Most-Preferred Voting

BTR has a close cousin that is significantly less susceptible to strategic manipulation of this sort. Like BTR, this variation, which we call

Table 2.3   Ranked-Choice Ballots with Strategic Voting to Illustrate *Survivor*-Style RCV

Percentage of Voters	First Choice	Second Choice	Third Choice
35	Scarlet	*Ultramarine*	*Purplish*
33	Ultramarine	Purplish	Scarlet
16	Purplish	Scarlet	Ultramarine
16	Purplish	Ultramarine	Scarlet

Note: Italics indicate transposed preferences due to strategic voting.

most-preferred voting (MPV), conducts a head-to-head face-off between the two least-preferred candidates and eliminates whichever one is preferred by fewer voters based on all preferences indicated on all ranked-choice ballots. And like BTR, this variation repeats this same elimination procedure until only the winner is left.

The only difference between BTR and MPV is how the methods define the two least-preferred candidates for the purpose of conducting head-to-head elimination matches. Whereas BTR defines them as the two candidates with the fewest first-choice votes, MPV defines them as the two candidates who are ranked higher than other candidates least often. To determine this, we can count the number of times a candidate is ranked higher than another candidate. If there are three candidates—as in our example of Scarlet, Ultramarine, and Purplish—a candidate who is ranked first on a ballot is ranked higher than two other candidates. A candidate who is ranked second is ranked higher than one other candidate, and a candidate who is ranked third (or is unranked) is ranked higher than no other candidate.

To make this calculation simple, we can give each candidate one "preference point" for each other candidate he or she is ranked above. Thus, being ranked first on a ballot secures two preference points, being ranked second secures one, and being ranked third (or unranked) secures zero. We then tally up each candidate's preference points from all the ballots. The two candidates with the fewest total preference points are the two least-preferred candidates.

Then, just like BTR, this variation conducts a head-to-head face-off between the two least-preferred candidates, eliminating the one ranked higher on fewer ballots. The elimination process continues until the winning candidate is preferred by more voters than the other candidate in the final face-off. This variation is also a Condorcet-compliant method because, as in BTR, a candidate who beats all other candidates in head-to-head face-offs necessarily wins this election, whether this candidate is involved only in the final face-off or any number of previous ones.

This variation is also normatively attractive insofar as it ensures that the candidate most preferred by the electorate will win. The final face-off in the procedure necessarily includes whichever candidate receives the most total preference points based on all the rankings on all the ballots. This candidate will also win the election unless another candidate is ranked higher by more voters (an unlikely but possible outcome). A candidate who beats the candidate with the most overall preference points head-to-head has a better claim to being the most preferred: between the two, more voters prefer this candidate. Thus, MPV truly elects the most-preferred candidate and for this reason can properly be called most-preferred voting.[55]

For anyone attracted to BTR for its simplicity, MPV emulates that attractiveness as much as possible while being far less susceptible to strategic manipulation. To use the example from before, suppose again that Scarlet's supporters rank Ultramarine second rather than third in the hopes of avoiding the election of Purplish (see Table 2.4).

This insincere strategy works in a BTR system, but it fails in an MPV one. To see this, we first calculate the preference points for each candidate:

Scarlet: 70 + 16 = 86
Ultramarine: 66 + 35 = 101
Purplish: 64 + 33 = 97

Scarlet and Purplish are the two candidates with the least preference points, and Purplish beats Scarlet in the initial head-to-head 65–35. Then, Ultramarine beats Purplish 68–32. Thus, not only does Scarlet fail to win the election, but Ultramarine prevails over Purplish when this insincere strategy is employed—a worse outcome in light of the

Table 2.4   Ranked-Choice Ballots with Strategic Voting to Illustrate MPV Method

Percentage of Voters	First Choice	Second Choice	Third Choice
35	Scarlet	*Ultramarine*	*Purplish*
33	Ultramarine	Purplish	Scarlet
16	Purplish	Scarlet	Ultramarine
16	Purplish	Ultramarine	Scarlet

Note: Italics indicate transposed preferences due to strategic voting.

true preferences of Scarlet's supporters. In this respect, strategic voting backfires under MPV, as it does under *Survivor*-style RCV.

Moreover, it is generally harder for candidates to figure out what might offer a strategic advantage under MPV, as opposed to BTR. The reason for this is that candidates need reliable polling only on first-choice preferences to determine the order of the head-to-head elimination rounds in a BTR system. By contrast, candidates need reliable polling on all the rankings on all the ballots to predict the preference points that will determine the order of the head-to-head elimination rounds under MPV. In a real-world election, especially one involving four or five candidates rather than three, it will be exceedingly difficult to make reliable predictions about each candidate's total number of preference points. Thus, voters may be more inclined to simply rank their ballots honestly to avoid the risk of an insincere strategy backfiring and causing a worse outcome from the perspective of their true preferences.[56]

A "Final Five" Form of Most-Preferred Voting

In considering alternative versions of ranked-choice voting, we have repeatedly invoked the same three-candidate hypothetical election involving two polarizing major-party candidates and a more moderate independent or third-party nominee somewhere in between the two extremes. But unless the electoral system is designed so that the general election is limited to only three candidates that emerge from some sort of primary election process, the ultimate choice that voters face will not always—or even often—be confined to just three candidates. We need to consider the possibility that voters will cast a ballot listing a larger number of candidates, and thus we must analyze how alternative versions of ranked-choice voting would handle a hyperpolarized electorate faced with this wider array of options.

For example, we can imagine voters in a general election choosing between five candidates seeking the same statewide office. Nevada is in the process of adopting this kind of electoral system, having voted for it once and now awaiting another referendum to confirm it.[57] If this measure takes effect, it will employ the LPR method of ranked-choice voting. But it is possible to imagine that Nevada—or another state—could instead implement a "final-five" system with a different version of ranked-choice voting, including MPV. These two forms of the "final-five" system would diverge sharply in their treatment of the same highly polarized electorate.[58]

Imagine a "final-five" election with one candidate from each of the five partisan "lanes"—or "hues" of partisanship—identified at the outset: Ultramarine, Blue, Purple, Red, and Scarlet. Suppose in this highly polarized electorate, the percentage of first-choice preferences among voters is as follows:

Ultramarine: 30 percent
Blue: 15 percent
Purple: 10 percent
Red: 16 percent
Scarlet: 29 percent

Suppose further, for sake of simplicity, that all 45 percent of voters who most prefer one of the Democrats (of either hue of blue) have as their second choice the other Democrat and that their preferences are otherwise linear in terms of degrees of partisan distance from the two Democrats. Conversely, the 45 percent of voters who most prefer one of the Republicans (of either shade of red) have as their second choice the other Republican, and they too have remaining preferences that are linear in terms of partisan distance from the two Republicans. Let's suppose that the voters who prefer Purple split slightly in favor of Republicans over Democrats but that they all prefer the more moderate Red and Blue major-party candidates over the more extreme Scarlet and Ultramarine candidates. Table 2.5 lists the ranked-choice ballots that result from those suppositions.

With these ballots, Scarlet wins the election using the LPR method. Purple is eliminated first,[59] then Blue, then Red, and finally Scarlet defeats Ultramarine 51 to 49 percent despite starting out with a smaller share of first-choice votes. In this way, LPR can elevate a more extreme candidate with very little first-choice support in a highly polarized election.[60]

By contrast, with these same ballots, MPV (like any Condorcet-compliant system) will elect Purple as the compromise candidate most representative of the highly polarized electorate's overall preferences—

Table 2.5   Ranked-Choice Ballots in a "Final Five" Election with MPV

Percentage of Voters	First Choice	Second Choice	Third Choice	Fourth Choice	Fifth Choice
30	Ultramarine	Blue	Purple	Red	Scarlet
15	Blue	Ultramarine	Purple	Red	Scarlet
4	Purple	Blue	Red	Ultramarine	Scarlet
6	Purple	Red	Blue	Scarlet	Ultramarine
16	Red	Scarlet	Purple	Blue	Ultramarine
29	Scarlet	Red	Purple	Blue	Ultramarine

taking into account all the preferences indicated on each voter's ranked-choice ballot, from first choices through last choices. MPV does this by first calculating the total number of preference points for each candidate:

Ultramarine: 120 + 45 + 4 = 169
Blue: 60 + 90 + 12 + 12 + 45 = 219
Purple: 40 + 90 + 90 = 220
Red: 64 + 105 + 8 + 45 = 222
Scarlet: 116 + 48 + 6 = 170

Given these totals, the first head-to-head matchup is between Ultramarine and Scarlet, which Scarlet wins 51–49. The second head-to-head is between Scarlet and Blue, which Blue wins 55–45. The third head-to-head is between Blue and Purple, which Purple wins 55–45.

The fourth and final head-to-head in the MPV procedure is between Purple and Red. Purple wins 55–45 and thus wins the election. This example is unusual in that the candidate with the most total preference points (Red) is preferred by fewer voters than another candidate (Purple). But because Purple is the candidate more voters preferred compared to any other in one-on-one matchups, it is the candidate that should prevail according to this method and its underlying philosophy.

Thus, the "final-five" system produces very different outcomes with the same set of ballots depending upon whether it uses the LPR method or a Condorcet-compliant method such as MPV. LPR elects one of the two most polarizing candidates, Scarlet, who loses head-to-head against every other candidate except Ultramarine and does not receive even 30 percent of first-choice votes. By contrast, MPV elects the least polarizing and most consensual candidate, Purple, whom more voters prefer compared to any of the alternatives.

This sharp divergence in outcome between these two methods is hardly an isolated instance. Rather, computer-simulated elections show a clear and pronounced pattern of divergence between the two systems. As we have seen (and summarized in Table 2.6), these computer simulations show a higher divergence in C-force scores between these two methods in a high-polarization electorate than in a low-polarization electorate.

The same type of computer simulations can also be conducted for profiles of the electorates in each of the fifty states. These profiles are constructed using available social science data on the partisan preferences of voters in each state,[61] and the computer simulated elections can be conducted using both methods. When 100,000 simulated elections are conducted for each state using each method, we see the same pattern

Table 2.6   Comparison of C-Force Scores Between LPR and MPV Methods in Simulated Elections

	C-Force, LPR	C-Force, MPV	C-Force Difference
Low polarization	0.517	0.751	0.234
High polarization	0.163	0.479	0.316

of divergence: the difference between C-force scores for LPR and MPV is largest in the most highly polarized states. In other words, the more polarized the state's electorate, the greater the difference in moderating extremism between the two methods of determining winners from the same ranked-choice ballots.

Take Nevada, for example.[62] It is the third-most polarized state, as measured by the average distance of its voters from its median voter (v): 0.293. Nevada is also the state for which the difference in C-force for these two electoral methods is the largest.[63] With LPR, the average distance of winners from the median voter (w) is 0.227, yielding a C-force of 0.225. With MPV, the average distance of winners from the median voter (w) is 0.147, yielding a C-force of 0.498—a difference in C-force of 0.273.[64] We can see this difference in visualizations of Nevada's electorate, LPR (typical IRV) winners, and MPV (Condorcet) winners, as depicted in Figure 2.25.

The same point applies to Arizona, the fourth-most polarized state,[65] where v = 0.292. LPR produces a w of 0.224 and a C-force of 0.232, whereas MPV produces a w of 0.148 and a C-force of 0.494. Figure 2.26 contains the visualizations of these results for Arizona.

The same point also applies to highly polarized states that are not evenly divided, such as Nevada or Arizona, but instead lean heavily to the right. Mississippi, for example, is actually the most polarized state, measured by the average distance of all its voters from the state's median voter (v): 0.296. For Mississippi, LPR elects winners with an average distance from the median voter (w) of 0.203, for a C-force of 0.313,[66] whereas MPV elects winners with a much smaller w of 0.129, for a much higher C-force of 0.562. The difference in C-force is 0.250, the fifth-largest C-force gap in the nation between these two methods of ranked-choice voting. With Mississippi's visualizations, in Figure 2.27, we can see both systems producing winners on the right side of the spectrum, but MPV, as a Condorcet-compliant system, on average produces winners far less extreme than LPR (the basic instant-runoff method):

If we plot each state's C-force score for these two electoral methods in relationship to each state's degree of polarization, we see that a state's C-force for LPR drops sharply as the state's level of polarization rises, as shown in Figure 2.28.[67]

By contrast, a state's C-force score for MPV drops much less sharply as a state's polarization increases (Figure 2.29).

Putting these two plots together, we see that the difference in C-force between LPR and MPV rises rapidly as the degree of a state's polarization increases (Figure 2.30).

Figure 2.25   Voters and Election Winners in Nevada

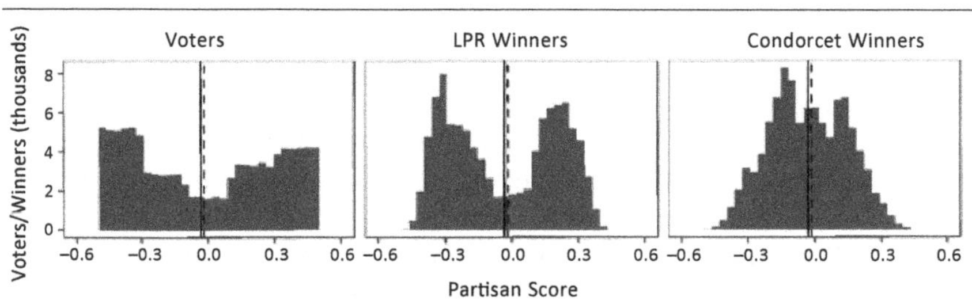

Figure 2.26   Voters and Election Winners in Arizona

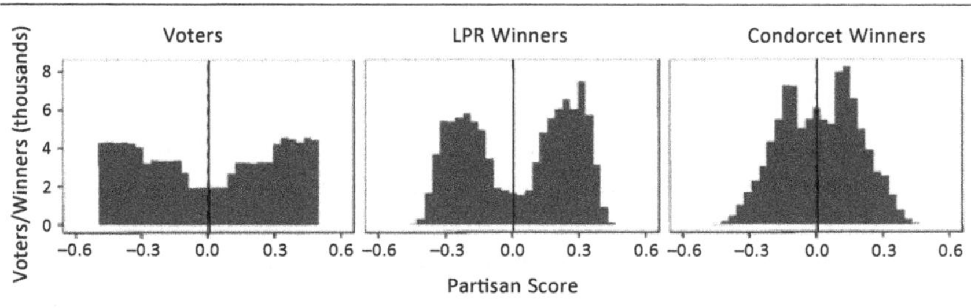

Figure 2.27   Voters and Election Winners in Mississippi

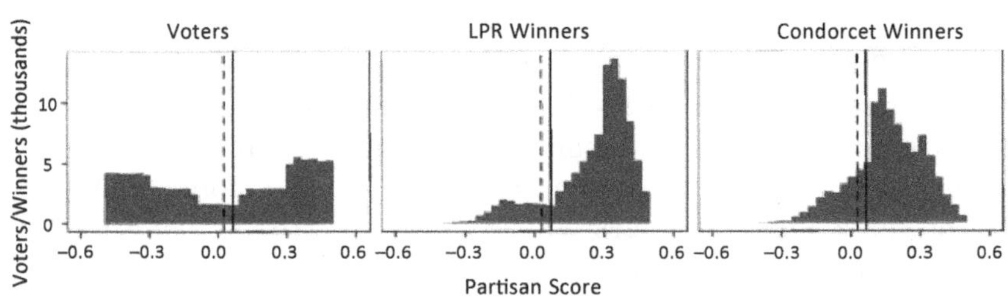

Figure 2.28   Electorate Polarization Versus LPR C-Force

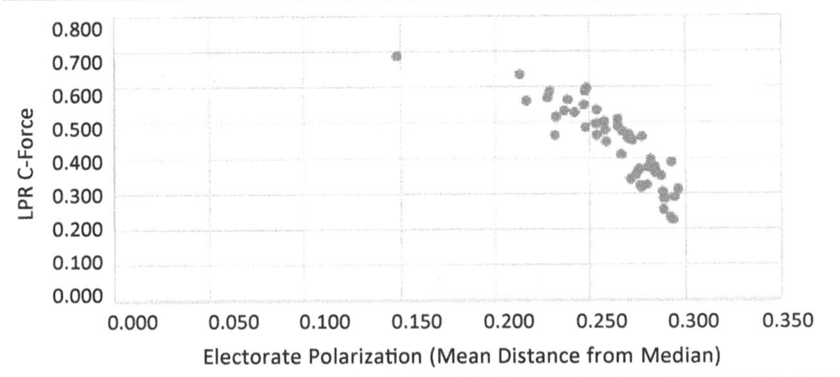

Figure 2.29   Electorate Polarization Versus Condorcet C-Force

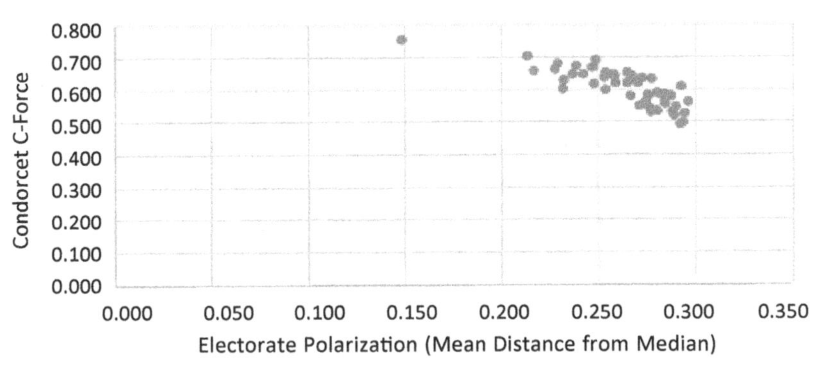

Figure 2.30   C-Force Difference (Condorcet Minus LPR)

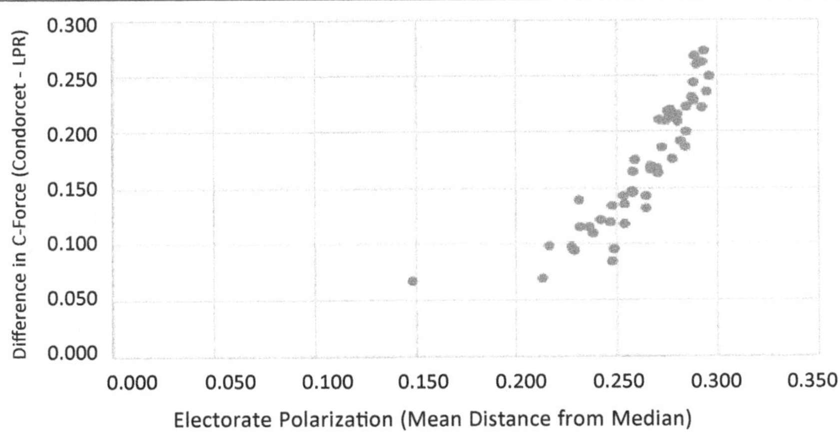

This relationship suggests that states with especially high levels of polarization would be particularly well-advised to consider the differences between LPR and MPV if and when they contemplate the adoption of a "final-four" or "final-five" system with ranked-choice voting (as Alaska has done and Nevada is doing). If a goal of this electoral reform is to reduce the frequency with which more extreme candidates win elections in such states, the sharp difference in C-force scores between the two methods of ranked-choice voting is a reason to consider whether adopting MPV rather than LPR would be more effective.[68]

One may wonder whether it is really desirable to elect a candidate for an important statewide office—say, governor or US senator—who, out of five finalist candidates, receives first-choice rankings of only 10 percent of all voters (as in our example above). That seems counterintuitive, given the electoral tradition of the United States. But is it really worse, in terms of representational fairness for all votes, than the outcome produced by the LPR method from the same set of ballots? That method, as we saw, produced a winner who had only 29 percent of first-choice votes—more than 10 percent to be sure, but nowhere near a majority, and not even the largest share, since Ultramarine had 30 percent but was leapfrogged by Scarlet. Between the two alternative methods, it would seem that MPV does a better job overall by taking account of all the preferences of all the voters— including the tribal desires of Democrats that more extreme Republicans do not win, and vice versa—than the LPR method. Yes, it lets a 10 percent first-choice candidate win by building coalitions on both sides, but that is preferable to a method that lets another relatively unpopular candidate prevail through solely one-sided support.[69]

Which candidate, once in office, is better positioned to govern on behalf of the electorate as a whole? Arguably, the moderate will pursue policies more broadly acceptable to the entire electorate, even if those policies are the first choice of relatively few voters. An extreme candidate, by contrast, will likely endeavor to pull policy toward the extreme, tending to alienate a large portion of the electorate and please only a narrow segment that forms their base of support.[70] The United States has certainly experienced the consequences of extremists attempting to dictate legislative outcomes, as exhibited by the collapse of Rep. Kevin McCarthy's speakership in the House of Representatives and the ensuing elevation of a Speaker who comes from the more extreme wing of his party.[71] Thus, for anyone concerned about the capacity of Congress to reach legislative compromises to address the nation's pressing problems, MPV may be a particularly attractive electoral method to employ in more polarized states.[72]

RCV Under Conditions of Asymmetrical Partisan Polarization

Our previous hypothetical examples, in order to illustrate basic principles, have been structured so that partisan polarization is roughly symmetrical: the spectrum that runs from blue to ultramarine is roughly as long as the spectrum that runs from red to scarlet. But as we saw above, the actual partisan polarization that has occurred in the United States over the last several decades has not been symmetrical. Although there has been polarization among both Democrats and Republicans, the shift toward the extreme has been much greater among Republicans than Democrats. One consequence is that many recent elections have exhibited a three-way split between a traditionally moderate Democrat, an extreme MAGA Republican, and a more moderate traditional Republican.

In this situation, deciding what method of ranked-choice voting to use has significant implications. In circumstances where the MAGA Republican is too extreme for the electorate's median voter, using the lowest-plurality runoff system to tabulate ranked-choice ballots will tend to cause the traditional Democrat to win. By contrast, with the same ranked-choice ballots, if the electorate overall is slightly more red than blue, then the use of most-preferred voting will tend to elect the more moderate traditional Republican.

Here is a set of hypothetical ranked-choice ballots that will illustrate this point. Suppose the three candidates are Blue (the traditional Democrat), Scarlet (the extreme MAGA Republican), and Crimson (a more moderate Republican like Senator Mitt Romney). Imagine the ranked-choice ballots involving these three candidates are listed in Table 2.7.

With these ballots, LPR elects Blue: Crimson is eliminated first; then Blue prevails over Scarlet 51–49. This is true even though only 40 percent of first-choice votes were cast for the Democrat, while 60 percent of first-choice votes were cast for either of the two Republicans.

Table 2.7   Ranked-Choice Ballots to Illustrate Difference Between LPR and MPV

Percentage of Voters	First Choice	Second Choice	Third Choice
40	Blue	Crimson	Scarlet
11	Crimson	Blue	Scarlet
14	Crimson	Scarlet	Blue
35	Scarlet	Crimson	Blue

The reason is that Scarlet is extreme enough that a significant fraction (although not a majority) of Crimson's supporters cross party lines to make Blue rather than Scarlet their second choice.

But if MPV—or any Condorcet-consistent procedure—is the method for tabulating these same ranked-choice ballots, then Crimson wins the election, defeating both Blue and Scarlet head-to-head. Thus, one of the two Republican candidates—the more moderate one—wins or loses depending on which tabulation method is used.

Something very similar to this hypothetical happened when Alaska first used its ranked-choice voting procedure in a 2022 special election for the state's single congressional seat. The three candidates were Mary Peltola, a traditionally moderate Democrat; Sarah Palin, an extreme Trump-endorsed MAGA Republican; and Nick Begich, a more traditional Republican. Peltola received 40 percent of first-choice votes, while the two Republicans split the remaining 60 percent, with Palin receiving more than Begich. Thus, under the LPR method, Begich was the first candidate eliminated. Palin got more of the second-choice votes from those who ranked Begich first, but Peltola received just enough of those second-choice votes from Begich's supporters to narrowly beat Palin 51.5 to 48.5 percent.

Democrats saw this result as a triumph of RCV's power to defeat an extremist like Palin. Republicans, however, saw it as a reason to repudiate RCV entirely: their two candidates got 60 percent of first-choice votes, and yet the Democrat won the seat. That result, from their perspective, meant that RCV was inherently flawed.

The problem was not the use of ranked-choice ballots, however. The problem was the particular tabulation method used to identify the winner from those ranked-choice ballots. The more moderate Republican in the race, Begich, was the Condorcet winner: he defeated both Peltola and Palin head-to-head. Yet he was the first to be eliminated with the use of LPR. Republicans were understandably upset about the unfairness of that outcome.

Unfortunately, Republicans have overreacted in their opposition to ranked-choice voting. Instead of condemning the particular tabulation method, they have attacked RCV in general without differentiating among tabulation methods. The Republican National Committee adopted a resolution "call[ing] on Congress, state legislatures, and voters to oppose ranked choice voting in every locality and level of government." Elected Republicans in various states have heeded this call and enacted or introduced legislation aimed at prohibiting the use of RCV.

The point here is not to advance an electoral method that favors one party or the other. Rather, the point is to identify the method that is fairest to all voters, regardless of their party affiliation or degree of partisanship. With respect to single-seat elections, the class of electoral methods that are Condorcet-consistent can be reasonably deemed the fairest because, by electing the candidate whom a majority prefers compared to every other candidate, these methods leave the fewest voters on the losing side of the outcome.

As we have seen, various forms of RCV are Condorcet-consistent, even though LPR is not. Thus, there is no need to object to RCV categorically. But insofar as some states may remain adamantly opposed to RCV, it is still possible to implement a Condorcet-consistent electoral method without using RCV at all.

A "Top-Three" General Election Without RCV

States wishing to reduce the risk of extreme winners in statewide elections without using any form of ranked-choice voting may wish to consider a "top-three" variation on California's "top-two" system. California's system, to recall, uses a nonpartisan primary (of the same type as Alaska's "top-four" system) to determine the two candidates who will proceed to the general election. It would be possible to use the same kind of nonpartisan primary but advance to the general election the three candidates who receive the most votes, rather than just the top two.

In the general election, voters would then express their preference between each pair of the three candidates: A versus B, A versus C, and B versus C. A candidate who receives more votes against each opponent in the general would win the election. For instance, if more voters prefer both B to A and B to C, then B wins. In this case, the procedure elects the Condorcet winner among the three general election finalists.[73]

There is, of course, a chance that one candidate is preferred by more voters over one of his or her general election opponents but not the other. In other words, more voters might prefer A to B, B to C, and C to A. In this case, there needs to be a rule for breaking a three-way tie.

Two straightforward tiebreaker rules are possible. One is simply to count all the votes that each candidate receives across all three sets of pairwise preferences, and the candidate with highest total number of votes wins.[74]

The other simple rule for breaking the tie is to elect the candidate whose single pairwise defeat has the smallest margin. Suppose A beats

B, 55–45; B beats C, 53–47; and C beats A, 51–49. In this case, A's margin of defeat against C, 2 points, is the smallest of the three margins of defeat, making A the winner according to this tiebreaker rule, which in the electoral science literature is (rather unhelpfully) called "minimax."[75] One normatively attractive quality of this tiebreaker rule is that it identifies the candidate closest to being the Condorcet winner when there isn't one: because it elects the candidate with the narrowest margin of defeat, it chooses the winner who comes closest to being preferred by a majority of voters over each other opponent. This attribute of the rule causes it to elect whichever of the three candidates is least divisive—or, to put the point more positively, is most unifying.

It is easy to see how this "top-three" system would counteract extremism. If two of the three finalists are relatively extreme but the third is not, the third is most likely to be preferred by more voters in head-to-head matchups against the other two and thus win the election. This is true whether the two more extreme candidates are on opposite sides of the third candidate or on one side of the partisan divide with the third closer to the electorate's median voter (either on the same or the opposite side of the partisan divide). In other words, in an electorate where the median voter is exactly Purple—equidistant from Blue and Red—the candidate closest to Purple, whether more Violet or more Fuchsia, will win, regardless of whether the other candidates are two more extreme shades of Blue, two more extreme shades of Red, or one extreme shade of Blue and one extreme shade of Red.

If this kind of "top three" system were adopted in states or districts where extreme candidates are currently able to win under the conventional electoral system of partisan primaries and plurality-winner general elections, moderate candidates would be more likely to prevail. Consider the cases of North Carolina and Ohio. In both states, an extreme election denier endorsed by Trump won the 2022 US Senate election: former Representative Ted Budd in North Carolina, who had promoted Trump's election denialism in the House, and J. D. Vance in Ohio, who embraced election denialism and other extreme positions in order to obtain Trump's endorsement in the state's Republican primary. Both candidates defeated their Democratic opponents in the conventional plurality-winner general election, and both would have prevailed even if their states had used California's "top-two" system or Alaska's "top-four" system with its lowest-plurality runoff procedure. But if these states had used the kind of "top-three" system described here, less extreme Republicans would have had a better chance of winning instead.[76]

In North Carolina, the extremist Budd defeated former governor Pat McCrory, a much more moderate Republican, in the primary. But if the state had used this "top-three" system with its nonpartisan primary, McCrory would have advanced to the general election along with Budd and the Democrat. In the general, McCrory almost certainly would have won: voters who preferred the Democrat to Budd (47 percent of the electorate) would have preferred McCrory to Budd, and voters who preferred Budd to the Democrat would also have preferred McCrory to the Democrat. Thus, McCrory would have been preferred by more voters when paired against both opponents and therefore prevailed in the "top-three" system.

Similarly, if Ohio had used the "top-three" system in 2022, the broadly popular incumbent, Rob Portman, would have been able to run for reelection without having to compete in a Republican primary dominated by Trump and his extremist MAGA supporters. In a "top-three" nonpartisan primary, Portman easily would have secured a spot on the general election ballot, along with Vance and the Democrat. Compared directly against Vance, Portman almost certainly would have been preferred by more voters, as the Democrat's supporters (also 47 percent of the electorate) would prefer the more moderate Portman to extremist Vance. Portman also would have been preferred by more voters compared to the Democrat, since Vance's supporters would prefer Portman to the Democrat. Thus, the "top-three" system would have allowed more moderate Republicans to win the 2022 US Senate elections in Ohio and North Carolina.[77]

The same point applies to House of Representative seats. Consider Arizona's second congressional district. In 2022, another Trump-endorsed election denier, Eli Crane, won the GOP primary against a more moderate Republican and then went on to win the general election against the Democrat. Crane would become one of the most extreme members of the House GOP caucus, where he was one of eight Republicans led by Matt Gaetz to topple Kevin McCarthy's speakership. But if Arizona had used the "top-three" system, the more moderate Republican most likely would have won the general election against both Crane and the Democrat.[78]

Used nationwide for congressional elections, the "top-three" system would tend to send fewer extremists to Congress. Overall, this would lead to a greater capacity to compromise, pass legislation, and govern in the national interest. It would also significantly reduce the likelihood of extremists in Congress, especially in the House of Representatives, engaging in the kind of antidemocracy behavior that former representative Liz Cheney has warned could occur if a leading election denier retains the speakership after the 2024 elections.[79]

This "top-three" system obviously comes with the cost of making voters in the general election vote three times to elect the winner of a single office. But this cost should be weighed against the benefit of effectively counteracting extremism, particularly if one seeks an alternative to ranked-choice voting. Both methods involve trade-offs. Ranked-choice voting makes it much easier for voters to select among more than three candidates. In an election with four candidates, a Condorcet-consistent election without ranked-choice ballots would require six direct pairwise comparisons, a prohibitive burden to impose on voters. But insofar as a choice among the top three candidates in a nonpartisan primary is sufficient to avoid the election of extremists—as indicated by the North Carolina, Ohio, and Arizona examples—having voters make three direct pairwise comparisons is not significantly more burdensome than having voters rank three candidates in order of preference.

Apart from the task of casting the ballot, the "top-three" system is easier for voters to understand than ranked-choice voting. It is also easier for election administrators to compute and for voters to follow on election night. As votes are counted, the running tally of A versus B, A versus C, and B versus C is reported. It is therefore easy to see immediately if one candidate is ahead of both opponents (or if a tiebreaker will be necessary). The "top-three" system requires no complicated calculation process involving the transfer of ballots from one candidate to another after candidates are eliminated, as required by a ranked-choice voting procedure.

This is not to say the "top-three" system is superior to ranked-choice voting. Some states might prefer the former, while others might prefer a version of the latter. Both are capable of counteracting extremism when coupled with the kind of nonpartisan primary used in California and Alaska—especially if the form of ranked-choice voting used elects Condorcet winners, as does the direct "top-three" system. Given their roles as laboratories of democracy, states can experiment with these different systems for avoiding the election of extremist candidates and learn through experience the detailed pros and cons of each alternative.

The Role of Parties in a Nonpartisan Primary System

Whether a state adopts a "top-four" or "top-five" nonpartisan primary as in Alaska or potentially Nevada, or instead the kind of "top-three" nonpartisan primary just discussed, there remains the question of how political parties interact with the chosen system. The nonpartisan primary can permit candidates to list the political party with which they are affiliated (as they do in California and Alaska). The nonpartisan primary could also permit candidates to indicate if they have been endorsed or nominated by their party in a preprimary party procedure, such as a caucus or a convention. A state could even permit a form of "fusion voting" in which a candidate's name could appear on the ballot—in either the primary, the general election, or both—as endorsed or nominated by more than one party.

Thus, the decision to use a nonpartisan primary does not by itself dictate the specific relationship between political parties and the electoral system. The nonpartisan primary functions essentially as the first round of a two-round electoral system operated by the government, similar to the two-round system that France uses for its presidential and national legislative elections. Political parties operate robustly in France, where voters know which candidates are endorsed or nominated by which parties for both rounds of the two-round system. The same could be true of a well-structured two-round system in the United States.

There remains the question of how many candidates should appear on the nonpartisan primary ballot and what method or rule should be used to determine their qualification. Forty-eight candidates participated in Alaska's first "top-four" primary, a special election to fill the state's single congressional seat, and thirty or more candidates often run in California's "top-two" primaries.[80] That is far too many candidates for voters to reasonably evaluate.

States could modernize the procedures by which candidates qualify for nonpartisan primary ballots, adopting an online system for electronic signature gathering to replace the old-fashioned pen-and-paper method currently employed. No aspect of today's electoral process is more antiquated than signature gathering for ballot access. A candidate's supporters, using their smartphones or tablets, could still go door-to-door to collect electronic signatures from registered voters. But registered voters could also go online themselves to sign any candidate's petition. Because signatures are not secret ballots, gathering them online does not raise the same internet security concerns as online voting.

States could set a reasonable threshold for the number of online signatures needed to qualify for the nonpartisan primary ballot. In a "top-four" or "top-five" system, a state might wish to have no more than a dozen or so candidates on the primary ballot, from which voters would winnow the field to four or five for the general election. For a "top-three" system, a state might wish to have no more than ten candidates in the primary.

A state could aim for these targets by setting the required number of signatures accordingly and adjusting them if necessary. For example, if a requirement of signatures from 1 percent of registered voters produced too many candidates, the state could raise the threshold to 2 percent or even higher for future elections. The Supreme Court upheld a 5 percent requirement before the invention of the internet,[81] and given the convenience of an online signature-gathering system—which would allow any candidate to post his or her petition—any threshold reasonably tailored to the state's target number of candidates would pass constitutional muster.

What voting procedure should be used in the nonpartisan primary itself to determine which candidates advance to the general election? In a "top-four" or "top-five" system that uses a form of ranked-choice voting in the general election, it would also be possible to use RCV in the nonpartisan primary to narrow the field to the specified number of finalists. Both lowest-plurality runoff and most-preferred voting could be adapted for this kind of nonpartisan primary. Doing so would tend to reduce the risk of extremists making it onto the general election ballot, especially if MPV were the particular method of RCV employed for this purpose.

But in a state that decided to adopt the direct "top-three" system described above in order to avoid using RCV in the general election, it seems unlikely that any form of RCV would be the preferred method for the nonpartisan primary.[82] If this is the case, the simplest procedure for the state to employ in the primary would be traditional plurality voting: voters select the one candidate they most prefer, and the candidates with the most votes advance to the general election. This is the procedure that both California and Alaska currently use for their nonpartisan primaries—California to identify two candidates for the general election and Alaska to identify four.

The "top-three" system could use exactly the same procedure to identify three finalists for the general election. Although there is some risk in an especially polarized primary electorate that the top three candidates will all be extreme partisans from either or both sides of the partisan divide, the examples from the 2022 election described above indicate that this risk is fairly low. Much more likely is that one of the three finalists will be relatively moderate, and this more moderate candidate will prevail against two more extreme opponents. Or, if two candidates are fairly moderate and only one extreme, as was often true of the top three candidates in the 2022 midterms, then at least one of the more moderate candidates would win and the sole extremist among the three finalists would not be elected.

Thus, a nonpartisan primary, whether part of a "top-four" or "top-five" system with RCV or a "top-three" system without RCV, can help protect against the election of extremists. But for states that insist on retaining partisan primaries, there is another possibility to discuss.

Party-Based RCV System

Rather than qualifying candidates for the general election ballot, an electoral system could qualify political parties. In a "top-five" system, that is, the top five qualifying parties could appear on the general election ballot, with the names of candidates listed only because they are party nominees. The parties could make their nominations through a primary or convention (or perhaps some other means). The nominated candidates would then be on the ballot by virtue of their parties having earned a spot that they are entitled to fill.

Maine operates something like this party-based RCV system.[83] Parties can qualify for the general election ballot, but so too can independent candidates. There is no specific limit on the number of parties or candidates that can qualify for the general election ballot. Rather, parties or candidates can qualify through separate threshold requirements. Whatever the number of candidates on the ballot, the lowest-plurality runoff form of RCV is used to elect the winner.

Maine's experience with this relatively new system is limited and thus gives us only a rudimentary sense of its capacity to promote moderation. The dominance of the two major political parties in Maine, as elsewhere in the United States, suggests that this version of RCV has only a modest capacity to counteract creeping polarization and extremism. As indicated above, a new centrist third party would not be competitive in Maine's system—with its use of LPR—unless the party's share of first-choice votes threatened to become large enough to move it into second place ahead of one of the two main parties.[84]

Nonetheless, using LPR rather than simple plurality voting within Maine's party-based system may cause the two major parties to stay closer to the center than they otherwise would.[85] Doing so would tend to keep the creation of a centrist third party in check. Moreover, LPR would reduce the pressure on major parties and their candidates to cater to the political extremes on either side, because as long as first-choice support for extremist parties stayed below that for Democrats and Republicans, then the process would eliminate the extremist party nominees and make the final choice between the Democrat and the Republican.

If polarization in a Maine-style system gets to the point where the two dominant parties are at the extreme ends of the political spectrum—say the twenty-yard lines or even closer to the end zones—and one or more third parties occupy the center but cannot attract enough support even through the LPR process to leapfrog either of the two extremist parties, it may be necessary to consider MPV (or some other Condorcet-compliant form of RCV) as a way to prevent elections from boiling down to a choice between these two extremist parties. MPV would be a suitable substitute for LPR in a Maine-style system, and regardless of how candidates qualify for the general election ballot, it could be used to determine the winner from the ranked-choice ballots.

For those who believe it is important to organize electoral competition around political parties rather than candidates, modifying Maine's version of RCV to employ MPV rather than LPR would open up the system to more centrist parties. To win over the median voter under the MPV procedure, parties and their nominees could not stray too far from the center of the electorate. If the Democrats and Republicans opened up a hole in the middle, another party would be able to fill it. If the Democrats and Republicans moved back toward the center in order to avoid the emergence of a competitive third party, the effect would still be to return electoral competition to between the forty-yard lines.

Fusion Voting Within an RCV System

It is also possible to incorporate fusion voting within a party-based ranked-choice voting system such as Maine's. Fusion voting permits a candidate on the general election ballot to be the nominee of more than one political party. All the votes cast for the candidate count toward his or her vote total regardless of which party nomination the voter chooses to support when casting the ballot. The same principle could apply when tallying preferences for a candidate on a ranked ballot—although it would be necessary to have a clear ballot design that prevents voters from attempting to give the same candidate two different rankings.

Some have advocated fusion voting in a simple plurality-winner electoral system, without ranked ballots, as a way to counteract polarization.[86] The theory is that in a fusion voting system a new middle-of-the-road party—let's call it the Moderate Party—could act as a kind of broker, co-nominating whichever major-party nominee stayed closer to the center of the electorate. The hope would be that some voters, who would not vote for a candidate labeled as a Democrat or a Republican, would be willing to vote for the same candidate if co-labeled as a Moderate.

While the idea is attractive in principle, there is little evidence that it would have a significant effect in practice. New York and Connecticut have used fusion voting for decades, but no Moderate Party has formed there to play this kind of brokering role. Instead, fusion voting has permitted more extreme parties—to the left of Democrats and to the right of Republicans—to play a leveraging role that risks pulling the major parties away from the center of the electorate rather than toward the middle.

In an RCV system, however, a different form of fusion might exert a more powerful centripetal effect. If a Moderate Party formed a fusion alliance with either the Democrats or the Republicans, they might be able to convince their respective voters to rank each other's preferred candidate second while still ranking their favored candidate first. In an RCV system with lowest-plurality runoff, if the Moderate Party's most-preferred candidate were to be eliminated first, the alliance might cause all the ballots ranking that candidate first to be transferred to the other party in the alliance. The attractiveness of this alliance might tend to pull the two major parties closer to the center than fusion voting would in a simple plurality-winner system.

A fusion alliance in an electoral system with most-preferred voting would likely have an even greater centripetal effect. If the Moderate Party and the Democrats, for example, convinced their supporters to rank each other's nominees first and second, it would be difficult for parties on the right side of the spectrum to prevail in a Condorcet-compliant system like MPV. Of course, the same holds true in the opposite direction: if the Moderate Party entered a fusion alliance with Republicans, it would be hard for Democrats to win. Thus, a new centrist party would be an especially effective powerbroker in the context of a Condorcet-compliant system that facilitated this kind of fusion alliance.

A form of fusion voting could also be incorporated into an electoral system like California's "top-two" system. Parties could nominate candidates prior to the first round of this two-round system. Then, if a party's nominee did not advance to the final round, that party could enter a fusion alliance with whichever advancing party's nominee it preferred. Thus, if the Moderate Party's candidate did not make it to the final round, the party could co-endorse whichever "top-two" finalist it considered most moderate. This kind of fusion in a "top-two" system would also have the greatest effect in offsetting polarization if the procedure for determining which "top-two" candidates advance to the final round is not a simple plurality vote but rather some form of RCV. If MPV is used in the first round of this system, the candidate with the most preference points will be one of the "top-two" finalists, a sign of being broadly acceptable to the entire electorate, and the other candidate will either have the second-most preference points or will have advanced through the elimination process by being preferred each time by more voters than the other candidate in contention.

Conclusion

Political polarization may reach a point where no electoral system can save a society from tearing itself apart. The United States arguably reached that point in the 1850s, in the lead-up to the Civil War, and some citizens—and even political scientists—fear that partisan animosity is once again reaching an unsustainable level.

The exploration of alternative electoral systems in this chapter is premised on the proposition that, as long as polarization has not yet reached a breaking point, our systems for aggregating electoral preferences and determining the winners of elections can be reformed to counteract, at least to some degree, the centrifugal forces pushing the two sides ever further apart.

There is no single electoral system that all states should adopt to counteract the rise of political extremism. Instead, there is a family of alternative electoral systems, each of which has the capacity to counteract polarization and extremism to varying degrees, and each of which involves its own particular set of policy trade-offs.[87] Some of these alternatives may be easier for the public to understand and accept than others—a factor that must be a key consideration apart from whatever theoretical benefits a system may have.

The "top-three" system offers considerable advantages, including its straightforward accessibility to voters and its simplicity to administer and report. Voters need not bother with the complexities associated with various forms of ranked-choice voting. Among the forms of RCV that counteract the effect of polarization, the *Survivor*-style Coombs method is probably the most accessible to the average citizen because of its similarity to the TV show's elimination method. The most-preferred voting method is arguably superior in terms of its ability to elect the candidate who performs the best against the competition, but insofar as it is less familiar and harder to comprehend, it may on balance be less attractive than the *Survivor*-style method.[88]

Different states suffer from different degrees of polarization. Each state has its own unique electoral profile, although some share similarities.[89] Thus, different states reasonably may wish to make different choices regarding what particular electoral reforms best suit their needs. Simply put, some states may need stronger antiextremism "medicine" than others. For example, the typical lowest-plurality runoff version of RCV may be enough to cure some states of their current bout of polarization. But in other, more polarized states—or if polarization gets worse in the future—a stronger dose of MPV (or some other Condorcet-compliant form of RCV) may be needed to counteract extremism.

Each state's choice will be partially a question of facts: Just how polarized is the electorate? But it also will be partially a question of values: Just how important is it to keep electoral competition within the traditional forty-yard lines? The combination of these considerations for each state necessarily means there is no "one-size-fits-all" solution.

States should be encouraged to experiment with alternatives, including those considered here. Even if there is no single perfect system for all states, it is fair to say that most would benefit from moving away—at least to some extent—from the prevailing system of partisan primaries followed by plurality-winner general elections. It is this system, combined with increased polarization in the electorate, that causes overrepresentation of extremism in Congress and state legislatures. Politics is no longer played within the forty-yard lines. Getting the competition back toward the middle of the field in most states will require some sort of structural reform of the electoral process along the lines we have considered here.

Notes

1. This chapter resulted from the deliberations of the task force's working group on ballot structures, which included Eric Maskin, Charles Stewart, Lisa Manheim, and Michael Kang. Although the chapter benefits greatly from those contributions, readers should not assume that the working group members agree with all of the content.

2. Georgia has a variation of a two-round system, which includes the possibility of a runoff between the top two vote getters in the general election if no candidate in the general election receives a majority of votes. Georgia's general election follows traditional partisan primaries and in this respect is more like most states than the "top two" system used in California and Washington. Although Georgia governor Brian Kemp and secretary of state Brad Raffensberger were able to defeat primary challenges encouraged by former president Donald Trump because of their role in resisting his efforts to overturn the 2020 presidential election in that state, the structure of Georgia's system as a general matter is unlikely

to more effectively counteract extremism than the "top two" system used in California and Washington. When extremist candidates win a partisan primary in Georgia's system, they can then win the general election—with or without a runoff—as long as they are more popular than the alternative, typically the nominee of the opposing major party.

France also uses a similar two-round system for its presidential and legislative elections, and in some key ways France's system resembles the one in California and Washington. The first round in France, as in those states, is nonpartisan in the sense that all candidates from all parties compete against each other, with the top two vote getters advancing to the second round. In France, however, there is only a single candidate from each party in the first round: a candidate who has received the party's nomination from an internal party procedure. Moreover, France holds the two rounds only two weeks apart, whereas in California and Washington the two rounds are separated by many months. Insofar as other states find a nonpartisan "top two" primary attractive, they should consider adopting some of the French system's specific features, which help increase turnout in the first round.

3. Richard H. Pildes, "Political Reforms to Combat Extremism," in *Our Nation at Risk: Election Integrity as a National Security Issue*, ed. Karen J. Greenberg and Julian E. Zelizer (New York: NYU Press, 2014), 70–92.

4. John Rawls, *Political Liberalism* (New York: Columbia University Press, 2025).

5. For an exploration of the value of alignment in the design and implementation of electoral systems, see Nicholas O. Stephanopoulos, *Aligning Election Law* (New York: Oxford University Press, 2024).

6. Nolan McCarty, *Polarization: What Everyone Needs to Know* (New York: Oxford University Press, 2019); Rachel Kleinfeld, *Polarization, Democracy, and Political Violence in the United States: What the Research Says* (Washington, DC: Carnegie Endowment for International Peace, 2023).

7. Joseph Bafumi and Michael C. Herron, "Leapfrog Representation and Extremism: A Study of American Voters and Their Members in Congress," *American Political Science Review* 104, no. 3 (2010): 519. https://doi.org/10.1017/S0003055410000316; Nathan Atkinson, Edward B. Foley, and Scott Ganz, "Beyond the Spoiler Effect: Can Ranked Choice Voting Solve the Problem of Political Polarization?," Georgetown McDonough School of Business Research Paper No. 4411173, *Illinois Law Review* (October 2024). http://dx.doi.org/10.2139/ssrn.4411173. An important new paper by Atkinson and Ganz demonstrates the degree to which this problem has become exacerbated in recent years. Nathan Atkinson and Scott Ganz, "Robust Electoral Competition: Rethinking Electoral Systems to Encourage Representative Outcomes," Georgetown McDonough School of Business Research Paper No. 4728225, *Maryland Law Review* (2024). http://dx.doi.org/10.2139/ssrn.4728225.

8. Cook Political Report with Amy Walter, Cook Partisan Voting Index.

9. The fact that Democrats cluster in cities while Republicans are dispersed throughout rural areas causes a district's median voter to diverge sharply from the statewide median voter even without any artificial manipulation of district lines due to partisan gerrymandering. When manipulative gerrymandering is added to the underlying divergence caused by legitimate geography, the degree of difference between a district's median and the state's can become even larger—and considerably so. See Stef W. Knight, "First Look: Battleground Imbalance," *Axios* (July 25, 2021) (describing study showing this difference in each state).

10. Appendixes to this chapter are available at https://kb.osu.edu/handle/1811/105337.

11. For an excellent explanation of why this is true, see Nathan Atkinson and Scott Ganz, "Robust Electoral Competition: Rethinking Electoral Systems to Encourage Representative Outcomes," Georgetown McDonough School of Business Research Paper No. 4728225, *Maryland Law Review* (2024).

12. Robert A. Dahl, *A Preface to Democratic Theory* (Chicago: University of Chicago Press, 2006), 98.

13. Robert A. Dahl, *A Preface to Democratic Theory* (Chicago: University of Chicago Press, 2006), 97–98.

14. Anthony Downs, *An Economic Theory of Democracy* (New York: Harper & Bros., 1957), 120.

15. Anthony Downs, *An Economic Theory of Democracy* (New York: Harper & Bros., 1957), 120.

16. Benjamin Reilly, "Centripetalism and Electoral Moderation in Established Democracies," *Nationalism and Ethnic Politics* 24, no. 2 (2018): 201.

17. Scott Ganz deserves credit for suggesting this metric.

18. Rachel Kleinfeld, *Polarization, Democracy, and Political Violence in the United States: What the Research Says* (Washington, DC: Carnegie Endowment for International Peace, 2023), 16, 21, 26.

19. John Sides, Chris Tausanovitch, and Lynn Vavrek, *The Bitter End: The 2020 Presidential Campaign and the Challenge to American Democracy* (Princeton, NJ: Princeton University Press, 2022).

20. Nathan Atkinson and Scott Ganz, "Robust Electoral Competition: Rethinking Electoral Systems to Encourage Representative Outcomes," Georgetown McDonough School of Business Research Paper No. 4728225, *Maryland Law Review* (2024).

21. A few states use multimember districts for their state legislatures, although they do not use proportional representation for these multimember districts. "State Legislative Chambers That Use Multi-member Districts," Ballotpedia.

22. Bill Bishop and Robert Cushing, *The Big Sort: Why the Clustering of Like-minded America Is Tearing Us Apart* (New York: Houghton Mifflin, 2008).

23. Dan Balz and Clara Ence Morse, "American Democracy Is Cracking. These Forces Help Explain Why," *Washington Post*, August 18, 2023.

24. As already suggested, the problem of "natural" gerrymandering also occurs on a statewide level relative to the nation as a whole. Even though the United States is relatively purple, many states are deep blue or deep red, and their statewide elections accordingly are uncompetitive. This is more the case for US Senate elections than for gubernatorial elections. Voters in a blue state like Massachusetts will occasionally vote for a Republican governor as a kind of check against Democrats becoming too extreme. But in US Senate elections, where partisan control of the entire chamber depends upon elections in all the states, voters are less likely to cross party lines in a way that would hurt their preferred party's overall share of Senate seats. To the extent that uncompetitive elections increase the power of political extremism, that extra factor compounds the problem analyzed in this chapter. For further analysis on this point, see the online appendix to this chapter, available at https://kb.osu.edu/handle/1811/105337.

25. These profiles come from Nathan Atkinson, Edward B. Foley, and Scott Ganz, "Beyond the Spoiler Effect: Can Ranked Choice Voting Solve the Problem of Political Polarization?," Georgetown McDonough School of Business Research Paper No. 4411173, *Illinois Law Review* (October 2024). (The profiles for all fifty states are in the online appendix to this chapter, available at https://kb.osu.edu/handle/1811/105337.)

26. Politics, of course, is not confined to the single dimension of traditional left-right competition. Still, as the eminent political scientist John Aldrich explained in his book *Why Parties?: A Second Look*, it is necessary to organize political competition along a single dimension, at least in the legislature if not in the electorate as a whole, so that some group can form that is able to secure a majority of votes. John H. Aldrich, *Why Parties?: A Second Look* (Chicago: University of Chicago Press, 2011). Moreover, as reductionist as it can sometimes seem, characterizing current American political competition as a battle between blue and red teams, with some purple voters in middle (and members of the blue and red teams varying in the degree of intensity to their blueness or redness), is a largely accurate depiction. See Anthony Fowler et al., "Moderates," *American Political Science Review* 117, no. 2 (2023) (most voters are identifiable on traditional left-right ideological spectrum). See also Nolan McCarty, *Polarization: What Everyone Needs to Know* (New York: Oxford University Press, 2019), 66 (discussing the increasing one-dimensionality of electoral competition).

27. See Jeremy Gelman, Evan Pristos, and Benjamin Reilly, "The Consequences of a Top-5/RCV System in Nevada: Advantaging Moderates but Sidelining Third Parties?," SSRN, April 27, 2024. https://dx.doi.org/10.2139/ssrn.4808131.

28. Nathan Atkinson and Scott Ganz, "Robust Electoral Competition: Rethinking Electoral Systems to Encourage Representative Outcomes," Georgetown McDonough School of Business Research Paper No. 4728225, *Maryland Law Review* (2024).

29. Different turnout percentages on each side, reflecting different degrees of enthusiasm, can also be a factor in electoral shifts back and forth between the two parties. John Sides, Chris Tausanovitch, and Lynn Vavrek, *The Bitter End: The 2020 Presidential Campaign and the Challenge to American Democracy* (Princeton, NJ: Princeton University Press, 2022), 6 (when there is partisan parity in a "calcified" electorate—whose partisan positions are rigid—small shifts in turnout percentages between the two sides can shift the election one way or the other).

30. Nathan Atkinson, Scott Ganz, and John Mantus, "A Simple Agent-Based Model for Simulating Single Winner Elections," SSRN, July 31, 2024.

31. Most self-identified "independent" voters, who do not officially affiliate with a political party as part of their voter registration, nonetheless act like partisan-leaning voters. "Political Independents: Who They Are, What They Think," Pew Research Center, March 14, 2019.

32. See Lee Drutman, "American politics has reached peak polarization," Vox, May 24, 2016, https://www.vox.com/polyarchy/2016/3/24/11298808/american-politics-peak-polarization.

33. For a dramatic visualization of this increased polarization over time, see "Political Polarization in the American Public," Pew Research Center, June 12, 2014, https://www.pewresearch.org/politics/2014/06/12/political-polarization-in-the-american-public/.

One can question the specific methodology underlying this visualization, but there is little doubt that a significant degree of increased "affective" polarization, or partisan "tribalism," has occurred in recent decades. Kleinfeld, *Polarization, Democracy*, 3.

34. See, e.g., Matt Bai, "Americans Always Need an Existential Threat. This Time, It's Each Other," *Washington Post*, July 17, 2024.

35. Nathan Atkinson and Scott Ganz, "Robust Electoral Competition: Rethinking Electoral Systems to Encourage Representative Outcomes," Georgetown McDonough School of Business Research Paper No. 4728225, *Maryland Law Review* (2024) (demonstrating this point with statistics).

36. See Nathan Atkinson and Scott Ganz, "Robust Electoral Competition: Rethinking Electoral Systems to Encourage Representative Outcomes," Georgetown

McDonough School of Business Research Paper No. 4728225, *Maryland Law Review* (2024).

37. In 2022, Andrew Yang and Christine Todd Whitman endeavored to form a moderate "Forward" party. Tim Reid, "Former Republicans and Democrats Form New Third U.S. Political Party," Reuters, July 27, 2022.

38. Whatever one thinks about the wisdom (or lack thereof) of the effort by the centrist No Labels group to qualify for the ballot with the view of potentially running a third-party presidential candidate, the fact that this effort occurred (before it failed to attract any viable candidate) is indicative of the belief that there is a gap in the center needing to be filled. Likewise, the fact that prominent politicians such as Mitt Romney, Joe Manchin, and Liz Cheney have talked openly about the idea of forming a third centrist party indicates the increasing appetite for this. Erin Doherty, "Romney's Third-Party Dance with Manchin Spills into View," Axios. September 13, 2023. In fact, Gallup polling shows the public's desire for a third major party is the highest it has ever been. Jeffery M. Jones, "Support for Third U.S. Political Party Up to 63%," Gallup, October 4, 2023.

39. On the actual prevalence of moderates within the American electorate despite increasing polarization, see Anthony Fowler et al., "Moderates," *American Political Science Review* 117, no. 2 (2023).

40. See Edward B. Foley and Eric Maskin, "How to Depolarize American Politics," *Project Syndicate*, February 8, 2024; Edward B. Foley, "A 'Top Three' Version of California's 'Top Two' Elections," *Common Ground Democracy*, February 11, 2024.

41. Arizona's 2024 US Senate election is arguably an example of this situation. Incumbent Kyrsten Sinema abandoned her reelection campaign as an independent centrist because she had no chance of winning in the existing first-past-the-post system, although she likely could have beaten either the Democrat or the Republican one-on-one.

42. Nathan Atkinson, Scott Ganz, and John Mantus, "A Simple Agent-Based Model for Simulating Single Winner Elections," SSRN, July 31, 2024.

43. Edward B. Foley, "The Nomination and Election of Statewide Candidates," *Illinois Law Review* (October 2024).

44. "2022 French Presidential Election: Official Results," *France 24*.

45. Benjamin Reilly, "Centripetalism and Electoral Moderation in Established Democracies," *Nationalism and Ethnic Politics* 24, no. 2 (2018): 201–221; Jeremy Gelman, Evan Pristos, and Benjamin Reilly, "The Consequences of a Top-5/RCV System in Nevada: Advantaging Moderates but Sidelining Third Parties?," SSRN, last revised April 27, 2024.

46. Glenn Wright, Benjamin Reilly, and David Lublin, "Assessing the Impact of Alaska's Top 4-RCV Electoral Reform" (paper presented at the American Political Science Association Annual Meeting, Los Angeles, California, September 2, 2023). It is important to note, however, that Giessel was a Condorcet winner who came very close to being eliminated by the lowest plurality runoff method. All three candidates received one-third of first-choice votes:

Cathy Giessel, the moderate Republican: 33.84 percent
Roger Holland, the more conservative Republican: 33.12 percent
Roselynn Casey, the Democrat: 33.04 percent

"RCV Detailed Report," Alaska Division of Elections. If Giessel had received just 135 fewer votes, she would have been the first candidate eliminated in Alaska's runoff, even though she still would have beaten both opponents head-to-head.

47. "RCV Detailed Report," Alaska Division of Elections.

48. Applying the Alaska system to a highly polarized 50–50 state is not the same thing as applying the system to Alaska itself. Murkowski was able to prevail over her Trump-endorsed MAGA opponent because Alaska is a red-leaning state where the Democratic Party is relatively weak, and thus Murkowski would be stronger than any Democrat even if she trailed the Trump-endorsed candidate. The same point does not apply to 50–50 states, such as Arizona, Wisconsin, or Pennsylvania, where the Democratic Party is much stronger than it is in Alaska.

A comparison of C-force scores for Alaska's system in Alaska itself versus Alaska's system in Arizona, for example, confirms this truth. Based on 100,000 simulated elections applied to a profile of the state's electorate, in Alaska itself the state's new system has a C-force of 0.4185. By contrast, in Arizona the same system has a much lower C-force of 0.0168.

49. Bernard Grofman and Scott L. Feld, "If You Like the Alternative Vote (a.k.a. the Instant Runoff), Then You Ought to Know About the Coombs Rule," *Electoral Studies* 23 (2004): 641.

50. Michael S. Kang, "Voting as Veto," *Michigan Law Review* 108 (2009): 1221.

51. The Coombs method will always elect the moderate compromise candidate as long as voters whose first choice is one of the two polarizing major-party nominees also make the opposing major-party nominee their last choice.

52. The Marquis de Condorcet was an eighteenth-century French theorist who proposed the idea that a candidate whom a majority prefers to each other candidate should win the election. Iain McLean and Fiona Hewitt, *Condorcet: Foundations of Social Choice and Political Theory* (Brookfield, VT: Edward Elgar, 1994). Unlike the other electoral methods considered below, including most-preferred voting, the specific procedure of the *Survivor*-style (Coombs) method is guaranteed to be Condorcet consistent only when voters are ideologically linear from left to right. See Bernard Grofman and Scott L. Feld, "If You Like the Alternative Vote (a.k.a. the Instant Runoff), Then You Ought to Know About the Coombs Rule," *Electoral Studies* 23 (2004): 647. Nonetheless, because the C-force numbers described in this report are based on models of electorates that are ideologically linear in this way, *Survivor*-style voting can be included among the class of Condorcet-consistent methods for the purposes of comparative C-force analysis.

53. Edward B. Foley, "The Constitution and Condorcet," *Drake Law Review* 70 (2022): 543, 560.

54. See James E. Green-Armytage, T. Nicholaus Tideman, and Rafael Cosman, "Statistical Evaluation of Voting Rules," *Social Choice and Welfare* 46, no. 1 (2016): 183, 201 (calling BTR "Condorcet-Coombs," because it modifies the Coombs elimination procedure in a way to be Condorcet compliant, and finding Condorcet-Coombs more vulnerable to strategic voting than other Condorcet-compliant electoral methods).

55. Most-preferred voting is also closely related to the total vote runoff method. See Edward B. Foley, "Total Vote Runoff: A Majority-Maximizing Form of Ranked Choice Voting," *New Hampshire Law Review* 21, no. 2 (2023): 323; Edward B. Foley and Eric Maskin, "Alaska's Ranked Choice Voting Is Flawed. But There's an Easy Fix," *Washington Post*, November 1, 2022. But most-preferred voting is even simpler insofar as it does not require the recalculation of preference points as part of its elimination procedure. Nor, in order to be a Condorcet-compliant method, does it require calculation for partial points for unranked candidates; instead, unranked candidates can be awarded zero points (as described in the text above), and the candidate who beats all others head-to-head still prevails.

56. See Foley, "The Nomination and Election of Statewide Candidates," *Illinois Law Review* (October 2024), for further development of most-preferred voting. There is another method, round-robin voting, which mathematically is very close to most-preferred voting but operates in a different way. See Edward B. Foley, "Tournament Elections with Round-Robin Primaries: A Sports Analogy for Electoral Reform," *Wisconsin Law Review* (2021): 1187.

57. Because this was a voter-initiated constitutional amendment, it must be endorsed by the voters in a second consecutive even-numbered election year, according to the provisions of Nevada's state constitution. "Nevada Question 3, Top-Five Ranked-Choice Voting Initiative (2022)," Ballotpedia.

58. See Nathan Atkinson, Edward B. Foley, and Scott Ganz, "Beyond the Spoiler Effect: Can Ranked Choice Voting Solve the Problem of Political Polarization?," Georgetown McDonough School of Business Research Paper No. 4411173, *Illinois Law Review* (October 2024) (showing significant divergence between different tabulation methods of ranked-choice ballots when an electorate is highly polarized; although the computer simulations that show this divergence were based on a "final four" system of the kind used in Alaska, a "final five" system of the kind considered in Nevada would likely show a similar or even greater divergence, because a candidate close to the electorate's median voter is even more likely to be among the top five candidates in a nonpartisan primary than among the top four, and this candidate will prevail in a MPV form of RCV but would not prevail in an LPR form of RCV).

59. After Purple is eliminated, Blue has 19 percent of first-choice votes, and Red has 22 percent, but these two candidates still remain behind Ultramarine and Scarlet in the number of first-choice votes, who remain at 30 and 29 percent, respectively.

60. For further illustration of this point, see Nathan Atkinson and Scott Ganz, "Robust Electoral Competition: Rethinking Electoral Systems to Encourage Representative Outcomes," Georgetown McDonough School of Business Research Paper No. 4728225, *Maryland Law Review* (2024).

61. These profiles are derived from the Cooperative Elections Study (CCES). For a description of the methodology, see Nathan Atkinson, Edward B. Foley, and Scott Ganz, "Beyond the Spoiler Effect: Can Ranked Choice Voting Solve the Problem of Political Polarization?," Georgetown McDonough School of Business Research Paper No. 4411173, *Illinois Law Review* (October 2024).

62. Whether Nevada's electoral politics would immediately resemble the computer simulations if the "final five" system were adopted depends in part on factors such as the effect of incumbency and the self-selection of potential candidates. Nevada's two current US senators are fairly moderate Democrats, and therefore the advantage of incumbency may help to protect them from a serious challenge from more progressive Democrats to their left.

63. The computer simulations yielding these numbers were conducted for a "final four" rather than a "final five" system. But results would be similar in either case. If anything, a "final five" system would likely produce an even greater difference in C-force scores between LPR and MPV because adding a fifth candidate to a Condorcet-compliant election in a highly polarized electorate with a bimodal distribution of voters will give the Condorcet-compliant procedure one more candidate with a chance to be closest to the median voter, whereas this additional candidate is simply likely to be eliminated early in the LPR procedure.

64. A new and important paper on the potential effect of Nevada's "final five" system in that state suggests that there are specific factors associated with the state's political culture that mitigate the effect of its polarization. Most notably, unlike in

other states, former president Trump has tended to support more traditional Republican candidates rather than the kind of MAGA extremists he has supported elsewhere. As a consequence, LPR may be more successful in avoiding the election of extremist candidates in Nevada than in other states with similar levels of polarization. See Jeremy Gelman, Evan Pristos, and Benjamin Reilly, "The Consequences of a Top-5/RCV System in Nevada: Advantaging Moderates but Sidelining Third Parties?," SSRN, April 27, 2024.

65. Tied with Delaware.

66. The methodology assumes that there are ten candidates in the nonpartisan primary. These ten candidates are drawn (randomly) from the state's profile of voters. In the nonpartisan primary, voters then choose the single candidate closest to them (in either direction). This emulates the simple plurality method of Alaska's nonpartisan primary. The top four candidates then advance to the general election, as in the Alaska system. Because the Alaska system is nonpartisan, there is no assumption about number of parties.

67. The online appendix to this chapter contains the calculations derived from the simulations for all fifty states: https://kb.osu.edu/handle/1811/105337.

68. This analysis is in no way intended to suggest that Nevada voters should not adopt the pending proposal for a "final five" system as it is currently drafted. For one thing, the legal language that will take effect if the measure is adopted describes the state's RCV tabulation procedure in broad enough terms that it arguably could encompass the Condorcet "total-vote runoff" method that is very similar to the most-preferred voting method described in this chapter. The relevant legal language simply calls for eliminating the candidate with the "fewest votes" without specifying whether this phrase means fewest total votes or fewest first-choice votes. While it's most likely that this language was intended to convey the latter meaning (fewest first-choice votes), the plain text is obviously capacious enough to encompass the former meaning (fewest total votes). Adoption of the measure therefore leaves open the possibility that a Condorcet-compliant form of RCV may be employed as a way to implement the new system. Even if this were not the case, it would be harmful to building momentum for electoral reform in other states that would be Condorcet compliant for this specific electoral reform proposal to be defeated.

69. For an analysis of why Condorcet-compliant electoral methods are the fairest way to determine an election's winner based on the divergent set of voter preferences, see Edward B. Foley, "Maximum Convergence Voting: Madisonian Constitutional Theory and Electoral System Design," Ohio State Legal Studies Research Paper No. 868, *Florida Law Review* (forthcoming).

70. See Sarah E. Anderson, Daniel M. Butler, and Laurel Harbridge-Yong, *Rejecting Compromise: Legislators' Fear of Primary Voters* (New York: Cambridge University Press, 2020).

71. Speaker Mike Johnson's condemnation of the bipartisan border bill as "dead on arrival" in the House of Representatives was undoubtedly a consequence of the existing electoral system (partisan primaries followed by plurality-winner general elections). See Briana Reilly, "Johnson Calls Senate Border Deal 'Dead on Arrival' in House," *Roll Call*, January 26, 2024. If the House were elected by means of a Nevada-style system of a nonpartisan "final five" primary followed by RCV, especially if the RCV method were Condorcet compliant, there is every reason to think that the bipartisan border bill would be able to secure passage in the House led by a Speaker who governed according to median rather than extreme right-wing preferences.

72. Eric Maskin has proposed a form of Condorcet-consistent voting that, under certain specified conditions, is resistant to strategic manipulation. See Eric Maskin, "A Condorcet Voting Rule That Is Strategy-Proof," Scholars at Harvard, February 2023. This method deserves further development and consideration, but given the need to educate the public on the basic principles of Condorcet-consistent electoral procedures, discussion of the distinctive features of Maskin's proposal—which involve eliminating candidates based on the heterogeneity of lower-ranked preferences among voters who rank a particular candidate first—is best deferred until after simpler Condorcet-consistent methods gain a significant degree of public acceptance.

73. If voters abstain from the one-on-one that does not include their preferred candidate, then they risk having the election decided without their participation. Suppose, for example, that Blue beats Red 51 percent to 49 percent because Purple's supporters weigh in on this matchup, but proponents of both Blue and Red abstain in the Purple-versus-Red and Purple-versus-Blue matchups, respectively. Then, if Blue's supporters are 40 percent of the electorate, and Red's are 35 percent, then the result of the Purple-versus-Red matchup will be Red defeating Purple 35 percent to 25 percent, and the result of the Purple-versus-Blue matchup will be Blue defeating Purple 40 percent to 25 percent. This outcome will make Blue the election's winner, having defeated both opponents one-on-one, an outcome that is obviously worse from the perspective of Red's supporters than if Purple had won. Thus, Red's supporters have an incentive not to abstain in the Purple-versus-Blue matchup, in order to have Purple prevail. Likewise, if Blue's supporters can't be sure that Blue will beat Red 51–49, then Blue's supporters also have an incentive to support Purple in the Purple-versus-Red matchup. Thus, supporters of both Blue and Red have an incentive to participate in a way that will cause Purple to be the Condorcet winner, rather than to abstain in the hope of defeating the Condorcet winner.

74. Duncan Black proposed this method for electing a candidate when there is no Condorcet winner who is preferred by more voters over each other candidate. Duncan Black, *The Theory of Committees and Elections* (New York: Cambridge University Press, 1958). Round-robin voting is a slight modification of Black's method; see Edward B. Foley, "Tournament Elections with Round-Robin Primaries: A Sports Analogy for Electoral Reform," *Wisconsin Law Review* (2021): 1187.

75. Edward B. Foley, "Maximum Convergence Voting: Madisonian Constitutional Theory and Electoral System Design," Ohio State Legal Studies Research Paper No. 868, *Florida Law Review* (forthcoming).

76. These two examples from the 2022 midterms, and others like them, show the danger of relying on data from previous elections where lowest-plurality runoff has been used to argue that this method will virtually always elect the Condorcet winner. See Nicholas Stephanopoulos, "Finding Condorcet," *Washington and Lee Law Review* (forthcoming). The problem with relying on this previous data is that it does not account for two key factors: first, the increasing partisan polarization of the electorate making it increasingly difficult for a moderate candidate close to the electorate's median voter to win a lowest-plurality runoff election; second, and perhaps even more important, moderate candidates have no incentive to run in a lowest-plurality runoff election where they will be eliminated before the two more extreme candidates. A candidate like Rob Portman has no more incentive to run in a lowest-plurality runoff election than in the current system of partisan primaries followed by a plurality-winner general election. On these key points, see Nathan Atkinson and Scott Ganz, "Robust Electoral Competition: Rethinking Electoral Systems to Encourage Representative Outcomes," Georgetown McDonough School of Business Research Paper No. 4728225, *Maryland Law Review* (2024).

77. Edward B. Foley and Eric Maskin, "How to Depolarize American Politics," *Project Syndicate*, February 8, 2024.

78. Edward B. Foley, "A 'Top Three' Version of California's 'Top Two' Elections," *Common Ground Democracy*, February 11, 2024.

79. Liz Cheney, *Oath and Honor: A Memoir and a Warning* (New York: Little, Brown & Co., 2023).

80. "U.S. House of Representatives Special Election in Alaska, 2022 (June 11 Top-Four Primary)," Ballotpedia.

81. *Jenness v. Fortson*, 403 U.S. 431 (1971).

82. One possible, and partial, exception to this point would be a procedure in which voters in the primary identified only a first and second choice among the candidates on ballot. A candidate marked as a voter's first choice would receive one vote, and a candidate marked as a voter's second choice would receive half a vote. The three candidates whose total sum of these full and half votes would advance to the general election. The simplicity of this procedure would make it a suitable component of the "top three" system, and it has the advantage of tending to reward less-polarizing candidates. Even if a candidate does not receive as many first-choice votes as some others, by accumulating a large number of half votes as a well-liked second choice of many voters, this candidate might beat out for one the top three spots a more polarizing opponent who, despite more first-choice votes, has far fewer second-choice votes.

83. See *Maine Republican Party v. Dunlap*, 324 F.Supp.3d 202 (D. Me. 2018).

84. In 2018, the use of RCV in Maine enabled a centrist Democrat, Jared Golden, to defeat a more extreme Republican, Bruce Poliquin, in a race for one of the state's congressional seats. See "Maine's 2nd Congressional District Election," Ballotpedia, 2018. But that race did not involve a significant third-party challenge by a moderate attempting to fill the gap between two polarized major-party nominees. Instead, the additional candidates in the race were fringe figures who could only play the role of spoiler. The true test of Maine's system will be in a statewide election where there isn't an established centrist incumbent like Susan Collins or Angus King but instead a genuine three-way race between Blue, Purple, and Red candidates vying for an open seat.

85. Benjamin Reilly, "Centripetalism and Electoral Moderation in Established Democracies," *Nationalism and Ethnic Politics* 24, no. 2 (2018): 201–221.

86. See William A. Galston, "Fusion Voting Could Lower the Temperature," *Wall Street Journal*, October 3, 2023; Daniel Cantor and William Kristol, "What Is 'Fusion Voting'? Just a Way to Save the Country, That's All," *New Republic*, June 15, 2024; "Open Letter from Scholars in Support of Re-legalizing Fusion Voting," *Medium*, July 11, 2024.

87. From the voter's perspective in terms of casting a ballot, all ranked-choice voting systems operate in the same way: the voter ranks candidates in order of preference. The difference is solely in the method of determining a winner based on all the preferences on all the ballots. As a matter of election administration, given existing computer technology, there shouldn't be any significant difference in the computational demands of the different methods under consideration here. The delay associated with any RCV method is caused not by the computation itself but by the need to receive all mailed ballots in order to conduct the computation. While media outlets can more easily project (in other words, predict) winners in a simple plurality election before all mailed ballots have been counted, it is more difficult for the media to make such projections (predictions) in RCV systems given that a candidate's lead can change in more complicated ways because of the multiple rankings

on each ballot. Officially certified results take essentially the same amount of time, because they require counting all the valid mailed ballots. Finally, if any form of RCV is thought to be too burdensome or complicated for voters (contrary to the experience of voters in Alaska, Maine, Australia, and elsewhere), then there are other innovative electoral systems that attempt to emulate Condorcet-compliant methods more simply. See Foley, "The Nomination and Election of Statewide Candidates," *Illinois Law Review* (October 2024).

88. Additional research needs to be done on various Condorcet-consistent RCV systems. One new idea suggested by Wes Holliday is to employ an Alaska-style "top four" system and elect either the Condorcet winner, if there is one; if not, then, between the two candidates who suffer only one head-to-head defeat against another candidate (because with four candidates and no Condorcet winner, mathematically there must be two and only two of these), to elect the candidate whose single head-to-head defeat has the smallest margin. Wesley H. Holliday, "A Simple Condorcet Voting Method for Final Four Elections," *SSRN* (July 7, 2024). https://dx.doi.org/10.2139/ssrn.4758509. This proposal is a version of the "minimax" method applied to a four-candidate election. Like any version of minimax, it has the virtue of electing the candidate who is either the Condorcet winner or the candidate closest to being a Condorcet winner. See Foley, "Maximum Convergence Voting: Madisonian Constitutional Theory and Electoral System Design," *Florida Law Review* 76 (forthcoming).

89. See Nathan Atkinson, Edward B. Foley, and Scott Ganz, "Beyond the Spoiler Effect: Can Ranked Choice Voting Solve the Problem of Political Polarization?," Georgetown McDonough School of Business Research Paper No. 4411173, *Illinois Law Review* (October 2024).

3

Proportional Representation

Lee Drutman

Electoral system choice is a central and extensively studied issue in political science. Recently, proportional representation (PR) has caught the attention of political reformers in the United States as a potential solution to multiple threats to US democracy.

Advocates believe that using multimember districts with PR for the US House of Representatives and state legislatures could reduce harmful polarization by breaking up binary conflicts. PR could help new center-right parties emerge, diminishing the influence of authoritarian extremism on the right. By allowing more parties, it could shift US politics away from its current hyperpartisan state. More directly, PR would blunt gerrymandering by eliminating the single-member district (SMD), which makes it possible to manipulate the boundaries of political constituencies to favor one political party.

However, some scholars and analysts are concerned that PR could fragment the US party system and make it harder to form majority coalitions. Others are concerned that the multimember districts needed for PR would weaken the direct connection between individual voters and their district representatives.

In this chapter, we aim to assess these claims by answering three key questions about proportional representation:

1. Can PR reduce affective polarization?

William Galston, Rachel Kleinfeld, Nolan McCarty, Jennifer McCoy, and Hans Noel contributed substantially to this chapter.

2. Can PR undermine the power of political extremists?
3. How might PR impact government performance and effectiveness?

We also address how proportional representation could impact gerrymandering and constituency representation.

Electoral System Families and How to Measure Proportionality

Political scientists have categorized electoral systems into three main types: majoritarian, mixed, and proportional. Figure 3.1 lays this out, with some country examples. Briefly, however, the systems can be described as follows:

Majoritarian systems: Majoritarian systems use single-winner districts to elect representatives. A core property of such districts is that they can only have one winner and so tend to feature two dominant parties. We know this as "Duverger's law." However, it is more of a tendency than a law. For example, Canada and India both have multiparty systems, despite single-winner elections. This is because different parties in these countries have different regional strengths.

Figure 3.1   Electoral Systems and Party Systems

| Majoritarian | | Mixed | | Proportional | |
Higher Thresholds, Fewer Parties		Some of Each		Lower Threshholds, More Parties	
Single-member plurality	Two-round instant run-off	Mixed majoritarian	Mixed proportional	Low-magnitude proportional	High-magnitude proportional
USA	France	Italy	Germany	Spain	Netherlands
UK	Australia	Hungary	New Zealand	Denmark	Israel
Canada		Japan		Ireland	

Proportionality Design Choices
Direct magnitude (larger = more permissive)
Remainder formula (round up or round down?)
Party list (open [candidate] or closed [partly only]?)
Voting choice (single mark or preferential ranked?)
Threshold for small parties / Bonus for large parties?

Some majoritarian systems use plurality voting. We call these single-member plurality, or "first-past-the-post," systems. France uses a two-round voting system, while Australia uses instant-runoff voting for its House of Representatives. The two-round system in France fosters modest multipartyism. In Australia, House elections usually involve two major parties, while Senate elections feature multiple parties because the Senate uses PR.

Proportional systems: Proportional systems use multiwinner districts to elect representatives and allocate seats by party. So, for example, in a ten-member district, a party that wins 20 percent of the votes will get 20 percent of the seats.

In most proportional systems, parties submit lists of candidates who run together, but voters can choose from the list. All votes count toward that party, and parties get seats in proportion to the total votes cast for all the parties' candidates. If a party wins two seats, its two most popular candidates will represent it in the legislature.

Some countries use a closed list, in which voters can only vote for the party. The party advances candidates from its own internal list. A few countries use an instant-runoff form of PR, called the single-transferable vote. This allows voters to rank candidates across multiple parties.

Proportional systems come in many varieties. No two countries use the same system, and systems change. The biggest variation across systems is district magnitude. Having larger districts lowers the threshold for parties to win representation. In a three-member district, for example, a party would need at least a quarter of the vote (plus one) to win a seat. In a ten-member district, a party would need only slightly more than 9 percent of the vote. Some other design choices include party list type, remainder formula, preferential voting options, national threshold, and treatment of coalition parties. In short, some proportional systems are more permissive and multiparty than others.

Mixed systems: Several countries use a combination of single-winner districts and PR to achieve a balance. Germany and New Zealand, for example, prioritize proportionality and are considered to have proportional systems even though they have some single-member districts. Hungary and Japan, by contrast, prioritize majoritarian features and are usually classified as more majoritarian despite having some multimember districts. The exact balance and the type of PR offer additional design choices.

Majoritarian and proportional systems are ideal types. In reality, countries exist along a continuum that can be measured in different ways. Some analyses use district magnitude, since larger districts create more permissively proportional systems. Other analyses use effective number of parties, either in the legislature or in the electorate. Additional measures include legislative party fractionalization, electoral party fractionalization, and disproportionality.

Collectively, these measures describe a general continuum—larger district magnitudes create more permissive systems that encourage more parties to form and compete because they are more likely to win seats in proportion to their vote share. However, the relationship is not perfectly correlated, as Figure 3.1 shows. For example, more permissive systems can sometimes encourage more parties to compete, such that several smaller parties fail to meet the threshold and waste votes. The key point is that not only does proportionality exist on a continuum but the effects of voting rules on party systems vary across countries and over time. Thus, in evaluating the effects of voting systems on political outcomes, we should not treat all proportional systems as the same. Some systems work much better than others.

Measures of the proportionality continuum can be defined as follows:[1]

• District magnitude: This is the total number of seats allocated divided by the total number of electoral districts. Since this variable is heavily right-skewed (a few countries use the entire legislature as one district), we will use the natural log in analyses.

• Effective number of parties on the seat level (enps): This is calculated for legislative seats according to the formula proposed by Markku Laakso and Rein Taagepera.[2]

• Effective number of parties on the votes level (envs): This is calculated for vote shares according to the formula proposed by Laakso and Taagepera.

• Legislative fractionalization of the party system (leg_fractional): This is an index of legislative fractionalization of the party system according to the formula proposed by Douglas Rae.[3] The index ranges between 1 (maximal fractionalization) and 0 (minimal fractionalization).

• Electoral fractionalization of the party system (elect_fractional): This is an index of electoral fractionalization of the party system according Rae's same formula.

• Disproportionality: This is an index of electoral disproportionality, following the formula proposed by Michael Gallagher.[4] This compares parties' votes to the legislative seats they are given. Higher numbers on the Gallagher Index indicate a greater disparity between votes and seats, meaning that elections have produced more disproportionate outcomes.

All these measures correlate reasonably well with each other, although some do so more closely than others. All capture slightly different dimensions of electoral and party systems. The effective-number-of-parties and fractionalization measures are the most closely correlated. Considering our focus on governing, legislative fractionalization will be our main variable of interest, along with district magnitude. Legislative fractionalization describes the actual party and governance situation, while district magnitude captures the level of proportionality most directly. These two are related to each other. But legislative fractionalization more directly appears to affect measurable outcomes we care about.

Electoral Engineering in a Complex World

All political systems are complex, with many interacting structures and actors. The goal of electoral interventions should be to create a better political environment, not to guarantee a particular outcome. However, different electoral rules suggest different winning strategies, in the same way that different rules in any game shape player behavior. In politics, rules affect how people behave and strategize, and winners sometimes change the rules for future rounds.

Democratic resilience requires a balance between consistent and flexible rules. Ultimately, to survive, any political system must be considered legitimate. And to be considered legitimate, it must be both somewhat responsive and somewhat stable. However, responsiveness and stability are in tension with each other. A system that is too responsive is not stable, because it changes too much in response to demands. And a system that is too stable is not responsive. Thus, some volatility and change is a sign of a healthy system. But too much too quickly can cause a system to collapse.

It is especially important that elections are seen as legitimate, since most democratic breakdowns occur around elections. If a large and consequential political minority stops respecting the rules because it doesn't win, violence and authoritarianism may take over as alternatives to elections.

A healthy political system can withstand a fair amount of conflict and contestation. Risks arise when the conflict becomes too intense for losers to accept election results and winners to consider the possibility of losing in the future. Persistently high and growing levels of political extremism, deep levels of affective polarization (out-partisan hatred), and the success of illiberal leaders are all signs of a democracy on the brink of collapse and in need of substantial intervention.

We should view political systems as having different states or dynamics, just as we do economic systems. We think of economies as being in depression, recession, recovery, or overexpansion. In each of these states, individual economic actors and firms make decisions based on their expectations of how others will behave. In a depression, investment slows because firms expect limited demand. To shock an economy out of depression, central bankers cut interest rates, and policymakers expand stimulus spending. In an economy that is booming, central bankers raise interest rates to suppress growth, and policymakers dial back economic stimulus. Modern economic management attempts to balance competing pressures using monetary policy interventions. Typically, these adjustments are minor. In extreme economic conditions, policymakers must take more dramatic measures to improve the state of the economy.

Our politics is currently in a more extreme state—a spiraling us-versus-them dynamic that undermines the shared faith in elections and government legitimacy on which healthy liberal democracy depends.[5] As Delia Baldassarri and Scott Page have explained, "Each type of polarization strengthens the other through feedbacks."[6] When everything reinforces everything else, they argue, "no sequence of small interventions will likely reverse our course." The core problem is a flattening of dimensionality, a fancy way of saying that everything has been reduced to a single us-versus-them dimension, distributed bimodally. And they stress, "As a rule, a bimodal distribution for anything suggests that something strange is afoot." Several papers in the December 14, 2021, issue of *Proceedings of the National Academy of Sciences of the United States of America* on the dynamics of polarization also note that bimodal distributions are almost always signs of impending collapse across many types of systems.

"So what is to be done?" Baldassarri and Page ask. "How do we escape our current situation? First, we must be aware of why we cannot chip away at this problem. We must take substantial actions."[7] Once politics tips into this bimodal state (of two separate distributions), small interventions become ineffective. Worse, they may even be counterproductive: "Once in a polarized state, well-intentioned attempts to improve interaction between groups may increase rather than decrease polarization, by encouraging the behaviors that pull people apart. . . . Even if we could turn tolerance up to 11, so to speak, the polarized equilibrium cannot be escaped."[8]

One factor unites almost all the causal processes driving polarization: "Once categorical boundaries between 'us and them' are drawn, a whole host of destructive social processes may kick in."[9] But try to break the causal chain apart, and everything affects everything. An exhaustive review of recent literature on political polarization similarly found a complex web of reinforcing causal mechanisms and cognitive biases driving partisan polarization.[10] Even perceiving the party system as polarized leads to higher levels of affective polarization.[11]

In this perniciously polarized state, extremism may become a property of the system as a whole, not of any particular actor. Certainly, some individuals respond more extremely to the conditions than others and stake out more radical, antisystem positions: "Extremism refers to the belief that an in-group's success or survival can never be separated from the need for hostile action against an out-group," writes J. M. Berger in attempting to define the concept. "The hostile action must be part of the in-group's definition of success."[12] High levels of group polarization and high uncertainty are core drivers of political extremism.[13] And closely divided razor's-edge elections contribute to high levels of uncertainty.

Extremists gain power by escalating conflicts and heightening contradictions. This further undermines effective governance. It drives distrust and antisystem attitudes, which further stoke hyperpartisan polarization and extremism. It is these dynamics we hope to arrest, and even reverse, through electoral system reform.

Can PR Reduce Affective Polarization?

Hyperpartisan polarization poses a significant challenge to American democracy. A growing share of partisans now deny the legitimacy and even the humanity of their political opponents. This antipathy, dehumanization, and openness to violence appears to follow from high levels of affective polarization: Democrats and Republicans, in particular, really dislike each other.

Can anything be done about this problem? A growing number of comparative studies have documented a relationship between voting systems and affective polarization. As a general pattern, more proportional systems, with more parties, have lower levels of affective partisan polarization than more majoritarian systems with fewer parties. In this section, we examine the threat affective polarization poses to liberal democracy and explore the observed relationships between party systems and affective polarization.

The Dangers of Affective Polarization

High levels of affective polarization pose a unique threat to democratic societies. Fear and loathing of out-partisans is associated with political intolerance, politicized facts, and less support for democracy.[14] The statistical relationship between affective polarization and democratic backsliding appears quite robust.[15]

The causal mechanisms that link affective polarization and democratic backsliding involve partisans tolerating, rationalizing, and even supporting antidemocratic actions by elites on their side. Although it is illiberal political elites who ultimately roll back democratic norms and freedoms (more on this in the next section), they are more likely to do so when they expect public support, or at least tolerance, for such transgressions.

This is now a well-documented pattern. Partisans tolerate or even applaud antidemocratic activities by their side, even when they report enthusiastic support for the underlying principles being violated. Whether we describe this as a "partisan double standard"[16] or "democratic hypocrisy,"[17] this pattern shows up across many surveys. The stronger the out-party hatred (at both an individual and a country level), the more pronounced the double standard.[18] As Suthan Krishanarajan concludes, "When violations of democracy are indisputably clear, many citizens find ways to not perceive undemocratic behavior as undemocratic if they agree with it politically. This might provide one explanation for why democratically elected leaders in today's democracies are so often able to get away with violations of democracy without facing electoral backlash."[19]

Partisans often justify their actions by claiming their political opponents are undermining democracy. Alia Braley and colleagues explain that "aspiring autocrats may instigate democratic backsliding by accusing their opponents of subverting democracy. . . . Would-be authoritarians' ability to weaponize the subversion dilemma may depend on a larger set of mutually reinforcing polarizations. These include increasing partisan identity strength, polarized views on policy, dislike of opposing partisans, dehumanization of opposing partisans, stereotypes of opposing partisans, and ethnic antagonism."[20] Braley and colleagues warn that this dilemma can "result in a death spiral for democracy."

Higher affective polarization leads to stronger perceptions of extremism from the other side.[21] Affective polarization also sharpens partisan cue taking: in a deeply polarized partisan environment, voters are more likely to rely exclusively on informational cues from one side, which heightens the power of such cues.[22] When partisans have strong negative views of their opponents, they are often ready to believe the worst about them.

The threat arises specifically from affective polarization in this context; ideological polarization is something separate and only weakly correlated to affective polarization.[23] The United States, for example, is not as ideologically polarized as many other democracies.[24] In these democracies, the ideological range of policy views represented in the legislature is much wider. A relationship between ideological polarization and affective polarization exists. More ideological polarization leads citizens to see sharper differences between parties, thus changing how they feel about the stakes of elections and which parties they perceive as on their "side."[25] The larger the divides, the more political elites can harness disagreements and frame them in existential terms.[26]

Multiparty democracies have long been associated with more ideological polarization. More parties make room for wider ideological dispersion of policy platforms.[27] The dispersion reaches its maximum at five parties; beyond that, additional parties do not bring forth a wider range of policy platforms.[28]

Nevertheless, majoritarian systems are more sensitive to dispersion of parties. When mainstream parties move away from the center, the polarizing effects are more pronounced.[29] In a two-party system, you can think of the main political parties as big magnets in a field where voters are small pieces of metal. When the magnets are in the middle, they attract lots of metal pieces from all around. But if one magnet moves toward an edge, it pulls many metal pieces with it. This makes the field look very divided. By contrast, a more proportional system can be thought of as having more magnets of varying sizes. So if one small magnet moves to an edge, the metal pieces (voters) have other magnets nearby and don't all follow the one that moved.

In simple terms, when the dominant parties and most voters are moderate, the voting system doesn't matter. But when major parties have diverging opinions, a majoritarian system amplifies these differences. That is because in this type of system, voters often follow the lead of the big parties, creating a more ideologically polarized electorate.

Can PR Reduce Affective Polarization?

Scholars have noticed that countries with proportional voting systems and more political parties have less affective polarization than countries with majoritarian systems and fewer parties. This finding is robust across different measures of affective polarization. As Jennifer McCoy and Murat Somer have observed, "The most extreme cases of polarization among our countries emerge in contexts of majoritarian electoral systems that produce a disproportionate representation for the majority or plurality party, and . . . once in power, the polarizing parties and incumbents attempt, and often succeed, in engineering additional constitutional and legal changes to enhance their electoral advantage."[30]

In *American Affective Polarization in Comparative Perspective*, Noam Gidron, James Adams, and Will Horne find a clear link between voting system proportionality and affective polarization. Simply put, the more disproportional the system, the stronger the dislike for opposing parties and even one's own party.[31]

Jonathan Rodden offers another way of viewing this. He considers voters' perceptions of their proximity to their preferred party and to other parties. In both cases, the United States stands out. Americans feel furthest from the party they support among citizens of comparable countries. Americans also feel furthest from the parties they oppose. Americans are the most cumulatively alienated from all parties. Higher alienation correlates with fewer parties.[32]

Here is one way to understand this dynamic: Assume any ideological distribution in the electorate. The more parties, the more evenly the parties can locate themselves throughout the electorate. With more parties, more voters will find a party close to their values—and perceive other parties as less far away. The consequences for affective polarization are significant. When partisans view each other as distant, elections feel more intense and threatening. This increases affective polarization. Perceived distance is the accumulation of issue differences between parties, not their average distance. So the more policy disagreements, the further the opposing parties seem, making them more threatening and hated. This corresponds to flattened issue dimensionality. Ideological and affective polarization, although distinct, mutually reinforce each other by amplifying perceptions of distance and disagreement.

The relationship between party system and affective polarization has become more pronounced in recent years as social and cultural issues have dominated politics more. The United States has had a remarkably sharp increase in affective polarization since 1990, even as affective polarization has remained roughly flat (or even decreased) in many other Western democracies.[33] The United States also appears unique in the extent to which voter antipathy is directed at individual candidates rather than parties.[34] This is likely because the United States has a distinctly candidate-centered politics.

Measuring affective polarization can be challenging in a multiparty context, because of the abundance of potential dyads and the various measures available. However, one consistency across all multiparty systems is that far-right parties are universally disliked by the rest of the electorate, and the feeling is mutual (supporters of far-right parties hate other partisans).[35]

Affective polarization is also increasing in Canada[36] and the United Kingdom,[37] both of which have majoritarian electoral systems, but not as fast as in the United States.[38] The comparison with Canada and the United Kingdom raises the obvious question: Why have neither of these countries experienced similarly dramatic spikes in affective polarization?

One possible reason is that affective polarization in the United States is driven not solely by first-past-the-post elections but rather by the interaction among first-past-the-post elections, geographic sorting of parties, and persistently close national competition that fuels intensifying two-party rivalry. After all, until relatively recently, the United States had a perfectly functional two-party system, with broad geographic overlaps among the parties. Canadian and British parties may be moving in the direction of American parties, although they are not as geographically separated.

A second possible reason is that Canadian and British parties control their own candidate nominations, unlike American parties. The direct primary system in the United States makes American parties distinctly weak and uniquely vulnerable to extremist takeovers. Relatedly, the US system of private financing of elections also makes parties (and candidates) uniquely vulnerable to extremist donors. (See discussions of campaign finance and primary elections in Chapter 7.)

A third possible answer is that Canada and the United Kingdom are both parliamentary systems, so they always, by definition, have unified government, which allows them to govern more effectively, with clearer accountability. The United States is a presidential system. This system often produces divided government, which can undermine effective governing in polarized times. The United Kingdom is essentially unicameral as well. Canada has a Senate, although one not nearly as formidable as that of the United States. When two major parties are evenly matched, the US system of separately elected chambers and a separately elected president may be particularly ill equipped to manage divisions.

A fourth possible answer is that both the United Kingdom and Canada have modest multipartyism, despite their first-past-the-post systems, giving frustrated voters the option to channel extremist activity into smaller fringe parties instead of pushing them to take over major parties. Canada also benefits from more variety in local parties and more political power at the provincial level. In the United States, federalism was long a source of political harmony through diversity—until the recent nationalization of US politics.

Figure 3.2 shows legislative fractionalization among Anglo countries, adding Australia and New Zealand for comparison. Australia uses PR for its senate while New Zealand moved to PR in 1996. The United States is the most dominantly binary political system.

Notably, there are active campaigns in both the United Kingdom and Canada to advance PR. Following a highly disproportionate 2024 election, in which Labour won 411 out of 650 seats in the House of Commons (63.2 percent) with just 33.7 percent of the vote, British commentators began discussing electoral system reform again. And Cana-

Figure 3.2   Legislative Fractionalization Among Anglo Countries, 1990–2020

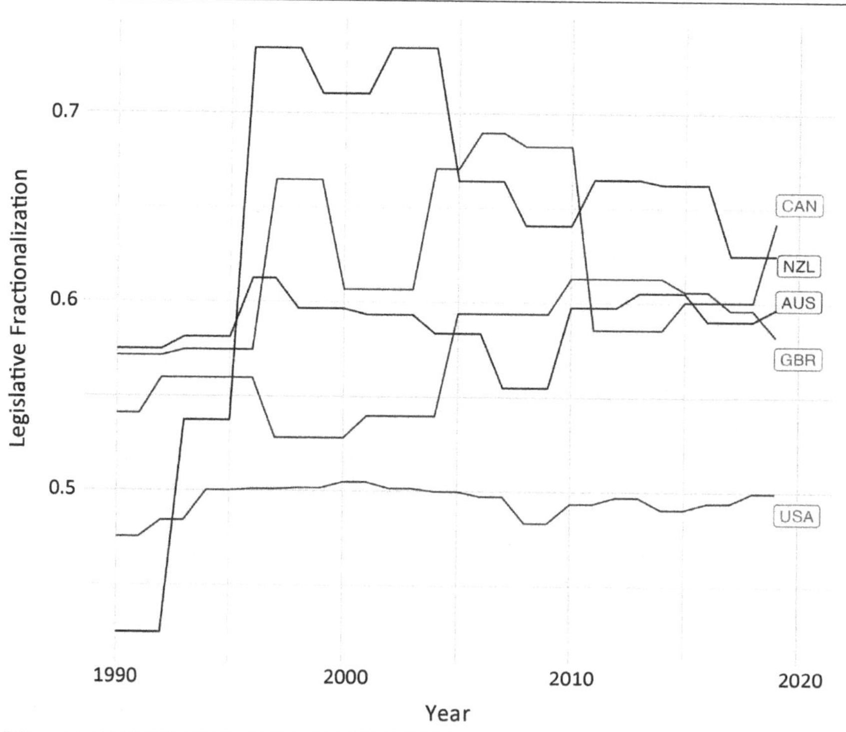

Source: Quality of Government Institute.

dian prime minister Justin Trudeau campaigned in 2015 on ending first-past-the-post elections but has since backtracked on this promise.[39]

It is likely that all four possible explanations (and perhaps others as well, such as the racial diversity of the country and the role of a single national public media) factor into the United States' uniquely high levels of affective polarization. This is an important enough question to merit a separate research project. It also shows the difficulty of comparing countries based solely on their electoral systems, without considering other important institutional factors.

Can PR Reduce Affective Polarization?

What explains the relationship between the electoral system and affective polarization? Broadly speaking, scholars have put forward four major hypotheses linking proportional multiparty democracy to lower affective polarization:

1. PR generates an "affective bonus" of parties being in coalitions together.
2. PR keeps geographic and partisan polarization somewhat distinct.
3. PR allows for more multidimensional issue politics.
4. PR makes it more likely that race and ethnicity crosscut partisanship.

The "affective bonus" of being in coalition together. Multiple recent studies have found that proportional multiparty governments have shifting coalitions with few permanent enemies and many occasional allies. In multiparty systems, parties form coalition governments and voters feel warmly toward other parties in their coalition.[40]

When coalitions shift, as they typically do from election to election, the positive feelings remain. As Will Horne and colleagues explain, "Governing parties' supporters feel much more warmly toward their coalition partner(s) than we can explain based on policy agreement alone. Moreover, these warm affective evaluations linger long after the coalition itself has dissolved."[41] Put another way, parties in the same coalition gain an "affective bonus" that endures even after the coalition dissolves. This also applies to parties that are in a shared opposition.[42]

The basic mechanisms here are straightforward. Being on the same team creates a sense of shared fate and superordinate identity.[43] Parties in a coalition share resources and say nice things about each other. They work together to compromise on policies. Voters view coalition partners in a positive light, assuming they share values.[44] Because proportional systems have "much denser networks of (current and past) co-governance than do disproportional systems . . . proportionality is associated with warmer aggregate levels of out-party evaluations across Western publics," Horne and colleagues conclude.[45]

In a majoritarian system with two nonoverlapping parties, each election reinforces the same conflict and psychological dynamics. This is particularly true in a majoritarian presidential system, such as the US system, where so much attention is focused on an extremely powerful winner-take-all office. Although the United States often winds up with a kind of coalition government (or what we more commonly call "divided government"), partisan conflict centers on winning one-party dominance. Potential compromises fall prey to political leaders believing they need to sharpen the differences between the parties ahead of the next election.

The relationship between geography and partisanship. In the United States, a leading explanation for the worsening of partisan polarization is that the two major parties have "sorted" by geography, values, and ideology.[46] In an earlier era, the two major US parties were broad, overlapping coalitions, each with liberal and conservative factions. But the nationalization of US politics led to the isolation and disappearance of conservative Democrats and liberal Republicans. Democrats became the party of urban, cosmopolitan cultural liberalism; Republicans became the party of rural, traditionalist conservatism. In a politics defined by a cosmopolitan/urban versus traditional/rural divide over moral values and national identity, a compromise middle ground is harder to find. When social identities align with partisan, geographic, and cultural sorting, affective polarization increases, turning party affiliation into a "mega-identity" that combines multiple identities.[47] Even though many battleground districts are in the suburbs, these districts have neither more moderates nor more swing voters than other districts. They are merely districts where both sides of the partisan density divide are represented in roughly equal proportions.[48]

The urban-rural divide and the rise of "postmaterialist" cultural-issue cleavages are not unique to the United States. They appear nearly universal among advanced democracies. Urban-rural cultural divides in majoritarian democracies reinforce partisan divisions, exacerbating disagreements.[49] Without crosscutting cleavages, politics collapses into a single dimension, and affective polarization increases.[50]

This political realignment also maps onto the economic effects of globalization. In many Western countries, "rust belts" and more rural areas that once provided manufacturing jobs are struggling. They are thus most vulnerable to a "politics of resentment"[51] and the appeals of far-right populism.[52]

Over two generations, cities have attracted more highly educated individuals, many of whom have "open" personality types and seek the novelty and variety of urban living. By contrast, rural areas have remained home to more "closed" personality types who do not wish to leave for cities or even for higher education. And to some extent, outer suburbs have drawn individuals out of cities who prefer a more predictable environment. This sorting by personality type and living preference does not always amount to an intentional partisan choice. Yet it has strengthened divisions between urban and rural areas by reinforcing cultural and lifestyle differences.[53] This, of course, makes affective partisan polarization much worse in a two-party system that reinforces these divides.

The multidimensionality of issue politics. The range of issues that national governments deal with has expanded in recent years. When new issues such as today's cultural issues become nationally salient, political parties must respond and take positions on them. The two parties in the United States take opposite positions as they compete. Thus, partisan polarization has grown through a process of "conflict extension."[54]

However, many issue extensions make procrustean pairings within party coalitions (for example, there is no obvious reason why opposition to abortion and opposition to higher taxes naturally go together). In two-party systems, parties must pitch very big tents to negotiate compromises.

Parties represent the diversity of public opinion in a society. In two-party systems, major parties are limited by their competing support coalitions. If these coalitions do not overlap, the parties will not converge. In two-party systems with nonoverlapping partisan support coalitions, the average distance between parties is likely to be higher, even if the overall dispersion among all parties is lower. In multiparty systems, parties can locate more evenly across an ideological spectrum so that no party is too far from its closest competitor.[55]

In the United States, leaders in both parties try to form alliances and make compromises by downplaying certain issues or highlighting differences with the opposing party on others, such as abortion, guns, immigration, or tax policy. In other words, rather than seeing parties as pulling apart on a single left-right continuum, we should see politics as a multidimensional issue space and treat polarization as the sum of parties' differences across all issues. Thus, a politics in which parties differ on twenty issues feels much more divided than a politics in which they differ on ten. If we simplify the ideology score, the distance between the parties would appear the same. But to voters, it feels more intense when there are twenty disagreements instead of ten. As Jonathan Rodden explains,

> Affective political polarization intensifies when new issue dimensions are added. In a two-party system, the parties will appear to be moving further from the average voter, and further from one another, if they offer ever-more heterogeneous and incoherent bundles of platforms over time as new issues are politicized. In the United States, as a result, increasing hostility toward the out-party goes hand in hand with increased ambivalence about the in-party. Meanwhile, the parties become increasingly internally fractious. In a multi-party system, on the other hand, when new issues emerge, parties can position themselves throughout the multi-dimensional issue space. As a result, voters feel closer not only to their in-party but also to the average out-party. In this way, I suggest that multi-party systems can reduce overall levels of affective polarization.[56]

Perception feeds reality. The more affectively polarized voters are, the more likely they are to misperceive the extremism of their political opponents. And when voters overestimate the extremism of their opponents, they view politics as a more intense group conflict.[57] Affective polarization has a reinforcing quality, especially within the constraints of a majoritarian system. Proportional multiparty systems offer greater variety of issue combinations and less limitation on issues than two-party majoritarian systems. Parties can compete on differing issues without demonizing one another, since they are not overextending their natural support base. Moreover, demonizing an opposition party is not always a winning strategy in a multiparty system.

Negative campaigning is thus less overwhelming in multiparty systems. This could reduce affective polarization,[58] since high-stakes elections with negative campaigning appear to be the most consequential force fueling this type of polarization.[59] High levels of negative campaigning also reduce feelings of political efficacy and undermine popular support for the political system, suggesting another consequence of sustained negative campaigns.[60]

Partisanship and race. A final and crucial aspect of affective polarization in the United States involves the question of race. As social and cultural issues have come to the center of American politics, questions around changing demography have collided with the party system in a zero-sum manner, leading to two competing visions for the country's future.

Whereas majoritarian democracies tend to collapse political conflict into a single dimension, proportional democracies tend to multiply dimensions through shifting coalitions and alliances, so that no electoral contest feels so all-or-nothing. For this reason democracy scholars have typically recommended proportional systems for diverse societies that might be prone to ethnic conflict.[61] As Frank Cohen explains,

> Under proportional arrangements, conflict is likely to take more frequent but less intense forms due to the institutional means available and accessible to dissatisfied minorities. By dispersing authority and victory, proportional institutions endear dissatisfied ethnic groups to the regime—that is, to the institutional status quo. They socialize them enough to prevent their use of extreme measures to engage the regime. . . . Under majoritarian arrangements, dissatisfied ethnics will not have the proximity to authority and victory they would have under proportional arrangements.[62]

Additionally, more proportional systems tend to allow for the kinds of shifting coalitions and crosscutting cleavages that reduce affective polarization, as described above. Rather than encourage ethnic voting, proportional systems spread ethnic voting across parties.[63] Cohen finds proportional systems do better at managing ethnic conflict than plurality systems, an empirical finding that is generally replicated,[64] although not entirely.[65] Obviously, there is only so much an electoral system can accomplish.

In *Designing Democracy in a Dangerous World*, Andrew Reynolds offers this nuanced assessment:

> Proportional electoral systems are akin to antibiotics. In the vast majority of cases PR systems are helpful aids in fighting the social ailments of minority exclusion and interethnic hostility. They tend to help stabilize unhealthy states and if used appropriately can bring a different and more constructive tone to political competition. But just like antibiotics PR elections systems will not be successful in every case. Sometimes the social ailment is antibiotic resistant, while in other cases the body politic has learnt how to counter the effects over time. Politicians and voters may find new ways of evading the incentives for accommodation and inclusion that proportional systems offer.

This is the important caution to any form of electoral engineering. Institutions can only change so much. Thus, as David Lublin and Shaun Bowler conclude in a review of the literature on electoral systems and ethnic minority representation,

> While the sense of the literature as a whole leans more toward PR as a conflict management tool, there are two important caveats to make. First . . . it is far easier to address issues of racial and ethnic division before society descends into ethnic violence. It is much easier to keep Humpty Dumpty on the wall than to put him back together again. . . . Second, and following on from that, it is hard to see that electoral institutions alone are enough to head off ethnic conflict. It is crucial to think about electoral institutions in combination with other institutions.[66]

While there are many reasons to believe PR might be better able to restrain racial conflicts, there are no guarantees. Still, this logic follows the long-standing political science wisdom that the best way to manage societal diversity is through crosscutting cleavages. When racial, ethnic, and other core identities align with partisan affiliation, affective polarization is much worse. When identities cut across partisanship such that different members of the same ethnic group support different political parties, politics becomes less all-or-nothing.[67] Thus, crosscutting political identities generate the "capacity to see that there is more than one side to an issue, that a political conflict is, in fact, a legitimate controversy with rationales on both sides."[68]

American racial and ethnic groups are not monoliths, a fact that recent Republican gains among minorities have made clear. Were more parties to exist in the United States, we would expect to see more heterogeneity in voting patterns among racial and ethnic groups. Such diverse voting is an important aspect of making multiracial, multiethnic democracy successful.[69]

Importantly, the governing institutions of the United States reflect the ideal of crosscutting coalitions, with multiple institutions sharing power and checking one another, both within and across different levels of government. James Madison's political theory got this crucial insight of democratic stability. Unfortunately, the partisan nationalization of American politics (unforeseen by Madison or any of the Framers) clashes with this institutional design principle, fostering all-or-nothing partisan electoral conflict atop institutions that make all-or-nothing partisan governing more difficult and leading to deep frustrations and gridlock.

Still, fragmented authority across levels and branches of government also makes the United States more resistant to capture by one dominant faction than more unicameral, centralized parliamentary democracies. This may be the result of a mismatch between the country's electoral and party systems (which are decidedly majoritarian) and its governing institutions (which are more oriented toward negotiation and consensus).[70]

Could Moving to PR Reduce Affective Polarization in the United States?

Let us consider the causal mechanisms that appear to be driving the empirical patterns. One possible causal mechanism is identified by the "shifting-coalitions" theory, which argues that high affective polarization is a downstream effect of repeated partisan opposition. Partisan voters feel warmly toward other parties that govern in coalition with their preferred party—or even perhaps in opposition. These warm feelings last beyond the duration of the coalition. If PR in the United States caused different parties to form coalitions and govern together in various ways, it could decrease polarization among voters.

When the United States was less affectively polarized, Democrats and Republicans worked together in Congress, and voters learned from politicians that bipartisanship was a good thing. When political elites publicly praise opposing partisans and openly work with them, voters are more likely to conclude that opposing partisans are decent and even good people. Affective polarization is lower under such circumstances. When political elites publicly demonize opposing partisans, however, voters are likely to infer that they are evil and dangerous. This learning process may take a few electoral cycles to sink in, but it can heighten affective polarization.

These party dynamics would change with a multiparty House, even though presidential and Senate elections would still be single winner. The overwhelming majority of presidential democracies use PR in their legislatures. However, their presidential elections typically center around two major preelectoral coalitions, reflecting a two-bloc dominant politics that provides some fluidity across electoral cycles. Indeed, given the Senate and the presidency, US multiparty politics would likely retain this two-bloc dominance common among many proportional systems. However, by being more flexible with coalitions, a multiparty system could avoid rigid partisanship.

The second possible causal mechanism is the relationship between geography and partisan alignment. In proportional multiparty systems, parties of the Left and the Right vie for votes across geographic regions. In majoritarian systems, left-leaning parties focus more on urban areas, while right-leaning parties focus more on rural areas. This divide has become clearer in an era in which social and cultural issues have grown more salient in national politics, and it seems likely to endure as long as these issue cleavages remain dominant. If rural-left and urban-right votes are given more weight, this could reduce polarization between Left and Right.

The third causal mechanism is the gradual buildup of issues that widen the gap between parties. A multiparty system could create room for more issue bundles, potentially leading voters to feel closer to multiple parties even if they are particularly enthusiastic about one. Demonization and negative campaigning would be less effective under such conditions, and voters may come to see opposing partisans in a less negative light.

The fourth mechanism explores how a two-party system can reinforce racial and ethnic divides through ongoing partisan conflict along those lines. Again, a multiparty system could foster partisan splits within racial and ethnic groups, which are often more heterogeneous than two-party politics might allow for. Although some may worry about the emergence of "ethnic parties," the evidence suggests that these rarely form in proportional systems.

Thus, this literature suggests that two things would need to happen for affective polarization to decline in the United States. First, more parties would have to form. Second, to change citizens' partisan views, parties would have to introduce new issue bundles and disrupt existing coalitions. This would be a gradual unwinding that might take several electoral cycles.

Would or could this happen? The presence of latent demand in both the electorate and the elite political class determines the extent of new party and issue-bundle formation. One sign of latent demand in the United States is that for more than a decade, polls have shown that around 45 percent of the electorate self-identifies as "Independent," and between 60 and 65 percent of the electorate expresses a desire for more than two parties. We can also observe factions within the major parties during primary elections.

The main question is whether different coalitions would form under an alternative voting system, thereby changing the nature of US politics. Models of multiparty systems suggest a fair amount of issue dynamism— parties evolve and change to adapt to shifting political opportunities.[71] But much of this behavior depends on the entrepreneurship of political elites, who can mobilize and alter public opinion.

This leads to new research questions: What coalitions or parties might form, and how might they realign the political system? What principles should guide electoral reform to reduce affective polarization? If PR can dampen affective polarization, it will do so through certain mechanisms. To prevent democratic backsliding, PR systems should reduce the link between geography and partisanship and encourage diverse political issues and flexible coalition governments.

Can PR Reduce Political Extremism?

The rise of political extremism and authoritarianism poses a challenge to democracy in the United States and around the world. But democracies have varied in their resilience to this threat. The question here is whether PR improves the resilience of democracies in handling the threats of extremism.

Theorizing the Relationship Between Electoral Systems and Political Extremism

For decades, comparative democracy scholars have argued over what type of political system better manages extremism. A common argument for a two-party system is that it prevents extremism by encouraging parties to create broad coalitions. To win elections, both parties must converge on the median voter. A party that moves to a political extreme will pay an electoral price. Thus, major parties should have an incentive to police extremism in their ranks.

A common argument for a proportional multiparty system is that if support for extremism exists, it is better to isolate that support into its own party. In a proportional multiparty system, extremist parties will sometimes have electoral success. This is a feature of PR. If extremist views exist within the population, a party will organize to represent that sentiment. However, the existence of a fringe party with extremist views does not necessarily present a serious problem for democracy. Some scholars have argued that it is better for antisystem voters to feel represented and have a stake in the system than for them to turn their frustration into more radical action, including violence.[72] A presence in a legislature, even in opposition, can help curb extremism by giving citizens an outlet to cast protest votes and be represented.[73] However, in societies where politics is both divided and fragmented, small parties on the extremes can sometimes have disproportionate leverage.[74]

In proportional multiparty systems, mainstream parties have two ways of responding to extremist parties. The "cordon sanitaire" is one approach. The second is the "taming" approach: mainstream parties invite extremist parties into government coalitions but effectively tame them by sharing the responsibility of governing, draining away some of the support for extremist parties that merely reflected a desire for change.

Implicit in both approaches is the idea that the overall political system is self-correcting and that enough voters prefer moderation to extremism to make the latter a political loser, while enough political elites are motivated to preserve the democratic system that they will reassess their partisan commitments and strategies in the face of extremist threats. Managing political extremism depends on the choices of voters and elites: Will they oppose extreme behavior?

However, much depends on the extent to which an extremist party is gaining support. An extremist party with 5 or 10 percent support is different from one with 25 percent support, which is where the danger zone starts. In a more proportional system, an extremist party with the support of a quarter of the electorate will get 25 percent of the seats in the legislature. This is high, but it still gives other parties opportunities to maneuver. In a two-party system, however, an extremist faction with 25 percent support could take over a major party.

Let's imagine a two-party system in which Party A wins 51 percent of the vote to Party B's 49 percent, thus gaining control of the government. However, Party A is split between two factions, Faction 1 and Faction 2. Faction 1 represents 51 percent of Party A, giving it control of the party. In a simple majority system, this faction, which represents just 26 percent of the country's electorate, would have total control of the government.

To be fair, this assumes that none of Faction 2 would defect to Party B, which may not be realistic. A minority faction may need to be larger to gain total control. But an even smaller faction could gain total power if only a plurality of support is needed because a few smaller parties take away votes without winning seats. Let's say Party A gets 45 percent of the vote, giving it control of a majority of seats. If Party A has three factions—one with 40 percent support and two with 30 percent—it would be possible for a faction with the support of just 22.5 percent of the electorate to gain total power.

There are many ways to shift around the math. But a general problem is that when a more extreme minority faction gains control of a major party, the losing moderate faction may wind up politically homeless. This describes the trajectory of Republican moderates in the United States over the last decade. Few have joined the Democratic Party. Most have remained reluctant Republicans, updating their positions to align with their party's in order to remain in good standing. They cannot operate as their own party in a two-party system.

If an extreme minority faction gains control of a major party, it often labels its opposition as more extreme to keep its moderate supporters. Again, this has happened with the Republican Party. Once Donald Trump took hold of the party, he provoked conflicts to exacerbate differences. Polarization is a common strategy of extremist authoritarians. They strategically choose conflicts designed to push their political opponents into more extreme positions in response. They force moderates to choose sides. This can tip a political system into escalating extremism.

It is easy to see this problem through the lens of primary elections, in which the "base" selects nominees who come from the political extremes—or at least have to cater to the extremes (see Chapter 5 on primary elections). But distortion from narrow candidate selection is a more generalized problem in a two-party system. Two parties will have separate "selectorates"—networks of donors, elites, activists, and voters who are responsible for elevating particular candidates over others. If a party is divided into competing factions, as a big-tent party in a two-party system is likely to be, those factions will compete for dominance, with the winner likely to set the agenda and priorities for that party. Even if it is a majority of a majority, the dominant faction will still be a minority. The US system, which strips party leaders of any formal authority in candidate selection, appears uniquely prone to this problem of an extremist faction taking over a major party in the current political climate.

In a two-party system, failure to eliminate extremism within either party can have devastating effects. Party leadership acts as a defense against extremism, and breaching this defense puts the system in grave danger. In a proportional system, by contrast, the failure of a single party to police its ranks against extremism is not catastrophic in the same way. In this sense, there is more resilience in a multiparty system, such that if one party becomes extreme, other parties can adjust. It is very unlikely that a single party will gain a majority of seats in the legislature in such a system, which means that parties typically have to form governing coalitions. Thus, far-right parties cannot govern on their own unless they win a majority of seats.

As noted above, mainstream parties have two ways to deal with extremist parties: the cordon sanitaire, in which mainstream parties form a "grand coalition" to keep extremist parties out of power, and the taming strategy of inviting extremists into coalition to force them to moderate. The latter approach appears to have two distinct advantages.

First, being part of a government coalition typically has a moderating effect on smaller far-right parties. Such parties usually soften their positions in exchange for governing responsibility.[75] This compromising, in turn, blunts their appeal. Populist parties that start off as political outsiders shed their antisystem credibility by becoming political insiders.[76] Because public opinion is thermostatic, parties in power often lose support in the following election. This makes for a double hit to far-right parties. Meanwhile, parties that moderate their positions typically gain back seats in the next election.[77] Extremist parties cannot deliver on their impossible promises of dramatic change, thus leaving their supporters disappointed in the next election.

Crucially, both strategies depend on the strength and democratic commitments of mainstream parties. The taming approach can work if a mainstream party is strong enough to keep the upper hand in the coalition. A cordon sanitaire approach can work if mainstream parties can navigate challenging times together. If mainstream parties are weak and hollow, neither approach will work very well.

Choosing the right approach depends on the specific country situation and election results.[78] Because the cordon sanitaire can lead to backlash, mainstream parties must be careful to take extraordinary measures only when the extremist party is truly illiberal and antisystem. Casting disagreement and dissent as extremism can reinforce alienation and extremism.[79]

But one benefit of a multiparty PR system is that mainstream parties have options and flexibility. The taming strategy can work in part because mainstream parties do not need extremist parties to form a governing majority. Mainstream parties can instead build a grand coalition to exclude extremist parties, which have nowhere near a majority of support and so depend on more mainstream parties to govern with them. The result is that mainstream parties have more bargaining leverage. Crucially, this is because the bargaining happens *between* parties, so different possible coalitions can form.

Proportional democracies are obviously not immune from democratic backsliding. But when they do backslide, it is typically under conditions of high societal polarization. Center parties struggle under such conditions, leading to the collapse of party systems into two governing coalitions—left and right. When only two governing coalitions are possible, extreme factions gain power and push moderate parties to adopt more radical positions, leading to increased polarization in society.[80]

If a PR system does collapse into two distinct and polarized blocs, there is still an opportunity for a new center party to form without displacing a major party, because a new center party could gain representation with as little as 10 or 15 percent of the vote. By contrast, in a two-party first-past-the-post system, a new center party would be unlikely to win any seats with that level of support, unless it had a particularly strong geographic concentration.

Measuring and Charting Extremist Parties

Extremism, such as polarization, is a problem much discussed but rarely defined clearly. As with polarization, extremism has multiple dimensions. A political party can be ideologically extreme (because it holds views far from the mainstream) but also supportive of liberal, pluralist democracy. Conversely, a political party can be ideologically moderate on most issues but extreme in its opposition to liberal, pluralist democracy. However, this second combination is unlikely. Typically, policy extremism goes along with illiberalism. Nationalism and xenophobia often go with authoritarian extremism. And populism, which is more appropriately described as a style of politics than as an ideology, also tends to go with authoritarianism. On their own, populism and nationalism can be compatible with liberal democracy. But when combined with authoritarianism, they become a threatening package that challenges key tenets of liberal pluralism, including minority rights and dissent.

Western democracies are currently experiencing a "fourth wave" of populism, with populist parties emphasizing anti-immigrant and antiglobalization views. The first wave (1945 to 1955) comprised "neofascist" parties that represented the last gasp of totalitarian movements from the 1930s and faded quickly. The second wave (1955 to 1980) reflected a more antiestablishment mood with a few "flash parties," such as the Farmers Party in the Netherlands and the Poujadism movement in France, which came and went swiftly. The third wave (1980 to 2000) occurred during a time of economic disruption and high unemployment. It was marked by the rise of the Front National in France and the Freedom Party in Austria.

The current wave has been the most successful so far, but it is much more heterogeneous than previous ones. It features more diverse types of parties and organizations, although these generally focus on cultural concerns, particularly a backlash against immigration. Most new populist parties in Europe have distanced themselves from violence and antidemocratic norms, despite their ethnonationalist rhetoric.[81]

Entrepreneurial populist leaders have seized on preexisting concerns about immigration and globalization. These issues became salient during the financial crisis of 2008–2009 and the migrant crisis of the mid-2010s.[82] However, the relative success of these parties does not reflect a sudden change in public opinion. If anything, citizens in European democracies have become more supportive of immigration, although public opinion is mostly flat. As Larry Bartels has documented, "The familiar specter of a 'populist wave' sweeping contemporary Europe is, at least when it comes to overall public opinion, wholly illusory." Instead, populist nativist right-wing sentiment has been consistent for decades. A reservoir of support has always existed. It is just that new parties have emerged to make these issues more salient. Still, as Bartels notes, "to suppose that a reservoir of right-wing populist sentiment is enough to constitute a crisis of democracy is unduly alarmist." The danger, Bartels notes, is when mainstream parties turn antidemocratic. Few voters in democracies want to support authoritarianism outright. But sometimes, they do without realizing what they are doing.

Multiparty democracies have long been associated with more ideological polarization.[83] However, ideological dispersion does not equate to success for extremist parties. Repeated studies have found no link between proportionality and extremist party success.[84] Nor are proportional systems associated with more success for anti-immigrant parties.[85] Most effects are null. However, at least one study found that majoritarian systems were associated with more party extremism.[86] Multiparty systems may even slightly benefit moderate parties.[87]

Evidence for these claims can be found in recent data from the V-Dem Institute, which asked country experts to assess the extent to which the parties in question show a lack of "commitment to democratic norms prior to elections."[88]

The V-Dem experts find the US Republican Party to be more illiberal than such European populist parties as the Austrian Freedom Party, the Danish People's Party, the True Finns Party, the Front National, the Dutch Party for Freedom, and the Swedish Democrats. This is largely because, although these parties are strongly anti-immigration, they have retained support for basic aspects of liberal democracy. The US Republican Party is more in line with the German Alternative for Deustchland, the Italian Northern League, the Hungarian Fidesz, and the Polish Law and Justice Party. Of these parties, only Fidesz and Law and Justice have been as successful as the Republican Party.

A more comprehensive measure of illiberalism's reach within a country is the overall amount of liberalism in its party *system*. To measure this, we take a weighted average of the antipluralism index across all parties in a system, which averages the scores of all parties that gain seats in the legislature and then weights the average by each party's share of seats. Looking at the relationship between district magnitude and the weighted illiberalism (antipluralism) index in the party system, we find that there appears to be a slight relationship, with more proportional systems having less party-system illiberalism, but considerable variation exists that district magnitude alone cannot explain.

Legislative fractionalization is more closely related to the overall success of illiberal parties than is district magnitude. Put simply, the more binary a legislative party system (closer to 0.5 on the fractionalization score), the more illiberalism exists within the party system. This relationship became especially pronounced in the 2010s, the decade in which Western democracies came under the most stress.

Legislative fractionalization is a property of the party system and a second-order property of the electoral system. The observed patterns are consistent with the theory. In a less fractionalized party system, with fewer parties and more binary competition, if one party becomes illiberal, it represents a much larger share of the legislature. In a more fractionalized party system, illiberalism can more easily be contained in one party without contagion. However, at the extremes of fractionalization, there does appear to be more illiberalism. In other words, a system that permits too many parties can give extremism too much of a foothold or make it too hard for liberal parties to coordinate against a concentrated threat.

Thus, the V-Dem data suggest that a moderate level of fractionalization might be best at managing extremism. However, we need to better understand the relationship. In the following section, we look briefly at the trajectories of two countries where backsliding occurred, Hungary and Poland. Both trajectories suggest a potential causal relationship, because in both countries the party system became much more binary (less fractionalized) immediately before the backsliding took place. We also look at a third country, Colombia, where the party system became more fractionalized prior to a democratic improvement.

Can PR Limit Political Extremism?

In a two-party system, moderates battle against extremism *within* their own parties. In a sense, mainstream partisan leaders who oppose extremism have the same two options—either cast extremists out of the party (the cordon sanitaire) or moderate extremism through responsibility (taming). The internal cordon sanitaire can work for a while, but it raises the same problems of backlash. With no smaller "release-valve" party, extremists nurture their disaffection and gain strength from it.[89]

If extremism can intensify in the absence of a release valve, it can grow within a party. In pursuit of a narrow majority, a major party may need to placate and even indulge the demands of an extremist faction to win elections. This leads to major parties courting extremists, which then polarizes the electorate. As the electorate polarizes, leaders of mainstream parties have fewer options to build a broad coalition, making them more reliant on extremists.

In a two-party system, coalitions are much longer lasting and less flexible. If we assume parties represent distinct policy perspectives and politicians care about policy as well as winning elections, sophisticated models and consistent empirical evidence show no median convergence. Instead, two-party competition leads just as easily to extremism.[90]

This is broadly the story of the Republican Party. For a long time, moderates had the upper hand. But starting in the 1990s, extremism within the party grew. Party leaders could not ignore the more extreme elements within the coalition. They tried but failed to manage these elements through messaging and symbolic politics. By 2010, the extremists had built a new movement within the party, the Tea Party, and had enough leverage to exert significant pull. By 2017, they had taken over the presidency in the person of Donald Trump. Other members of the party had two equally unappealing options: capitulate or leave. Most stayed and appeased Trump because they enjoyed being in power (or had convinced themselves that they could do more good by sticking around than by leaving).

Trump was not initially popular among most Republicans. There are still many Republicans, particularly Republican elites, who would like to move on from Trump's distinct brand of confrontational, polarizing politics. But polarization and conflict escalation have been Trump's reliable strategy. Over his political career, he has constantly tested the limits. When confronted, he always doubles down on a polarizing conflict strategy. Each time, other Republicans have rallied to his side rather than give Democrats a "victory."

Trump's success here depends on affective polarization and the two-party system. He can only rally support to his side because, for many Republicans, the possibility of letting Democrats win is simply intolerable. In reluctantly backing Trump, Republicans rationalize that Democrats are even worse, thus compounding affective polarization. Eric Groenendyk identified the "lesser-of-two-evils" defense as a key factor in partisan animosity in the United States.[91]

The Republican Party shares similarities with successful right-wing parties in Hungary and Poland. All three countries share two important things in common: they have grown perniciously polarized across geographic divides in the twenty-first century, and their turn toward political illiberalism has been a top-down process. In none of these countries did a majority of voters want a democratic rollback, and many to this day have rationalized developments as appropriately democratic.

The United States has long had a two-party system, but since 2000 the geographic sorting of the two political parties has increased the level of polarization significantly. Meanwhile, Hungary and Poland both followed a trajectory of legislative consolidation before falling into illiberalism. First, the level of legislative fractionalization declined.

Then, the countries' V-Dem scores fell. The timing suggests a possible causal relationship (consolidation, then decline), but the reality is obviously more complicated than that. Likely, the legislative consolidation was a symptom of societal polarization, which in turn contributed to democratic decline.

Hungary is a paradigmatic case of "pernicious polarization" across urban-rural lines. Although Hungary has had a multiparty system since the end of the Cold War, the divide between its right and left blocs has never been bridged. That divide has been primarily cultural and symbolic, not economic. Starting in the late 1990s, the cleavage moved towards a stronger "us-versus-them" logic. Prior to the 2010s, Fidesz was a moderate party, and Viktor Orban showed few signs of being an autocrat. Fidesz supporters did not willingly vote to weaken democracy. They voted for change at a time of political scandal.[92] Upon gaining a majority, the party strengthened executive power and weakened checks and balances considerably, centralizing power.

Poland followed a similar trajectory. Law and Justice won the presidency and majorities in both chambers of parliament in 2015, going on to overhaul the judiciary, limit civil rights, increase surveillance, and fill state jobs with party loyalists. Decision-making power was consolidated by the party chairman, Jarosław Kaczyński. In a "change" election, the party campaigned around child-tax credit, prescription drugs for the elderly, and frustration with the status quo—not widespread illiberalism. But with polarizing elite rhetoric, Law and Justice split the country, drawing support overwhelmingly from the poorer and more rural eastern half.

One notable explanation for why Fidesz has been successful in Hungary is that it united a heterogeneous coalition of diverse interests who all opposed the political Left, but for different reasons. In a polarizing party system organized around two blocs, mobilizing a heterogeneous coalition based on fear became a winning strategy.[93] Nothing unites like a common enemy. When political conflict is flattened into two issue bundles and one dimension, "us-versus-them" political strategies are at their most potent.

Bartels notes another commonality across the United States, Hungary, and Poland: "Popular support for authoritarian nationalism was greatly magnified in two distinct respects—first by co-opting the existing support of established mainstream conservative parties, and second by benefiting from significant disproportionality in the translation of electoral seats into political authority."[94]

How much can be explained by electoral system design? In Hungary, Fidesz gained majority control in 2011 under a mixed system in which roughly half of seats were elected through single-member districts and half through proportional representation. Fidesz then used its majority to transform the electoral system. It increased the share of single-member districts, gerrymandered many of those districts, and reduced the overall number of seats in the legislature. The gambit worked. In the next election, Fidesz won 67 percent of the seats with 45 percent of the vote. This "majoritarian turn" in the rules of the electoral system almost certainly helped Fidesz solidify power.[95] In 2022, the party won 135 out of 199 seats in the legislature, benefitting from a favorable electoral law.

Poland has a 5 percent national threshold atop a system of multi-member districts, such that a party that does not get 5 percent nationally does not get any seats.[96] Poland also has an 8 percent threshold for parties campaigning as a bloc. Seats that go unclaimed as a result go to the largest parties. This threshold was put in place to prevent excessive fragmentation and encourage more majoritarian outcomes. However, in the 2015 election, it had a perverse effect. A group of center-left parties campaigned as a bloc that year but fell just short of the threshold with 7.7 percent of the vote nationwide. Because this bloc and other smaller parties forfeited their seats, Law and Justice was able to win 51.1 percent of the seats in the Polish Sejm (parliament) with just 37.6 percent of the popular vote. It was again able to win 51.1 percent of the seats in the Sejm in 2019, despite winning 43.6 percent of the national vote. This disproportionality allowed Law and Justice to govern without partners, imposing a form of minority rule.

A driving force of democratic backsliding is deep societal polarization, fueled by opportunistic political elites. Under certain circumstances, polarizing strategies can be very effective for parties hoping to win majority control. However, it is important to note that neither Fidesz nor Law and Justice began as far-right illiberal parties; nor were they elected on a promise to build a more authoritarian society. Instead, once they gained single-party majority power, they used it to further entrench their control. The more concentrated the party system is into two dominant parties, the more likely it is that one party can win an outright majority and control of government. Certainly, the United States is not Poland or Hungary. The United States has a more robust democratic history and culture, and both separation of powers and federalism provide some bulwarks against one-party dominance across the entire country. But one party can do considerable damage to political institutions if it gains unified control of Congress, the Senate, the presidency, and many state governments.

In a divided society, PR provides the flexibility for unlikely coalitions of pro-democracy parties to campaign together by appealing to different societal groups and interests. This is the story of Poland's 2023 election, held under a proportional rule, in which three opposition parties ran as a loose coalition and won a majority of seats. As Anne Applebaum observed, "The existence of three opposition parties meant that different messages were heard by different parts of the electorate, on the center-right as well as the center-left. Some of the candidates attacked [Law and Justice]. . . . Some used the language of unity and called for an end to polarization."[97]

In both Poland and Hungary, leaders were much more successful in eliminating checks and balances and strengthening executive power than they have been in the United States. The United States has the advantage of more deeply institutionalized checks and balances. However, it is notable that in all three countries, the electoral system allowed a political party to win majority control without winning a majority of the votes, and in a binary party system, few voters believed they were voting against democracy.

Democratic backsliding is a complex phenomenon with many causes. The party system and the electoral system merely provide one institutional framework. Ultimately, much depends on how political elites respond to challenges and on the strength and democratic commitments of major-party leaders. However, the core question here is whether different electoral systems dampen or amplify threats of extremism, particularly in the current era, in which urban-rural polarization poses a significant threat to democratic stability. In a recent study of democratic backsliding, Michael K. Miller argues that winner-take-all elections make democratic backsliding more likely because of the ways in which they allow winners to consolidate power.[98]

One notable exception to the democratic backsliding of recent decades is Colombia, a country that has been on the democratic upswing. Colombia's politics were deeply polarized in the 1990s, the peak years of the FARC Fuerzas Armadas Revolucionarias de Colombia) conflicts.[99] But starting that decade, the country adopted a series of electoral reforms that opened up its political system, effectively breaking up the dominance of its two major parties by denationalizing politics, reducing corruption, and expanding participation. Particularly consequential was a 2003 reform that moved the system in a much more party-proportional direction, replacing a candidate-centered electoral system that was akin to the single nontransferable vote but slightly different. Although the once-dominant parties remained players after 2003, new parties become important too.

Colombia's democratic improvements and party-system expansion followed the exact opposite trajectory of Poland and Hungary, where party-system narrowing preceded democratic decline.[100] Again, we should be cautious about interpreting these changes. Much else was happening in Colombia at the time, including an effective crackdown on guerillas, which enabled more people to participate in politics without fear of violence. There was also a fair amount of decentralization and localism, which encouraged more parties and sectors to get involved in politics.

A more detailed analysis would demand more research on the other factors driving change in these countries' party systems. However, it is notable that the three Organization for Economic Cooperation and Development (OECD) countries that have seen the most significant changes in their V-Dem scores in recent decades (two negative, one positive) all show the same suggestive patterns across these two variables, although in opposite directions. Hungary changed its electoral laws to move in a more majoritarian direction. Colombia changed its electoral laws to move in a more proportional direction. While party systems alone cannot explain the democratic shifts in these countries, they did provide significant opportunities for actors to behave as they did.

Extremism, Losers' Consent, and Satisfaction with Democracy

Democracy depends on the consent of losers, who must accept the outcome of elections. One of the most robust findings in political science is the gap between electoral winners and losers. Electoral winners report being more satisfied with democracy than electoral losers do. This is especially true in majoritarian democracies, because the distinction between winners and losers is much sharper in such countries. The satisfaction gap is even wider under conditions of polarization.[101] By contrast, in proportional democracies, the difference between winning and losing in elections is less stark, and the divide between opposition and governing coalitions is sometimes less clear. Thus, PR is associated with more satisfaction with democracyand more confidence in the electoral process.[102]

Certainly, context matters here. Countries with high-quality governments experience lower satisfaction among winners and higher satisfaction among losers. This indicates the influence of government quality on closing the gap. Presumably, this is because a robust civil service and strong rule of law place guardrails on what any governing majority can accomplish.[103] Low levels of corruption also help close the gap.[104]

The information environment matters as well. In divided democracies, electoral losers more often hear arguments claiming the election was unfair. Biased and polarized media are more commonly found in low-quality democracies.[105]

Currently, a major threat to American democracy concerns electoral legitimacy. Trump's campaign against the 2020 election result has turned into a broader partisan fight, causing significant harm to the US electoral system. This high-stakes presidential election environment interacts with affective polarization in ways that make it more easily exploitable by an authoritarian who wants to abuse it to stay in power. To be sure, all presidential elections are winner-take-all, which makes presidential democracies more vulnerable to the losers' consent problem. But under circumstances of high affective polarization, a close election can be dry tinder for an illiberal autocrat who wants to burn down democratic structures.

Could PR Reduce the Power of
Illiberal Extremism in the United States?

Different systems create different strategic landscapes for moderates to build coalitions. Regardless of the system, much depends on party leadership. Multiparty systems provide more flexibility to manage extremism when it gains representation.

Adopting a more proportional system in the United States would likely lead to the emergence of a far-right extremist party, as it has in other proportional democracies. A more proportional system would also allow a center-right party to organize and provide voters with an alternative right-of-center option. Historically, pushbacks against antisystem extremism have depended on broad cross-ideological coalitions, which are more difficult to build in binary two-party systems. Poland's recent election proves that proportional systems can allow multiple parties to unite and win as a pro-democracy coalition.

Illiberal extremists have had the most success in deeply divided party systems with high levels of affective polarization. In such polities, citizens are most likely to overlook democratic norm violations by their own side.

To the extent illiberal extremist parties have achieved government control, it is not because their illiberal extremist policies or governing approaches were popular. It is because they won majority government control with banal promises of political change and then became more extreme. They have maintained their power both by making institutions more biased in their favor (typically, more executive centered and thus more majoritarian) and by pursuing a polarizing strategy to make their political opponents seem more dangerous and extreme. As long as affective polarization is high, they face a low electoral price for antidemocratic activity.

Extremist parties running on extremist platforms are unpopular throughout Western democracies. Although such parties may sometimes gain the support of up to 20 percent of the electorate, the other 80 percent strongly opposes them. Extremist parties can't take over governments without support from mainstream parties, so they have to either stay in opposition or make compromises to join a coalition. This reduces their power to harm democracy, even if it leads to more anti-immigrant or isolationist policies. Only under certain conditions, such as extreme polarization, do mainstream parties capitulate to the demands of small extremist parties in exchange for support in forming governing coalitions.

Without electoral reform, two unlikely possibilities exist for managing extremism within the American two-party system. Either moderates regain the upper hand within the Republican Party or Democrats become a dominant big-tent moderate party. Perhaps these outcomes are more likely than passing reforms to adopt PR; perhaps not. But given the current trajectory of American politics, MAGA's continued dominance within the Republican Party, and the likelihood of more close national elections, neither of the above possibilities seems likely.

Reducing political extremism is challenging in a society where it has gained significant power. But a proportional system offers more possibilities.

How Does PR Impact Quality of Governance?

Theories of Governance Under Majoritarian and Proportional Systems

In this third section, we assess the relationship between electoral systems and government performance. Do proportional or majoritarian systems provide for more effective governance? One argument for majoritarian systems being more effective focuses on accountability. The argument is that under a majoritarian system, voters can empower a single party to govern. A unified party can enact its program, and then voters can judge the result. If voters are happy, they can re-empower the governing party at the next election. If voters are unhappy, they can vote in the opposition party, assuming they like its proposals better. The threat of being tossed out of power should make parties more responsive in the majoritarian system.

An argument for proportional multiparty systems is that they allow for more diverse representation, leading to effective policymaking through bargaining. By providing voters with more choices, a proportional system can create a more representative legislature. Elected lawmakers can then negotiate to reach broadly accepted policies that represent diverse constituents.

This argument for proportional multiparty systems also involves a critique of the case for majoritarian systems. First, it suggests that the supposed accountability benefits of majoritarian systems are merely theoretical. The state of the economy, the most important factor in electoral outcomes, is often influenced by factors beyond the control of the party in power. However, the governing party does have levers to stimulate short-term growth ahead of an election (such as major stimulus), which can encourage irresponsible fiscal policy. Second, if most voters are partisans, they will not be neutral observers. They will cheerlead the policies of their party no matter what. Instead, a small group of mostly uninterested voters will decide elections, driven by a "throw-the-bums-out" mentality. If the parties are far apart, this can lead to wild swings in policy.

In the United States, moreover, the electoral system might be majoritarian, but the governing rules are antimajoritarian. Therefore, voters struggle to evaluate party performance as compromise is prevalent across governing institutions, often controlled by opposing parties, making it difficult to assess policy and performance. Voters might blame the president, but especially under divided government, the president is limited by the legislature. This could prompt the opposition-led legislature to oppose the president, with the goal of achieving unified government for its side. All of this becomes very confusing for voters: Whom do they hold accountable in a system that is supposed to encourage accountability?

Supporters of majoritarian systems argue that such systems provide clear choices for potential governing coalitions, as they must form into two competing parties prior to elections. In contrast, proportional systems often form coalitions after elections, giving voters less influence and making it harder to achieve electoral accountability. Because majoritarian systems give parties a majority, the government can get to work immediately, whereas in proportional systems, parties can sometimes take months to form a government.

Supporters of proportionality could respond that their preferred system provides greater flexibility to stay aligned with the political center.

Preelectoral coalitions are common in proportional systems, especially in proportional presidential systems. This helps voters understand their options and gives them more control over which part of the coalition they want to support. Furthermore, a proportional advocate may claim that the two choices seem arbitrary and voters should have more options for better responsiveness.

The theory debate could go back and forth for pages. Much also depends on the parties, their leaders, and their disagreements. Electoral systems can shape the parameters of negotiation and affect the conditions and motivations for reaching compromises.

Next we turn to the evidence, starting with the differences between presidential and parliamentary PR systems. PR presidentialism has some distinct governing dynamics.

How Does PR Work with Presidentialism?

Europe's parliamentary systems are commonly used as a reference point for proportional multiparty democracy. But the United States has a presidential system. The main difference between presidential and parliamentary systems is that, in presidential systems, presidents are elected independently from the legislature. In parliamentary systems, the legislature chooses the head of government. Some parliamentary systems are majoritarian, such as that of the United Kingdom

Among relatively stable liberal democracies, majoritarianism is much more common in parliamentary systems than in presidential systems (see Table 3.1).

The overwhelming majority of presidential systems are either proportional (fifteen of twenty-four) or mixed (five of twenty-four). Only four presidential democracies use a majoritarian electoral system for the legislature. Alongside the United States, the other three are Ghana,

Table 3.1   Distribution of Liberal Democracies by System of Government and Lower-Chamber Electoral System

	Majoritarian	Proportional	Mixed
Parliamentary	12	15	3
Presidential	4	15	5
Semipresidential	2	17	5

Note: Liberal democracies are defined as countries whose V-Dem liberal democracy scores have consistently exceeded .50 for the past decade.

Liberia, and Sierra Leone. And the second two barely make the cutoff. France has a majoritarian semipresidential system.

Thirty years ago, the combination of presidentialism and a multiparty legislature was widely viewed as "difficult."[106] The worry was that presidents would have a hard time garnering legislative support for their programs, resulting in immobilism and gridlock, which in turn could lead to either corrupt vote buying, executive overreach, or both. Without a doubt, there were occurrences of this, especially in the 1970s and 1980s.

But more recent evidence suggests these assessments were too pessimistic. For at least a decade now, the growing conventional wisdom has been that presidentialism and PR can work well together. Examples of robust, stable democracies that use this combination include Costa Rica, Cyprus, Chile, and Uruguay.

Recent scholarly assessments are similarly positive. As Paul Chaisty and colleagues observe, "Twenty years of research have shown presidentialism to be remarkably durable, and in particular its multiparty variant has vastly overperformed relative to early predictions."[107] José Antonio Cheibub and coauthors likewise note, "Government coalitions are less frequent under presidentialism than under parliamentarism, but the difference is one of degree, not of kind. Highly fractionalized legislatures turn out to promote coalitions in both systems. Single-party minority governments are not less successful in the legislature than coalition governments, minority or majority. Legislative paralysis appears to be a rare phenomenon."[108]

According to Carlos Pereira and Marcus André Melo, "The ability of multiparty presidentialism to subsist with sustainable democracy is beyond dispute. . . . [M]ultiparty presidentialism has boosted political stability, and has not degenerated into systemic corruption as long as robust political competition and a set of strong autonomous institutions exist alongside it to keep its potential excesses within bounds."[109]

Responding to Juan Linz, who warned of the dangers of presidentialism, Christian Arnold and colleagues argue, "The Linzian interpretation of presidentialism is probably too pessimistic. Presidents in Latin America are not always the inflexible and imperial leaders previously characterized by Linz."[110] And Eduardo Alemán and George Tsebelis conclude, "We do not find dominant or deadlocked presidents; instead, we observe differences in the extent to which presidents succeed in enacting their programs and, perhaps more interestingly, how this is achieved."[111]

Naturally, some multiparty presidential countries have performed better than others. Some presidents have been more successful than others.

Since presidential democracies vary considerably across institutional design and economic conditions, it is possible to offer some tentative conclusions. Broadly speaking, they are as follows:

1. Presidents with fewer formal constitutional powers must bargain more with legislators, which might lead to more democratic stability.[112]
2. A modest multiparty system without excessive fragmentation seems to work best. Some party diversity is helpful. Extreme party-system fragmentation is more problematic.[113]
3. Binary political divisions and high levels of polarization are dangerous no matter what.
4. Individual presidential character and talent matter.

In multiparty systems, presidents have various ways to build majorities. The most common and effective way is through multiparty cabinets. To help facilitate a governing coalition in the legislature, presidents typically allocate positions and portfolios in their cabinet, often in proportion to party strength. Scholars refer to this as coalition presidentialism.

Often presidents can hold together multiparty coalitions across the executive and legislative branches, which allows them to pass preferred policy and govern. Cabinets form more easily when coalitions are smaller and have more ideological overlap.[114]

But a "minority government" does not necessarily lead to immobilism. On the contrary, presidents can bargain with opposing parties on an ad hoc basis.[115] In some ways, this can be desirable. A minority government that forms coalitions around each individual issue is more likely to represent the majority's views on those issues. However, this situation can also lead to deadlock.

Preelectoral coalitions are common in multiparty presidential democracies and regularly affect how cabinet posts are allocated. Parties endorsing candidates from another party provide infrastructure, connections, and funds. In exchange, they get policy concessions and coalition appointments, including at the cabinet level.[116]

Presidents can use pork barrel politics to build coalitions. Plenty of coalition partners are available for a price.[117] To be sure, "particularistic benefits" can sometimes grow indistinguishable from outright corruption. This is one reason an overly fragmented or weak party system can be problematic.

Still, the broad takeaway is that concerns about immobilism and deadlock in multiparty presidential systems have been overblown: As

José Antonio Cheibub and colleagues conclude, "Whatever is wrong with presidentialism, is not due to the difficulty of forming coalitions."[118] The real perils of presidentialism stem from illiberal elites, not from multipartyism—and in this sense, the situation is similar to parliamentary democracies.

The United States presents a different environment for building coalitions. A president who confronts a Congress with one chamber controlled by the opposing party will encounter significant opposition and more limited legislative leeway.[119] With just two parties and elections that are always neck and neck, this is a regular event. It is unlikely that a president will win opposing-party support through cabinet appointments or policy concessions when facing an adversarial Congress. The effectiveness of pork barrel politics has significantly diminished. Due to high polarization, the binary US party system limits presidents' ability to form cross-party alliances.

Thus, the most dangerous threat to a presidential democracy appears to be deep partisan polarization—a dynamic that raises the already high stakes for winner-take-all presidential elections to impossible levels. In a recent essay, Lee Drutman and Scott Mainwaring explain why PR can be successful with presidentialism:

> The United States now experiences many of Juan Linz's warned-about "perils of presidentialism." Gridlock, immobilism, and the problem of "dual legitimacy" (presidents and legislatures claiming competing mandates) are present under divided government, and are weakening US democracy. Conversely, when the same party controls the White House and Congress in this era of intense polarization, congressional checks on the president are too weak. . . .
>
> Whatever concerns about presidentialism exist, there is no evidence that a two-party system makes presidentialism function better. If a two-party system works well with presidentialism, it is only when that two-party system produces non-ideological, moderate parties. Whatever risks exist in combining presidentialism and multipartyism in the United States, they are far fewer than doing nothing and maintaining the divisive us-against-them status quo.[120]

How Governing Coalitions Form in Multiparty Systems

All legislatures require majority votes to pass legislation. In multiparty systems, multiple parties join to form a governing coalition. Sometimes, these multiparty coalitions form before elections, particularly in presidential multiparty systems. In parliamentary systems, coalitions usually come together after elections, although in some instances they form beforehand.

The postelection coalition-formation process is often high drama, full of political wheeling and dealing. Typically, the party that wins the most seats plays the role of "formateur"—and gets the first shot at building a coalition. The process of coalition formation involves much public and private back-and-forth, some of it performative, some of it genuine. In the end, a governing coalition forms, often with a written agreement (which takes time to work out).[121]

On average, the postelection negotiation process takes less than a month (shorter than the two-month period between US elections and the seating of a new Congress). However, the duration can vary. The Netherlands, which has the most proportional system in Europe and typically the most legislative parties, usually takes the longest to form a government—on average, about three months.[122] Generally, high polarization and excessive legislative fragmentation contribute to longer negotiation periods.[123] Parties form coalitions more easily when they mostly agree on the important issues or have different issues they care about and so can effectively logroll. Coalitions also form more easily when individual leaders have more experience in office.[124] Generally, partisan coalitions reflect a broad agreement that strikes a compromise among parties based on their vote share.[125]

Although postelection coalitions are more common in parliamentary systems, about a quarter of all governments that form in such systems emerge from preelection coalitions. That is, multiple parties agree that if they win a majority of seats between them, they will govern as a coalition. This helps voters pick the government they want to support early on and improves the chances of a smooth coalition formation postelection.[126]

Preelection coalitions are more common in multiparty presidential systems. According to one recent study, 56 percent of multiparty presidencies were supported by a preelectoral coalition.[127] Because presidents are elected by a majority vote, this puts a higher premium on preelectoral coordination. If different parties work together for one presidential candidate, these efforts boost that candidate's chances of winning. Supporting a presidential candidate can give smaller parties benefits such as policy concessions, support for lower-level candidates, cabinet positions, and other appointments.[128]

Generally, coalitions that form more easily stay together more easily. Since most parliamentary democracies do not have fixed elections, the collapse of a coalition can bring about a new election, while a "caretaker" government keeps the lights on until a new government is formed. Presidential systems are more rigid (or stable, depending on your perspective), so a broken-down coalition can mean immobilism and gridlock.

Occasionally, proportional multiparty countries have failed to form governments. For example, in the Netherlands, it took a record 225 days (nine months) to form a new government following the 2021 election. After the 2017 Dutch election, forming a government took seven months. But during these periods, caretaker governments still operated, as is typically the case in parliamentary systems during the coalition-formation process.

As a general pattern, governments in western Europe form relatively quickly, usually within a few weeks. However, the average formation time has been creeping up lately, and the number of coalitions taking more than sixty and even ninety days to form has increased.

Another general trend in recent years has been toward more new party activity in proportional systems. However, this has only translated into modest increases in legislative fractionalization.

In the United States, a new Congress is not seated until two months after an election, which would give American parties time to work out potential coalitions if the country adopted a more proportional system. However, the recent drama around the selection of the House Speaker has prompted some to question whether such a system would make this even more difficult.

Yet there are two things to keep in mind. One is that the role of the House Speaker has varied over time, and the current role is uniquely powerful. At various times, the Speaker has been a much less powerful actor. For example, from 1937 to 1961, the House was effectively led by a powerful Rules Committee, which itself was led by a (mostly conservative) coalition across party lines. Individual committees were also more powerful.

The second consideration is that in an era of narrow congressional majorities and two polarized parties, small groups can have tremendous leverage. Given that there are many ways for the House of Representatives to operate and many possibilities for a more committee-based internal governance system, we should be able to imagine alternative organizing structures that would work better with a more proportional system. Indeed, our own history suggests many recipes from periods in which our party system contained multitudes.

Nonetheless, the dynamics of changed legislative organization under PR would merit further study. Shifting to a more proportional system of voting without thinking through legislative organization would be extremely shortsighted and potentially disastrous.

Can Proportional Systems Better Govern from the Center?

Once a government is formed, there are many ways to evaluate its performance. One common evaluative framework asks whether government policymaking corresponds broadly to citizen preferences. Typically, this is measured by correspondence with the median voter.

In a majoritarian two-party system, the expected convergence mechanism is strategically electoral, or "Downsian": major parties are expected to converge on the political middle, with both parties offering moderate, center-oriented policy programs in accordance with the theory proposed by Anthony Downs. Obviously, this convergence mechanism is not operative in the American party system.[129] It also does not appear to be operative in other majoritarian democracies, casting considerable doubt on the theory.[130] There are many potential reasons for this disconnect. There is also considerable debate over the underlying prediction of the theory and whether it is flawed, either because it makes too many unrealistic assumptions about how parties and candidates behave or because various institutional mechanisms are standing in the way of convergence.[131] We will put those debates to the side for now and only observe that parties in the United States are clearly not converging on a political middle.

In a proportional multiparty system, the expected convergence mechanism is mathematical and coalitional. A winning multiparty coalition on a single dimension must, by definition, include the median party. The median party represents the policy of the median voter (or something close to it). This gives the median party considerable leverage.[132] Thus, Michael Laver and Norman Schofield argue, "the party controlling the median legislator . . . is effectively a dictator on policy. . . . It makes no difference if it goes off on holiday to Bermuda and sits on the beach getting a suntan. If we confine ourselves to one-dimensional accounts of coalition bargaining, then the core position of the party controlling the median legislator implies that its policies should be enacted whatever it does."[133] The formal results correspond to empirical evidence. Policy outputs in proportional multiparty systems do, on balance, correspond better to median voter preferences than policy outputs in majoritarian two-party systems.[134]

Of course, the reduction of politics to a single dimension is an oversimplification. As previously discussed, multidimensionality is crucial for resilience in all systems, including political ones. If we value multidimensionality, a two-party system becomes more brittle, since it can really only handle one dimension of conflict at a time, leading to more dramatic realignments as issue dimensions change.[135] One-dimensional politics is especially prone to binary polarization, as, ironically, Downs showed. He spells out his median voter theory on page 118 of his 1957 *An Economic Theory of Democracy*. On page 119, Downs lays out a different distribution, one that is more bimodal. In this case, single-winner elections give extremists too much power.

Here is the logic: "If voters' preferences are distributed so that voters are massed bimodally near the extremes, the parties will remain poles apart in ideology," Downs writes. Under such conditions, "abstention is rational for extremist voters who are future oriented. They are willing to let the worse party win today in order to keep the better party from moving towards the center, so that in future elections it will be closer to them. . . . Abstention thus becomes a threat to use against the party nearest to one's own extreme position so as to keep it away from the center."[136]

Once the center collapses, parties move to extremes:

> In such a situation, unless voters can somehow be moved to the center of the scale to eliminate their polar split, democratic government is not going to function at all well. In fact, no government can operate so as to please most of its people; hence the situation may lead to revolution. . . . The once centralized distribution begins to polarize into two extremes as the incumbents increasingly antagonize those who feel themselves oppressed. When the distribution has become so split that one extreme is imposing by force policies abhorred by the other extreme, open warfare breaks out.[137]

In this way, a minority massed at the extreme of one party can effectively rule by strategic use of leverage.

This pattern resembles the "base"-dependent strategy of mobilization now dominant in American politics, particularly on the right. The base—a political minority—can threaten to withhold support from a more moderate candidate. The fewer moderates in the electorate, the more potent this threat becomes. And the more parties pull to extremes, the fewer moderates remain. Under such circumstances, a logical partisan strategy is "demonization" (discussed above), in which party leaders try to mobilize extreme voters not by moderating themselves but by demonizing their political opponents and raising the stakes of the election. This leads to more affective polarization, which further threatens democratic stability.

Multiparty systems allow for more multidimensional coalitions, such that politics is more likely to stay around the political center—the so-called heart of politics. This is because when coalitions are more flexible, extreme positions on any single dimension are harder to sustain.[138]

How Does PR Relate to Government Quality and Effectiveness?

Theories of coalition formation and governing provide admittedly indirect ways of understanding the core question here: How do voting systems relate to government performance? Thus far, the literature has suggested mostly that coalition formation is different under different types of systems, all of which have pros and cons. There are also differing theories on median convergence. Proportional systems are better at achieving a policy orientation toward the political middle.

Now we turn more directly to measures of government performance. A challenge here is that government performance is subjective. Nonetheless, democracy scholars have developed many metrics for measuring performance. Here, we assess how three measures of performance are related to district size and legislative fragmentation.

The first is the "Good Governance" measure of the Quality of Governance Institute, which assesses "a political system in terms of its executive capability and accountability."[139] The relationship between good governance and district magnitude (a measure of proportionality) in the 2010s suggests no significant relationship, save that countries with very large district magnitudes have worse governance on this measure. The relationship between legislative fragmentation and good governance is relatively weak, although as a general pattern, OECD countries with greater legislative fragmentation perform marginally better on the Good Governance measure.

The second measure is the same institute's "Government Effectiveness" score, which focuses on the capacity of government to "to produce and implement good policies and deliver public goods." Its components include "the quality of public service provision, the quality of the bureaucracy, the competence of civil servants, the independence of the civil service from political pressures, and the credibility of the government's commitment to policies."[140]

Looking first at district magnitude, the relationship suggests a slight boost in effectiveness in the mid-range of district magnitude, although nothing approaching statistical significance. With regard to legislative fractionalization, we see a statistically significant relationship in the 2010s, with more legislatively fragmented OECD countries performing better on the Government Effectiveness score. This relationship appears to continue into the current decade, although with fewer observations, statistical significance disappears.

The third measure is the "Functioning of Government" score from Freedom House, which assesses the accountability, openness, and transparency of governments.[141] Here again, there is a slight boost in the middle range of district magnitude, although short of statistical significance. In the first decade of the twenty-first century, the most legislatively fragmented countries had slightly worse functioning than those in the middle range. But in the 2010s and into the 2020s, it is the most legislatively fragmented countries that have the highest degree of government functioning.

All these measures show considerable variation across electoral systems, even though a relationship exists. Indeed, the strongest predictor of government quality, effectiveness, and functioning is gross domestic product (GDP). Rich countries perform better on all these measures than poor countries.[142] However, if we plot per capita GDP against each measure of government performance, we see a steady pattern. The United States consistently falls short of the level of government performance one would expect for a nation of its wealth. This underperformance is highest in the 2010s, reflecting worsening hyperpartisan polarization and the Republican Party's drift toward illiberalism (at least according to V-Dem scores). The overall relationship is a steady linear increase up to a point. Once a country hits a per capita real GDP of around $50,000, there are no additional gains in government quality from additional wealth.

What conclusions should we draw from these relationships? As with the previous analysis of extremism in the party system, we see that party systems in the upper-middle range of fractionalization perform the best. The relationship between district magnitude and performance variables is more tenuous and unclear.

To the extent these analyses can guide us, they strongly suggest that legislative fractionalization, not proportionality directly, is the key variable for a healthier political system. However, legislative fractionalization is difficult to engineer, and too much fragmentation can be problematic as well. Moving toward a more modestly proportional system could facilitate healthy levels of legislative fractionalization.

However, concerns about fragmentation undermining the functioning of governing are not supported here or in other studies.[143] If deep polarization is the most vexing problem, there is also no evidence that more fragmented party systems are more polarized.[144]

The Bottom Line: Party System and Quality of Government

Majoritarian and proportional systems organize around different theories of governance. The majoritarian vision believes that governance works best when one party has majority control, can implement its preferred policies, and is directly accountable for its performance. The proportional vision believes that effective governance involves considering numerous perspectives, even if doing so makes it difficult for voters to deliver a decisive mandate.

Practically, the United States is not a fully majoritarian system, given the many veto points in the system. The United States is also a presidential democracy. Although PR and presidentialism together were once viewed negatively, recent studies indicate that the combination can function effectively. Contrary to earlier assessments, it is no longer considered a difficult combination.

Majoritarian and proportional systems have different approaches to coalition formation, but the distinctions are often overstated. Many proportional democracies, especially presidential ones, form preelectoral coalitions. And in the United States, frequently divided government means that, in practice, much governing winds up being done by reluctant de facto coalitions.

Various measures of government performance do not show that proportionality (as measured by district magnitude) has any statistical correlation with government performance. Moderate to high levels of legislative fragmentation are linked to better government performance, indicating that the party system is more important than proportionality per se.

Eliminating Gerrymandering and Improving Constituency Representation

Two other issues related to PR do not fit neatly into any of the sections above. The first is an important benefit of proportional representation: its ability to eliminate gerrymandering. The second is a commonly raised concern about PR: that it will undermine constituency representation.

Single-Member Districts and Gerrymandering

Under single-member districts, the translation of national party votes into congressional seats depends on how voters are spread across districts. This enables gerrymandering. It also leads to distortions even without intentional gerrymandering.[145] As one literature review sums up the problem, "One well-evidenced feature of electoral systems that employ single-member districts is that legislative contest outcomes are almost invariably disproportional, irrespective of any explicit political involvement in the drawing of district boundaries."[146] Recent US elections have been roughly proportional at the national level. But within many states, representation is extremely disproportional.

Under certain conditions, it is possible for a party that wins a minority of votes statewide to still win a majority of legislative seats. This is called a "plurality reversal," and it is a documented feature of single-winner districting. It does not happen often, but it can happen enough to raise questions about electoral fairness.[147] The Electoral College demonstrates the same dynamic of accumulated winner-take-all elections. A candidate can prevail, even if he or she did not win the popular vote, by gaining support in specific geographic areas.[148] A similar electoral inversion happened in 2012, when Republicans won a majority of seats in the House of Representatives, even though Democratic candidates received more votes than Republican candidates.

Typically, state-level plurality reversals are a product of active gerrymandering, which usually exacerbates the disproportionality of vote-to-seat ratios. But some of this distortion happens naturally. Sometimes, voters distribute themselves "inefficiently." For example, if Democratic voters overwhelmingly cluster into urban districts, many Democratic votes will be "wasted."

Single-member districts make gerrymandering especially profitable. Mapmakers can draw tens of thousands of possible maps and then choose the one that maximizes their preferred metric. If that metric is partisan bias, they can maximize it, as many have. Sometimes, extreme partisan gerrymanders wind up being struck down by courts.

However, because single-member districts generate many naturally occurring distortions in proportionality, scholars have struggled to find a clear standard to differentiate between normal bias and gerrymandering. Despite at least eighteen proposed metrics, scholars have not agreed on a standard for deciding where to draw the line between expected distortions within a normal range and obviously intentional gerrymandering.[149] This failure reflects the reality that some distortion is inherent in single-member districting. The party that more efficiently distributes its voters has an unfair advantage.

Attempts to make maps "fair" are also complicated by other normative values of districting: competitiveness, compactness, keeping communities of interest together, and ensuring adequate minority representation through majority-minority districts. Competitiveness poses the biggest challenge to partisan fairness. Imagine a scenario in which every district is a 51–49 district. In this scenario, every district would also be very competitive. However, the smallest national swing would dramatically shift the balance of power—a hypermajoritarian result.

Or consider the opposite end of this spectrum. To ensure a 51–49 balance of power based on voter registration data, Party A could get 51 districts that are safe for Party A, and Party B could get 49 districts safe for Party B. Under such a scenario, perfect proportionality would be achieved, but not a single seat would be contested. In this respect, partisan fairness and competitiveness are often in tension. The more districts that are evenly balanced, the greater the potential distortion from small shifts in partisan support.

In the United States today, the reality is far closer to the partisan-fairness end of this continuum, although it may not feel that way. By most estimates, about 90 percent of districts are uncompetitive. This puts a ceiling on how big a majority either party can hope to win in Congress. However, control of the chamber rests on the remaining 10 percent of districts. Moreover, because most single-member districts are uncompetitive, primary elections become disproportionately important.

How might this change under proportional representation? PR in legislative elections allows for multiple candidates and multiple parties to represent the same district. Seats are won by parties in close proportion to their share of the vote. The larger the district magnitude, the lower the percentage of the vote a party needs to win at least one seat. Lower thresholds make districts more proportional but also allow more viable parties.

Cross-nationally, gerrymandering is a much more significant problem in majoritarian democracies than in proportional ones. As proportionality increases, gerrymandering becomes irrelevant and insignificant.[150] Single-member districts lead to more wasted votes and increase the chances of districting manipulation. Larger districts waste fewer votes, because they allow for more winners. Single-member districts often result in only two parties, making it easier for mapmakers to predict election outcomes based on past voting patterns. In multiparty systems, voters are less predictable, making it harder to anticipate the consequences of alternative districting schemes.

Were the United States to adopt PR for House elections, the number of wasted votes would decline. Parties would be motivated to compete more extensively, allowing more voters to have a say. Gerrymandering would become irrelevant.

District Size and Constituency Service

A commonly voiced concern about PR is that multimember districts undermine constituency-representative relationships. Certainly, a single representative is easier for voters to identify, and single-member districts clearly incentivize the cultivation of a "personal vote" by doing good constituency service—for instance, by helping citizens navigate federal programs and services. Several studies have shown that representatives from single-member districts prioritize constituency service more than those from multimember districts.[151]

However, the quality of constituency service in single-member districts can be highly variable, especially in safe districts. Representatives from competitive and swing districts prioritize constituency service. With greater electoral safety, representatives place less importance on serving their constituents and are less likely to respond to their requests.[152] Since around 90 percent of elected US representatives come from safe districts, prioritizing constituency service is largely optional. Some representatives do; others don't.[153] As Brian Crisp and Scott Desposato note, "In SMDs, incumbents only compete with challengers who often lack experience, funding, and other perks necessary to pose a real threat. In MMDs, incumbents have to face other incumbents in the same district."[154]

In the United States, minority constituents are also less likely to receive responses to constituent service requests, particularly from Republican legislators.[155] Latino constituents are especially likely to be ignored.[156] However, when the legislator is a member of a minority community, response rates for that community go up.[157]

In an exhaustive study, Daniel J. Butler finds that "politicians exhibit favoritism toward some constituents over others" and "are less responsive to constituents who are not from their racial group."[158] Importantly, Butler argues that much of this unresponsiveness cannot be explained by strategic behavior, suggesting significant limits on the ability of competition to drive better constituency service. As Butler explains, "Politicians come to office with different information, knowledge, and sets of experiences that make it easier for them to work on issues important to people like them. . . . [P]oliticians' personal knowledge allows them to more easily help those most like them. This is exactly the behavior we expect from rational officials: they should work on the issues for which their personal knowledge makes it is less costly to do so."[159]

Butler suggests that multimember districts can improve representation by providing diverse citizens with more diverse representation. "A major benefit of multi-member districts is that each legislator comes to office with unique experiences and information on different topics. Legislators in multi-member districts can use that knowledge to specialize in different issues that are important in the district and provide Pareto-improving representation."[160] (i.e., better representation for everyone)

In a single-member district, the quality of constituency service depends on both the characteristics of that district (is it competitive?) and the particular experiences and demographics of the representative (which constituent groups does he or she care about?). By contrast, in a multimember district, constituents have multiple representatives and thus a greater chance of finding one who shares their values and concerns.

The level of emphasis representatives place on constituent service in multimember districts depends on the presence of "candidate-specific" voting on ballots. Open-list PR and single-transferable vote (STV) systems enable voting for specific candidates and incentivize constituency service. Closed-list systems do not. Thus, under open-list and STV systems, where representatives can pay a price for poorly attending to their districts, candidates spend more time addressing the concerns of their constituents.[161] If they don't, they are more likely to lose.

The idea behind multimember districts is that having a diverse group of representatives is beneficial for a large and diverse population. Rather than splitting a large geographic area into several smaller constituencies, each with one representative, it is better to let several representatives simultaneously represent the entire geography. Different representatives will inevitably bring different perspectives and better represent different subconstituencies.

The US Congress has long had multimember districts for the Senate: each state is a two-member district whose senators are usually elected nonconcurrently. Historically, many states have elected senators from opposing parties, although this has become rarer recently. Senators from the same state often have different representation styles, focusing on different issues and constituencies. As Wendy Schiller concludes in discussing multimember district representation in the US Senate, "If we incorporate the two-person nature of Senate delegations and the multidimensionality of legislative behavior into our evaluation of Senate representation, we can conclude that representation in the U.S. Senate is better than it is commonly believed to be. When two senators from the same state are viewed as a pair, it is clear that their combined representational agendas include a wide range of interests and opinions that exists among constituents in their state."[162]

Schiller finds that senators from the same state establish a distinct identity, particularly when they come from the same party. Same-state senators seek out different voter groups, sectors, interest bodies, and geographical constituents. Their campaigns, committee assignments, sponsored bills, senate speeches, and roll-call votes all provide evidence of this.

In a single-member district, each party can only choose one representative. This means that parties (or party voters in a primary) often choose the most generically "electable" representative. Practically, this means somebody who meets the stereotypical view of what a representative should look like: white, male, older, and personally wealthy. By contrast, in a multimember district, parties can offer a slate of candidates that appeal more broadly to distinct subsets of voters in the hope of improving their overall vote share.[163] In turn, individual candidates can more specifically prioritize the concerns of subconstituencies that might otherwise have their issues ignored.[164] By contrast, "focusing on issues that are not salient for all voters is not a viable strategy where a candidate must win a large proportion—a plurality or even a majority—of votes to get elected."[165]

The US Congress has certainly become more diverse across race and gender over time. However, the United States lags behind many peer nations in equal representation, particularly across gender.

A related feature of constituency representation involves bringing federal spending to home districts. Like constituency service, this is a nonideological means of serving a district and cultivating a personal vote. However, to the extent that cities are split into separate districts, individual representatives may have a more difficult time coordinating to secure citywide funding projects. James Snyder and Michiko Ueda find that "dividing large 'natural economic communities' into many single-member districts may reduce the effectiveness of these communities' legislative delegations, providing an argument for the use of multimember districts."[166]

Similarly, Justin Kirkland finds that having shared responsibility for a multimember district creates a basis on which representatives can work together. As he explains, "Multi-member districts provide legislators with natural allies that should help them swing legislative outcomes in favor of their home district. Legislators from single-member districts lack allies expressly interested in helping them benefit their home districts. Additionally, by creating an electoral environment where legislators have incentives to work across party lines the party cohesion within a legislature (a result supported by Adams 1996) and create more ideologically diverse political parties."[167]

In a study of multiple European democracies, Audrey Andre and Sam Depauw find that under open-list systems (where candidate-specific voting is allowed), larger district magnitude increases representatives' "likelihood of promoting the collective needs of a territorial or social sub-constituency" and "probability of engaging in project work and social group representation."[168] However, larger district size is associated with "a negative impact on the perceived effectiveness of assisting constituents in their private dealings with public authorities in open-list and closed-list systems alike."[169] Although arguments for single-member districts highlight the importance of direct constituency linkages, a recent study concluded, "(Perhaps surprisingly) single-member (SM) district systems do not have more geographically representative legislatures than multi-member (MTM) district systems."[170]

The bottom line is that in a single-member district, both parties settle on one candidate, and the two nominees compete to be the sole representative of that district. This provides clarity and unity of direct representation, but at the expense of diversity (across multiple dimensions). A multimember district allows more diversity of representation for a geographic area.

Moreover, because many single-member districts are not competitive, many voters in those districts will not have voted for the representative who won. In early 2024, only 55 percent of Americans said that their representative was deserving of reelection.[171] However, most incumbent members of Congress win by much larger margins because most districts are not competitive.

Many single-member districts also do not necessarily correspond to meaningful constituencies. Within larger catchment areas, representatives can serve different constituency groups with distinct identities.

Conclusions and Recommendations

The consequences of electoral system design have been the subject of innumerable political science studies. Yet electoral system change is never entirely predictable. All electoral systems interact with the underlying dynamics of societies. Electoral systems also reflect choices among values and priorities. As the 2013 American Political Science Association task force on electoral system design argued, "The choice of an electoral system has normative consequences, requiring a clarification of priorities, acceptance of tradeoffs, and perhaps even the sacrifice of a competing value. Electoral rules go a long way toward shaping the way democracy develops. They determine whether relevant perspectives are included in decision making, the nature of the government that emerges, the ways in which the public can hold this government accountable, and the pressures on parties to pursue certain modes of socioeconomic redistribution (or not)."[172]

Each country is different, and the United States is especially different.[173] Moreover, no reform is truly exogenous. The existing political system affects what kinds of reforms are even possible and how they are likely to be implemented. Changing from a majoritarian to a proportional system is a consequential change, and one that should be approached with significant caution.

Implementing a proportional system in the United States would give a center-right party the chance to organize. The essential assumption here is that enough voters on the right would support such a party, were there an opportunity to do so in a way that would lead to getting a proportional share of seats in the legislature. There are reasons to expect this would be the case, given the growing desire that many Americans express for more parties and the frustrations many report having with partisan extremes. However, much would depend on the ability of leaders to step forward and organize new parties with pro-democracy values. The recent elections in Poland show how a diverse pro-democracy coalition can unite under a proportional system while still targeting different voter groups.

On balance, we see evidence that a more proportional multiparty system could have significant benefits. It would offer a framework for realigning partisan politics in ways that could reduce affective polarization (which is driven by the repeated binary zero-sum nature of sorted partisan conflict) and marginalize extremist factions (the extremist faction on the right has a significant advantage in having captured one of the two major parties and not having to face a more center-oriented conservative party). Implementing a PR system in the United States is arguably the best way to counter the extreme Right and empower a pro-democracy center-right party.

The relationship between PR and quality governance is less certain, although countries with medium to medium-high legislative fractionalization score highest on various measures of effective and functioning government. However, to the extent one believes, first, that much of the recent deterioration of US governance flows from hyperpartisan affective polarization and political extremism and, second, that PR can ameliorate these concerns, it may follow that a proportional system could improve governing quality. At the very least, there is no systematic evidence that countries with more legislative fractionalization are performing worse across measures of government quality, functioning, and effectiveness.

Although a more proportional, multiparty system could create opportunities for political actors to realign and moderate US politics, there are no guarantees. There are also lots of institutional design choices to consider, which we do not weigh in on here because we do not agree sufficiently, although we encourage further and more extensive research on the trade-offs of different design choices, such as district magnitude, voting methods, and remainder formulas. The analyses presented in this chapter suggest that a PR system with moderate legislative fractionalization would be effective for promoting healthy governance.

Ultimately, however, we can only go on the evidence we can observe. We can assess the data, but we must also let ourselves think about the behaviors that are possible under different rules. In politics, there are no guarantees. But there are tendencies and probabilities.

Broadly, the group agrees on two main recommendations.

1. *Congress should amend the 1967 Uniform Congressional Districting Act and allow states to choose PR for their congressional delegations if they wish to, prohibiting at-large bloc voting.* Currently, states are prohibited from electing their congressional delegations under multimember districts by a 1967 law that was intended to curb at-large bloc voting, which posed a significant risk to Black voters in the South. We agree this law should be updated to allow states to choose to elect their delegations through proportional multimember districts. Such a reform would enable ballot initiatives on behalf of PR. It would also enable state courts to impose PR as a remedy in gerrymandering cases. The Constitution is silent on district magnitude. Congress has repeatedly passed legislation instructing states on districting, including the 1967 law. None of these laws have been challenged as unconstitutional. Up through the 1840s, states regularly elected congressional delegations through multimember districts.

2. *Individual states should move toward proportional, multimember districts for their legislatures.* PR would be applicable for any state legislature. States could demonstrate how PR could work by electing their legislatures under a proportional voting rule.

We disagree on other options. Some of us agree on the value of a national mandate for PR for Congress, while others would prefer an incremental approach right now. We reached no universal recommendation.

We also acknowledge the limitations of our initial recommendation. Moving toward PR on a state-by-state basis could temporarily disrupt the balance of power, depending on which states implement these changes.

But state experimentation can also facilitate a gradual transition. By putting this option on the table, we encourage a new pathway for reform.

Additionally, to the extent we move toward a system of PR in the United States, our group would encourage different states to make institutional design choices most appropriate for their geographies and political cultures.

We would like to see future research into and exploration of different approaches to PR, including the appropriate district magnitude and whether to use the single-transferable vote, a party-list system, or other variations of proportional representation. We recognize that each of these systems has pros and cons, and there is no perfect system for elections.

We have questions about how different rules could affect party systems and how PR in the House would work with single-winner elections for the Senate. The question of how Congress might function under a multiparty system also demands further study.

We would encourage more research into how governance might change under PR and how a multiparty House might interact with the presidency and a Senate that would still be elected under a single-winner electoral system.

We believe more research should be devoted to all these questions. Given the trajectory of American democracy, an opportunity for significant electoral change may open up. The more research and thought we put into institutional design in advance, the more thoughtful the national debate will be.

Notes

This chapter is the product of deliberations among the Task Force Working Group on Proportional Representation, which was chaired by Lee Drutman and included Larry Diamond, William Galston, Rachel Kleinfeld, Nolan McCarty, Jennifer McCoy, and Hans Noel.

1. The source for the data in all these measures but the last one (disproportionality) is the Quality of Government Institute.

2. Markku Laakso and Rein Taagepera, "'Effective' Number of Parties: A Measure with Application to West Europe," *Comparative Political Studies* 12, no. 1 (April 1, 1979): 3–27. https://doi.org/10.1177/001041407901200101.

3. Douglas Rae, "A Note on the Fractionalization of Some European Party Systems," *Comparative Political Studies* 1, no. 3 (October 1, 1968): 413–418. https://doi.org/10.1177/001041406800100305.

4. Michael Gallagher, "Proportionality, Disproportionality and Electoral Systems," *Electoral Studies* 10, no. 1 (1991): 33–51. This formula uses the standard least squares method for comparing the relationship between two samples. The source for

this index is Christopher Gandrud, "Gallagher Electoral Disproportionality Data, 121 Countries, 1945–2014, Current version: v2, Data Updated: 20 March 2015."

5. See, generally, Jennifer McCoy and Murat Somer, "Toward a Theory of Pernicious Polarization and How It Harms Democracies: Comparative Evidence and Possible Remedies," *ANNALS of the American Academy of Political and Social Science* 681, no. 1 (2019): 234–271. https://doi.org/10.1177/0002716218818782; Murat Somer, Jennifer L. McCoy, and Russell E. Luke, "Pernicious Polarization, Autocratization and Opposition Strategies," *Democratization* 28, no. 1 (2021): 1–20. https://doi.org/10.1080/13510347.2020.1865316.

6. Delia Baldassarri and Scott E. Page, "The Emergence and Perils of Polarization," *Proceedings of the National Academy of Sciences of the United States of America* 118, no. 50 (December 14, 2021). https://doi.org/10.1073/pnas.2116863118.

7. Delia Baldassarri and Scott E. Page, "The Emergence and Perils of Polarization," *Proceedings of the National Academy of Sciences of the United States of America* 118, no. 50 (December 14, 2021).

8. Delia Baldassarri and Scott E. Page, "The Emergence and Perils of Polarization," *Proceedings of the National Academy of Sciences of the United States of America* 118, no. 50 (December 14, 2021).

9. Keith E. Stanovich, Richard F. West, and Maggie E. Toplak, "Myside Bias, Rational Thinking, and Intelligence," *Current Directions in Psychological Science* 22, no. 4 (August 2013): 259–264. https://doi.org/10.1177/0963721413480174.

10. Such is the takeaway from an exhaustive review on "cognitive-motivational mechanisms of political polarization." The review cites 345 articles documenting causal pathways in every direction and a long list of cognitive biases that exacerbate binary partisan polarization once it gets underway. For example, as the authors note, "longitudinal research demonstrated that ideological consistency at time 1 predicted affective polarization at time 2, and affective polarization at time 1 predicted ideological consistency at time 2, all other things being equal." Keith E. Stanovich, Richard F. West, and Maggie E. Toplak, "Myside Bias, Rational Thinking, and Intelligence," *Current Directions in Psychological Science* 22, no. 4 (August 2013): 259–264. https://doi.org/10.1177/0963721413480174.

11. Aida Just, "Partisanship, Electoral Autocracy, and Citizen Perceptions of Party System Polarization," *Political Behavior*, December 2, 2022. https://doi.org/10.1007/s11109-022-09839-6.

12. J. M. Berger, *Extremism* (Cambridge, MA: MIT Press, 2018), 43.

13. J. M. Berger, *Extremism* (Cambridge, MA: MIT Press, 2018).

14. Eelco Harteveld et al., "The (Alleged) Consequences of Affective Polarization: Individual-Level Evidence and a Survey Experiment in 9 Countries," OSF Preprints, October 1, 2022; Eli J. Finkel et al., "Political Sectarianism in America," *Science* 370, no. 6516 (October 30, 2020): 533–536.

15. Yunus Emre Orhan, "The Relationship Between Affective Polarization and Democratic Backsliding: Comparative Evidence," *Democratization* 29, no. 4 (May 19, 2022).

16. Matthew H. Graham and Milan W. Svolik, "Democracy in America? Partisanship, Polarization, and the Robustness of Support for Democracy in the United States," *American Political Science Review* 114, no. 2 (May 2020): 392–409. https://doi.org/10.1017/S0003055420000052.

17. Gabor Simonovits, Jennifer McCoy, and Levente Littvay, "Democratic Hypocrisy and Out-Group Threat: Explaining Citizen Support for Democratic Erosion," *Journal of Politics* 84, no. 3 (2022): 1806–1811.

18. John Carey et al., "Who Will Defend Democracy? Evaluating Tradeoffs in Candidate Support among Partisan Donors and Voters," *Journal of Elections, Pub-*

lic Opinion and Parties (July 7, 2020): 1–16. https://doi.org/10.1080/17457289 .2020.1790577; Caterina Chiopris, Monika Nalepa, and Georg Vanberg, "A Wolf in Sheep's Clothing: Citizen Uncertainty and Democratic Backsliding," *Journal of Politics* (forthcoming); Matthew H. Graha, and Milan W. Svolik, "Democracy in America? Partisanship, Polarization, and the Robustness of Support for Democracy in the United States," *American Political Science Review* 114, no. 2 (May 2020): 392–409. https://doi.org/10.1017/S0003055420000052; Zhaotian Luo and Adam Przeworski, "Democracy and Its Vulnerabilities: Dynamics of Democratic Backsliding," SSRN Scholarly Paper, Rochester, NY, December 31, 2021. https://doi.org/10.2139/ssrn.3469373; Jennifer McCoy, Tahmina Rahman, and Murat Somer, "Polarization and the Global Crisis of Democracy: Common Patterns, Dynamics, and Pernicious Consequences for Democratic Polities," *American Behavioral Scientist* 62, no. 1 (January 2018): 16–42. https://doi.org/10.1177 /0002764218759576; Michael K. Miller, "A Republic, If You Can Keep It: Breakdown and Erosion in Modern Democracies," *Journal of Politics* 83, no. 1 (January 1, 2021): 198–213. https://doi.org/10.1086/709146; Jon Kingzette et al., "How Affective Polarization Undermines Support for Democratic Norms," *Public Opinion Quarterly* 85, no. 2 (October 1, 2021): 663–77. https://doi.org/10.1093/poq /nfab029; Yunus Emre Orhan, "The Relationship Between Affective Polarization and Democratic Backsliding: Comparative Evidence," *Democratization* 29, no. 4 (May 19, 2022): 714–35. https://doi.org/10.1080/13510347.2021.2008912; Elisabeth Gidengil, Dietlind Stolle, and Olivier Bergeron-Boutin, "The Partisan Nature of Support for Democratic Backsliding: A Comparative Perspective." *European Journal of Political Research* 61, no. 4 (2022): 901–29. https://doi.org/10.1111 /1475-6765.12502.

19. Suthan Krishnarajan, "Rationalizing Democracy: The Perceptual Bias and (Un)Democratic Behavior," *American Political Science Review* 117, no. 2 (2023): 474–496. https://doi.org/10.1017/S0003055422000806.

20. Alia Braley et al., "The Subversion Dilemma: Why Voters Who Cherish Democracy Participate in Democratic Backsliding" (working paper, OSF Preprints, August 18, 2022), 45.

21. Dalston G. Ward and Margit Tavits, "How Partisan Affect Shapes Citizens' Perception of the Political World," *Electoral Studies* 60 (August 1, 2019).

22. Affective polarization heightens the power of such cues (see James N. Druckman et al., "Affective Polarization, Local Contexts and Public Opinion in America," *Nature Human Behaviour* 5, no. 1 [January 2021]: 28–38. https://doi.org /10.1038/s41562-020-01012-5).

Affectively polarized partisans feel a need to signal their partisan identity, distinguishing themselves from the other party. This leads to directional motivated cognition and more partisan cue taking Lavine, Johnston, and Steenbergen 2012; Lavine, Johnston, and Steenbergen 2012). When a Republican is in the White House, the more affectively polarized Republican voters are, the less they will support democratic norms, particularly those concerning constitutional protections that limit executive power (see Kingzette, Jon, James N Druckman, Samara Klar, Yanna Krupnikov, Matthew Levendusky, and John Barry Ryan. "How Affective Polarization Undermines Support for Democratic Norms." *Public Opinion Quarterly* 85, no. 2 (October 1, 2021): 663–677. https://doi.org/10.1093/poq/nfab029).

Under high affective polarization, "partisans may take cues from the behaviour of party elites" (Elisabeth Gidengil, Dietlind Stolle, and Olivier Bergeron-Boutin, "The Partisan Nature of Support for Democratic Backsliding: A Comparative Perspective," *European Journal of Political Research* 61, no. 4 (2022): 901–929. https://doi.org/10.1111/1475-6765.12502).

23. "It is crucial to recognize that affective polarization is distinct from ideological polarization—the extent to which citizens disagree on matters of ideology and issue positions. This relation is endogenous and not straightforward (Iyengar et al. 2018; Ward and Tavits 2019). While affective polarization has grown according to most accounts, there is less evidence for surging ideological polarization: regarding most topics, Americans' and Europeans' actual views have become less, rather than more, divided (Baldassarri and Gelman 2008; Adams et al., 2012; Nuesser et al., 2014). Indeed, Reiljan (2020) and Gidron et al. (2019a) find a weak or inconsistent relation between ideological polarization on affective polarization. Individual-level evidence is mixed too (Rogowski and Sutherland 2016; Bougher 2017). All in all, it is clear that affective polarization depends partly—perhaps mostly—on other factors than the strength of ideological disagreement between camps. This points the way towards explanations rooted in the relations between political camps as social groups, including their social sorting. Still, ideological polarization functions as a key benchmark to compare any other correlate of affective polarization to." Eelco Harteveld, "Ticking All the Boxes? A Comparative Study of Social Sorting and Affective Polarization," *Electoral Studies* 72 (August 1, 2021): 2.

24. Ideological polarization at the mass level is not exceptionally high in the United States. Anthony Kevins and Stuart N. Soroka, "Growing Apart? Partisan Sorting in Canada, 1992–2015," *Canadian Journal of Political Science/Revue canadienne de science politique* 51, no. 1 (March 2018): 103–133; Andres Reiljan, "'Fear and Loathing Across Party Lines' (Also) in Europe: Affective Polarisation in European Party Systems," *European Journal of Political Research* 59, no. 2 (2020): 376–396.

25. Jon Rogowski and Joseph Sutherland, "How Ideology Fuels Affective Polarization," *Political Behavior* 38, no. 2 (2016): 485–508. https://doi.org/10.1007/s11109-015-9323-7; Paul M. Sniderman and Edward H. Stiglitz, *The Reputational Premium: A Theory of Party Identification and Policy Reasoning* (Princeton, NJ: Princeton University Press, 2012).

26. Andres Reiljan, "'Fear and Loathing Across Party Lines' (Also) in Europe: Affective Polarisation in European Party Systems," *European Journal of Political Research* 59, no. 2 (2020): 376–396.

27. PR systems produce "greater ideological dispersion." Jay K. Dow, "Party-System Extremism in Majoritarian and Proportional Electoral Systems," *British Journal of Political Science* 41, no. 2 (April 2011): 341–361. https://doi.org/10.1017/S0007123410000360. "The empirics show that more proportional systems support greater ideological dispersion, while less proportional systems encourage parties to cluster nearer the centre of the electoral space. This finding is maintained in several sub-samples of national elections and does not depend on the inclusion of highly majoritarian systems (such as the United Kingdom)." Konstantinos Matakos, Orestis Troumpounis, and Dimitrios Xefteris, "Electoral Rule Disproportionality and Platform Polarization," *American Journal of Political Science* 60, no. 4 (2016): 1026–1043. https://doi.org/10.1111/ajps.12235.

28. Josephine T. Andrews and Jeannette Money, "The Spatial Structure of Party Competition: Party Dispersion Within a Finite Policy Space," *British Journal of Political Science* 39, no. 4 (October 2009): 805–824. https://doi.org/10.1017/S0007123409990172.

29. Lawrence Ezrow, "The Variance Matters: How Party Systems Represent the Preferences of Voters," *Journal of Politics* 69, no. 1 (2007): 182–192. https://doi.org/10.1111/j.1468-2508.2007.00503.x.

Ezrow's Voter Diversity Hypothesis (H1) suggests that changes in the diversity of voters' policy preferences cause corresponding changes in the diversity of policy positions presented by the competing parties. This concept of dynamic distributional representation is significant as it impacts party positioning strategies. The Electoral Laws Result (H2), another key finding, posits that party system dispersion is more responsive to voter dispersion in countries with less proportional electoral systems. However, this does not imply that parties in proportional systems are completely unresponsive to shifts in the diversity of their voters' policy opinions.

30. Jennifer McCoy and Murat Somer, "Toward a Theory of Pernicious Polarization and How It Harms Democracies: Comparative Evidence and Possible Remedies," *ANNALS of the American Academy of Political and Social Science* 681, no. 1 (January 2019): 234–271. https://doi.org/10.1177/0002716218818782.

31. Noam Gidron, James Adams, and Will Horne, *American Affective Polarization in Comparative Perspective* (Cambridge: Cambridge University Press, 2020) (noting, "Partisans residing in countries with majoritarian, single-winner voting systems tend to dislike opposition parties more intensely, and like their own party less, than do partisans in countries with proportional voting systems").

32. Jonathan Rodden, "Keeping Your Enemies Close: Electoral Rules and Partisan Polarization," in *Who Gets What? The New Politics of Insecurity*, ed. Frances Rosenbluth and Margaret Weir. SSRC Anxieties of Democracy (Cambridge: Cambridge University Press, 2021), 129–160.

33. Levi Boxell, Matthew Gentzkow, and Jesse M. Shapiro. "Cross-Country Trends in Affective Polarization," *Review of Economics and Statistics* 106, no. 2 (2024); Noam Gidron, James Adams, and Will Horne, *American Affective Polarization in Comparative Perspective* (Cambridge: Cambridge University Press, 2020); Diego Garzia, Frederico Ferreira da Silva, and Simon Maye, "Affective Polarization in Comparative and Longitudinal Perspective," *Public Opinion Quarterly* 87, no. 1 (spring 2023): 219–231. https://doi.org/10.1162/rest_a_01160. Gidron, Adams, and Horne similarly report, "Since the mid 1990s, affective polarization has intensified more sharply in the United States than in most other Western publics. . . . We find that American affective polarization has intensified over time, and moreover, that this rise is driven by Americans' growing dislike of partisan opponents, rather than by warming attachments to their own party. Furthermore, our comparative analyses suggest that America's intensifying affective polarization is not part of a cross-national trend: instead we find that affective polarization in other Western publics has remained steady (on average) across this period." Garzia, da Silva, and Maye also find that the United States is the most affectively polarized, and the trends in the United States are strongest, among similar countries.

34 Diego Garzia and Frederico Ferreira da Silva, "The Electoral Consequences of Affective Polarization? Negative Voting in the 2020 US Presidential Election," *American Politics Research* 50, no. 3 (May 1, 2022): 303–311; Andres Reiljan et al., "Patterns of Affective Polarization Toward Parties and Leaders Across the Democratic World," *American Political Science Review*, June 29, 2023, 1–17. https://doi.org/10.1017/S0003055423000485.

35. Markus Wagner, "Affective Polarization in Multiparty Systems," *Electoral Studies* 69 (February 1, 2021): 102199. https://doi.org/10.1016/j.electstud.2020.102199.

36. Anthony Kevins and Stuart N. Soroka, "Growing Apart? Partisan Sorting in Canada, 1992–2015," *Canadian Journal of Political Science/Revue canadienne de science politique* 51, no. 1 (March 2018): 103–133. https://doi.org/10.1017/S0008423917000713.

37. Sara B. Hobolt, Thomas J. Leeper, and James Tilley, "Divided by the Vote: Affective Polarization in the Wake of the Brexit Referendum," *British Journal of Political Science* 51, no. 4 (October 2021): 1476–1493. https://doi.org/10.1017/S0007123420000125; Nahema Marchal and David Watson, "The Rise of Partisan Affective Polarization in the British Public," SSRN Scholarly Paper, October 25, 2019. https://doi.org/10.2139/ssrn.3477404.

38. Levi Boxell, Matthew Gentzkow, and Jesse M. Shapiro, "Cross-Country Trends in Affective Polarization," *Review of Economics and Statistics* 106, no. 2 (2024): 557–565.

39. "Justin Trudeau Vows to End 1st-Past-the-Post Voting in Platform Speech," CBC News, October 6, 2015.

40. Hyeonho Hahm, David Hilpert, and Thomas König, "Divided We Unite: The Nature of Partyism and the Role of Coalition Partnership in Europe," *American Political Science Review* 118, no. 1 (February 2024): 69–87. https://doi.org/10.1017/S0003055423000266.

41. Will Horne, James Adams, and Noam Gidron, "The Way We Were: How Histories of Co-governance Alleviate Partisan Hostility," *Comparative Political Studies* 56, no. 3 (2023). https://doi.org/10.1177/00104140221100197.

42. Noam Gidron, James Adams, and Will Horne, "Who Dislikes Whom? Affective Polarization Between Pairs of Parties in Western Democracies," *British Journal of Political Science* 53, no. 3 (July 2023): 997–1015. https://doi.org/10.1017/S0007123422000394.

43. Hyeonho Hahm, David Hilpert, and Thomas König, "Divided We Unite: The Nature of Partyism and the Role of Coalition Partnership in Europe," *American Political Science Review* 118, no. 1 (February 2024): 69–87. https://doi.org/10.1017/S0003055423000266.

44. Citizens employ a coalition heuristic to infer that cogoverning parties share more similar ideologies than is implied by their manifestos. David Fortunato and Randolph T. Stevenson, "Perceptions of Partisan Ideologies: The Effect of Coalition Participation," *American Journal of Political Science* 57, no. 2 (2013): 459–477. https://doi.org/10.1111/j.1540-5907.2012.00623.

45. Will Horne, James Adams, and Noam Gidron, "The Way We Were: How Histories of Co-governance Alleviate Partisan Hostility," *Comparative Political Studies* 56, no. 3 (2023). https://doi.org/10.1177/00104140221100197.

46. Matthew Levendusky, *The Partisan Sort: How Liberals Became Democrats and Conservatives Became Republicans* (Chicago: University of Chicago Press, 2009).

47. Lilliana Mason, "A Cross-Cutting Calm: How Social Sorting Drives [US] Affective Polarization," *Public Opinion Quarterly* 80, no. S1 (2016): 351–377; Lilliana Mason and Julie Wronski, "One Tribe to Bind Them All: How Our Social Group Attachments Strengthen Partisanship," *Political Psychology* 39 (February 2018): 257–277.

48. Nolan McCarty et al., "Geography, Uncertainty, and Polarization," *Political Science Research and Methods* 7, no. 4 (October 2019): 775–794. https://doi.org/10.1017/psrm.2018.12.

49. Jonathan Rodden, "Keeping Your Enemies Close: Electoral Rules and Partisan Polarization," *Who Gets What? The New Politics of Insecurity*, ed. Frances Rosenbluth and Margaret Weir. SSRC Anxieties of Democracy (Cambridge: Cambridge University Press, 2021), 129–160.

50. Eelco Harteveld, "Ticking All the Boxes? A Comparative Study of Social Sorting and Affective Polarization," *Electoral Studies* 72 (August 1, 2021): 102337.

51. Katherine J. Cramer, *The Politics of Resentment: Rural Consciousness in Wisconsin and the Rise of Scott Walker* (Chicago: University of Chicago Press, 2016).

52. Jason S. Spicer, "Electoral Systems, Regional Resentment and the Surprising Success of Anglo-American Populism," *Cambridge Journal of Regions, Economy and Society* 11, no. 1 (March 10, 2018): 115–141. https://doi.org/10.1093/cjres/rsx029.

53. Will Wilkinson, "The Density Divide: Urbanization, Polarization, and Populist Backlash," Niskanen Center, June 26, 2019, provides the most comprehensive summary of this development.

54. Geoffrey C. Layman and Thomas M. Carsey, "Party Polarization and 'Conflict Extension' in the American Electorate," *American Journal of Political Science* 46, no. 4 (October 2002): 786–802.

55. Josephine T. Andrews and Jeannette Money, "The Spatial Structure of Party Competition: Party Dispersion Within a Finite Policy Space," *British Journal of Political Science* 39, no. 4 (October 2009): 805–824. https://doi.org/10.1017/S0007123409990172.

56. Jonathan Rodden, "Keeping Your Enemies Close: Electoral Rules and Partisan Polarization," in *Who Gets What? The New Politics of Insecurity*, ed. Frances Rosenbluth and Margaret Weir. SSRC Anxieties of Democracy (Cambridge: Cambridge University Press, 2021).

57. Dalston G. Ward and Margit Tavits, "How Partisan Affect Shapes Citizens' Perception of the Political World," *Electoral Studies* 60 (August 1, 2019): 102045. https://doi.org/10.1016/j.electstud.2019.04.009.

58. Christian Elmelund-Praestekaer, "Beyond American Negativity: Toward a General Understanding of the Determinants of Negative Campaigning," *European Political Science Review* 2, no. 1 (March 2010): 137–156. https://doi.org/10.1017/S1755773909990269; Christian Elmelund-Praestekaer, "Negative Campaigning in a Multiparty System," *Representation* 44, no. 1 (April 1, 2008): 27–39; Annemarie S. Walter, "Negative Campaigning in Western Europe: Similar or Different?," *Political Studies* 62 (April 2, 2014): 42–60.

59. Enrique Hernández, Eva Anduiza, and Guillem Rico, "Affective Polarization and the Salience of Elections," *Electoral Studies* 69 (February 1, 2021): 102203. https://doi.org/10.1016/j.electstud.2020.102203.

60. Richard R. Lau, Lee Sigelman, and Ivy Brown Rovner, "The Effects of Negative Political Campaigns: A Meta-analytic Reassessment," *Journal of Politics* 69, no. 4 (November 2007): 1176–1209.

61. See, among many others, Frank S. Cohen, "Proportional Versus Majoritarian Ethnic Conflict Management in Democracies," *Comparative Political Studies* 30, no. 5 (October 1, 1997): 607–30. https://doi.org/10.1177/0010414097030005004; Arend Lijphart, "Constitutional Design for Divided Societies," *Journal of Democracy* 15, no. 2 (April 8, 2004): 96–109; Pippa Norris, *Electoral Engineering: Voting Rules and Political Behavior* (Cambridge: Cambridge University Press, 2004); Pippa Norris, *Driving Democracy: Do Power-Sharing Institutions Work?* (Cambridge: Cambridge University Press, 2008); Andrew Reynolds, *Designing Democracy in a Dangerous World* (Oxford: Oxford University Press, 2011).

62. Frank S. Cohen, "Proportional Versus Majoritarian Ethnic Conflict Management in Democracies," *Comparative Political Studies* 30, no. 5 (October 1, 1997): 614. https://doi.org/10.1177/0010414097030005004.

63. John D. Huber, "Measuring Ethnic Voting: Do Proportional Electoral Laws Politicize Ethnicity?," *American Journal of Political Science* 56, no. 4 (2012): 986–1001 (finding that using survey data to implement four measures of "ethnicization"

in forty-three countries, "proportional electoral laws are associated with lower levels of ethnicization—the opposite of what is widely assumed").

64. Stephen M. Saideman et al., "Democratization, Political Institutions, and Ethnic Conflict: A Pooled Time-Series Analysis, 1985–1998," *Comparative Political Studies* 35, no. 1 (February 1, 2002): 103–129; Gerald Schneider and Nina Wiesehomeier, "Rules That Matter: Political Institutions and the Diversity—Conflict Nexus," *Journal of Peace Research* 45, no. 2 (March 2008): 183–203; David Lublin and Shaun Bowler, "Electoral Systems and Ethnic Minority Representation," in *The Oxford Handbook of Electoral Systems*, ed. Erik S. Herron, Robert J. Pekkanen, and Matthew S. Shugart (Oxford: Oxford University Press, 2018), 158–174. "Saideman et al. (2002), for example, examine data on ethnic conflict and rebellion between 1985 and 1998 to show that proportional representation helps to suppress ethnic conflict. The finding is consistent with Schneider and Wiesehomeier (2008), who show that majoritarian electoral institutions promote conflict in divided societies, while more inclusive ones are beneficial (Schneider and Wiesehomeier 2008, 198). These findings are in line with the kinds of steps taken by divided societies in practice" (Lublin and Bowler, 2018, 10).

65. Joel Selway and Kharis Templeman., "The Myth of Consociationalism? Conflict Reduction in Divided Societies," *Comparative Political Studies* 45, no. 12 (December 2012): 1542–1571. https://doi.org/10.1177/0010414011425341.

66. David Lublin and Shaun Bowler., "Electoral Systems and Ethnic Minority Representation," in *The Oxford Handbook of Electoral Systems*, ed. Erik S. Herron, Robert J. Pekkanen, and Matthew S. Shugart (Oxford: Oxford University Press, 2018), 158–174. https://doi.org/10.1093/oxfordhb/9780190258658.013.26.

67. Lilliana Mason, "A Cross-Cutting Calm: How Social Sorting Drives Affective Polarization," *Public Opinion Quarterly* 80, no. S1 (2016): 351–377; Eric A. Nordlinger, *Conflict Regulation in Divided Societies* (Washington, DC: University Press of America, 1984), 93; G. Bingham Powell, "Political Cleavage Structure, Cross-Pressure Processes, and Partisanship: An Empirical Test of the Theory," *American Journal of Political Science* 20, no. 1 (1976): 1–23; Gabriel A. Almond, "Comparative Political Systems," *Journal of Politics* 18, no. 3 (1956): 391–409; Robert Alan Dahl, *Pluralist Democracy in the United States: Conflict and Consent* (Chicago: Rand McNally, 1969); Ralf Dahrendorf, *Class and Class Conflict in Industrial Society* (London: Routledge & Kegan Paul, 1976); Karl Deutsch, *Nationalism and Social Communication: An Inquiry into the Foundations of Nationality* (Cambridge, MA: MIT Press, 1966); David Easton, *Systems Analysis of Political Life* (New York: John Wiley & Sons, 1965), chap. 15; Seymour Martin Lipset, *Political Man: The Social Bases of Politics* (New York: Doubleday, 1960), chaps. 3–4; Frank A. Pinner, "Cross-Pressure," in *International Encyclopedia of the Social Sciences*, ed. David L. Sills (New York: Macmillan, 1968), 3:116–118.

68. Diana C. Mutz, "Cross-Cutting Social Networks: Testing Democratic Theory in Practice," *American Political Science Review* 96, no. 1 (2002): 122.

69. Lee Drutman, "Elections, Political Parties, and Multiracial, Multiethnic Democracy: How the United States Gets It Wrong," *New York University Law Review* 96 (2021): 36.

70. For a discussion of how diffusion of power and countermajoritarian institutions contribute to negotiation and consensus, see Arend Lijphart, "Negotiation Democracy Versus Consensus Democracy: Parallel Conclusions and Recommendations," *European Journal of Political Research* 41, no. 1 (2002): 107–113. https://doi.org/10.1111/1475-6765.00005.

71. Michael Laver and Norman Schofield, *Multiparty Government: The Politics of Coalition in Europe* (Oxford: Oxford University Press, 1990); Michael Laver and Ernest Sergenti, *Party Competition: An Agent-Based Model* (Princeton, NJ: Princeton University Press, 2011).

72. G. Bingham Powell Jr., "Extremist Parties and Political Turmoil: Two Puzzles," *American Journal of Political Science* 30, no. 2 (1986): 357–378. https://doi.org/10.2307/2111101; Arthur H. Miller and Ola Listhaug, "Political Parties and Confidence in Government: A Comparison of Norway, Sweden and the United States," *British Journal of Political Science* 20, no. 3 (1990): 357–386.

73. Elisabeth Carter, "Does PR Promote Political Extremism? A Rejoinder," *Representation* 41, no. 1 (January 2004): 63–66. https://doi.org/10.1080/00344890408523290; see also Elisabeth Carter, "Does PR Promote Political Extremism? Evidence from the West European Parties of the Extreme Right," *Representation* 40, no. 2 (January 2004): 82–100.

74. Israel may come to mind here as an example. However, the Israeli system is distinct in the number of parties, since Israel has an extremely large district magnitude and a closed list system.

75. "Anti-immigration parties that were not ostracised became more moderate, whereas those that were treated as outcasts continued to be extremist." Joost Van Spanje and Wouter Van Der Brug, "The Party as Pariah: The Exclusion of Anti-immigration Parties and Its Effect on Their Ideological Positions," *West European Politics* 30, no. 5 (November 2007): 1022–1040.

76. Peter Mair, *Ruling the Void: The Hollowing of Western Democracy* (New York: Verso Books, 2013); Pedro Riera and Marco Pastor, "Cordons Sanitaires or Tainted Coalitions? The Electoral Consequences of Populist Participation in Government," *Party Politics* 28, no. 5 (September 2022): 889–902. Populist parties tend to lose support for being in government. Parties generally lose support for being in a governing coalition, especially junior parties. It's worse for populist parties since they draw their strength from being outsiders. "Since the populist appeal lies in the 'widening gap between rulers and ruled'" (Mair, 2013: 18–19), if they participate in government, they can no longer resort to this feeling of lack of political representation among the electorate to win votes and they become part of the problem rather than the solution in the eyes of the citizens" (Riera and Pastor, 2022, 899).

77. James Adams and Zeynep Somer-Topcu, "Moderate Now, Win Votes Later: The Electoral Consequences of Parties' Policy Shifts in 25 Postwar Democracies," *Journal of Politics* 71, no. 2 (April 2009): 678–692. https://doi.org/10.1017/S00223381609090537.

78. William M. Downs, Carrie L. Manning, and Richard N. Engstrom, "Revisiting the 'Moderating Effects of Incumbency': A Comparative Study of Government Participation and Political Extremism," *Journal of Contemporary European Studies* 17, no. 2 (August 1, 2009): 151–169. https://doi.org/10.1080/14782800903108627.

79. "Determining whether or not a given party can be successfully brought into the system is of course difficult, but it is crucial to try." Sheri Berman, "Taming Extremist Parties: Lessons from Europe," *Journal of Democracy* 19, no. 1 (2008): 5–18.

80. Kim Lane Scheppele, "The Party's Over," in *Constitutional Democracy in Crisis?*, vol. 1 (Oxford: Oxford University Press, 2018), 495–515. https://doi.org/10.1093/law/9780190888985.003.0028. Scheppele describes a pattern that involves the "convergence of party systems on fewer and fewer parties, followed by a collapse of the traditional parties, along with the conventional markers of what is Left and what is Right."

81. For a general overview of populism in postwar Europe, see Matthew Goodwin, "Extreme Politics: The Four Waves of National Populism in the West," in *Extremes*, ed. Duncan Needham and Julius Weitzdörfer, 1st ed. (Cambridge: Cambridge University Press, 2019), 104–123. https://doi.org/10.1017/9781108654722.007; Cas Mudde, "Three Decades of Populist Radical Right Parties in Western Europe: So What?," *European Journal of Political Research* 52, no. 1 (2013): 1–19. https://doi.org/10.1111/j.1475-6765.2012.02065.x; Cas Mudde, "The Far-Right Threat in the United States: A European Perspective," *ANNALS of the American Academy of Political and Social Science* 699, no. 1 (2022): 101–115. https://doi.org/10.1177/00027162211070060.

82. See, e.g., Abdelkarim Amengay and Daniel Stockemer, "The Radical Right in Western Europe: A Meta-analysis of Structural Factors," *Political Studies Review* 17, no. 1 (2019): 30–40. https://doi.org/10.1177/1478929918777975; Kai Arzheimer and Carl C. Berning, "How the Alternative for Germany (AfD) and Their Voters Veered to the Radical Right, 2013–2017," *Electoral Studies* 60 (August 2019): 102040. https://doi.org/10.1016/j.electstud.2019.04.004; J. Lawrence Broz, Jeffry Frieden, and Stephen Weymouth, "Populism in Place: The Economic Geography of the Globalization Backlash," *International Organization* 75, no. 2 (2021): 464–494; Elias Dinas et al., "Waking Up the Golden Dawn: Does Exposure to the Refugee Crisis Increase Support for Extreme-Right Parties?," *Political Analysis* 27, no. 2 (2019): 244–254. https://doi.org/10.1017/pan.2018.48; Albana Shehaj, Adrian J. Shin, and Ronald Inglehart, "Immigration and Right-Wing Populism: An Origin Story," *Party Politics* 27, no. 2 (2021): 282–293. https://doi.org/10.1177/1354068819849888.

83. Ernesto Calvo and Timothy Hellwig, "Centripetal and Centrifugal Incentives Under Different Electoral Systems," *American Journal of Political Science* 55, no. 1 (2011): 27–41; Jay K. Dow, "Party-System Extremism in Majoritarian and Proportional Electoral Systems," *British Journal of Political Science* 41, no. 2 (April 2011): 341–361. https://doi.org/10.1017/S0007123410000360.

84. Lawrence Ezrow, "Parties' Policy Programmes and the Dog That Didn't Bark: No Evidence That Proportional Systems Promote Extreme Party Positioning," *British Journal of Political Science* 38, no. 3 (July 2008): 479–497; Elisabeth Carter, "Does PR Promote Political Extremism? Evidence from the West European Parties of the Extreme Right," *Representation* 40, no. 2 (January 2004): 82–100; see also G. Bingham Powell, "Ideological Trends and Changing Party System Polarization in Western Democracies," in *Politics in South Asia: Culture, Rationality and Conceptual Flow*, ed. Siegfried O. Wolf et al. (Cham: Springer International Publishing, 2015), 17–30. https://doi.org/10.1007/978-3-319-09087-0_2.

85. Wouter Van Der Brug, Meindert Fennema, and Jean Tillie, "Why Some Anti-immigrant Parties Fail and Others Succeed: A Two-Step Model of Aggregate Electoral Support," *Comparative Political Studies* 38, no. 5 (June 1, 2005): 537–573. https://doi.org/10.1177/0010414004273928.

86. See Kai Arzheimer and Elisabeth Carter, *Explaining Variation in the Extreme Right Vote: The Individual and the Political Environment*, Keele University School of Politics, International Relations and the Environment (2003); Kai Arzheimer and Elisabeth Carter, "Political Opportunity Structures and Right-Wing Extremist Party Success," *European Journal of Political Research* 45, no. 3 (2006): 432. https://doi.org/10.1111/j.1475-6765.2006.00304.x.

87. Lawrence Ezrow, "Are Moderate Parties Rewarded in Multiparty Systems? A Pooled Analysis of Western European Elections, 1984–1998," *European Journal of Political Research* 44, no. 6 (2005): 881–898. https://doi.org/10.1111/j.1475-6765.2005.00251.x.

88. For more details on how this measure is conceptualized, see Anna Lührmann, Juraj Medzihorsky, and Staffan I. Lindberg, "Walking the Talk: How to Identify Anti-pluralist Parties," Varieties of Democracy Institute, March 2021.

89. "The evidence presented above lends support to the proposition that excluding the extremists by institutional means may actually cultivate extremism rather than suppress it." Elisabeth Carter, "Does PR Promote Political Extremism? A Rejoinder," *Representation* 41, no. 1 (January 2004): 65. https://doi.org/10.1080/00344890408523290.

90. Oleg Smirnov and James H. Fowler, "Policy-Motivated Parties in Dynamic Political Competition," *Journal of Theoretical Politics* 19, no. 1 (January 1, 2007): 9–31. https://doi.org/10.1177/0951629807071014; Donald Wittman, "Candidate Motivation: A Synthesis of Alternative Theories," *American Political Science Review* 77, no. 1 (March 1983): 142–157. https://doi.org/10.2307/1956016.

91. Eric Groenendyk, "Competing Motives in a Polarized Electorate: Political Responsiveness, Identity Defensiveness, and the Rise of Partisan Antipathy," *Political Psychology* 39 (February 2018): 159–171; Eric Groenendyk, "Justifying Party Identification: A Case of Identifying with the 'Lesser of Two Evils.'" *Political Behavior* 34, no. 3 (September 2012): 453–475.

92. Federico Vegetti, "The Political Nature of Ideological Polarization: The Case of Hungary," *ANNALS of the American Academy of Political and Social Science* 681, no. 1 (January 1, 2019): 78–96; Kim Lane Scheppele, "The Party's Over," in *Constitutional Democracy in Crisis?*, vol. 1 (Oxford: Oxford University Press, 2018); Larry M. Bartels, *Democracy Erodes from the Top: Leaders, Citizens, and the Challenge of Populism in Europe* (Princeton, NJ: Princeton University Press, 2023), chap. 7.

93. Natasha Wunsch and Theresa Gessler, "Who Tolerates Democratic Backsliding? A Mosaic Approach to Voters' Responses to Authoritarian Leadership in Hungary," *Democratization* 30, no. 5 (July 4, 2023): 914–937. https://doi.org/10.1080/13510347.2023.2203918.

94. Larry M. Bartels, *Democracy Erodes from the Top: Leaders, Citizens, and the Challenge of Populism in Europe* (Princeton, NJ: Princeton University Press, 2023).

95. Matthijs Bogaards, "De-democratization in Hungary: Diffusely Defective Democracy," *Democratization* 25, no. 8 (November 17, 2018): 1481–1499. As Bogaards has explained, "The majoritarian turn in the electoral system has served as a tool for ensuring the long-term electoral success of the dominant party" (Bogaards, 2018, 1485). https://doi.org/10.1080/13510347.2018.1485015.

96. Christian B. Jensen and Daniel J. Lee, "Potential Centrifugal Effects of Majoritarian Features in Proportional Electoral Systems," *Journal of Contemporary Central and Eastern Europe* 29, no. 1 (January 2, 2021): 1–21. https://doi.org/10.1080/25739638.2021.1928879; Victoriano Ramírez González, Blanca Luisa Delgado Márquez, and Adolfo López Carmona, "Electoral System in Poland: Revision and Proposal of Modification Based on Biproportionality," *Representation* 51, no. 2 (April 3, 2015): 187–204. https://doi.org/10.1080/00344893.2015.1056217.

97. Anne Applebaum, "Poland Shows That Autocracy Is Not Inevitable," *The Atlantic* (blog), October 16, 2023.

98. Michael K. Miller, "A Republic, if You Can Keep It: Breakdown and Erosion in Modern Democracies," *Journal of Politics* 83, no. 1 (January 1, 2021): 198–213. https://doi.org/10.1086/709146.

99. Juan Albarracín, Laura Gamboa, and Scott Mainwaring, "Deinstitutionalization Without Collapse: Colombia's Party System," in *Party Systems in Latin America*, ed. Scott Mainwaring, 1st ed. (Cambridge: Cambridge University Press, 2018),

227–254. https://doi.org/10.1017/9781316798553.009; Erika Moreno, "Whither the Colombian Two-Party System? An Assessment of Political Reforms and Their Limits," *Electoral Studies* 24, no. 3 (2005): 485–509. https://doi.org/10.1016/j.electstud.2004.08.001; Matthew S. Shugart, Erika Moreno, and Luis E. Fajardo, "Deepening Democracy by Renovating Political Practices: The Struggle for Electoral Reform in Colombia," in *Electoral Systems and Political Transformation in South America*, edited by Scott Mainwaring and Timothy R. Scully, 1st ed. (Cambridge: Cambridge University Press, 2004), 80–108.

100. Due to data availability, this chart uses effective number of parties, not fractionalization. However, the two measures are closely correlated.

101. Christopher J. Anderson et al., *Losers' Consent: Elections and Democratic Legitimacy* (Oxford: Oxford University Press, 2005); Stefan Dahlberg and Jonas Linde, "Losing Happily? The Mitigating Effect of Democracy and Quality of Government on the Winner–Loser Gap in Political Support," *International Journal of Public Administration* 39, no. 9 (July 28, 2016): 652–664. https://doi.org/10.1080/01900692.2016.1177831; Matthew Germer, "Restoring Losers' Consent: A Necessary Step to Stabilizing Our Democracy," R Street Institute, September 2021; Sergio Martini and Mario Quaranta, "Political Support Among Winners and Losers: Within- and Between-Country Effects of Structure, Process and Performance in Europe," *European Journal of Political Research* 58, no. 1 (2019): 341–361. https://doi.org/10.1111/1475-6765.12284; Richard Nadeau and Andre Blais, "Accepting the Election Outcome: The Effect of Participation on Losers' Consent," *British Journal of Political Science* 23, no. 4 (1993): 553–563; Richard Nadeau, Jean-François Daoust, and Ruth Dassonneville, "Winning, Losing, and the Quality of Democracy," *Political Studies* 71, no. 2 (May 1, 2023): 483–500. https://doi.org/10.1177/00323217211026189; Julian Bernauer and Adrian Vatter, "Can't Get No Satisfaction with the Westminster Model? Winners, Losers and the Effects of Consensual and Direct Democratic Institutions on Satisfaction with Democracy," *European Journal of Political Research* 51, no. 4 (2012): 435–468. https://doi.org/10.1111/j.1475-6765.2011.02007.x.

102. Sarah Birch, "Electoral Institutions and Popular Confidence in Electoral Processes: A Cross-National Analysis," *Electoral Studies* 27, no. 2 (June 1, 2008): 305–320, finds that "elections that include a proportional representation component are rated more highly than those that do not." Christopher J. Anderson, "Parties, Party Systems, and Satisfaction with Democratic Performance in the New Europe," *Political Studies* 46, no. 3 (August 1, 1998): 572–588.

103. Stefan Dahlberg and Jonas Linde, "Losing Happily? The Mitigating Effect of Democracy and Quality of Government on the Winner-Loser Gap in Political Support," *International Journal of Public Administration* 39, no. 9 (July 28, 2016): 652–664. https://doi.org/10.1080/01900692.2016.1177831; Richard Nadeau, Jean-François Daoust, and Ruth Dassonneville, "Winning, Losing, and the Quality of Democracy," *Political Studies* 71, no. 2 (May 1, 2023): 483–500. https://doi.org/10.1177/00323217211026189.

104. J. Anderson and Y. V. Tverdova, "Corruption, Political Allegiances, and Attitudes Toward Government in Contemporary Democracies," *American Journal of Political Science* 47, no. 1 (2003): 91–109. doi:10.1111/1540-5907.00007.

105. Richard Nadeau, Jean-François Daoust, and Ruth Dassonneville, "Winning, Losing, and the Quality of Democracy," *Political Studies* 71, no. 2 (May 1, 2023): 488. https://doi.org/10.1177/00323217211026189.

106. Scott Mainwaring, "Presidentialism, Multipartism, and Democracy: The Difficult Combination," *Comparative Political Studies* 26, no. 2 (July 1, 1993): 198–228.

107. Paul Chaisty, Nic Cheeseman, and Timothy Power, "Rethinking the 'Presidentialism Debate': Conceptualizing Coalitional Politics in Cross-Regional Perspective," *Democratization* 21, no. 1 (January 2, 2014): 72–94. https://doi.org/10.1080/13510347.2012.710604.

108. José Antonio Cheibub, Adam Przeworski, and Sebastian M. Saiegh, "Government Coalitions and Legislative Success Under Presidentialism and Parliamentarism," *British Journal of Political Science* 34, no. 4 (October 2004): 579. https://doi.org/10.1017/S0007123404000195.

109. Carlos Pereira and Marcus André Melo, "The Surprising Success of Multiparty Presidentialism," *Journal of Democracy* 23, no. 3 (July 2012): 156–170. https://doi.org/10.1353/jod.2012.0041.

110. Christian Arnold, David Doyle, and Nina Wiesehomeier, "Presidents, Policy Compromise, and Legislative Success," *Journal of Politics* 79, no. 2 (April 2017): 392. https://doi.org/10.1086/688080.

111. Eduardo Alemán and George Tsebelis, *Legislative Institutions and Lawmaking in Latin America* (Oxford: Oxford University Press, 2016), 225.

112. This is Shugart and Carey's argument: Matthew Soberg Shugart and John M. Carey, *Presidents and Assemblies: Constitutional Design and Electoral Dynamics* (Cambridge University Press, 1992). Argelina Cheibub Figueiredo and Fernando Limongi make the opposite argument for the Brazilian case. In the context of high party system fragmentation, strong constitutional powers—especially presidential decree powers—help enable presidents govern. Without strong constitutional powers, the president would face a daunting task. Argelina Cheibub Figueiredo and Fernando Limongi, "Presidential Power, Legislative Organization, and Party Behavior in Brazil," *Comparative Politics* 32, no. 2 (2000): 151–170. https://doi.org/10.2307/422395.

113. Eduardo Mello and Matias Spektor, "Brazil: The Costs of Multiparty Presidentialism," *Journal of Democracy* 29, no. 2 (2018): 113–127. https://doi.org/10.1353/jod.2018.0031.

114. Johannes Freudenreich, "The Formation of Cabinet Coalitions in Presidential Systems," *Latin American Politics and Society* 58, no. 4 (2016): 80–102.

115. José Antonio Cheibub, Adam Przeworski, and Sebastian M. Saiegh, "Government Coalitions and Legislative Success Under Presidentialism and Parliamentarism," *British Journal of Political Science* 34, no. 4 (October 2004): 565. https://doi.org/10.1017/S0007123404000195.

116. Johannes Freudenreich, "The Formation of Cabinet Coalitions in Presidential Systems," *Latin American Politics and Society* 58, no. 4 (2016): 80–102. https://doi.org/10.1111/laps.12003.

117. Christian Arnold, David Doyle, and Nina Wiesehomeier, "Presidents, Policy Compromise, and Legislative Success," *Journal of Politics* 79, no. 2 (April 2017): 383; see also Lori Ann Post, Amber N. W. Raile, and Eric D. Raile, "Defining Political Will," *Politics & Policy* 38, no. 4 (August 25, 2010): 653–676. doi:10.1111/j.1747-1346.2010.00253.x.324.

118. José Antonio Cheibub, Adam Przeworski, and Sebastian M. Saiegh, "Government Coalitions and Legislative Success Under Presidentialism and Parliamentarism," *British Journal of Political Science* 34, no. 4 (October 2004): 565. https://doi.org/10.1017/S0007123404000195.

119. Certainly Congress still enacts bipartisan legislation, even in divided government. See James M. Curry and Frances E. Lee, *The Limits of Party: Congress and Lawmaking in a Polarized Era* (Chicago: University of Chicago Press, 2020). But Congress also fails to resolve many significant issues, leading to distrust and frustration with government. Sarah Binder, "The Dysfunctional Congress," *Annual*

Review of Political Science 18, no. 1 (2015): 85–101; Jeremy Gelman, *Losing to Win: Why Congressional Majorities Play Politics Instead of Make Laws* (Ann Arbor: University of Michigan Press, 2020); Philip A. Wallach, *Why Congress* (Oxford: Oxford University Press, 2023).

120. Scott Mainwaring and Lee Drutman, "The Case for Multiparty Presidentialism in the US: Why the House Should Adopt Proportional Representation"(Washington DC: New America and Protect Democracy, December 2024).

121. Heike Klüver, Hanna Bäck, and Svenja Krauss, *Coalition Agreements as Control Devices: Coalition Governance in Western and Eastern Europe* (Oxford: Oxford University Press, 2023).

122. Alejandro Ecker and Thomas M Meyer, "The Duration of Government Formation Processes in Europe," *Research & Politics* 2, no. 4 (October 1, 2015): 2053168015622796. https://doi.org/10.1177/2053168015622796.

123. Sona N. Golder, "Bargaining Delays in the Government Formation Process," *Comparative Political Studies* 43, no. 1 (January 1, 2010): 3–32. https://doi.org/10 .1177/0010414009341714. Lanny W. Martin and Georg Vanberg, "Wasting Time? The Impact of Ideology and Size on Delay in Coalition Formation," *British Journal of Political Science* 33, no. 2 (April 2003): 323–332. https://doi.org/10.1017 /S0007123403000140.

124. Alejandro Ecker and Thomas M. Meyer, "Coalition Bargaining Duration in Multiparty Democracies," *British Journal of Political Science* 50, no. 1 (January 2020): 261–280. https://doi.org/10.1017/S0007123417000539.

125. Lanny W. Martin and Georg Vanberg, "Parties and Policymaking in Multiparty Governments: The Legislative Median, Ministerial Autonomy, and the Coalition Compromise," *American Journal of Political Science* 58, no. 4 (2014): 979–996. https://doi.org/10.1111/ajps.12099.

126. Sona Nadenichek Golder, "Pre-electoral Coalition Formation in Parliamentary Democracies," *British Journal of Political Science* 36, no. 2 (April 2006): 193–212. https://doi.org/10.1017/S0007123406000123; Mihail Chiru, "Early Marriages Last Longer: Pre-electoral Coalitions and Government Survival in Europe," *Government and Opposition* 50, no. 2 (April 2015): 165–188. https://doi.org/10 .1017/gov.2014.8; Kaare Strøm and Wolfgang C. Müller, "The Keys to Togetherness: Coalition Agreements in Parliamentary Democracies," in *The Uneasy Relationship Between Parliamentary Members and Leaders*, ed. Lawrence D. Longley and Reuven Y. Hazen (London: Frank Cass, 2000), 255–282.

127. André Borges, Mathieu Turgeon, and Adrián Albala, "Electoral Incentives to Coalition Formation in Multiparty Presidential Systems," *Party Politics* 27, no. 6 (November 1, 2021): 1279–1289. https://doi.org/10.1177/1354068820953527.

128. Adrián Albala, André Borges, and Lucas Couto, "Pre-electoral Coalitions and Cabinet Stability in Presidential Systems," *British Journal of Politics and International Relations* 25, no. 1 (February 2023): 64–82. https://doi.org/10.1177 /13691481211056852.

129. Jacob S. Hacker and Paul Pierson, "After the 'Master Theory': Downs, Schattschneider, and the Rebirth of Policy-Focused Analysis," *Perspectives on Politics* 12, no. 3 (September 2014): 643–662.

130. See, e.g., Johanan D. Mussel and Henry Schlechta, "Australia: No Party Convergence Where We Would Most Expect It," *Party Politics*, July 21, 2023. https:// doi.org/10.1177/13540688231189363.

131. For a long list of reasons why two-party convergence might fail, see Bernard Grofman, "Downs and Two-Party Convergence," *Annual Review of Political Science* 7, no. 1 (2004): 25–46.

132. Massimo Morelli, "Demand Competition and Policy Compromise in Legislative Bargaining," *American Political Science Review* 93, no. 4 (1999): 809–820.

133. Michael Laver and Norman Schofield, *Multiparty Government: The Politics of Coalition in Europe* (Oxford: Oxford University Press, 1990), 111.

134. G. Bingham Powell, "Election Laws and Representative Governments: Beyond Votes and Seats," *British Journal of Political Science* 36, no. 2 (2006): 291–315; G. Bingham Powell and Georg S. Vanberg, "Election Laws, Disproportionality and Median Correspondence: Implications for Two Visions of Democracy," *British Journal of Political Science* 30, no. 3 (2000): 383–411; Michael D. McDonald and Ian Budge, *Elections, Parties, Democracy: Conferring the Median Mandate* (Oxford: Oxford University Press, 2005); Michael D. McDonald, Silvia M. Mendes, and Ian Budge, "What Are Elections for? Conferring the Median Mandate," *British Journal of Political Science* 34, no. 1 (2004): 1–26.

135. Gary Miller and Norman Schofield, "Activists and Partisan Realignment in the United States," *American Political Science Review* 97, no. 2 (2003): 245–260; Gary Miller and Norman Schofield, "The Transformation of the Republican and Democratic Party Coalitions in the U.S," *Perspectives on Politics* 6, no. 3 (2008): 433–450; Norman Schofield, Gary Miller, and Andrew Martin, "Critical Elections and Political Realignments in the USA: 1860–2000," *Political Studies* 51, no. 2 (June 1, 2003): 217–240.

136. Anthony Downs, *An Economic Theory of Democracy* (New York: Harper & Bros., 1957), 119.

137. Anthony Downs, *An Economic Theory of Democracy* (New York: Harper & Bros., 1957), 120.

138. Anthony J. McGann and Michael Latner, "The Calculus of Consensus Democracy: Rethinking Patterns of Democracy Without Veto Players," *Comparative Political Studies* 46, no. 7 (July 2013): 823–850; Norman Schofield, ed., *Collective Decision-Making: Social Choice and Political Economy*, Recent Economic Thought 50 (Berlin: Springer Science & Business Media, 2013).

139. The Governance Index examines how effective governments are in directing and implementing policies appropriate to these three goals.

140. https://datafinder.qog.gu.se/variable/wbgi_gee.

141. The variable examines to what extent the freely elected head of government and a national legislative representative determine the policies of the government; if the government is free from pervasive corruption; and if the government is accountable to the electorate between elections and operates with openness and transparency.

142. In multiple regression analysis, country GDP explains considerable variance across countries.

143. The relationship between legislative fragmentation and democratic outcomes is unclear and probably nonexistent. It is also difficult to measure. Vicente Valentim and Elias Dinas, "Does Party-System Fragmentation Affect the Quality of Democracy?," *British Journal of Political Science* 54, no. 1 (January 2024): 152–178. https://doi.org/10.1017/S0007123423000157.

144. Pippa Norris, "'Things Fall Apart, the Center Cannot Hold': Fractionalized and Polarized Party Systems in Western Democracies," *European Political Science*, January 31, 2024, concludes, "Party system fractionalization and polarization should be treated as two distinct and unrelated dimensions of party competition."

145. Ernesto Calvo and Jonathan Rodden, "The Achilles Heel of Plurality Systems: Geography and Representation in Multiparty Democracies," *American Journal of Political Science* 59, no. 4 (2015): 789–805. https://doi.org/10.2307/24582948; R. H. Brookes, "The Analysis of Distorted Representation in Two-Party

Single-Member Elections," *Political Science* 12, no. 2 (September 1960): 158–167. https://doi.org/10.1177/003231876001200204; Graham Gudgin and Peter J. Taylor, *Seats, Votes, and the Spatial Organisation of Elections* (Colchester, UK: ECPR Press, 2012); David W. Brady and Bernard Grofman, "Sectional Differences in Partisan Bias and Electoral Responsiveness in US House Elections, 1850–1980," *British Journal of Political Science* 21, no. 2 (1991): 247–256.

146. Lisa Handley and Bernard Grofman, *Redistricting in Comparative Perspective* (Oxford: Oxford University Press, 2008), 222.

147. For discussions, see R. H. Brookes, "The Analysis of Distorted Representation in Two-Party Single-Member Elections," *Political Science* 12, no. 2 (September 1960): 158–167. https://doi.org/10.1177/003231876001200204; William Bunge, "Gerrymandering, Geography, and Grouping," *Geographical Review* 56, no. 2 (1966): 256–263. https://doi.org/10.2307/212882; Edward R. Tufte, "The Relationship Between Seats and Votes in Two-Party Systems," *American Political Science Review* 67, no. 2 (1973): 540–554; Drew A. Linzer, "The Relationship Between Seats and Votes in Multiparty Systems," *Political Analysis* 20, no. 3 (2012): 400–416. https://doi.org/10.1093/pan/mps017.

148. Robert S. Erikson, Karl Sigman, and Linan Yao, "Electoral College Bias and the 2020 Presidential Election," *Proceedings of the National Academy of Sciences of the United States of America* 117, no. 45 (November 10, 2020): 27940–27944. https://doi.org/10.1073/pnas.2013581117.

149. Gregory S. Warrington, "A Comparison of Partisan-Gerrymandering Measures," *Election Law Journal* 18, no. 3 (September 2019): 262–281, https://doi.org/10.1089/elj.2018.0508.

150. Ferran Martínez i Coma and Ignacio Lago, "Gerrymandering in Comparative Perspective," *Party Politics* 24, no. 2 (March 1, 2018): 99–104. https://doi.org/10.1177/1354068816642806. S; see also Alex Keena et al., *Gerrymandering the States: Partisanship, Race, and the Transformation of American Federalism* (Cambridge: Cambridge University Press, 2021), https://doi.org/10.1017/9781108995849.

151. Valerie Heitshusen, Garry Young, and David M. Wood, "Electoral Context and MP Constituency Focus in Australia, Canada, Ireland, New Zealand, and the United Kingdom," *American Journal of Political Science* 49, no. 1 (2005): 32–45.

152. Valerie Heitshusen, Garry Young, and David M. Wood, "Electoral Context and MP Constituency Focus in Australia, Canada, Ireland, New Zealand, and the United Kingdom," *American Journal of Political Science* 49, no. 1 (2005): 32–45; Kyle Dropp and Zachary Peskowitz, "Electoral Security and the Provision of Constituency Service," *Journal of Politics* 74, no. 1 (January 2012): 220–234, https://doi.org/10.1017/S0022381611001216; Brian F. Crisp and William M. Simoneau, "Electoral Systems and Constituency Service," in *The Oxford Handbook of Electoral Systems*, ed. Erik S. Herron, Robert J. Pekkanen, and Matthew S. Shugart (Oxford: Oxford University Press, 2018), 344–364. https://doi.org/10.1093/oxfordhb/9780190258658.013.18. For theory, see Scott Ashworth and Ethan Bueno de Mesquita, "Constituency Services with Electoral and Institutional Variations," University of California Working Papers, April 22, 2004; See also J. Vincent Buck and Bruce E. Cain, "British MPs in Their Constituencies," *Legislative Studies Quarterly* 15, no. 1 (1990): 127–143. https://doi.org/10.2307/440006.

153. There may be a partisan difference. A recent study, drawing on a dataset of congressional correspondence with all federal agencies, finds that "Republicans provide less overall constituency service" and, in particular, that "electing Republican causes a 14.8 percent decrease in the amount of constituency service targeted at low-income individuals." Rochelle Snyder et al., "Who Gets Constituent Service?" (working paper, 2021), 26.

154. Brian F. Crisp and Scott W. Desposato, "Constituency Building in Multi-member Districts: Collusion or Conflict?," *Journal of Politics* 66, no. 1 (February 2004): 136–156. https://doi.org/10.1046/j.1468-2508.2004.00145.x.

155. Micah Gell-Redman et al., "It's All About Race: How State Legislators Respond to Immigrant Constituents," *Political Research Quarterly* 71, no. 3 (September 1, 2018): 517–531. https://doi.org/10.1177/1065912917749322.

156. Mia Costa, "How Responsive Are Political Elites? A Meta-analysis of Experiments on Public Officials," *Journal of Experimental Political Science* 4, no. 3 (December 2017): 241–254. https://doi.org/10.1017/XPS.2017.14.

157. Mia Costa, "How Responsive Are Political Elites? A Meta-analysis of Experiments on Public Officials," *Journal of Experimental Political Science* 4, no. 3 (December 2017): 241–254.

158. Daniel M. Butler, *Representing the Advantaged: How Politicians Reinforce Inequality* (Cambridge: Cambridge University Press, 2014).

159. Daniel M. Butler, *Representing the Advantaged: How Politicians Reinforce Inequality* (Cambridge: Cambridge University Press, 2014), 118.

160. Daniel M. Butler, *Representing the Advantaged: How Politicians Reinforce Inequality* (Cambridge: Cambridge University Press, 2014), 124.

161. Brian F. Crisp and William M. Simoneau, "Electoral Systems and Constituency Service," in *The Oxford Handbook of Electoral Systems*, ed. Erik S. Herron, Robert J. Pekkanen, and Matthew S. Shugart (Oxford: Oxford University Press, 2018); for a review, see also Audrey André and Sam Depauw, "District Magnitude and Home Styles of Representation in European Democracies," *West European Politics* 36, no. 5 (September 2013): 986–1006; John M. Carey and Matthew Soberg Shugart, "Incentives to Cultivate a Personal Vote: A Rank Ordering of Electoral Formulas," *Electoral Studies* 14, no. 4 (December 1, 1995): 417–439.

162. Wendy J. Schiller, *Partners and Rivals: Representation in US Senate Delegations* (Princeton, NJ: Princeton University Press, 2000), 165.

163. Brian F. Crisp and Patrick Cunha Silva, "The Role of District Magnitude in When Women Represent Women," *British Journal of Political Science* 53, no. 3 (July 2023): 1061–1069; M. Shugart, M. Valdini, and K. Suominen, "Looking for Locals: Voter Information Demands and Personal Vote-Earning Attributes of Legislators Under Proportional Representation," *American Journal of Political Science* 49, no. 2 (April 2005): 437–449; Y. Kweon and J. M. Ryan, "Electoral Systems and the Substantive Representation of Marginalized Groups: Evidence from Women's Issue Bills in South Korea," *Political Research Quarterly* 75, no. 4 (2021): 1065–1078.

164. Facing such incentives, instead of perceiving themselves as responsible for the interests of at least 50 percent + 1 of the constituents in their districts, legislators may feel they can specialize. Brian F. Crisp and Patrick Cunha Silva, "The Role of District Magnitude in When Women Represent Women," *British Journal of Political Science* 53, no. 3 (July 2023): 1062. See also H. Coffee, "MPs' Representational Focus in MMP Systems: A Comparison Between Germany and New Zealand," *Representation* 54, no. 4 (2018): 367–389; J. A. MacDonald and E. E. O'Brien, "Quasi-experimental Design, Constituency, and Advancing Women's Interests: Reexamining the Influence of Gender on Substantive Representation," *Political Research Quarterly* 64, no. 2 (2011): 472–486; M. Tremblay, "Women's Political Representation: Does the Electoral System Matter?," *Political Science* 57, no. 1 (June 2005), 59–75.

165. Brian F. Crisp and Patrick Cunha Silva, "The Role of District Magnitude in When Women Represent Women," *British Journal of Political Science* 53, no. 3 (July 2023): 1062.

166. James M. Snyder Jr. and Michiko Ueda, "Do Multimember Districts Lead to Free-Riding?," *Legislative Studies Quarterly* 32, no. 4 (2007): 667.

167. Justin H. Kirkland, "Multi-member Districts' Effect on Collaboration Between U.S. State Legislators," *Legislative Studies Quarterly* 37, no. 3 (2012): 334.

168. Audrey André and Sam Depauw, "District Magnitude and Home Styles of Representation in European Democracies," *West European Politics* 36, no. 5 (September 2013): 986–1006.

169. Audrey André and Sam Depauw, "District Magnitude and Home Styles of Representation in European Democracies," *West European Politics* 36, no. 5 (September 2013): 999.

170. Leonardo Carella and Andrew Eggers, "Electoral Systems and Geographic Representation," *British Journal of Political Science* 55, no. 1 (January 2024): 40–68, p. 41.

171. "U.S. Voters: Biden, Most in House Don't Deserve Another Term," Gallup.

172. John Carey et al., "Between Science and Engineering: Reflections on the APSA Presidential Task Force on Political Science, Electoral Rules, and Democratic Governance: Political Scientists as Electoral System Engineers," *Perspectives on Politics* 11, no. 3 (September 2013): 827–840.

173. Steven L. Taylor et al., *A Different Democracy: American Government in a 31-Country Perspective* (New Haven, CT: Yale University Press, 2014).

4

Why Proportional Representation Could Make Things Worse

Richard H. Pildes

We have deep reservations about any proposal to replace our current system of single-member districts (SMDs) and first-past-the-post (FPTP) elections by amending federal law to permit or require states to use multimember districts (MMDs) to elect members of Congress. For proponents, the point of doing so would be to achieve proportional representation (PR) in the US House of Representatives.[1] In the fall of 2020, some 200 academics sent an open letter to Congress urging it to permit states to do so.[2] The Fair Representation Act,[3] introduced in the House in 2021, would, among other things, require states with two or more congressional districts to elect House members from MMDs using a form of PR based on ranked-choice voting (a system otherwise known as the single-transferrable vote [STV]).

The purpose of such proposals is to enable the creation of a House comprised of five or six political parties. To the extent that Chapter 3 might be read as encouraging such changes, we would not want our silence to be taken as an endorsement. We will refer here to proposals for MMDs for Congress as proposals for PR.

PR proponents argue that the hyperpolarized nature of our two-party system and the toxic, tribalistic political culture of our current era compel a shift to PR. Their proposal is thus a response to the specific nature of democratic politics in the United States today. The desire to find a silver bullet that would free us from a state of politics that few consider healthy is understandable. But we are concerned that the diagnosis that

---

Larry Diamond and Frances Lee contributed substantially to this chapter.

single-member districts and FPTP elections lie at the heart of America's descent into toxic politics may not be correct. More importantly, we worry that electing House members through PR could well make our political institutions even more dysfunctional. We also believe it is important to understand the concrete institutional details of what a shift to PR in the House would entail. The details are important, because looking closely at how PR would actually work in the United States reveals significant issues not readily apparent in more abstract debates about the merits of such proposals.

How PR Would Work for Congress: Threshold Issues

Proponents of MMDs for the House suggest that such districts should be designed to send five to seven members to Congress. This would require new federal legislation because current federal law requires single-member districts for Congress. One reason proponents argue for MMDs, rather than a more straightforward system of statewide PR, is their belief that Americans should be able to identify an individual representative as "their" representative; many people, particularly lower-income citizens, rely on congressional offices for assistance with Social Security or other public entitlements and benefits.

Under the system of MMDs proposed in the Fair Representation Act, a state such as North Carolina, with fourteen representatives, would be divided into three districts, two of which would elect five members and one of which would elect four. In the general election, ten or more candidates would presumably be on the ballot for the five seats in a five-member MMD. Currently, the average population of a congressional district is about 761,000 people. Under the proposed system, North Carolina would have two districts of 3.805 million people and one with 3.044 million. If the entire state were a single electoral district, there would be no natural and statutory connection between the state's fourteen house members and its nearly 11 million residents. Hence, the choice of MMDs rather than statewide PR is to enable residents to continue to feel connected to "their" representatives and hold them accountable. Whether either of those aims would be realistic in districts with 3 million people is an initial question.

Moreover, to make this system work, the method by which we vote would have to change in fairly substantial ways. Thus, one of the requirements reformers sometimes pair with the introduction of MMDs is ranked-choice voting (the single transferrable vote system mentioned above). Voters rank as many of the ten or more candidates as they prefer. In a five-member MMD, any candidate who wins more than a sixth of the vote (close to 17 percent) is immediately elected. The seats that remain empty after this initial round are filled by winnowing down the rest of the field: the candidates with the fewest first-preference votes are eliminated and their votes are transferred to whichever candidate is ranked immediately below the eliminated candidate on each ballot, until five candidates have cleared the one-sixth-plus-one-vote threshold. In a seven-member MMD, the threshold for victory is one-eighth of the vote (12.5 percent) plus one. The fewer members elected from a district, the higher the minimal winning threshold.[4] Proponents believe an electoral system composed of moderately sized districts (say, of up to five members each) would generate a Congress of five or six parties, with perhaps a green party, a socialist party, and a moderate Democratic Party on the left and a religious party, a libertarian party, and a business-oriented Republican Party on the right.

Recognizing the informational burden this system would put on voters, PR proponents instead sometimes suggest using a party-list voting system. This system would even more dramatically change the way we vote. First, it would do away with primary elections for choosing a party's nominees. Instead, each party would choose, through whatever internal processes it preferred, a slate of candidates and rank order them on the ballot. Voters would then cast a single vote for their preferred party. In a "closed-list" system, voters could not vote for a specific candidate or alter the rank ordering of the candidates on the list. In a partially or fully "open-list" system, voters could vote for a specific candidate on the party-chosen list, which would also count as a vote for that party, or they could simply vote for a particular party without identifying any specific candidate. Under party-list PR, political parties receive a number of seats in the legislature proportionate to their vote share. While we might be sympathetic to a system in which parties regain more control over selecting their nominees, the shift to a list PR form of party-based voting would be a radical one in the American context.

Several additional issues related to the mechanics of this system should be noted. One immediate problem is that twenty-one states, nearly half of them, have fewer than five representatives. If five representatives is the ideal number for each MMD—enabling the desired level of multiparty competition in all states—the introduction of PR would have to be paired with a massive expansion of the House (which has been set at 435 representatives since 1929). Seven states currently have only one representative. To give those states five representatives, the House would need to have 2,175 members. Again, even PR proponents are not enamored of that much representation. They typically propose a House of 700 members, roughly the size of the lower chambers in Germany and the United Kingdom. At this size, the thirteen states that today have just one or two representatives would not be able to constitute a single five-member MMD. Thus, parties capable of crossing the electoral threshold with 17 percent of the vote in some states would not win a single seat in smaller states with that same 17 percent.

As noted above, new congressional legislation would be required to adopt any version of MMDs. But a critical question is whether any such legislation should merely permit states to shift to MMDs or require them to. While the Fair Representation Act mandates MMDs with PR for all states with multiple representatives, many reform proponents advocate permitting, but not requiring, states to use MMDs. This is surely a concession to political realities, for a shift even to voluntary use of MMDs would be a heavy political lift. But in a voluntary system, partisan calculations would undoubtedly shape legislative decisions about whether to shift to MMDs, along with calculations about the choices other states would be anticipated to make. The legislative majority in any one state would have to decide to weaken its power by shifting to MMDs without any guarantee that other states would do the same. State-by-state partisan calculations would drive those choices. Such dynamics are precisely why Congress concluded in 1842, and reaffirmed in 1967, that a uniform national requirement for congressional districts is required. The proposed system of MMDs for the House, then, would be unlikely to get off the ground or to remain stable unless Congress mandated it uniformly. That is most likely why the Fair Representation Act would require states to use MMDs for Congress.

Another question is whether MMDs would actually generate multiparty democracy in the United States. Senators and the president would continue to be elected as they currently are, given hardwired provisions of the Constitution. Because two-party competition will continue to dominate these higher offices, how many ambitious politicians would run under other party labels for the House?

In sum, under these proposals PR would concretely mean either a 700-member House of around six parties or a House closer to (or exactly) the current size with less proportionality, alongside two-party competition for the presidency and the Senate. Voters would choose among ten or so candidates in districts of around 2.4 million to 3.8 million people (about three to five times the size of current districts). For a voting system, they would use STV or an open-list PR system for either one candidate or one political party. The practical range and nature of the changes required to implement such a system within the constraints of American institutions would be major considerations if Congress ever seriously debated requiring or permitting MMDs and PR.

Is the Diagnosis on Which PR Proposals Rest Accurate?

PR proponents argue that under the current SMD/winner-take-all electoral system for the House, two-party competition is responsible for the toxic "us-versus-them" political culture that has emerged. And these proponents maintain that a six-party Congress would encourage more compromise-oriented politics, rather than simply making legislation more difficult. Because no party would be likely to win an outright legislative majority, governing would require coalition building. Parties would purportedly recognize that they have to compromise to get anything done, and more extreme, uncompromising parties could be left on the margins of legislative work. Different coalitional majorities, so the theory goes, would be assembled for different issues. But forming a coalition without the party or parties of the political center would be difficult. With more parties, more viewpoints would have to be considered.

But there are good reasons to question whether PR proponents have the correct diagnosis: that FPTP elections are a primary cause of our current political disease. FPTP systems do tend to generate two-party politics (with some qualifications), but no other FPTP system is characterized by the toxic tribal politics and affective polarization that have come to characterize the United States.

In the United Kingdom, the birthplace of FPTP, politics have long been consensual, moderate, and pragmatic, despite major differences over policy. The Margaret Thatcher years saw intense conflict, but between then and Brexit, political scientists noted, "in contrast to American elites' policy polarization, British politics witnessed dramatic depolarization, that is, policy convergence between the elites of the two dominant political parties."[5] Brexit, of course, roiled British politics for half a decade after voters in 2016 approved the referendum to depart the European Union, but it was an existential issue that countries rarely confront. More importantly, Brexit did not entail tribal political conflict between the two major parties; both were internally riven over Brexit and related issues.

The current leaders of both major British parties are again generally viewed as technocratic and pragmatic. Although the constituencies of the left and right parties in the United States and the United Kingdom share much in common—the same stark educational divide, the same rural/urban split—little in Britain resembles the affective polarization of the United States, despite policy conflicts. As a leading British political commentator put it in 2023, the United Kingdom is "Europe's haven of moderation."[6] Indeed, that commentator warned, "Those in the UK who campaign for proportional representation should view contemporary Europe as a warning, not a template."[7] The United Kingdom's most recent elections handed the governing reins to a modern left-of-center Labour Party.

Similarly, one hardly would view Canada, the other major Western democracy using FPTP elections, as afflicted by a toxic political culture of affective polarization akin to that of the United States. As a major comparative study concluded, the rise of affective polarization in the United States since the 1990s is "not part of a cross-national trend." In other Western democracies, affective polarization was fairly stable, and much lower than in the United States, during this period.[8]

If our system no longer produces moderate, pragmatic parties, we should ask what other institutional features of our elections or political culture could be causing FPTP to behave so differently. Likely candidates include unique aspects of the ways we organize our democratic process: our use of primary elections, our system of privately financed campaigns, and our presidential nomination process that denies elected party figures any formal role in choosing the parties' nominees—issues that other parts of this book address.

Chapter 3 offers data showing that affective polarization tends to be greater in countries with FPTP elections. But we do not find this data significant. No one thinks the United Kingdom, Canada, or Australia has anything like the affective polarization that currently characterizes the United States; nor is affective polarization a serious problem in those countries. Indeed, one study's general conclusion is that American affective polarization, while above average, is not even "exceptionally intense" in comparative perspective.[9]

Is the Cure Worse Than the Disease?

A major challenge that the United States and other Western democracies face is restoring faith in their ability to deliver effective governance on issues citizens care most about—and actually delivering that governance.[10] According to proponents of MMDs, this system would produce a five- or six-party House. Our major concern is that this fragmentation of parties would make the political process more, not less, dysfunctional. Given the depth of dissatisfaction with government today, this is a particularly pressing concern. When democratic governments fail to deal effectively with issues that matter most to voters, that failure can lead to distrust, alienation, withdrawal, anger, and resentment. Even worse, it can fuel desires for a strongman figure who promises to cut through the dysfunction and deliver where democratic governments have not.

The best place to examine how a five- or six-party Congress might function is in the PR democracies of western Europe. But the way these democracies have functioned over the last decade or so—the same period in which politics in the United States has become so much more divisive—is very different from how they functioned for most of the period from World War II until about ten years ago. For this reason, assessments of western European PR democracies from before this past decade are outdated and can be misleading.[11]

From World War II until around ten years ago, many of the PR democracies in Europe that are formally multiparty systems had functioned, in effect, as two-and-a-half-party systems.[12] Either one of the two large, dominant parties won an outright majority, or it governed with the support of one smaller party. This generated fairly stable and continuous government, even as control might shift from one of the two dominant parties to the other. The impression many have of how well PR worked in these countries might well be based on this long period of relatively stable politics.

But that era is now gone. Just as the last decade or so has brought continual dissatisfaction with government in the United States, it has brought continual dissatisfaction with government in western Europe. This in turn has generated turbulent politics across much of the continent, including the rise of "antisystem" politics and parties in many countries.[13]

Over the last decade, the long-stable two-and-a-half-party structure has collapsed in most of western Europe. The inability of governments to address their citizens' most pressing concerns has led to a hemorrhaging of support for the long-dominant European parties, such as Germany's center-right Christian Democrats and center-left Social Democrats. As a result, support for the major parties has fractured, and new insurgent parties of various ideologies have emerged while previously minor parties, some of them populist or more ideologically extreme, have gained greater support. We are seeing in western Europe exactly the kind of splintering of those larger parties that PR advocates claim would be a virtue for the United States. Several of these systems, which functioned in effect as two-and-a-half-party systems for decades, have become five- or six-party systems.

One of us (Richard H. Pildes) has extensively detailed the rise of these newly fragmented multiparty political systems in western Europe and Scandinavia and shown how dysfunctional many of these governments have become.[14] A standard summary measure of the fragmentation of a country's party system is the "effective number of parliamentary parties."[15] While this measure is based on a mathematical formula, it gives an intuitive sense of how many parties matter in a legislature for the purpose of assembling a majority. In FPTP systems, the number is generally under 3 (in the United States it is 2, and in parliamentary systems it tends to be 3; it is about 2.4 in the United Kingdom, 2.8 in Canada, and 3.2 in Australia). In most of Europe's PR systems, the effective number ranges from 5 to 7; in parliamentary Belgium, which has had chronic problems forming governments, it is nearly 10. In Germany, the number has risen from under 4 in 1990 (and 3 in the former West Germany) to 5.5 today.[16]

In general, the more fragmented party systems that have emerged in Europe have had at least three effects on governance that those who advocate adopting PR in the United States have underestimated. These effects need to be carefully considered before embracing the goal of a five- or six-party US House.

First, it now takes much longer to form a governing majority in European parliaments, as bargaining drags on for many months between the various parties and potential coalitional partners. Second, voters can lack a clear sense of the government and policies they are voting for, since coalitions between a number of parties are often cobbled together after elections and on terms not always foreseeable in advance. Elites bargain after elections to forge a governing majority (and hence policy), although sometimes these coalitional pairings are made clear to voters in advance. Such coalitions are also more likely to be ideologically incoherent, since the multiple parties that comprise them often have strongly divergent views on major issues.

Third, when these coalitional governments do manage to form, they are more fragile. The departure of one or more minor parties from the coalition can cause the government to collapse. This outcome has become more likely, since conflicting ideologies among multiparty coalitions can cause fissures that lead one or more to abandon the coalition. As a result, some of these democracies have had to hold repeated national elections in an effort to find a governing majority. Others have lost votes of no confidence.

These developments are powerful signs of continual dissatisfaction with nearly all the PR governments of western Europe. Newly fragmented party systems in these countries reflect the strong frustrations of so many citizens with their governments' inability to deliver on issues they care about. And yet, at the same time, this fragmentation makes it even harder for governments to function effectively, since they are more divided, fragile, and difficult to form in the first place. Democratic governments in much of the West are now caught in this perverse dynamic. The prospect of importing these struggles to the United States should give pause to those advocating PR for the House.

To make the transformation of Europe's PR systems more concrete, consider the case of Germany, which until recently was considered a bastion of stability and good governance among European democracies. Since World War II, it had been a typical two-and-a-half-party system, with the traditionally large center-left party (the Social Democrats) and center-right party (the Christian Democrats) alternating in control of government. Between them, these parties regularly combined in the 1970s to receive over 90 percent of the vote.

But in recent years, Germany has splintered into a six-party system.[17] In the 2017 elections, the two previously dominant parties combined to receive just 53 percent of the vote,[18] and in 2021 they failed to achieve a combined majority. The votes these major parties shed were absorbed by smaller parties of various ideologies, such as the Alternative for Germany (AfD), the Free Democrats, the Greens, and the Left. After 2017, it took six months to form a government, the longest time since the creation of Germany's post–World War II democracy.[19]

Since its most recent elections, Germany has been governed by a three-party coalition for the first time. While that coalition has remained mostly united over Ukraine policy, the ideological conflicts between the three parties, particularly on domestic issues, have raised questions about whether even a three-party coalition can function effectively.[20] The coalition has proven highly unpopular, partly because the two smaller parties have been fiercely at odds.[21] Dissatisfaction with government in Germany remains extremely high; at the time of this writing, only 19 percent of people report being "satisfied" with the government.[22] Partly as a result, the hard-right AfD is currently the second-most popular party in Germany.[23] Commentators describe the country as "slipping further and further into crisis."[24]

Chapter 3 presents partial evidence suggesting that PR systems score well on expert assessments of "Good Governance" and "Government Effectiveness," as well as Freedom House's "Functioning of Government" measure. But these measures focus heavily on inputs to or general qualities of government, such as how transparent it is or how much corruption exists, rather than on how effectively government delivers policy solutions to pressing problems. We think the most meaningful evidence of how citizens feel about their governments is what economists call their "revealed preferences": the way they actually vote. And as voting patterns throughout western Europe demonstrate, citizens have been consistently dissatisfied with the performance of their governments and continually searching for new alternatives.

In the spirit of healthy skepticism, we offer Table 4.1, which presents the percentile scores on three often-used World Bank measures of governance quality—government effectiveness, control of corruption, and rule of law—for two sets of seven advanced industrial democracies: one predominantly majoritarian with an average effective number of parties of 2.49, and the other PR (and for the most part, highly proportional) with an average effective number of parties of 6.37.[25] As is apparent from the table, there is virtually no difference in the average quality of governance for the two systems. The majoritarian systems

Table 4.1 Governance Quality, Majoritarian and PR Systems, 2022 Percentile Scores

Country	Number of Effective Parties	Government Effectiveness	Control of Corruption	Rule of Law
Australia	3.15	93	95	91
Canada	2.76	94	93	93
United Kingdom	2.39	86	93	89
United States	2.0	87	83	89
Japan	2.69	96	91	92
Korea	2.09	90	77	85
Taiwan	2.38	91	83	87
Majoritarian Average	*2.49*	*91*	*88*	*89*
Belgium	9.7	85	89	88
Denmark	7.24	98	100	100
Germany	5.51	88	96	92
Israel	6.51	85	79	81
Netherlands	7.03	95	97	93
Spain	3.44	78	75	77
Sweden	5.18	95	98	94
Proportional Average	*6.37*	*89*	*91*	*89*

actually have the edge in government effectiveness with an average percentile rank of 91, compared to 89 for the PR systems; the PR systems do a bit better in controlling corruption (91 to 88); and the two systems have the same average percentile scores on rule of law (89).[26]

To be sure, the challenge of party fragmentation is greater in parliamentary systems than it would be in the American presidential system. In the United States, the government's existence wouldn't depend on a majority coalition. Nonetheless, a majority would have to be forged to elect a Speaker of the House and determine how committees would be structured.

The western European experience over the last decade or so is critical to understand because it illustrates the range of difficulties associated with putting together majority coalitions in systems with five or six political parties—and also puts to rest the notion that PR systems there are working smoothly and producing effective government with widespread public satisfaction.[27] Moreover, PR systems have always made it more likely that more extreme minority parties will gain representation. One way PR systems have contained that threat is by forging an agreement among major parties not to go into coalition with extremists (known as a "cordon sanitaire"). Yet that approach has widely broken down (though not in France), as these parties have grown in support through PR and coalitions have become dependent on more extreme parties to govern.[28]

The US party system is already fragmented. Even without a multiparty system, the Democrats and the Republicans are both sharply divided internally, particularly in recent years on the Republican side. These internal factional disputes, despite being confined within the two-party system, have already made governing substantially more difficult. Yet, as riven by conflict as the two major parties are at the moment, at least their quarrels take place within the two-party system, in which fellow party members have strong incentives to pull together.

Imagine if each party were split, as PR advocates would prefer, into three parties, generating a six-party Congress. First, there would be the issue of electing a Speaker of the House, through a majority vote of the whole chamber. This is not equivalent to forming a government in a parliamentary system, but it would be similar to forming a majority for the purpose of legislating. Now envision having to cobble together majority coalitions on specific policy issues in the likely event that no one party controls the chamber. Under these circumstances, each party would be incentivized to try to expand its base of support by making strategic judgments about whether being part of a majority coalition or refusing to go along on specific issues would be more likely to improve its electoral prospects. Each party would likely have its own red lines on what compromises it would refuse to make, lest it undermine its appeal to core supporters.

In addition to the possibility that such an arrangement could make Congress even more dysfunctional, at least two other potential drawbacks of the way multiparty systems function must be considered. First, as Frances Rosenbluth and Ian Shapiro document in *Responsible Parties: Saving Democracy from Itself*,[29] a significant cost of cobbling together governing majorities, particularly amid party proliferation, is that doing so frequently requires buying off smaller parties with policy concessions (or the provision of legislative pork, as in Brazil). Smaller parties represent, by definition, smaller segments of the electorate. Buying their support with policy concessions typically weakens aggregate social welfare, since their demands usually lack majority support. Voters also often perceive these payoffs to smaller parties as a form of vote buying, which fuels a sense that the political system is corrupt. A degree of this does take place in a two-party system, where parties must sometimes logroll between their factions, but the policy price is typically lower because these factions still retain a shared interest in the party's success. Rosenbluth and Shapiro's book is an extended analysis of why systems with two strong political parties (or two stable political coalitions in unfragmented PR systems) are more likely to enhance social welfare than fragmented PR systems of five or six parties.

A second consequence of PR is that it enables voters to remain ensconced in much smaller, ideologically narrow parties than in a two-party system. Committed environmentalists can silo themselves in a green party; other voters, in a socialist party or evangelical party, and so on. Voters can therefore remain more purist in their party affiliations and have to compromise less on the candidates for whom they vote. The process of negotiating, compromising, and bargaining among competing interests takes place largely among party leaders, after elections (or when party coalitions are formed in advance). This is an elite-driven practice of democracy.

In FPTP elections, by contrast, more of that process takes place among voters themselves; in deciding whether to support Bernie Sanders or Joe Biden in a Democratic primary, for example, a socialist voter has incentives to take into account which candidate has the broadest electoral appeal and would thus be more competitive in the general election. Much of the motivation for adopting PR among advocates is to end our tribalistic politics, but would enabling voters to sort themselves into narrower, more ideologically "pure" parties really diminish tribalism?

This chapter is not meant as a comprehensive critique of proposals for a PR House. It is intended merely to express our skepticism and to raise the major concerns we have about such a change. Any consideration of a shift to MMDs for the House must contend with the range and magnitude of the changes that would need to accompany this shift, including to the connection between representatives and constituents, to the size of the House, and to the way we vote. In addition, to the extent the principal justification for this transformation is that our FPTP election system is the primary cause of our current tribalistic and toxic political culture, we have doubts about that claim. Most fundamentally, we are concerned, based partly on the experience of Western democracies over the last decade or so, that a five- or six-party House would make the political process even more dysfunctional than it has been in recent years. Because inability to deliver effective government is driving the current crisis of democracy, we would not support a shift to MMDs and PR for Congress absent a convincing demonstration that such a shift would make the political process function more effectively rather than, as we fear, making it even more difficult for government to deliver on the issues citizens care most urgently about.

States are free to adopt MMDs and PR for their state legislatures, subject to compliance with federal constitutional requirements and statutory ones, such as the Voting Rights Act. If there is to be experimentation with such systems, they should begin at the state level.

To ease toxic polarization at the national level, we believe there is greater promise in replacing the traditional party primary with all-candidate, nonparty primaries (as outlined in Chapter 5), combined with various forms of instant-runoff voting (as discussed in Chapter 2). The traditional party primary makes it too easy for extreme or factional candidates to win office even when they lack the support of electoral majorities. These reforms to the structure of primaries and voting rules would enhance the prospects of candidates who do have majority support among the general electorate. These reforms also represent a more incremental, state-by-state approach and hence embody a more prudential form of experimentation. They might or might not substantially reduce polarization and extremism, but they also do not pose the risk that PR does of a national change that might make Congress more dysfunctional and would be difficult to undo. And in contrast to PR, these reforms might realistically be adopted by more US states in the coming decade. Whatever PR's merits, there is little practical prospect of the system becoming our method for electing members of Congress anytime soon. For those who believe the need for political reform is urgent to diminish extremism and polarization in our national politics, we cannot afford to wait for the day Congress might adopt PR, even if that were a desirable reform path.

An Additional Note on "Self-Districting" by Edward B. Foley

My views on proportional representation lie between those expressed in Chapters 3 and 4. I am skeptical that PR can be a panacea in the United States for the problems of polarization and extremism. Because neither the Senate nor the presidency is susceptible to PR, and even the House of Representatives is only partially susceptible to it since twenty-one states have four or fewer representatives, I believe that the most effective way to combat polarization and extremism will be through the adoption of nonpartisan primaries of the type now used in Alaska and California and a general election conducted according to a "Condorcet-consistent" method (as described in Chapter 2).

Nonetheless, I'm not as wary of PR as the contributors to Chapter 4 are. I believe it would be very valuable for states to experiment with various forms of PR for at least one of their legislative chambers. With states serving as they are supposed to as laboratories of democracy, the nation as a whole can beneficially learn from this experimentation. Even with respect to the US House of Representatives, I am not averse to experimenting with PR, although I would not support a federal statute to mandate PR.

Instead, I would encourage states to consider adopting a form of PR that I call "self-districting" in which voters themselves choose their district for purposes of representation. Because it is consistent with the single-member district requirement of current federal law, self-districting would not require any congressional legislation. States already have the power under Article I, § 4 of the Constitution to adopt this form of PR for their delegations to the House if they wish.

Moreover, I believe that self-districting is the form of PR most consistent with traditional American electoral practices and thus would be most agreeable to Americans if proposed as a ballot initiative. In a self-districting system, each voter would be a resident of a single specific congressional district, which would be represented by a single representative in the House. Thus, self-districting preserves the direct constituent-representative relationship that is so important to Americans, including for reasons of constituent service. Moreover, in a self-districting system, each voter in a regular general election gets to vote for which of several candidates on the ballot they want to be their representative. Consequently, self-districting also preserves the direct electoral connection between voters and their chosen representative that is so important to Americans' understanding of self-government.

What makes self-districting a form of PR is the method by which voters choose what electoral constituency, or district, they wish to be represented in. Because each self-selected constituency must have an equal number of voters, in order to comply with the constitutional principle of "one person, one vote," a constituency that attracts enough voters through the self-selection process for two or more districts will be allocated the number of districts that is in proportion to its share of the state's citizen voting-age population. If a state implements a self-districting system, political parties will compete for the allegiance of citizens in the state, just as they would in any other form of PR system, and these parties would control a share of seats in proportion to their share of the votes.

I have discussed the details of the self-districting system elsewhere, both in longer and shorter works.[30] I need not repeat those details here. Readers of this book interested in learning those details can find those other texts online (free of charge).

To be clear, I do not propose self-districting as a remedy for polarization or extremism. But I do not believe this system would exacerbate those problems in the United States, especially if a Condorcet-compliant form of ranked-choice voting were used to elect the single representative from each district. While it is foreseeable that a party espousing extremist views, such as election-denialist authoritarianism, would win a share of seats in a self-districting system—as it likely would under any districting system when a majority of voters in some districts hold such views—an extremist party could not gain control of Congress as long as these extremist views did not become the majority position statewide in any state (or at least not in a majority of congressional districts nationwide).

The benefits of a self-districting system, as I see it, lie in other features. First and foremost, self-districting entirely eliminates the problem of partisan gerrymandering because voters, and not the government, determine what districts the voters are in. In a self-districting system, the political parties are downstream, not upstream, of the districting system—or, if one prefers, the parties are servants of the districting choices made by voters, not the masters of the districting choices to which the voters must be supplicants.

Second, and almost as important, self-districting eliminates the difficult role that race currently plays in US districting decisions. In a self-districting system, the voters themselves decide whether they wish to make race a factor in their own districting decisions. And because this is a personal, not a governmental choice, it raises none of the constitutional difficulties that race-based districting by the government does. Moreover, because voters are empowered to make this choice themselves, they can avoid the problem of race-based vote dilution: if they wish, members of racial minorities can guarantee themselves a number of seats in proportion to their share of the population.

Finally, self-districting is in keeping with the American tradition of personal autonomy and individual empowerment. The American spirit of self-government is to let citizens control their own destinies insofar as possible. Self-districting is the method of districting that does this to the maximum extent feasible. Thus, I would encourage states to pursue PR and, in doing so, to consider self-districting as the form most suitable for the United States.

Notes

1. The material in this statement consists of excerpts taken from Richard H. Pildes, "Skepticism About Proportional Representation for Congress," *Illinois Law Review* (forthcoming 2024).

2. Scholars for Redistricting Reform, "Letter to Congress on Ending Single Member Congressional Districts and Adopting Proportional Representation," *Medium*, September 19, 2022.

3. "H.R. 3863—Fair Representation Act, 117th Congress (2021–2022)," Congress .gov.

4. There are two different methods for establishing the election threshold under STV. The Hare formula makes the election quota total votes/total seats. If this approach were used, the minimal threshold would be 20 percent in a five-member district. The Droop formula makes the quota total votes/(total seats + 1) + 1. For various reasons, most experts consider the Droop method the better one, and the STV systems in use in other countries use the Droop quota. Dylan Difford, "Hare vs Droop: How to Set the Quota Under STV," Electoral Reform Society, August 10, 2021. For five seats, the Droop method means dividing the number of votes by one-sixth (or 16.6 percent), then adding one to the total. That's where the 17 percent figure derives from. For an explanation and demonstration of this process for a general audience, see "How Proportional RCV Works," at "Proportional RCV Information," FairVote.

5. James Adams, Jane Green, and Caitlin Milazzo, "Has the British Public Depolarized Along with Political Elites," *Comparative Political Studies* 4, no. 4 (2012): 507–530.

6. Janan Ganesh, "Britain Is Europe's Haven from the Hard Right," *Financial Times*, October 3, 2023.

7. Janan Ganesh, "Britain Is Europe's Haven from the Hard Right," *Financial Times*, October 3, 2023.

8. See Levi Boxell, Matthew Gentzkow, and Jesse M. Shapiro, "Cross-Country Trends in Affective Polarization," *Review of Economics and Statistics*, January 25, 2022, 1–60.

9. Noam Gidron, James Adams, and Will Horne, *American Affective Polarization in Comparative Perspective* (Cambridge: Cambridge University Press, 2020), 70.

10. See Richard H. Pildes, "The Neglected Value of Effective Government," NYU School of Law, Public Law Research Paper No. 23-51, *University of Chicago Legal Forum* 2023, article 8 (2024): 185–210.

11. For example, the references in Chapter 3 to how well these systems satisfy median voter preferences all date to well before the past decade.

12. Alan Siaroff, "Two-and-a-Half-Party Systems and the Comparative Role of the 'Half,'" *Party Politics* 9, no. 3 (2003): 267–290.

13. Jonathan Hopkin, *Anti-system Politics* (Cambridge: Cambridge University Press, 2022), 3 (describing the rise of a "xenophobic Right and the anti-capitalist Left as part of a common global trend: anti-system politics").

14. See Richard H. Pildes, "Political Fragmentation in the Democracies of the West," *Brigham Young University Journal of Public Law* 37 (2023): 209–245; Richard H. Pildes, "Democracies in the Age of Fragmentation," *California Law Review* 110 (2022): 2051–2092.

15. "Effective Number of Parties," Wikipedia.

16. Aiko Wagner, "Party System Change in Eastern and Western Germany Between Convergence and Dissimilarity," *German Politics* 32 (2023); "Effective Number of Parties," Wikipedia.

17. Unless otherwise noted, the facts in this paragraph are taken from Richard H. Pildes, "Political Fragmentation in the Democracies of the West," *Brigham Young University Journal of Public Law* 37 (2023): 217.

18. Stefan Wagstyl, Guy Chazan, and Tobias Buck, "Merkel Wins Fourth Term but Far-Right Populists Make Gains," *Financial Times*, September 25, 2017.

19. Stefan Wagstyl, Guy Chazan, and Tobias Buck, "Merkel Wins Fourth Term but Far-Right Populists Make Gains," *Financial Times*, September 25, 2017.

20. "What Lies Ahead for Germany's Coalition Government," *Rane*, December 23, 2022; Sarah Marsh, "German Coalition, Beset by Crises, Could Get More Fractious After Vote," *Reuters*, October 10, 2022.

21. Rebecca Staudenmaier and Sabine Kinkartz, "Satisfaction in German Government Plummets," *DW*, September 1, 2023; see also Joseph de Weck, "Germany Is No Longer Exceptional," *The Atlantic*, July 22, 2023: "The three parties in Scholz's ruling coalition . . . squabble over everything, including whether to ban gas heating systems, how to deal with China, and whether to raise the child-benefits system. The result is neither calm nor order, at a time when inflation and the energy crisis are already destabilizing life in Germany."

22. Rebecca Staudenmaier and Sabine Kinkartz, "Satisfaction in German Government Plummets," *DW*, September 1, 2023.

23. Rebecca Staudenmaier and Sabine Kinkartz, "Satisfaction in German Government Plummets," *DW*, September 1, 2023.

24. Rebecca Staudenmaier and Sabine Kinkartz, "Satisfaction in German Government Plummets," *DW*, September 1, 2023.

25. One could quibble with the case selection, but even though Japan, Korea and Taiwan have PR components to their electoral systems, they function in mainly majoritarian fashion, as their low effective number of parties indicates, and the Australian lower house of parliament is single-member-district (using RCV). The seven PR systems include two of the most successful Scandinavian countries, so we are not trying to bias the sample.

26. Data on the percentile rankings come from the World Bank's Worldwide Governance Indicators; "Effective Number of Parties," Wikipedia.

27. Despite survey data showing voters in these countries responding with significant levels of satisfaction with government see "Democracy," at https://europa .eu/eurobarometer/surveys/detail/2966), the actual revealed behavior of these voters in elections shows continual dissatisfaction, which has driven the rise of new, insurgent parties and rapid decline in support of the traditional major parties and coalitions.

28. Martin Sandbu, "Europe's Cordon Sanitaire Against the Far Right May Not Work," *Financial Times*, June 30, 2024.

29. Ian Shapiro and Frances Rosenbluth, *Responsible Parties: Saving Democracy from Itself* (New Haven, CT: Yale University Press, 2018).

30. Edward B. Foley, "Self-Districting: The Ultimate Antidote to Gerrymandering," *Kentucky Law Journal* 111 (2023): 693, https://dx.doi.org/10.2139/ssrn .4328642; Edward B. Foley, "Self-Districting Solves the Problem of the Supreme Court's South Carolina Case," *Common Ground Democracy*, May 24, 2024.

5

Primary Elections

Robert G. Boatright

This chapter considers options for reforming primary elections. We have taken the existence of primaries as a given and assumed that political parties will continue to play some role in determining how primaries are conducted in most states. We do not mean to suggest that discussion of more radical restructurings of American elections, such as creating nonpartisan primaries or abolishing primaries altogether, should be considered out of bounds. However, each of us has some interest or expertise in the development of primary elections over the past century, and we have therefore sought to explore what improvements are possible within the framework of the contemporary system.

A defining feature of the early years of the American direct primary (the era between roughly 1900 and 1920) is the primary's overwhelming popularity. Once primaries were introduced, it became very hard for states to do away with them. There is some debate about when the first primaries were used; several states or local jurisdictions experimented with them during the late nineteenth century.[1] Statewide mandatory primaries were first adopted in Minnesota and Wisconsin during the first decade of the twentieth century, and by 1917 they were used in all but three states. They spread so rapidly in part because proponents argued they were more democratic and less corrupt than other means of choosing nominees.[2] They also spread because, even though they appeared to

---

Sunshine Hillygus, Ray La Raja, Seth Masket, Hans Noel, and Caroline Tolbert contributed substantially to this chapter. Research assistance was provided by Nathan Micatka and Sarah Kersting-Mumm.

be a major step toward democracy and away from the rule of party bosses, primaries were not in practice a substantial threat to political parties, which quickly learned to use primary rules to their advantage.[3] Every time a state moved to abandon the primary, it was quickly reinstated, either by a party or through an initiative or referendum process.[4] Today, every state uses some sort of primary.

This poses a dilemma. We agree that there are pathologies to the contemporary direct primary (used to choose nominees directly, as opposed to the delegate-selection primaries used to pick presidents). As early as the first decade of the 1900s, political scientists such as Henry Jones Ford warned that primaries would weaken parties, reward demagoguery, produce extreme or unrepresentative nominees, and ultimately reduce citizens' involvement in democratic politics.[5] These things have all come to pass: the power of party elites is weaker than at any point in the past century, parties are more polarized than at any point since the advent of the direct primary, and many of the most prominent members of Congress are known less for their legislative accomplishments than for their ability to stoke outrage. We would not necessarily argue that primaries are the principal cause of these problems, but they certainly bear some of the blame.

However, it has taken over a century for Ford's predictions to come true, and primary elections have become an entrenched part of the American political system. Given the popularity of the concept of primaries and the widespread public perception that they are the most democratic way to winnow the field of candidates prior to the general election, we believe our greatest contribution can be to focus on what is politically feasible in the short run. Accordingly, in this chapter we limit ourselves to considering how changes to the primary, short of abolition, might mitigate some of the ills about which Ford was so concerned.

Goals and Definitions

Before presenting our findings, it is important to clarify our goals. We would argue that there are four goals at stake in any proposed reform to the direct primary.

1. *Electing competent leaders who are representative of the general public:* The reader will note that there are in fact two considerations here: candidate quality should matter, but candidates should also reflect

the issue preferences, ideological positions, and perhaps other descriptive characteristics of the electorate.

2. *Reducing ideological extremity:* We acknowledge that there will be variations in voter preferences across states or districts, so the extremity of candidates chosen in primaries will likely be relative to the extremity of their districts. Such variation, if it is a problem, might be addressed through changes to legislative apportionment and redistricting, through the establishment of multimember districts, or even through resizing of the House or Senate, but such considerations fall outside our mandate. Nevertheless, certain reforms of direct primaries—such as the introduction of ranked-choice voting (RCV), open primaries, or nonpartisan primaries—may reduce the ideological extremity of candidates. (See Chapter 2 on ballot structures for further discussion of this point.)

3. *Increasing voter turnout in primaries:* Although primary turnout will often vary depending on the level of competition or the particular offices up for election in a given year, we generally believe that increasing voter turnout will improve the representativeness of candidates and increase public support for the political process.

4. *Giving voters (including independents) more choice in the selection of nominees:* While we support giving parties some role in the primary process, we believe that increasing voter choice in primaries will also increase public support for parties and the political system.

These goals are all related. We presume, for instance, that an increase in voter turnout will, beyond a certain point, lead to more representative nominees, and we presume that, for the most part, more representative nominees will be less ideologically extreme. There are mathematical questions about whether this is necessarily so, but we contend that there is ample evidence to support these assumptions.

It is also important to be clear about how we define extremism. As Table 5.1 (adapted from Cynthia Miller-Idriss's work) notes, there are three commonly used definitions of political extremism and three types of responses to it.[6] Extremism can be defined as a matter of ideology, which is to some extent a relative matter and will always be present within an electorate or an elected body; it can be seen as a matter of anti-democratic or antisystem ideas; and it can be seen as a matter of uncivil or excessively confrontational behavior, rhetoric, and actions.

Most of the research on primaries since the early 2000s has considered the relationship between primary elections and political polarization; that is, it has considered extremism only in the ideological sense.

Table 5.1   Types of and Responses to Extremism

Types of Extremism

1	Empirical	Defined relative to the status quo; no normative assessment of context. Some amount of extremism will likely always exist.
2	Normative	Defined based on content; includes antidemocratic attitudes or hostile or violent attitudes toward others.
3	Behavioral	Defined based on mode of presentation; includes uncivil and confrontational behavior, rhetoric, and actions; normative assessment of tactics but not necessarily of ideas expressed.

Responses to Extremism

A	Environmental	Prevent or minimize factors that cause extremism
B	Therapeutic	Treat symptoms of extremism
C	Platform based	Prevent the spread of extremist ideas

Historically, however, primary elections, particularly in the segregation-era South, have been associated with a sort of demagoguery and extremism that has little to do with ideology. We see it as part of our task to move the discussion away from a narrow focus on ideology and toward a broader discussion of whether electoral reforms can mitigate antisystem rhetoric or behavioral extremism.

The Standard Tools Don't Matter

We have reached a consensus about what doesn't work. The history of primary reform is a history of futility. The past century is replete with efforts to make primaries more or less open, earlier or later, or easier or harder to participate in. Figure 5.1 (adapted from Rob Boatright's work) shows that during the four decades after the establishment of direct primaries, an average of three to four states enacted changes to their primaries each legislative cycle. Black bars in this figure represent the number of states making rule changes per year; gray bars represent the average direction of reform—whether it was an "open" reform (coded as positive) that expanded citizen participation or a "closed" one that restricted citizen participation (coded as negative). Most of the narrower reform ideas under discussion today have been attempted in the past, with no obvious pattern or clear results. The main conclusion one might

Figure 5.1   Primary Law Changes, 1928–1970

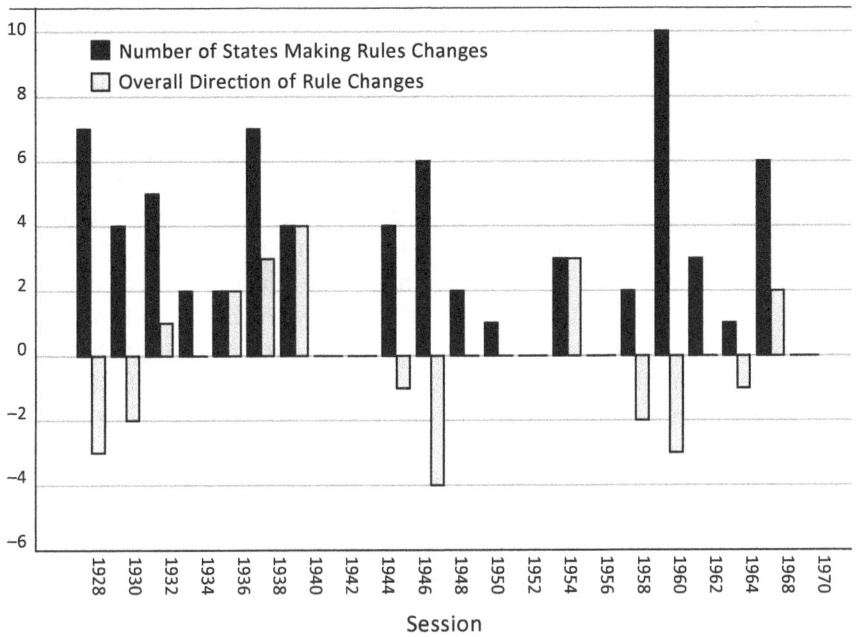

draw from these reforms is that politicians and political parties have a history of manipulating primary rules for short-term advantage, using specious normative claims.

This history suggests we should be cautious about proposing reforms that have been tried in the past.[7] Too often, these reforms have been implemented by politicians seeking short-term gain, and they have had minimal consequences. In addition, we have reached the following conclusions about how reforms adopted in the past might relate to contemporary political problems.

Most Primary Reforms Adopted in the Past Would Not Have Major Effects on Polarization

Many claims have been made in the media or by reform advocates about the effects of party primaries over the past twenty years. Most of these claims have been about congressional primaries, and most have had to do with how primaries are said to exacerbate polarization in Congress. The evidence for these claims is mixed. For instance:

- It has been argued that primary electorates are ideologically extreme, composed of strong liberals and strong conservatives. Survey evidence on primary electorates has been elusive, however. Some studies of Democratic and Republican primary voters have found little ideological difference between them and Democratic and Republican voters in general elections, while others have found evidence that primary voters are more extreme than the full electorate (including nonvoters). There is little consensus in this literature about what a substantial difference would be or what the relevant comparison group is. We do know that primary voters are different from general election voters in other ways (such as age, income, race, political knowledge, and so forth), and we have evidence that many candidates *believe* the primary electorate to be more extreme than it is in fact.[8] Some recent studies have focused on subtler differences, such as voters' preference for candidates who will seek compromise.[9]

- It has been argued for decades that open primaries (in which any registered voter can cast a ballot for a candidate of either party) produce less ideologically extreme or more representative nominees than closed primaries (where participation is limited to registered party members and voters can only choose among the candidates of their party). There is again little evidence to support this claim, and some have argued that the relationship is in fact the reverse.[10] To be clear, open primaries, which choose a party's nominee, are different from nonpartisan primaries that advance candidates to a general election regardless of party affiliation. Therefore, the evidence that open primaries do not effectively reduce extremism has no bearing on the potential of nonpartisan primaries, such as Alaska's "top-four" system, to do the same.

- People have also argued for over a century about when primaries should be held. Some contend that staging them closer to the general election will produce higher turnout (and hence a more representative electorate) while others argue the reverse. There is no strong evidence that it matters either way; contemporary scholarship suggests that primary timing has a minimal effect if other things are held constant.[11]

- Several studies have also addressed the perception that incumbent moderates have increasingly been challenged in primaries. Boatright argued in 2013 that there was little evidence to support this claim at that time, although his more recent work has found that moderate Republicans are indeed increasingly challenged in primaries.[12] In *Rejecting Compromise: Legislators' Fear of Primary Voters*, Sarah Anderson, Daniel Butler, and Laurel Harbridge-Yong have persuasively argued that what matters is perception: incumbents preemptively change their positions because they perceive they will be challenged.[13] Donald Trump has made effective use of this type of threat, boasting about eliminating through primary challenges Republican incumbents he believes to be insufficiently committed to his "MAGA" movement. Consequently, the fear of drawing a primary challenge from a Trump-endorsed opponent has been offered as an explanation for why so many Republican incumbents have embraced Trump's claims that the 2020 presidential election was stolen even though they did not believe those claims themselves.

There is more work to be done on these issues, but the conclusion we draw is that more modest primary reforms don't really make a difference. If there is a problem, it is with the primary itself, and that is harder to fix short of abolition.

Changing Primary Laws May Not Address Problems Manifested in Primaries

Some of us are skeptical that primary elections are the major driver of polarization or the rise of political extremism. Some problems are manifested differently in primary elections than they are in general elections. For instance, changes in campaign finance laws and practices have affected primaries differently than they have general elections. In an era of high political polarization where voters see partisanship as a social identity, voters will respond to party cues in general elections. But such cues are absent in partisan primaries, and voters may therefore be susceptible to appeals based on ideology or candidate traits. Knowing this, interest groups and factional movements (including the MAGA movement loosely connected to Trump) may adopt different strategies in primary elections than in general elections.[14] If one is concerned about such activities, changing campaign finance law may be one appropriate response.

Similar arguments may be made about other activities that take place in primaries. Elections are integrated systems, where redistricting laws, voter-access laws, election administration, campaign finance, and other laws interact with primary election laws. Changing primary election laws while leaving all of these other things constant may therefore not have an impact on polarization or extremism.

National-Level Primary Reform May Be Difficult to Achieve

The federal government has historically shown limited interest in changing primary election laws. Although Congress and the national parties have the power to formally or informally influence how state primaries are conducted, the most likely venue for reform is at the state level and, in some cases, within state political parties. As noted above (and shown in Figure 5.1), states have changed primary laws repeatedly, sometimes for idiosyncratic reasons, sometimes out of broader normative concerns—for instance, to increase participation or make nominees more representative. These changes have not always had lasting results.

Efforts to influence primaries often interact with aspects of state political culture. Some reforms may have a short-term effect on candidate emergence or voting behavior, but these effects may dissipate over time. This does not mean that reforms are not worthwhile, but we are wary of the consequences of mobilizing the public around reforms that will not bear fruit or of the possibility that (as was arguably the case with the introduction of primaries in the first place) reforms that have negative consequences may prove "sticky" and be difficult to repeal.[15]

Despite these qualifications, we note that analyses of polarization and extremism frequently discuss primaries, and many extant reform proposals are framed with reference to polarization or extremism.[16] This means two things. First, reforms will happen regardless of whether there is any national consensus or movement in favor of them. We should therefore endeavor to prevent such reforms from making matters worse and ensure that we know how to measure their results as effectively as possible. And second, the problems of polarization and extremism are substantial enough that we should be open to changes even without complete certainty about whether primaries are the cause of these phenomena. We should also be open to the possibility that short-term changes may be valuable even if in the long run the political system adapts and the effects of reforms decay.[17]

What Might Work

There are three principal ways in which primaries *might* produce unrepresentative or extreme nominees; we offer our reform proposals with reference to the subject areas around them.

1. *Barriers to voting:* If voter turnout is low or unrepresentative of the state or district electorate, the nominee might therefore not be representative of the voting population in terms of ideology or other relevant characteristics. This may be a particular concern in areas dominated by one party.

2. *The selection mechanism:* Primaries may produce candidates who win multicandidate races with a plurality but not a majority of the vote. Such candidates may again not be representative of the electorate, and they might have lost to one or more of the other candidates in a head-to-head matchup.

3. *The role of parties:* It has been shown that parties can winnow the field so that the two problems outlined above are less consequential; they can do so by reducing the number of viable candidates or by making their own preferences clear.[18] This power can be abused, but when parties use it judiciously, they can reduce extremism. Parties vary across states in their ability to do this, and some scholars have argued that parties have generally grown less able to shape the candidate pool. However, partisan primaries may still produce ideologically unrepresentative nominees even when parties are functioning well. Polarized parties may produce nominees who do not reflect the median voter of the full electorate, and if parties lack the ability or the desire to limit who can enter primaries, candidates (particularly incumbents) may adopt ideologically extreme positions to ward off primary challenges.

There are many arguments both for and against reforms within each of these areas, and their normative implications are not necessarily limited to addressing extremism. In the discussion below, we address possible reforms in each of these domains, by discussing what political scientists know about them, what we still need to find out, and what changes would address problems. We propose that reforms in each area map onto the goals outlined above in the manner illustrated in Table 5.2.

Turnout and Representation

What we know. Turnout in state-level primaries has increased since 2016, but it is still extremely low. According to an estimate by the

Table 5.2   Effects of Different Types of Primary Election Reforms

	Elect Competent Leaders	Reduce Ideological Extremity	Increase Turnout	Increase Voter Choice
Reduce barriers to voting		+	+	
Change selection mechanism		+	+/−	+
Change (increase) role of parties	+	+	+/−	−

Bipartisan Policy Center, 21.3 percent of eligible voters participated in the 2022 midterm primaries.[19] Figure 5.2 shows turnout in congressional primaries in nonpresidential years since 1930, drawn from reports from the Center for the Study of the American Electorate (1930–2012) and the Bipartisan Policy Center (2014–2022).[20] Primary turnout fluctuates wildly across jurisdictions, such that candidates winning House primaries often do so with the support of less than 10 percent of the electorate. Primary turnout in the House also tends to be driven by the elections at the top of the ticket: by concurrent presidential primaries, ballot initiatives, or other competitive statewide primaries.[21] Fluctuations resulting from these factors tend to swamp any swings that might result from primary type or timing, although it is hard to separate these factors from other characteristics of state party culture.

As discussed above, we also know that the voters who participate in partisan primaries are not representative of the overall electorate. Some studies show that the primary electorate is older, whiter, wealthier, and more conservative than the population as a whole, but other studies conclude that the ideological views of primary voters differ little from those of voters who support their party's nominee in the general election.[22] We know that the composition of the primary electorate varies from

Figure 5.2   Congressional Primary Turnout in Midterm Election Years, 1930–2022

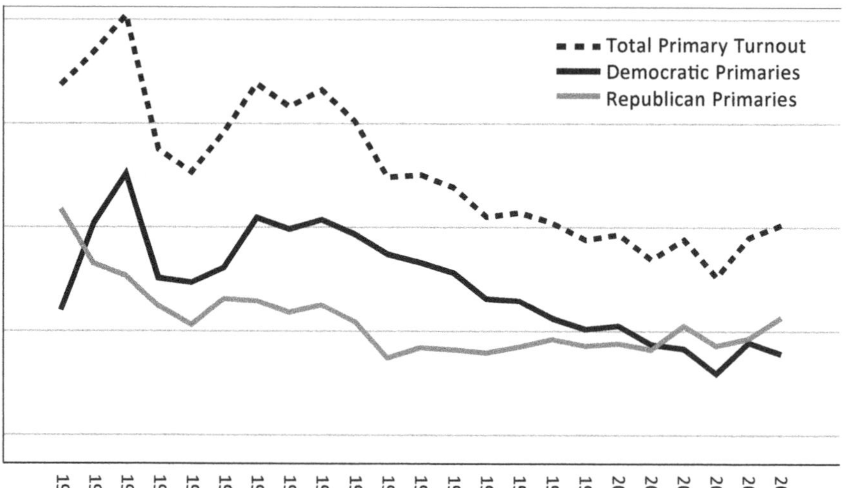

year to year and from state to state, depending on the nature of the races on the ballot.

There have been major advances in studying primary voters in recent years. While we once knew next to nothing about the national primary electorate, we now have the ability to make precise claims about who votes based on the full voter file as opposed to survey samples (thanks to the Cooperative Election Study [CES] and Catalist data made available for academic use). As part of this book project, we have begun our own research on primary voters. Table 5.3 shows our estimates of some important characteristics of the congressional primary electorate over the past three midterm elections (characteristics are harder to estimate for presidential election years) using a Catalist national voter file built from the fifty state voter files and augmented with commercial and campaign data. This table shows that conservative voters are more likely to take part in primaries, a finding that has no consistent correlate in general elections. If conservatives are more likely to vote in primaries, there is a risk that this will skew Republican primaries to the right. But the extent of this skew depends on how fractured the Republican field is and whether this rise in conservative turnout is a national phenomenon or confined to particular areas of the country. Liberal voters are also more likely to vote in Democratic primaries than are more moderate Democrats, but this tendency was less pronounced in 2014 and 2018. The primary electorate also tends to be older, whiter, and wealthier than the general electorate—in line with the studies we mentioned above. As turnout increased between 2014 and 2022, these gaps narrowed slightly among primary voters.

Four states currently hold nonpartisan primaries, and two employ a variant of ranked-choice voting. In most cases, these systems are new enough or the states idiosyncratic enough that it is hard to draw firm conclusions or generalize from their election results, especially regarding voter turnout. Research on California's nonpartisan primary has been mixed but tends to show it encourages more moderate candidates. Studies of the nonpartisan primary in Washington have tended to minimize its impact. And the few studies of Louisiana's much older nonpartisan primary system have concluded that the system encourages moderation.[23]

Alaska's system, which includes both a nonpartisan primary and a ranked-choice general election that can feature multiple candidates of the same party, is the subject of several recent research projects. Some of these projects have touted ways that the system can advantage more broadly popular and less ideologically extreme candidates.[24]

Alaska saw heightened voter turnout in its 2022 primary, but this shift could have stemmed from the novelty of the system or the fact that a special election for the House took place the same day. Although many candidates were eliminated in the House and Senate primaries, very few candidates were eliminated in the state's legislative primaries. Some analyses of the 2022 election have drawn on the state legislative results to argue that nonpartisan "top-four" primaries will (by design) serve a very different function than primaries that result in candidate nominations.

Finally, even though Table 5.3 shows that the primary electorate became slightly more representative as turnout increased, we should be cautious about always assuming that any increase in voter turnout is beneficial for representation. We know that increased primary turnout is associated with the nomination of more moderate legislators among Democrats, but there is no similar relationship among Republicans.[25] Studies of very low-turnout races at the municipal level show that when turnout is below 10 or 15 percent, for instance, small increases can make the representation problem worse. This is not the case when the starting point is 40 percent or higher,[26] which indicates that turnout is much more strongly affected by preference intensity in low-turnout races. Merely relying on candidate- or party-driven efforts to increase turnout will not necessarily increase representation.

What we need to know. Given the overrepresentation of ideologically extreme voters in the primary electorate, increasing primary turnout could be one way to combat extremism. But if we are seeking to increase primary turnout, we need to know what the advantage of doing so would be beyond merely involving more people in the political process. This means we need to be able to say more about the primary electorate, beyond ideology or demographics. We support efforts to survey primary voters on topics that go beyond demographics, ideology, or partisanship.[27] More research in this area will help us know what to expect if turnout increases and to identify any potential trade-offs associated with such a shift.

National data on the characteristics of primary voters can be misleading, because primary elections do not take place at the national level but rather feature fifty different state electorates. Thus, it is also important to understand the effect that political competition and individual candidates have on primary voter turnout. Consider Table 5.4 on midterm election year primaries in Ohio since 2014, which shows that the electorate varies substantially from one primary to the next.

Table 5.3 Percentage of Voters by Demographic Groups in the 2014, 2018, and 2022 Congressional Primaries

	Voted 2014 (%)	Voted 2018 (%)	Voted 2022 (%)
Age			
Below 25	5.03	6.37	8.17
25–39	5.71	8.65	10.20
40–54	12.33	14.44	16.24
55–73	25.16	26.04	28.71
73+	12.59	23.23	24.38
White (non-Hispanic)	15.58	19.74	22.76
Black	9.39	13.03	12.55
Latino	8.30	9.30	9.35
Asian	10.67	11.34	13.03
Male	13.43	17.16	19.06
Female	13.83	17.59	19.44
College degree	18.65	22.35	25.96
No college degree	12.03	15.97	17.49
Conservative ideology	28.68	29.35	26.11
Moderate ideology	7.68	6.44	7.20
Liberal ideology	24.76	24.64	33.92
Republican	23.52	28.62	34.84
Democrat	18.64	23.08	23.57
Married	21.55	21.77	24.67
Not married	8.61	12.73	13.79
Income			
Less than $20,000	10.35	6.24	5.04
$20,000–$29,999[a]	13.11	9.67	9.21
$30,000–$49.999[a]	9.60	13.9	15.13
$50,000–$74,999[a]	16.51	19.86	22.36
$75,000–$99,999[a]	17.58	24.3	27.81
$100,000–$149,999[a]	18.03	27.28	31.46
$150,000 and above[a]	19.82	31.91	35.60

Notes: Percentages shown are the "yes" responses for each category; they should not sum to 100 across category types (e.g., we are showing that 26.11 percent of conservatives voted in the 2022 primary, not that 26.11 percent of 2022 primary voters were conservative). Data drawn from 2015, 2020, and 2023 1 percent Catalist file, national voter file, administrative data.

a. For 2014, income categories are: under $20,000; $20,000–$39,999; $40,000–$59,999; $60,000–$79,999; $80,000–$99,999; $100,000–$119,999; and $120,000+.

Although Ohio leans slightly Republican, Republicans are substantially more likely to vote in primaries than are Democrats—a tendency that contributes to making the primary electorate whiter and more conservative than the state as a whole. This imbalance, however, appears to be largely a product of heightened competition in Republican primaries:

Table 5.4   Percentage of Voters by Demographic Groups in the 2014, 2018, and 2022 State Primaries in Ohio

	Voted 2014 (%)	Voted 2018 (%)	Voted 2022 (%)
Age:			
Below 25	3.18	5.17	6.87
25–39	3.53	6.03	8.07
40–54	9.42	11.74	14.29
55–73	20.83	24.56	29.00
73+	12.45	23.13	23.75
White (non–Hispanic)	11.94	16.94	20.11
Black	6.59	8.93	8.80
Latino	3.40	3.89	5.36
Asian	4.30	3.22	4.69
Male	10.95	15.88	18.86
Female	10.85	15.59	17.77
College degree	15.67	20.31	24.29
No college degree	9.75	14.66	16.92
Republican	23.16	28.40	39.06
Democrat	15.35	20.54	19.69
Conservative ideology	26.07	28.73	30.80
Moderate ideology	4.80	1.77	2.89
Liberal ideology	25.61	25.05	27.43
Married	18.00	20.78	24.76
Not married	6.03	10.04	11.06
Income:			
Less than $20,000	6.50	3.37	2.99
$20,000–$29,999[a]	10.53	7.00	7.24
$30,000–$49,999[a]	8.68	11.92	13.01
$50,000–$74,999[a]	14.17	19.66	22.50
$75,000–$99,999[a]	15.69	23.82	28.81
$100,000–$149,999[a]	15.17	25.68	31.27
$150,000 and above[a]	15.33	28.46	33.26
All	11.30	16.00	18.10

Notes: Percentages shown are the "yes" responses for each category; they should not sum to 100 across category types (e.g., we are showing that 26.07 percent of conservatives voted in the 2014 primary, not that 26.07 percent of 2022 primary voters were conservative). Data drawn from the 2015, 2020, and 2023 1 percent Catalist file, national voter file, administrative data.

a. For 2014, income categories are: under $20,000; $20,000–$39,999; $40,000–$59,999; $60,000–$79,999; $80,000–$99,999; $100,000–$119,999; $120,000+.

there was little competition in Democratic primaries for governor or senator in any of these years, while Republicans had a competitive gubernatorial primary in 2018 and a very competitive senate primary in 2022. Republicans, in other words, simply had more reason to vote than did Democrats.

Individual candidates may also have played a role in stimulating turnout in these elections. Such disparities spread across multiple states can influence what the primary electorate looks like at the national level in a given year, and they can ultimately lead to the nomination of candidates who are unrepresentative of their party. It seems problematic to us, however, to argue that there is a core primary electorate in either party, let alone to blame this phenomenon on characteristics of primary voters. According to our analysis of Catalist data, only 56.01 percent of 2022 primary voters voted in the 2018 primaries, and only 55.89 percent of 2018 primary voters voted in the 2014 primaries.[28] This is a substantial degree of churn from one election year to the next, and it cannot be explained solely by changes in competitiveness. It suggests that within states the characteristics of primary voters can change dramatically over time. It is therefore hard to make the case that any particular voting reform will change competition or outcomes in partisan primaries.

One conclusion we can draw, however, is that to make primary voters more representative of the general public, it would be necessary to attract voters who have little interest in the primaries themselves. Many citizens vote in general elections out of habit, out of commitment to the democratic process, or because they see differences between the parties but know little about the candidates. It is possible that such voters could improve the quality of primary campaigns or pull primary candidates away from the political extremes, but we are far from knowing how this might work.

Reforms that would increase turnout and representation. Below, we list some reforms that we believe are worth considering to increase turnout and representation:

1. *Encouraging states to cluster primaries:* There are many ways in which the number of different primary dates could be reduced. One way would be to hold more state primaries on the same day as presidential primaries. These concurrent primaries would increase turnout, but the turnout increase would depend on the competitiveness of the presidential primaries. Concurrent primaries could also potentially increase turnout in idiosyncratic ways—for instance, by drawing more voters who strongly support one of the presidential candidates but have little interest in down-ballot races. This arrangement would not necessarily have as great an impact on turnout in midterm election years as it would in presidential years, but it would still ultimately result in fewer primary election dates and thus might be an improvement on the status quo.

2. *Establishing a national congressional primary day:* If states were induced to hold primaries on a particular day, these elections would attract more media attention and therefore stand a better chance of turning out less attentive voters, even if their own primaries were not particularly competitive. We expect that this reform would increase turnout while at the same time making the primary electorate more representative. A same-day national primary would limit the ability of interest groups or other nonparty organizations to selectively target individual early primaries in order to shape the national narrative about a given year's elections, and thus there might be some support for this idea among incumbent legislators.[29] Such a system might resemble that of France, which holds primaries for all legislative seats simultaneously. The establishment of a national primary day would not necessarily influence the presidential primary calendar.

3. *Instituting compulsory voting:* Some democratic nations have compulsory voting, generally with the option of submitting a blank ballot. Such a policy would increase the size of the electorate, although it would be odd to push for compulsory voting in primaries before making the case for it in general elections. Any effort to establish compulsory voting would require that primaries first be made open or nonpartisan.[30]

4. *Holding nonpartisan primaries:* Because so few states have adopted nonpartisan primaries, we do not yet have definitive evidence that they would have a major impact on extremism. However, we have seen no empirical or theoretical evidence that nonpartisan primaries would increase extremism. We believe more state-level experimentation with nonpartisan primaries, such as those held in Alaska, would increase our understanding of their effects and help us determine whether and how they should be more broadly adopted. We note that some members of our task force feel strongly that this chapter should have made a stronger case for nonpartisan primaries. We explain our reluctance to do so in Appendix A.

5. *Encouraging use of RCV systems for primaries:* While we are unconvinced that ranked-choice voting will fundamentally change primaries, we are open to the possibility that it could. In theory, RCV might give candidates greater incentive to appeal to voters who are unlikely to rank them first on the ballot, thus reducing the possibility that candidates will only mobilize strong supporters. And using RCV in primaries would not require states to use it in the general election. In many states, parties could adopt RCV on an ad hoc basis, as was the case in the Virginia Republican gubernatorial primary in 2021.

6. *Making primaries optional:* Many studies of voter turnout contend that Americans are called upon to vote far more often than citizens of other democracies and that the frequency of elections reduces turnout. Allowing states or parties to cancel primaries if certain conditions are not met would enable voters to be called upon only when the stakes are higher—potentially increasing turnout and producing a less ideologically extreme electorate. Currently, some states hold primaries even when an office is uncontested; other states hold them for low-profile offices when races closer to the top of the ballot are uncontested or not seriously contested. Allowing for party conventions rather than primaries in such instances might improve the quality of nominees and save the activity of voting for more important moments.

7. *Deeming primary election wins valid only if a turnout threshold is met:* It is common in some elective bodies to consider a result binding only if, for instance, half of all eligible voters have cast ballots. We have not considered the details of how this might work—if a separate election would be required or if an alternate selection mechanism should be used when the threshold is not met.

These reforms have varying degrees of public support, both in terms of their overall popularity and their popularity within partisan groups. (We consider public opinion about primary reforms in more detail later in this chapter.) These reforms also vary in their current political feasibility, and in terms of whether responsibility for their implementation would reside with state governments, the federal government, or political parties.

The Selection Mechanism

What we know. It has long been established that multicandidate, plurality-winner elections lead to the selection of candidates who do not represent the median voter. In addition, the more ideologically distinct partisan electorates become, the less likely they are to choose nominees who represent the full electorate's median voter.[31] This is by no means a novel claim, but there are disputes about whether political parties have the ability to informally solve this problem or whether voters in fact vote strategically or mitigate the problem by voting on the basis of candidate traits other than ideology.[32] However, most recent studies of candidate selection indicate that party nominees have become less representative of their districts over the past two or three decades.[33]

We know as well that congressional elections featuring plurality winners are not uncommon. Over the past fifty years, an average of 11 percent of challenger primaries and 36 percent of open-seat primaries have been won with a plurality of the vote. Plurality primary winners performed slightly worse in general elections than nominees who received a majority of the primary vote. In other words, parties pay a penalty in the general election for selecting plurality winners in competitive districts. But the data suggest three reasons that extremism might still proliferate in uncompetitive districts. First, extreme candidates of the dominant party are at less of a disadvantage in the general election in these districts. Second, the fact that these districts are uncompetitive to begin with means that their degree of extremity relative to the statewide or nationwide electorate is already higher. And third, the value of the nomination in these districts is presumably greater because it is more likely to lead to a general election victory, so absent party intervention, more candidates will emerge in open-seat races in these districts. Formal or informal efforts to resolve multicandidate competition thus will lead to candidates with greater general election support, who will presumably be more representative of their districts.

What we need to know. Other than the evidence offered above, there is little data on what becomes of plurality primary winners.[34] Anecdotal stories abound of politicians who won their initial races for Congress with less than 50, 40, or even 30 percent of the vote. According to the nonpartisan electoral reform lobby group FairVote, six of the eight Republican House members who supported the motion to vacate against Speaker Kevin McCarthy in October 2023 initially won their primaries with less than a majority of the vote.[35] Then again, many long-serving members of Congress, including former Speaker Tip O'Neill, initially won their seats with a plurality of the vote. We do not know whether plurality winners perform worse over time. It is entirely possible that they become more representative or conventional or that they struggle to win future elections and ultimately lose their seats. It could also be that the incentive system in Congress used to pull ideologically extreme plurality winners toward the center but no longer does so. We also do not know whether plurality winners are more common in some places than others or whether they share any other features. Nonetheless, it is well established that divisive primaries can be problematic for political parties.[36] It is also easy to draw on anecdotal evidence to make the case that plurality winners can cause broader problems in terms of extremism or unrepresentativeness.

Reforms that would change the selection mechanism. Many of the proposals that would change the primary selection mechanism overlap with other categories of reform in that they would influence voter participation, change the role of parties in primaries, or offer parties more discretion in how to conduct primaries. We recognize that these reforms are part of a much larger debate about the appropriate role of parties in contemporary American politics and that the success of any of these reforms may depend in part on the health of the two major parties.

1. Requiring or allowing the use of RCV in primaries: As noted above, parties could be encouraged or required to use ranked-choice voting in primaries or otherwise allowed greater discretion in establishing primary rules.

2. Encouraging parties to hold preprimary conventions: These could be used to limit ballot access, endorse candidates before the primary, or engage in other winnowing procedures. Many states use such procedures today, and some case studies have shown that they can produce more moderate nominees.[37] However, party organizations can antagonize internal factions by playing a role in selecting candidates, and parties may therefore have good reason not to want this responsibility.

3. Expanding the use of runoff elections: Runoffs, currently used in ten states (all in the South), would solve the problem of plurality winners. But some studies have noted that runoffs can be expensive for jurisdictions and candidates and that voter turnout often declines between the initial primary and the runoff, thus introducing representation problems.[38]

4. Allowing or encouraging fusion balloting: Fusion balloting, currently used in New York, allows multiple nominations for the same candidate. That means a minor party can nominate the same candidate as the Democratic or Republican parties. Advocates of fusion balloting argue that it can enhance voter choice, improve voter knowledge about candidates on the ballot, and increase the power of minor parties while reducing the likelihood of their acting as "spoilers." However, in the 1997 case *Timmons v. Twin Cities Area New Party*, the Supreme Court permitted states to outlaw this practice.[39]

5. Eliminating sore loser laws: Sore loser laws, which prohibit defeated primary candidates from running as independent or third-party candidates in subsequent general elections, are currently used in forty-seven states.[40] Eliminating such laws can offer a path for defeated primary candidates to make their case to a broader electorate. For instance, if a moderate candidate is defeated in a party primary but has substantial support among independent or opposite-party voters or among voters who did not participate in the primary, he or she would have an alternate path to victory.

6. Requiring nonpartisan primaries: This is the lone selection-mechanism change that would explicitly limit party discretion. However, nonpartisan primaries can and have allowed parties to play a role in endorsing candidates, holding preprimary conventions, and developing criteria for how party labels will be used on the ballot.

As with the reforms aimed at improving turnout and representation discussed above, we offer these possible electoral changes not because all of us fully endorse them but because we see them as plausible responses to the problem of extremism. We also offer them without regard to their political feasibility or their popularity among voters or politicians.

Giving Parties More Power

What we know. Many histories of primary elections have argued that the leaders of national or state political party organizations have intervened, both formally and informally, in their party's primaries to increase the likelihood that party nominees will be strong general election candidates.[41] According to this argument, the problem of extreme candidates being nominated is a consequence not necessarily of primary election rules but of the declining ability of parties to influence primary results. One avenue for addressing extremism, then, would be to strengthen political parties.

For decades, political scientists have studied variations in levels of party organization across US states. Measures of party organization and party culture created in the 1980s or earlier by David Mayhew and Daniel Elazar still have some predictive value.[42] More recently, Hans Hassell has documented the ways in which party leaders coalesce around their chosen candidates before primaries begin.[43] Various studies of party-allied super political action committees (PACs) have also documented their role in shaping primary competition.[44] Today, some of the states that were initially the most skeptical of direct primaries are occasionally able to make primaries optional or to determine whether to open or close them. We know as well that in countries such as Mexico, where primaries are optional, parties use primaries selectively, holding them when it benefits them to do so.[45]

What we need to know. Although it is possible to document the methods by which parties have converged around moderate nominees, we lack the ability to determine whether, when, and how parties that have the capacity to block extremists actually do so. We can observe instances when party organizations or party-allied groups seek to offer an advantage to candidates they deem more electable, but electability is not necessarily the same thing as moderation. In 2022, for instance, multiple House and Senate candidates endorsed by Donald Trump won nominations despite concerns among other Republican leaders about their moderation or electability—only to lose to Democrats in competitive states and districts. At the same time, party leaders in other states (notably New York) were able to coalesce around moderate candidates who ultimately won both the nomination and the general election.

States with partisan primaries also vary in the latitude they give political parties in structuring the nomination process. Although most of this information is publicly accessible, we lack a comprehensive state-by-state accounting of the legal constraints on party control of primaries. Some states have statutory requirements, while others are bound by constitutional restrictions, either dating back to the adoption of their constitutions or enacted later through ballot initiatives. (Appendix B lists state constitutional provisions relating to primary elections.) Before undertaking any effort to give parties more leeway in primaries, however, we would need to know more about what is possible and what such reforms would entail.

There are also concerns about what parties would do with this responsibility. It is possible to find anecdotal evidence of parties using this responsibility sensibly, as when Virginia Republicans used a ranked-choice vote to block the least palatable candidate in the 2021 governor's race.[46] But there are also numerous examples of state parties that have been radicalized and might well choose more extreme nominees than would rank-and-file voters. To our knowledge, there exists no good analysis of the degree of practicality or extremism among state parties and state party leaders, although several recent works explore characteristics of local parties.[47] There are, moreover, questions we should be asking about the difference between the short-term and long-term effects of any change in party power: Will granting more decisionmaking power over nominees to ideologically extreme state party organizations ultimately prompt those organizations to become more practical? And are the short-run costs of any such changes worth the long-term benefits?

Reforms that would change the role of parties in primaries. Many of the same reform proposals noted above are relevant here. These include:

1. *Allowing RCV in primaries, encouraging parties to hold preprimary conventions, and/or expanding the use of instant-runoff elections:* All of these reforms were listed above as options to change the selection mechanism. Here, we would emphasize the possibility of giving parties greater discretion to use such methods rather than requiring them.

2. *Clarifying the role state parties might play following the adoption of a nonpartisan primary system:* In the previous section, we noted ways in which parties might still play a role in nonpartisan primaries by offering endorsements, holding preprimary conventions, or making other official statements about their preferences before the primary is held.

3. *Other efforts to invigorate state or local political parties:* These could include changing campaign finance laws to incentivize contributions to and from the parties or changing rules governing party coordination with candidates.

As the next section indicates, however, the public is skeptical of election reforms that grant parties greater power. And as noted above, we explore some alternative arguments about the role of parties in primaries in our discussion of nonpartisan primaries in Appendix A.

Public Support for Primary Election Reform

To measure public sentiment on the reform ideas discussed in this chapter, our task force commissioned a YouGov survey. The survey, fielded in March 2023, had 3,000 respondents and included fifteen questions on frequently discussed reform proposals.

The responses indicate strong public support for many different types of reforms. However, a substantial number of respondents—roughly one-fourth to one-third per question—had no opinion on these reforms, and many questions showed a gap in support between Democrats and Republicans. Overall, respondents were most favorable toward reforms that could be framed as more democratic or "open" and were least favorable toward reforms that would enhance the power of political party organizations. This is a finding of other surveys on political reform, and it corresponds with early public attitudes about primaries as well.[48]

Table 5.5 shows the percentage of respondents in favor of each proposed reform, excluding respondents who had no opinion. Two of the questions here ("national primary" and "rotate primary") pertained to presidential primaries and were included for validation purposes; the responses to these questions track closely with the responses in a 2020

Table 5.5   Support for Congressional Primary Reform Among Those Expressing an Opinion, by Party Identification, 2023

Electoral Reform	Full Sample (%)	Democrats (%)	Independents (%)	Republicans (%)
None (supports status quo)	61.31	59.82	53.86	72.60
Open primaries	80.95	83.56	83.98	73.00
Optional primaries	75.45	75.88	75.90	74.29
Runoff elections	74.54	79.21	72.42	71.02
National congressional primary day	74.07	77.08	72.01	72.60
15 percent candidate threshold	64.04	65.92	60.82	65.43
Nonpartisan primary	59.50	66.87	60.69	48.26
Ranked-choice voting (RCV)	57.78	68.15	58.59	42.35
Sore loser laws	57.72	67.53	48.37	56.45
Party endorsements	54.46	62.49	42.94	58.02
Voter threshold	51.20	54.94	51.62	45.78
State party conventions	36.73	36.78	35.29	38.51
Comparison to presidential primary reforms				
National primary	80.78	83.71	78.60	79.57
Rotate primary	72.81	77.66	72.18	66.65
Approximate percentage of sample	100.00	36.63	37.43	25.93

Note: Numbers are calculated using survey weights.

CES survey that focused on presidential primary reform.[49] And one question ("sore loser") was phrased such that a favorable answer indicated that the respondent was in favor of sore loser laws—that is, in favor of the status quo.

Table 5.5 shows the partisan and ideological differences among respondents. It is evident here that ranked-choice voting has taken on a partisan aspect: Democrats support it while Republicans oppose it. A majority of Republicans support maintaining the status quo while a majority of Democrats oppose doing so. Most of the other questions show a partisan split, but few show Democrats and Republicans on opposing sides. And partisans are more likely to support reforms that enhance party power than are independents. The lone reform that shows substantial and relatively consistent support among Democrats,

Republicans, and independents is a national congressional primary day. It is also noteworthy that very few differences in responses can be attributed to race and that younger respondents are more supportive than older respondents of most reforms.

In future research sponsored by our task force, we will offer a more detailed interpretation of these results. We offer them here, however, to show that there is public appetite for reform, although the reforms the public favors are not necessarily the same ones we favor. Party-enhancing reforms will not garner public support, and it should worry advocates of ranked-choice voting that there is such a partisan split on that question. It is encouraging that there is strong and bipartisan support for establishing a same-day national congressional primary.

Future Research

To summarize, there were several issues raised in the course of writing this chapter that the task force was able to address and others that we are not actively studying but which we hope other political scientists can address. The former category includes:

• *Public attitudes toward primaries and primary reform:* We have offered some data from our YouGov survey on voter attitudes toward reform and on the determinants of these attitudes, and we have recently concluded a more complete study of the survey results. In this chapter, we raised concerns about the politicization of many reform ideas. More research should be done to determine political obstacles to primary reform proposals and propose ways to frame some of these ideas to generate bipartisan support.[50]

• *Characteristics of primary voters:* As noted above, one challenge in studying primary voters is that the primary electorate varies from one cycle to the next, depending on the competitiveness of state-level or presidential primaries on the same ballot. Another project supported by the task force is our study of Catalist data on primary voters in different years and different states. We anticipate completing a more detailed study of this subject in the coming months as well.

The latter category of issues includes:

• *The characteristics of state parties:* It is not evident what state party leaders might do were they given more control over primaries. We would benefit, however, from a study of state parties that pays particular attention to primaries and from an effort to measure state party strength, pragmatism, professionalism, or propensity to be captured by ideological factions. In short, we need to know which state parties would be able to improve primaries if given the tools to do so and which would not.[51]

• *Laws governing state adoption of primary election law changes:* We need a better state-by-state analysis of the constraints on modifying primaries. This information is all readily available from individual states, but to our knowledge there is no compendium of it.[52]

• *Political ambition:* Studies such as those by Anderson, Butler, and Harbridge-Yong, as well as forthcoming work by Danielle Thomsen, emphasize the importance of candidate perceptions about primaries.[53] This scholarship is somewhat related to much earlier work on political ambition.[54] While much of the research discussed elsewhere in this chapter addresses the effects of legal changes on primary election results, studies of political ambition emphasize that perceptions about what will happen in primaries can determine who runs for office (and can thereby shape election outcomes) irrespective of primary laws or other facts surrounding primaries.

• *State legislative primaries:* Almost all the findings we have presented are about primaries for federal office—for House and Senate seats—and, in a few instances, for governorships. Although there is some scholarship on state legislative primaries and on polarization within state legislatures, more research is needed on how primary elections relate to political extremism at this level and on how our recommendations might apply.[55]

Recommendations

The aforementioned reforms are all means of pursuing the goals of reducing or discouraging political extremism. They all involve trade-offs, which we have noted, and they vary substantially in the magnitude of change they would entail and the amount of public support they enjoy. In many instances, they are not reforms we enthusiastically support; rather, they are reforms we are open to and encourage states or state parties to consider. By way of summary, however, we offer a short list of the reforms we believe are most promising. All of these reforms received strong support from our task force subcommittee members.

1. *Establish a national primary day.* We believe that having a single date for all state primaries (excluding presidential primaries) would offer a number of benefits. It would increase voter turnout by focusing citizens' attention on the primary election regardless of the competitiveness of their particular state. It would direct media attention more broadly across all primaries, rather than toward just a handful of idiosyncratic races from which the public might draw erroneous lessons. It would prevent super PACs and other groups from using the sequential nature of primaries to shape the national narrative. And it would potentially alter the relationship between state and national party organizations. We are uncertain about how advocacy for such a primary day might work. States could be offered incentives from Congress or the national parties to converge on a particular day, or perhaps legislation could be enacted establishing rules for primaries. We note that Congress has the constitutional authority under Article I, Section 4 to mandate a nationally uniform primary date for congressional elections. We are agnostic about when such a day might fall, although the standard reform recommendation for decades has been to hold primaries in the early autumn.[56] We recognize the political challenges that any effort to establish a national primary day would face. In our judgment, advocacy for the idea would have two major benefits even if it is unsuccessful: it would help focus attention on the problem of low primary turnout, and it might encourage states to consider clustering their primaries, which would still be beneficial.

2. *Encourage continued experimentation with alternative primary models.* We do not yet know whether ranked-choice voting or nonpartisan primaries would reduce political extremism, but new research is promising and shows they can lead to candidate moderation and reduce polarization. Until the recent Maine and Alaska reforms, RCV had not been tested at the state or federal level in the United States, and variants adopted at the municipal level have not always succeeded.[57] However, we are optimistic that the "top-four" or "top-five" models discussed in Chapter 2 might be able to avoid some of the problems that plagued mid-twentieth-century experiments with RCV and the single transferable vote. We see no reason why any of these reforms would be worse than the status quo, and as parties and voters adapt to them across different state political cultures, we are interested in whether the systems become more popular with the public. There will be work to do to convince Republicans and conservatives that they, too, can benefit from RCV, "top-two" primaries, or other such reforms.[58]

3. *Take steps to strengthen political parties.* These would include measures to give parties greater flexibility to use alternate types of pri-

maries. We would support providing state parties with the ability to alter primary laws to fit their unique circumstances. For instance, we believe RCV would be appropriate in primaries in heavily partisan districts, and we see little reason for states to prohibit parties from adopting open primaries or optional primaries if they choose to do so. We also think parties can have a potentially salutary impact on the nomination process if they strengthen their gatekeeping functions to deter unfit and politically extreme candidates. We would encourage parties to hold preprimary conventions to limit ballot access, endorse candidates before the primary, or engage in other winnowing procedures that give voters a choice among candidates who would be effective representatives of the party and its adherents. Notwithstanding a populist culture that strongly embraces candidate nominations by voters, many partisans appear to acknowledge that parties have an important role to play in shaping the nomination. Indeed, the vast majority do not believe that voters should have exclusive influence.[59] Parties can also be strengthened by granting them a greater role in financing their candidates (see the recommendations in Chapter 7). Studies indicate that parties tend to support more moderate candidates than do other kinds of donors and that these candidates tend to do better in general elections.[60]

4. *Eliminate sore loser laws.* Although many of the reforms we support would enhance the power of party leaders, we were divided on this one. However, some of us felt that if the goal of increasing party flexibility is to encourage parties to nominate electable candidates, then these candidates should be able to win in general elections regardless of their opponents. Moreover, sore loser laws have historically been used to block candidates who have substantial support among independents or voters of the opposing party. We note that our survey results show that the public does not support abolishing sore loser laws, but there may be ways to frame the issue that would change public attitudes. We further note that eliminating sore loser laws might effectively be coupled with adopting RCV or an instant-runoff system if there is concern about a defeated primary candidate running as a "spoiler" in the general election.

Conclusions

In closing, we wish to comment on four topics that have come up during our discussions. First, we want to reiterate that many of the problems associated with primaries are the result of other changes in our politics. It is important to be clear about the causes of polarization and extremism.

Often, things that play a role in primaries—such as super PACs, lopsidedly partisan districts, or social media—cause problems. But the issue is not necessarily the primary itself or its rules. Primaries have existed for over a century, while many of the problems associated with them are more recent. We should not assume that primary election reforms will solve these problems. Nor should we lose sight of the benefits primaries of all types offer some voters in terms of candidate choice and political engagement—or of the Progressive-era goal of reducing the potential for corrupt bargaining within parties over nominations.

Second, the reforms we have presented here follow two paths. One is rooted in Progressive Era ideas about the role of the public in democratic politics. If we are serious about allowing voters to play a role in primaries, it is important that we extend this opportunity to all voters. Hence our interest in making it easier to vote and in encouraging habitual voting. The second path is distinctly pro-party. We take seriously concerns that party organizations have been weakened to the point that they can no longer serve their traditional function of aggregating interests and that some party organizations have been so radicalized that they will use any additional powers they receive to steer their nominees further away from the electorate's preferences—or even from democratic norms. History (as well as many theoretical models) suggests that parties are punished by voters when they do this. If such retribution is no longer possible—if party organizations are irrevocably broken, in other words—then more radical changes may be necessary. But we have framed this chapter as a survey of options that would retain a role for parties.

Third, it is important to think about the time frame for reform. Those who think extremism is an immediate threat to the political system may well conclude that changes that yield a short-term benefit are worth pursuing even if the benefit dissipates as the system adapts, eventually rendering the changes meaningless. For instance, one could argue that the adoption of "top-four" ranked-choice voting in Alaska prevented a particular candidate with antisystem views (Sarah Palin) from winning a House seat and that this single election may have had further implications for the activities of the 118th Congress. Perhaps a few changes like that matter even if in the long run RCV does not have any strong effects. We do not have a good theory about how to balance short-term and long-term interests in election reform.

Fourth and finally, we have offered a relatively conservative slate of reforms. We have concentrated on changes we think are achievable in the somewhat near future, and we have done so for two reasons. First, one lesson we have taken from the history of primaries is that they are hard to get rid of and that the public will generally support things that sound democratic, even if in fact they are not. Second, as Bruce Cain and others have argued, mobilizing the public around any sort of process reform risks exhausting people, and a reform that shows no consequences three or four elections out can lead to disillusionment and to reform "cycles" that become increasingly more radical and futile.[61] This suggests we should be cautious about what is achievable and recognize that citizens have myriad political interests; distracting them with false hopes can have serious repercussions for assembling political movements in pursuit of other types of policy changes that might be more effective in solving the very real problems our nation faces.

Some readers may find our suggestions too cautious. We emphasize that this is not an argument against more ambitious plans for rethinking American elections. But citizens, political parties, and state governments have a range of tools at their disposal to tame political extremism and reduce polarization, and reforming primaries is just one of them. We believe that primary elections can be improved without abandoning an institution that has proved malleable enough to meet the needs of different state governments and, on balance, been an asset to American democracy for much of the past century.

Appendix A: Nonpartisan Top-Two, Top-Four, or Top-Five Primaries— Why Not Give Parties Less Power?

Some members of our task force have argued strongly for recommending the adoption of nonpartisan primaries. As we have noted, the nonpartisan primary has been implemented in four states: California, Washington, Louisiana, and Alaska. California and Washington use nonpartisan primaries to winnow the field to two candidates for their general elections. Louisiana holds a jungle primary on the day of the general election and a runoff in December. In 2022 Alaska implemented a nonpartisan primary, from which the top four candidates proceed to an RCV general election. Nevada voters approved a "top-five" nonpartisan primary and RCV general election in 2022 and voted on it a second time in 2024.[62]

In theory, nonpartisan elections should encourage moderation. They allow candidates to appeal to voters of both parties, and they can lead to the election of candidates who might otherwise have failed to receive a majority or plurality of votes in a party primary. Political parties can still play a role in nonpartisan primaries, moreover. They can hold conventions beforehand to endorse candidates. Party labels can be used on the primary ballot to inform voters, and the ballot can note which candidates have received a party endorsement. The ballot can also indicate which candidate is the incumbent. In their capacity as private associations, parties and organizations allied with parties (such as interest groups and super PACs) can still communicate with voters or engage in other campaign activities, as can private individuals with ties to parties.

Our lack of a strong endorsement for nonpartisan primaries is based on both empirical observations and normative concerns. First, let us consider the empirical evidence. All the states that use nonpartisan primaries have idiosyncratic politics. California has a history of particularly weak political parties; for much of the twentieth century, it allowed for cross-filing: candidates could simultaneously run for the Democratic and Republican nomination. California used a blanket primary, which is in practice nearly identical to a nonpartisan "top-two" primary, for two election cycles in 1996 and 1998. Evidence of its effectiveness was mixed, but some argued that the system didn't have time to mature before being struck down by the Supreme Court in *California Democratic Party v. Jones* in 2000.[63] The state's "top-two" primary was established by referendum in 2010. That same year, California enacted (again by referendum) a nonpartisan redistricting commission. It has trended strongly Democratic over the past two decades. Early studies of the "top-two" primary contended that it had little effect, although they acknowledged it was difficult to separate the effects of the primary from those of the state's redistricting efforts.[64] Arguments for the effectiveness of the "top-two" primary rest largely on one study, which considered the behavior of the state's members of Congress from 2003 to 2018.[65] It would be consistent with the results of this study to argue that it took nearly a decade for adaptations of candidates, voters, and parties to the "top-two" primary to become evident.

Washington adopted its "top-two" primary by voter initiative in 2004. The state had used a blanket primary from 1935 to 2000 and an open primary during the brief period after the Supreme Court's *California Democratic Party v. Jones* decision but before its adoption of the "top-two" primary. Todd Donovan argues that the "top-two" system has had few noticeable effects, in part because it was not a radical break from the systems that preceded it.[66]

Louisiana also has a history of weak political parties, although conventional measurements place it in a different category than Alaska, California, or Washington. Louisiana adopted a nonpartisan jungle primary in 1975. This primary was enacted legislatively, at the behest of recently elected governor Edwin Edwards, reportedly out of frustration that he had been forced to run in a primary as well as a runoff prior to the general election while his Republican opponent had not. Unlike other nonpartisan-primary states, Louisiana separates state and federal elections. State elections, held in odd-numbered years, feature a primary in October and a runoff in November. Federal primaries are held on the same date as the general election, with a runoff in December if necessary. Current US senator John N. Kennedy won his seat in 2016 after receiving less than 25 percent of the primary vote, and turnout for the subsequent runoff was more than 50 percent lower than for the primary. Some recent studies have argued that the state's legislature has been less polarized and more effective than those of other southern states.[67] And in recent years, Louisiana has had more two-party competition at the state level than its immediate neighbors, but its congressional delegation is not noticeably less extreme than those of other southern states. Speaker of the House Mike Johnson, the ultimate choice of those who unseated Kevin McCarthy, first won his Louisiana seat after receiving 25 percent of the vote in the 2016 primary.

Alaska, which adopted its "top-four" ranked-choice voting system in 2022, has a long history of nonpartisan electoral politics. It used a blanket primary from 1967 to 1992 and again from 1996 to 2000.[68] Alaska also has a long history of Republican Party factionalism, and it has politics that revolve around resource extraction (unlike other extractive states, however, it also has a very large percentage of union members). Both chambers of the legislature have a history of establishing bipartisan coalitions; currently, the state senate governing coalition includes 85 percent of the chamber. Arrangements such as these substantially reduce the need for political parties to play a role in elections at all. As we have noted above, early evidence from Alaska does suggest that the "top-four" system provided advantages to more moderate candidates in the 2022 US House and Senate elections and in at least two state legislative races.[69]

All these states have a history of weak political parties, according to standard political science metrics, and all but Louisiana enacted nonpartisan primaries by referendum.[70] Not all states have direct democracy provisions, and the historical weakness of parties in slating candidates or otherwise organizing politics in California, Washington, Louisiana, and Alaska may be one reason why nonpartisan primaries passed there in the first place. These states' experiences therefore offer little guidance on how nonpartisan primaries would function in states with stronger parties. If we uncritically accept all the claims made about these states, we have four different trajectories: it took nearly a decade for the effects of California's primary law change to become evident and perhaps longer for the effects of Louisiana's reform to become noticeable; little changed in Washington; and there were immediate changes in Alaska, but these changes might well fail to persist if the state's Republican Party effectively adapts to them.

One simple way to measure how state legislative election systems can adapt to changes such as the nonpartisan primary is to consider how states using this system fit into Boris Shor and Nolan McCarty's measurements of state legislative polarization.[71] Shor and McCarty compare average levels of polarization in each state from 1996 to 2020. They provide no evidence that the introduction of the "top-two" primary led to less polarization. Some proponents of these systems argued that California and Washington polarized at a slower pace than other states following the introduction of the "top-two" primary, but Shor and McCarty's data do not show this to be the case.[72] This does not mean that a small number of extreme candidates were not defeated; nor does it suggest that the change had no effect on other types of extremism as defined earlier in this chapter. And none of these states had a long enough experience with the "top-four" ranked-choice voting system for us to make claims about its effect on polarization. We concede that the "top-four" RCV system differs in important ways from the "top-two" primary, and we look forward to seeing what results it might have in Alaska or other states.

Critics might also respond that all states are idiosyncratic in their own ways. We agree with this. Our point, however, is that the states that have used nonpartisan primaries are, with the exception of Louisiana, all idiosyncratic in the same way: they are weak-party states with direct-democracy provisions. Their atypicality may well be the reason they introduced nonpartisan primaries. We encourage state experimentation and would be willing to reconsider our views in the event that more nonpartisan primaries, RCV systems, or other untested reforms were implemented.

There is, however, also a compelling normative case against the nonpartisan primary. Political parties play a vital role in organizing legislative politics. If candidates do not have to seek the support of their party's leaders and voters, they have little reason to play a constructive role in putting forward their party's policies in government. This, in turn, deprives voters of their most effective tool for holding politicians accountable. As noted above, political parties can still play a role in nonpartisan primaries by endorsing candidates, taking other steps to communicate their preferences to voters, or boosting their preferred candidates. These signals, however, are most likely to be understood by politically engaged and knowledgeable voters, and in some instances, they can read as the same sort of corrupt "behind-the-scenes" politics that progressives objected to at the time the direct primary was created. Less informed voters—who often tend to be poorer or less ideologically extreme—are less likely to perceive these signals. In this sense, elections without partisan cues or with partisan cues only some people can read can actually be less democratic. This is one reason, scholars argue, why nonpartisan elections tend to have very low turnout.[73]

The practical case against the nonpartisan primary lies in its limited effectiveness and in the trade-offs that advocacy for it would entail. In theory, it makes sense that nonpartisan primaries could encourage bipartisanship and discourage extremism. But if the changes they spur are subtle and take a decade or more to materialize, they may not be powerful enough to effectively combat contemporary extremism. The logic behind the nonpartisan primary is based on a unidimensional model of political ideology that captures neither the characteristics of "moderate" voters nor the characteristics of political extremism that we described at the beginning of this chapter. As we have documented above, moreover, political parties have historically used a range of tools to discipline or remove extremists: party leaders can sanction individual officeholders for egregious behavior, parties can hold preprimary conventions to winnow the field, and party-allied donors can coalesce around their preferred candidates. If parties are too weak to do these things today, our preferred approach is to incentivize parties to behave more responsibly rather than to limit their ability to influence elections. If parties are too broken to be repaired—a possibility we think is worth continuing to discuss—then antiparty reforms may be more appropriate. But in that case, we would argue that a range of other reforms (including many discussed in other chapters of this book) have more promising track records than do nonpartisan primaries.

Appendix B: State Constitutional Provisions Regarding Primaries

State	Citation	Year of Adoption	Content
Alabama	§182	1901	Disqualifies people who make or offer "to make a false return in any election by the people or in any primary election to procure the nomination or election of any person to any office" from registering to vote or from voting.
Alabama	§183	1901	"No person shall be qualified to vote, or participate in any primary election, party convention, mass meeting, or other method of party action of any political party or faction, who shall not possess the qualifications prescribed in this article for an elector, or who shall be disqualified from voting under the provisions of this article."
Alabama	§190	1901	"The legislature shall also make provision by law, not inconsistent with this article, for the regulation of primary elections, and for punishing frauds at the same, but shall not make primary elections compulsory. The legislature shall by law provide for purging the registration list of the names of those who die, become insane, or convicted of crime, or otherwise disqualified as electors under the provisions of this Constitution, and of any names which may have been fraudulently entered on such list by the registrars; provided, that a trial by jury may be had on the demand of any person whose name is proposed to be stricken from the list."
Alaska	Article XV, §6	1956	Requires governor to take necessary measures to hold primary and general elections.
Alaska	Article XV, §7	1956	"The primary election shall take place not less than forty nor more than ninety days after the proclamation by the governor of the Territory. The general election shall take place not less than ninety days after the primary election. The elections shall be governed by this constitution and by applicable territorial laws."
Arizona	Article VII, §17	1962	Requires primary when there is a vacancy in congress.
Arizona	Article VII, §10	Amended 1998	"The legislature shall enact a direct primary election law, which shall provide for the nomination of candidates for all elective state, county, and city offices, including candidates for United States Senator and for Representative in Congress. Any person who is registered as no party preference

State	Citation	Year of Adoption	Content
			or independent as the party preference or who is registered with a political party that is not qualified for representation on the ballot may vote in the primary election of any one of the political parties that is qualified for the ballot."
Arkansas	Article III, §13	Undetermined	Procedures for elections with only one candidate apply to primary elections.
Arkansas	Amendment 29, §5	Undetermined	"Only the names of candidates for office nominated by an organized political party at a convention of delegates, or by a majority of all the votes cast for candidates for the office in a primary election, or by petition of electors as provided by law, shall be placed on the ballots in any election."
Arkansas	Amendment 39, §1	Undetermined	"The General Assembly shall have power to enact laws providing for a registration of voters prior to any general, special, or primary election, and to require that the right to vote at any such election shall depend upon such previous registration."
Arkansas	Amendment 51, §§1–2, 10	Undetermined	Asserts that all rules related to voter registration in general elections also apply to primary elections.
Arkansas	Amendment 76, §1	Undetermined	Sets forth rules for general congressional elections that also apply to primary elections.
California	Article II, §5	Amended 2010	Defines rules for primary elections.
Colorado	Article XXVIII, §§2–3, 5–6	Undetermined	Defines campaign finance laws for general and primary elections.
Connecticut	Article XXXI	2008	Allows electors who will be eighteen years old by the general election to vote in primary elections.
Florida	Article IV, §5(a)	Undetermined	Allows candidates for governor and lieutenant governor to run without a running mate in primary elections but requires them to have a running mate for the general election.
Florida	Article VI, §5(b)	Undetermined	"If all candidates for an office have the same party affiliation and the winner will have no opposition in the general election, all qualified electors, regardless of party affiliation, may vote in the primary elections for that office."
Hawaii	Article II, §4	Amended 1978	"Secrecy of voting shall be preserved; provided that no person shall be required to declare a party preference or nonpartisanship as a

State	Citation	Year of Adoption	Content
			condition of voting in any primary or special primary election."
Hawaii	Article II, §8	Amended 1978	Allows primary elections to be held so long as they are more than forty-five days before the general election.
Hawaii	Article III, §4	Amended 1988	Asserts that a candidate elected by a primary election unopposed in the general election is considered elected by the primary election.
Kentucky	§151	1891	Prohibits people guilty of fraud, intimidation, bribery, or corrupt practice from being nominated or elected to office.
Maine	Article IV §4	Undetermined	"No person may be a candidate for election as a member of the House of Representatives unless, at the time of the nomination for placement on a primary, general or special election ballot, that person is a resident in the district which the candidate seeks to represent."
Michigan	Article II, §4(2)	Amended 2018	"No law shall be enacted which permits a candidate in any partisan primary or partisan election to have a ballot designation except when required for identification of candidates for the same office who have the same or similar surnames."
Minnesota	Article VII, §9	1980	"The amount that may be spent by candidates for constitutional and legislative offices to campaign for nomination or election shall be limited by law. The legislature shall provide by law for disclosure of contributions and expenditures made to support or oppose candidates for state elective offices."
Mississippi	Article XII, §247	Undetermined	"The legislature shall enact laws to secure fairness in party primary elections, conventions, or other methods of naming party candidates."
Nevada	Article II, §10(2)	1996	Limits campaign spending in primary and general elections.
New Hampshire	Part 1, Article XI	1956	Allows for absentee voting in primary elections.
New Mexico	Article VII, §5	Undetermined	Does not allow runoff elections for primaries.
New York	Article I, §1	Amended 2001	Allows citizens to be disenfranchised from voting in primary elections in certain circumstances.
North Dakota	Article II, §1	Undetermined	Assures secrecy in voting for all elections, including primaries.

State	Citation	Year of Adoption	Content
North Dakota	Article II, §3	Undetermined	Allows only qualified electors to participate in all elections, including primaries.
Ohio	Article V, §7	Amended 1976	Requires primary elections for all elective state, district, county, and municipal offices except for municipal elections that are in towns of a certain size.
Oklahoma	Article III, §3	1976	Gives the legislature the ability to create a mandatory primary system.
Rhode Island	Article IV, §9	Undetermined	"The general assembly shall require each candidate for general office in any primary, general or special election to report to the secretary of state all contributions and expenditures made by any person to or on behalf of such candidate, provided however, that the general assembly may limit such disclosure to contributions or expenditures in excess of such an amount as the general assembly shall specify."
Rhode Island	Article IV, §10	Undetermined	"The general assembly shall adopt limitations on all contributions to candidates for election to state and local office in any primary, general or special election and shall provide for the adoption of a plan of voluntary public financing and limitations on total campaign expenditures of campaigns for governor and such other general officers as the general assembly shall specify."
South Carolina	Article II, §10	Amended 1971	Requires the general assembly, to among other things, "provide for the nomination of candidates."
South Dakota	Article VII, §3	Undetermined	Requires the general assembly, to among other things, provide for the nomination of candidates.
Vermont	Chapter II, §4	Undetermined	Entitles everyone qualified to vote to vote in primaries.
Virginia	Article II, §3	Amended 1995	Ensures that there can be write-in candidates, but does not make the guarantee for primaries.
Virginia	Article II, §1	Undetermined	Entitles everyone qualified to vote to vote in primaries.
Virginia	Article II, §4	Undetermined	"The General Assembly shall provide for the nomination of candidates, shall regulate the time, place, manner, conduct, and administration of primary, general, and special elections, and shall have power to make any other law regulating elections not inconsistent with this Constitution."

Notes

1. Alan Ware, *The American Direct Primary* (New York: Oxford University Press, 2002); Lawrence Jacobs, *Democracy Under Fire* (New York: Oxford University Press, 2022).

2. Charles Merriam and Louise Overacker, *Primary Elections* (Chicago: University of Chicago Press, 1928).

3. Alan Ware, *The American Direct Primary* (New York: Oxford University Press, 2002); Eric Lawrence, Todd Donovan, and Shaun Bowler, "The Adoption of Direct Primaries in the United States," *Party Politics* 19, no. 1 (2013): 3–18.

4. Alan Ware, *The American Direct Primary* (New York: Oxford University Press, 2002); Robert G. Boatright, *Reform and Retrenchment: A Century of Efforts to Fix Primary Elections* (New York: Oxford University Press, 2024).

5. Henry Jones Ford, "The Direct Primary," *North American Review* 190, no. 644 (1909): 1–14.

6. Nancy Rosenblum, "'Extremism' and Anti-extremism in American Party Politics," *Journal of Contemporary Legal Issues* 12 (2002): 843–886; Cynthia Miller-Idriss, *Hate in the Homeland* (Princeton, NJ: Princeton University Press, 2022).

7. See Robert G. Boatright, *Reform and Retrenchment: A Century of Efforts to Fix Primary Elections* (New York: Oxford University Press, 2024), 44, for details.

8. David Broockman et al., "Why Local Party Leaders Don't Support Nominating Centrists," *British Journal of Political Science* 51, no. 2 (2021): 724–749; Sarah E. Anderson, Daniel M. Butler, and Laurel Harbridge-Yong, *Rejecting Compromise: Legislators' Fear of Primary Voters* (New York: Cambridge University Press, 2020).

9. See, e.g., Andrew B. Hall and Daniel M. Thompson, "Who Punishes Extremist Nominees? Candidate Ideology and Turning Out the Base in US Elections," *American Political Science Review* 112, no. 3 (2018): 509–524; John Sides et al., "On the Representativeness of Primary Electorates," *British Journal of Political Science* 50, no. 3 (2018): 677–685; Rachel Porter, "Estimating the Ideological Extremity of Primary Electorates" (unpublished ms., Notre Dame University, 2023).

10. Barbara Norrander and Jay Wendland, "Open Versus Closed Primaries and the Ideological Composition of Presidential Primary Electorates," *Electoral Studies* 42 (2016): 229–236; Barbara Norrander and Kerri Stephens, "Primary Type and Polarization of State Electorates" (paper presented at the State Politics and Policy Conference, Houston, Texas, 2012).

11. Robert G. Boatright, Vincent G. Moscardelli, and Clifford Vickrey, "Primary Election Timing and Voter Turnout," *Election Law Journal* 19 (2020): 472–485; Gregg B. Johnson, Meredith-Joy Petersheim, and Jesse T. Wasson, "Divisive Primaries and Incumbent General Election Performance: Prospects and Costs in U. S. House Races," *American Politics Research* 38, no. 5 (2010): 931–955.

12. Robert G. Boatright, *Getting Primaried* (Ann Arbor: University of Michigan Press, 2013); Robert G. Boatright, "Congressional Primary Challenges and the Health of the Parties," in *The State of the Parties*, ed. John C. Green, 9th ed. (Lanham, MD: Rowman & Littlefield, 2022), 59–74.

13. Sarah E. Anderson, Daniel M. Butler, and Laurel Harbridge-Yong, *Rejecting Compromise: Legislators' Fear of Primary Voters* (New York: Cambridge University Press, 2020).

14. Sarah E. Anderson, Daniel M. Butler, and Laurel Harbridge-Yong, *Rejecting Compromise: Legislators' Fear of Primary Voters* (New York: Cambridge University Press, 2020); Robert G. Boatright, "Interest Group Activity in Congressional

Primaries," in *Interest Group Politics*, ed. Alan J. Cigler and Burdett A. Loomis, 9th ed. (Washington, DC: Congressional Quarterly Press, 2015), 176–206.

15. Lawrence Jacobs, *Democracy Under Fire* (New York: Oxford University Press, 2022); Bruce E. Cain, *Democracy More or Less: America's Political Reform Quandary*. Cambridge Studies in Election Law and Democracy (Cambridge: Cambridge University Press, 2014).

16. Rachel Blum, *How the Tea Party Captured the GOP: Insurgent Factions in American Politics* (Chicago: University of Chicago Press, 2020).

17. See, e.g., Seth E. Masket, *The Inevitable Party: Why Attempts to Kill the Party System Fail and How They Weaken Democracy* (New York: Oxford University Press, 2016).

18. Hans J. G. Hassell, *The Party's Primary: Control of Congressional Nominations* (New York: Cambridge University Press, 2018).

19. Joshua Ferrer and Michael Thorning, "2022 Primary Turnout," Bipartisan Policy Center, March 6, 2023.

20. The Center for the Study of the American Electorate data omit 1954.

21. Robert G. Boatright, *Congressional Primary Elections* (New York: Routledge, 2014), chap. 3.

22. John Sides et al., "On the Representativeness of Primary Electorates," *British Journal of Political Science* 50, no. 3 (2018): 677–685.

23. Christian R. Grose, "Reducing Legislative Polarization: Top-Two and Open Primaries Are Associated with More Moderate Legislators," *Journal of Political Institutions and Political Economy* 1 (2020): 267–287; R. Michael Alvarez and J. Andrew Sinclair, *Nonpartisan Primary Election Reform: Mitigating Mischief* (New York: Cambridge University Press, 2014); Todd Donovan, "The Top Two Primary: What Can California Learn from Washington?," *California Journal of Politics and Policy* 4 (2012): 1–22; Richard Barton, "Louisiana's Long-Term Election Experiment," Unite America Institute, November 2022.

24. See, e.g., Benjamin Reilly, David Lublin, and Glenn Wright, "Alaska's New Electoral System: Countering Polarization or 'Crooked as Hell'?," *California Journal of Politics and Policy* 15 (2023).

25. Danielle Thomsen, "Primary Turnout and Partisan Polarization in the U.S. House" (unpublished ms., Syracuse University, 2017).

26. Zoltan Hajnal and Jessica Trounstine, "Where Turnout Matters: The Consequences of Uneven Turnout in City Politics," *Journal of Politics* 67, no. 2 (2005): 515–535.

27. Jennifer Wolak, *Compromise in an Age of Party Polarization* (New York: Oxford University Press, 2020).

28. Robert Boatright, Caroline Tolbert, and Nathan Micatka, "How Much Variation Is There in State Primary Electorates, and Why Should We Care?" (paper presented at the Southern Political Science Association Annual Meeting, New Orleans, Louisiana, January 10–13, 2024).

29. An interest group with limited resources may find it attractive to spend money in an early primary in order to establish its clout and use whatever attention it receives for that effort to raise money for intervention in a primary later in the year. See Robert G. Boatright, *Getting Primaried* (Ann Arbor: University of Michigan Press, 2013).

30. We note that a Brookings Institution task force convened in 2007 recommended compulsory voting in general elections but not in primaries. See Brookings Institution and Ash Center for Democratic Governance and Innovation, "Lift Every Voice: The Urgency of Universal Civic Duty Voting," Brookings Institution, July 20, 2020.

31. See, e.g., James Adam sand Samuel Merrill III, "Candidate and Party Strategies in Two-Stage Elections Beginning with a Primary," *American Journal of Political Science* 52 (2008): 344–359.

32. See, e.g., Eric McGhee et al., "A Primary Cause of Partisanship? Nomination Systems and Legislator Ideology," *American Journal of Political Science* 58 (2014): 337–351; Seth J. Hill, "Sidestepping Primary Reform: Political Action in Response to Institutional Change," *Political Science Research and Methods* 10 (2022): 391–407.

33. Seth J. Hill and Chris Tausanovitch, "A Disconnect in Representation? Comparison of Trends in Congressional and Public Polarization," *Journal of Politics* 77 (2015): 1058–1075.

34. One recent exception to this is Laurel Harbridge-Yong and Rachel Hutchinson, "The Plurality Problem: Plurality Primary Victors Hurt Parties in the General Election," SSRN Working Paper 4707767, January 26, 2024.

35. Rachel Hutchinson, "The 'Motion to Vacate' and Electoral Incentives," FairVote, October 4, 2023.

36. Jeffrey Lazarus, "Unintended Consequences: Anticipation of General Election Outcomes and Primary Election Divisiveness," *Legislative Studies Quarterly* 30 (2005): 435–461; Alan Ware "'Divisive' Primaries: The Important Questions," *British Journal of Political Science* 9 (1979): 381–384.

37. Andrew D. McNitt, "The Effect of Preprimary Endorsement on Competition for Nominations: An Examination of Different Nominating Systems," *Journal of Politics* 42 (1980): 257–266; John C. Green and Paul S. Herrnson, "Party Development in the Twentieth Century: Laying the Foundations for Responsible Party Government?," in *Responsible Partisanship: The Evolution of American Political Parties Since 1950*, ed. John C. Green and Paul S. Herrnson (Lawrence: University Press of Kansas, 2003), 37–60.

38. Charles S. Bullock and Loch K. Johnson, *Runoff Elections in the United States* (Chapel Hill: University of North Carolina Press, 1992); Alexander P. Lamis, "The Runoff Primary Controversy: Implications for Southern Politics," *PS: Political Science and Politics* 17 (1984): 782–787.

39. Eric Loepp and Benjamin Melusky, "Why Is This Candidate Listed Twice? The Behavioral and Electoral Consequences of Fusion Voting," *Election Law Journal* 21 (2022): 105–123.

40. Barry C. Burden, Bradley M. Jones, and Michael S. Kang, "Sore Loser Laws and Congressional Polarization," *Legislative Studies Quarterly* 39, no. 3 (August 2014): 299–305; Michael S. Kang and Barry C. Burden, "Sore Loser Laws in Presidential and Congressional Elections," in *Handbook of Primary Elections*, ed. Robert G. Boatright (New York: Routledge, 2018), 456–466.

41. Alan Ware, *The American Direct Primary* (New York: Oxford University Press, 2002); Hans J. G. Hassell, *The Party's Primary: Control of Congressional Nominations* (New York: Cambridge University Press, 2018); Seth E. Masket, *The Inevitable Party: Why Attempts to Kill the Party System Fail and How They Weaken Democracy* (New York: Oxford University Press, 2016).

42. Daniel J. Elazar, *American Federalism: A View from the States*, 2nd ed. (New York: Thomas Y. Crowell, 1972); David R. Mayhew, *Placing Parties in American Politics* (Princeton, NJ: Princeton University Press, 1986).

43. Hans J. G. Hassell, *The Party's Primary: Control of Congressional Nominations* (New York: Cambridge University Press, 2018).

44. Robert G. Boatright and Zachary Albert, "Factional Conflict and Independent Expenditures in the 2018 Democratic House Primaries," *Congress & the Presidency* 48 (2021): 50–77.

45. Kathleen Bruhn, "Party Primaries as a Strategic Choice: The Costs and Benefits of Democratic Candidate Selection," in *Routledge Handbook of Primary Elections*, ed. Robert G. Boatright (New York: Routledge, 2018), 354–368.

46. Raymond J. La Raja and Alexander Theodoridis, "How Ranked-Choice Voting Saved the Virginia GOP from Itself," *Washington Post*, November 5, 2021.

47. Byron E. Shafer and Regina L. Wagner, *The Long War over Party Structure* (New York: Cambridge University Press, 2019); David Broockman et al., "Why Local Party Leaders Don't Support Nominating Centrists," *British Journal of Political Science* 51, no. 2 (2021): 724–749; David Doherty, Conor M. Dowling, and Michael G. Miller, *Small Power: How Local Parties Shape Elections* (New York: Oxford University Press, 2022).

48. David M. Primo and Jeffrey D. Milyo, *Campaign Finance and American Democracy: What the Public Really Thinks and Why It Matters*, 1st ed. (Chicago: University of Chicago Press, 2020; Robert G. Boatright, *Reform and Retrenchment: A Century of Efforts to Fix Primary Elections* (New York: Oxford University Press, 2024).

49. Joseph Coll, Caroline J. Tolbert, and Michael Ritter, "Understanding Preferences for Comprehensive Electoral Reform in the United States," *Social Science Quarterly* 103 (2022): 1523–1538.

50. Robert G. Boatright, Caroline J. Tolbert, and Nathan K. Micatka, "Public Opinion on Reforming U.S. Primaries," *Social Science Quarterly* 105 (2024): 876–893.

51. See, e.g., David Doherty, Conor M. Dowling, and Michael G. Miller, *Small Power: How Local Parties Shape Elections* (New York: Oxford University Press, 2022).

52. One book that approaches doing this is Drew Kurlowski, *Election Law Revealed* (St. Paul, MN: West Academic, 2019).

53. Sarah E. Anderson, Daniel M. Butler, and Laurel Harbridge-Yong, *Rejecting Compromise: Legislators' Fear of Primary Voters* (New York: Cambridge University Press, 2020); Danielle M. Thomsen, "Competition in Congressional Elections: Money Versus Votes," *American Political Science Review* 117, no. 2 (2023): 675–691.

54. See, e.g., L. Sandy Maisel, *From Obscurity to Oblivion* (Knoxville: University of Tennessee Press, 1982); Joseph Schlesinger, *Ambition and Politics: Political Careers in the United States* (Chicago: Rand McNally and Co., 1966).

55. Steven Rogers, *Accountability in State Legislatures* (Chicago: University of Chicago Press, 2023); Robert E. Hogan, "Competition in State Legislative Primary Elections," *Legislative Studies Quarterly* 28 (2003): 103–126; Boris Shor and Nolan McCarty, "Two Decades of Polarization in American State Legislatures," *Journal of Political Institutions and Political Economy* 3 (2022): 343–370.

56. National Municipal League, *A Model Direct Primary Election System: Report of the Committee on the Direct Primary* (New York: National Municipal League, 1951).

57. Jack Santucci, *More Parties or No Parties* (New York: Oxford University Press, 2022).

58. See Kevin R. Kosar, "Conservatives Should Look More Closely at Systemic Election Reforms," American Enterprise Institute, October 3, 2023.

59. Zachary Albert and Raymond J La Raja, "Who Should Decide the Party's Nominee? Understanding Public Attitudes Toward Primary Elections," *Party Politics* 27, no. 5 (September 1, 2021): 928–941.

60. Hans J. G. Hassell, "Principled Moderation: Understanding Parties' Support of Moderate Candidates," *Legislative Studies Quarterly* 43, no. 2 (2018): 343–369; Brian F. Schaffner and Raymond J. La Raja, *Campaign Finance and Political*

Polarization: When Purists Prevail (Ann Arbor: University of Michigan Press, 2015); Andrew B. Hall and Daniel M. Thompson, "Who Punishes Extremist Nominees? Candidate Ideology and Turning Out the Base in US Elections," *American Political Science Review* 112, no. 3 (2018): 509–524.

61. Bruce E. Cain, *Democracy More or Less: America's Political Reform Quandary.* Cambridge Studies in Election Law and Democracy (Cambridge: Cambridge University Press, 2014).

62. Nevada law requires that constitutional initiatives be voted on in two successive general elections; see "Filing a Constitutional Initiative," Nevada Secretary of State Francisco V. Aguilar.

63. See the essays in Bruce E. Cain and Elisabeth R. Gerber, eds., *Voting at the Political Fault Line: California's Experiment with the Blanket Primary* (Berkeley: University of California Press, 2002).

64. For a summary, see R. Michael Alvarez and J. Andrew Sinclair, *Nonpartisan Primary Election Reform: Mitigating Mischief* (New York: Cambridge University Press, 2014).

65. Christian R. Grose, "Reducing Legislative Polarization: Top-Two and Open Primaries Are Associated with More Moderate Legislators," *Journal of Political Institutions and Political Economy* 1 (2020): 267–287.

66. Todd Donovan, "The Top Two Primary: What Can California Learn from Washington?," *California Journal of Politics and Policy* 4 (2012): 1–22.

67. Richard Barton, "Louisiana's Long-Term Election Experiment," Unite America Institute, November 2022.

68. For a history of state election law, see Gerald A. McBeath and Thomas A. Morehouse, *Alaska Politics and Government* (Lincoln: University of Nebraska Press, 1994). For a timeline of Alaska primary laws, see the Alaska Secretary of State website.

69. Sarah E. Anderson et al., "Top-4 Primaries Help Moderate Candidates via Crossover Voting: The Case of the 2022 Alaska Election Reforms," *The Forum* 21 (2023): 123–136; Benjamin Reilly, David Lublin, and Glenn Wright, "Alaska's New Electoral System: Countering Polarization or 'Crooked as Hell'?," *California Journal of Politics and Policy* 15 (2023); Gerald A. McBeath, "Alaska Electoral Reform: The Top 4 Primary and Ranked Choice Voting," *California Journal of Politics and Policy* 15, no. 1 (2023); Zachary Albert et al., "The Effect of Alaska's Top 4 / RCV System on Campaign Finance" (paper presented at the Southern Political Science Association Annual Meeting, New Orleans, Louisiana, January 10–13, 2024).

70. Daniel J. Elazar, *American Federalism: A View from the States*, 2nd ed. (New York: Thomas Y. Crowell, 1972); David R. Mayhew, *Placing Parties in American Politics* (Princeton, NJ: Princeton University Press, 1986).

71. Boris Shor and Nolan McCarty, "Two Decades of Polarization in American State Legislatures," *Journal of Political Institutions and Political Economy* 3 (2022): 343–370.

72. Richard Barton, "California's Top-Two Primary: The Effects on Electoral Politics and Governance," Unite America Institute, June 2023.

73. Zoltan Hajnal and Jessica Trounstine, "Where Turnout Matters: The Consequences of Uneven Turnout in City Politics," *Journal of Politics* 67, no. 2 (2005): 515–535.

6

Presidential Nominations

Richard H. Pildes and Frances Lee

The risks of political extremism are particularly great if a politically extreme figure can capture the presidency, with all its attendant actual and rhetorical powers. For the first 170 or so years of American history, this risk was mitigated by the need for party nominees to gain the support of elected party figures at all levels of government throughout the country. But with the shift in the 1970s to the system of direct primary elections for choosing party nominees, we believe the risk of more demagogic, extreme figures capturing the nomination of one or both parties—and hence the presidency—has increased. Given the US commitment to choosing nominees through direct primaries, however, we offer several potential means of working within the existing system to reduce the risk of more extremist candidates capturing a party's nomination.

We also offer suggestions for how to improve the primary debate process. Primary debates should play a significant role in informing party voters of the quality and policy positions of various candidates. Especially in large primary fields, which are increasingly common, these debates should help voters identify important distinctions among candidates within the party. We believe there are numerous ways of improving the primary debate process to enable it to play that role more effectively. The second part of this chapter provides those recommendations and the justifications for them.

The Context of the Problem

One of the most consequential and radical changes to the American electoral system of the last fifty years was the introduction in the 1970s of the direct primary to select major-party nominees. After more than a century and a half during which elected state, national, and local party figures from around the country played a major role in choosing their parties' candidates for president, we moved almost overnight to a purely voter-controlled method in which primary elections (and a small number of caucuses) determine party nominees. The candidate who wins a majority of convention delegates through these primary elections becomes the party's nominee. Elected party figures no longer have any direct decisionmaking role in the nominations process (except, in theory, for the Democratic Party's superdelegates, who are not permitted to vote in the first round of balloting at the party's convention).

This change has had a range of consequences. It is responsible for the large fields of candidates who frequently now run in the primaries. It has prompted more figures who know they have no prospect of winning the nomination to nonetheless declare themselves candidates in order to raise their profile for other purposes. (Almost anyone with minimal support and resources can run and generate media coverage.) It has given outsize weight to the states that hold early primaries. It has made it more likely that a candidate can capture the nomination by appealing only to one strong faction within a party rather than reflecting a compromise among various factions. But most importantly for our purposes, the shift to a more direct popular method of selection has significantly increased the risk that extremist, demagogic, or inexperienced candidates can capture the nomination of one or both major political parties.

When the shift to this popular selection process was underway, leading scholars of political parties expressed exactly that worry. As Nelson Polsby and Aaron Wildavsky cautioned in 1964, eliminating any role for elected party figures in the nomination process "might lead to the appearance of extremist candidates and demagogues, who, unrestrained by allegiance to any permanent party organization, would have little to lose by stirring up mass hatreds or making absurd promises."[1] Indeed, it was precisely this worry that led Martin Van Buren to establish the party convention as a vehicle for choosing the nominee.[2] Van Buren had concluded that, without a role for elected party figures, competition for the presidency would devolve into a system of highly personalized and factional politics that generated too many candidates and more extreme, demagogic campaign appeals, as individual candidates fought to distinguish their personal brands.[3] In Van Buren's view, unified national political parties and party nominating conventions were critical for fostering broad consensus because they forced compromise among cross-cutting cleavages and reined in personality-based politics.

Another virtue of the convention system was that delegates, selected by local party actors from across the country, would bring to the nomination process a diverse range of important qualities and perspectives. Many would have governing experience, and while they would certainly strive to advocate for constituencies within the party, they would also grasp the compromises necessary for a party to function.[4] In addition, many of these figures would have direct experience working with potential nominees, offering valuable perspective on their ability to govern the country.

Elected party figures from around the nation were also likely to represent the major interests and factions within the party; the need to gain their support would make it more likely that successful candidates would reflect that range of interests and factions.

We do not wish to romanticize such convention-run parties. While this system could bring voice to issues and constituencies across the country, it also had the effect of squelching discussions on slavery and civil rights for much of the nineteenth and twentieth centuries.[5] This political system was a product of its time and reflected the preferences of the nearly exclusively white and male memberships of both parties, seeking to protect and advance their interests.

Conventions are now much more inclusive, but the electoral system has evolved into one that primary voters dominate. Since we are unlikely to go back to the old system, the question is whether there are ways to improve the nominations process by leveraging some of the advantages elected party figures can provide while still accepting the central role of voters in choosing the nominees. This chapter addresses potential reforms to do so.

In addition, a crucial step along the path to nomination is the primary debate, where voters are able to see and evaluate competing candidates at the same time addressing the same issues. We therefore also address ways to improve the primary debate process to give voters more of the information they need to make well-informed decisions among candidates. First, however, it is important to put the current nominations process in historical context in order to understand how this system emerged.

The Historical Evolution of the Nominations Process

Most Americans take for granted, and perhaps even consider natural, our current direct popular method of choosing the parties' nominees. Little memory or understanding exists of how the prior selection system worked. Yet the dramatic shift to a fully voter-driven method of selection has profound effects on our system of government, including on the risk that more extremist forces can capture the presidency. Changing the method of choosing the parties' nominees inevitably shapes the kinds of candidates who run; the reasons candidates choose to run; the size of the primary election field; the role of prior name recognition or celebrity status; the kind of political figures most likely to succeed in capturing nominations and the White House; and, most importantly, the way government functions and the interests and political forces to which it is most likely to be responsive.

To provide context for the reforms discussed in this chapter, the next section describes how the nominations process worked up until the changes of the 1970s. We then describe those changes and the unintended consequences they produced. To offer a broader perspective on these issues, we briefly illustrate how much of an outlier our system of presidential-candidate selection is compared to other major democracies. The final section of this chapter then turns to several reform proposals that would help reduce the risk that an extremist candidate captures a party's nomination and, with it, potentially the White House.

The Historical Role of Peer Review

For most of American history until the 1970s, the nominations process included a significant role for "peer review" by existing officeholders and party officials who helped select their party's candidate for president. The first form of peer review emerged in the early nineteenth century.[6] This was the congressional caucus, which arose as the de facto means of preselecting credible presidential candidates in a world in which factional or partisan divisions had begun to emerge. In the caucus system, which lasted until 1824, members of Congress from a self-identified coalition— the Jeffersonian Republicans—would privately come to an agreement on the candidate they would endorse to the public as representing their views. The birth of this system reflected, in part, the fear that without such a filtering device, too many candidates would run, the Electoral College would be unable to select a clear winner, and the president would end up being chosen by the House of Representatives (where each state delegation has one vote).

But critics began to deride the method as "King Caucus." With such a small group in Congress carrying such decisive weight in identifying party candidates, the caucus system began to lose its legitimacy. Within a couple decades, it was replaced by the national party nomination conventions that (in vestigial form) remain with us today. Though the party convention was not invented by Van Buren, he quickly turned it into an enduring feature of American democracy, along with the mass national political party he created and legitimized. Of particular relevance here, Van Buren had concluded that in the vacuum created by the demise of the caucus system, competition for the presidency had devolved into a system of highly personalized and factional politics that generated too many candidates and more extreme, demagogic campaign appeals, as candidates struggled to create a distinct identity.[7] Unified national political parties and party nominating conventions were thought to be vehicles for fostering broad consensus by forcing compromise among cross-cutting cleavages and reining in personalized, and hence more demagogic, politics. By 1836, as James Ceaser has written, "the idea of partisan nominations was never again seriously challenged; it became part of the living constitution."[8]

The convention system involved a larger and more representative group of selectors than the caucus system, with state and local party leaders effectively controlling the conventions and the nomination process. They had considerable capacity to influence the choice of delegates (who were selected by party caucus, district convention, state convention, executive committee, or some combination of these and similar methods). Party leaders also led their own state delegations and essentially controlled how they voted.[9] Party leaders, who included state and national officeholders, had thick ties to their parties and their commitments; they had ongoing and long-standing ties to their parties and were professional politicians.[10] Thus, the convention system continued to provide peer-review filtering of potential nominees, albeit in more attenuated form than had the congressional caucus.

With certain incremental changes, party conventions provided this form of peer review and filtering all the way until 1972. The most significant adaptation of this system came during the Progressive Era with the push for direct primaries as a means of choosing party nominees for all levels of elected office. That introduced a limited role for a few direct presidential primaries to choose convention delegates. But most remarkable in hindsight is how little effect the direct primary movement had on the presidential nomination process, given how successful that movement turned out to be for elections at virtually every other level.

The direct primary was added as an element—but just an element—to the nomination system in 1912. Thirteen states ended up choosing their delegates through the direct primary for that year's Republican convention.[11] From then on, the nomination process was best understood as what scholars have called a "mixed system": primary elections to choose delegates from some states, alongside a continuing role for local, state, and national party figures selected in the more traditional ways. Although winning a primary could influence the selection process, most of the power to determine the nominees continued to rest with traditional party figures.[12]

As early as 1920, enthusiasm for the direct primary as part of the presidential nomination process had dissipated. Primaries became a contained feature of the system, with the dominance of the party organization resolidified.[13] After 1920, only twelve to eighteen states, depending on the year, used some form of primary to select delegates.[14] And as late as 1968, only fourteen states used primaries; they selected between 37 and 38 percent of the delegates, well less than the majority needed to control the choice of nominee.[15] Most importantly, many of these primaries were "favorite-son" contests that did not determine the presidential preference of the convention delegates. Primaries played a role in this mixed system for selecting presidential nominees, in other words, but elected party figures remained the dominant force.

The convention system had its flaws, to be sure. Accusations of insider dealing in secretive "smoke-filled" rooms dogged the practice. More damningly, this system tended to reinforce, rather than undermine, many of the exclusionary biases of the day. Politicians not wishing to address slavery or civil rights or to see those issues split their delicate party coalitions would work to exclude certain figures from the process. This was not purely a feature of early American history, either: Civil rights protesters targeted the 1964 Democratic convention precisely for refusing to seat Black southern delegates, and Shirley Chisholm's 1972 campaign ran into many of the same barriers. Peer review could serve as both a protector of the republic and a way to reinforce its hierarchies.

Even with these exclusionary tendencies, however, the twentieth-century mixed system functioned in more complex ways than is generally appreciated. Popular primaries and party figures turned out to check and balance each other's influence. Party figures continued to have incentives to put their weight behind candidates likely to hold the party's factions together, run a competitive election, govern effectively, and reflect the party's general ideology. But primaries also kept the system from being too closed: "outsiders" could challenge the existing party hierarchy and orthodoxy and force the party to remain responsive, at least up to a point. The system mixed elements of direct popular choice and peer review.

Primaries also enabled less tested candidates to show skeptical party leaders that they could win votes—as when John Kennedy won the 1960 West Virginia primary and proved that a Catholic could succeed in heavily Protestant areas.[16] Even an insurgent candidate like Barry Goldwater in 1964 could successfully work the mixed system.[17] But no candidate could succeed without also convincing enough institutional party figures throughout the country to support them. In 1960, for example, just sixteen states held Democratic primaries, and while Kennedy won ten of those, he still required the support of party regulars to gain the nomination. Primaries mattered, but so did the ability to build coalitions within the party.

Under this system, some candidates chose to "run" on the inside track and make their appeal primarily or even exclusively to the party figures who controlled convention delegates. Others took advantage of the outside track to demonstrate their popular appeal. The net effect of this mixed system was to keep the political parties (meaning party leaders from the national, state, and local levels) in control. As the most thorough recent study concludes about the convention process in the decades before it collapsed, in no nomination contest "was a party forced by strong candidates with large popular followings to choose a nominee it didn't want."[18] And as this study goes on to explain, "with the exception of the Republicans in 1964 and the Democrats in 1968, parties consistently attempted to find candidates who were broadly acceptable to party groups and able to compete well in the general election."[19]

Thus, for the first 170 or so years of American history, the selection of nominees for the presidency typically involved a high degree of control and peer review from national, state, and local party leaders from throughout the country. Party leaders retained the most significant power over presidential nominations, even as the precise form of peer review evolved, from selection by a small caucus in Congress to nominating conventions that eventually created a partial role for direct popular input.

The Inadvertent Creation of Today's Direct Presidential Primaries

The convention system unraveled in the aftermath of the 1968 Democratic convention in Chicago. Almost overnight, it was replaced by today's system of choosing party nominees exclusively through popular vote in primaries and caucuses. In many ways, this change was unintended; indeed, it transpired despite some of its architects intending to forestall exactly the changes their recommendations brought about. But within a decade, the United States had abandoned a 170-year-old peer-review selection system and replaced it with a purely voter-driven one.

The catalyst for this change was the explosive 1968 Democratic convention in the midst of the Vietnam War. Torn asunder by conflicts over the war, the convention ended up nominating the establishment candidate, Vice President Hubert Humphrey. Humphrey had entered the race too late to make it onto the ballot for any of the primaries but was nominated nonetheless through a vote by elected party figures.

To appease critics of his nomination, Humphrey agreed to a reform commission, known as the "McGovern-Fraser Commission," to advise on how to improve the nomination process for the 1972 convention. Its recommendations quickly led to the current system of primary elections and voter caucuses choosing the great majority of delegates. As Byron Shafer, the leading scholar of this transformation, put it, the reforms constituted "a revolutionary change in the mechanics of presidential selection, the greatest systematically planned and centrally imposed shift in the institutions of delegate selection in all of American history."[20] As a result, he added, "the official party has been *erased* from what was still nominally the party's nomination process."[21]

Strikingly, this dramatic shift to a "plebiscitary," primary-dominated selection process was not the aim of many reformers, including those on the McGovern-Fraser Commission.[22] The commission had intended to save the convention system by preserving a critical role for the party. It did not seek to create a primary-dominated selection system that essentially shut institutional party figures out of the process. But the changes that flowed from the commission's report ironically had the exact opposite of their intended effect.

Austin Ranney, a member of the commission who had spent much of his career as a political scientist trying to strengthen parties rather than hollow them out, described how the body's recommendations led inadvertently to the modern direct popular selection process:

> I well remember that the first thing [the commission] agreed on . . . was that we did not want . . . any great increase in the number of state primaries. Indeed, we hoped to prevent any such development by reforming the delegate-selection rules so that the party's non-primary process would be open and fair, participation in them would greatly increase, and consequently the demand for more primaries would fade away. . . . But we got a rude shock. . . . We accomplished the opposite of what we intended.[23]

The reforms had largely sought to preserve the legitimacy of the party by making the caucus system more accessible, transparent, and open. Up until then, it had been governed by baroque rules designed to enable only party insiders to participate. But for a variety of reasons, the state parties—first on the Democratic side and then on the Republican one—responded by rapidly expanding the role of primaries, which had the effect of putting the nomination in the hands of primary voters once a majority of delegates were selected that way.

In the first two elections after these changes were made, the Democrats nominated candidates, Jimmy Carter and George McGovern, who almost certainly would not have been selected under the convention system. For a few decades after that, the political parties found ways to work within the new selection process to nominate figures that party leaders and the establishment most preferred. But since 2004, a series of candidates have captured the nomination who would have been unlikely to do so under the convention system: John McCain, Barack Obama, and Donald Trump. McCain broke with party orthodoxy on some issues, and Obama lacked experience and clout within the party, but both garnered endorsements from elected officials well before their respective national conventions. Trump, by contrast, combined inexperience in government with inconsistency with traditional party priorities and won very little elite support until much later in the election season. The shift in types of successful candidates reflects the implications of the modern nomination system.

Other aspects of today's nomination process reflect the 1970s reforms. The extremely large field of candidates now regularly running, at least when there is no obvious frontrunner, is a product of these changes. Such an expansive field has occasionally forced primary debate platforms to be divided into a "main" debate stage, which can still have as many as ten figures on it, and a "junior varsity" debate stage. Candidates regularly enter the presidential primaries for purposes other than genuinely seeking their party's nomination; while these candidates know they have no realistic chance of winning, they run to raise their name recognition in pursuit of other aims—to score a potential cable television or book deal, for instance, or to emphasize idiosyncratic issues. Primary electorates may place less weight on prior government service than party elders in the convention system, and primary electorates are more likely to prefer "outsider" candidates. Most importantly for present purposes, the switch to a direct primary selection process has increased the risk that extremist or demagogic candidates will capture the nomination and the White House.

A Brief Comparative Perspective

The United States is an outlier among major democracies in employing such a voter-centered method for choosing nominees who then compete to become chief executive of the country. (In parliamentary systems, the selection process is for a party leader, who then becomes prime minister if his or her party wins a majority of seats in the parliament.) A brief comparative perspective is helpful to put the US system in context.

Several well-established democracies continue to rely exclusively on a peer-review system in which party members in parliament choose the party leader without any popular input (much like the congressional caucus system that once existed in the United States). Other major democracies employ a mixed system in which elements of peer review are combined with a vote by party members. However, these parties have many fewer members than US parties do, because the hurdles to becoming a party member are more significant than in the United States, where voters become party members simply by checking a box when they register to vote or arrive at the polls. In these countries, party membership often requires paying annual dues. Only a small minority of democracies have moved to mostly plebiscitary selection methods, but even in these countries, the percentage of ordinary voters who participate is far lower than in the United States. To be sure, some of these are parliamentary systems, but nothing intrinsic to the presidential system requires direct popular selection of nominees, as the pre-1970s experience in the United States illustrates.

The Australian Liberal Party and the New Zealand National Party both use exclusively peer-review methods. The leaders of these two center-right parties continue to be elected solely by their parliamentary peers and colleagues.[24] In Germany, party leaders are required by law to be elected by delegates to the party's national conference every two years. Typically, the major figures in the parties reach a consensus beforehand and present a united front at the conference in a "coronation" of the uncontested leader.

The United Kingdom offers a good example of a mixed system. In the Conservative Party, the parliamentary party plays an initial gatekeeping role. It uses successive ballots to winnow the field of candidates down to two that are voted on by the full party membership, which currently consists of around 150,000 individuals.[25] A candidate for Labour Party leader, meanwhile, must be a member of Parliament and must first receive support from 20 percent of Labour members of Parliament (and there are further requirements of internal party support). Candidates who gain that level of peer support are then voted on by Labour Party members.

Canada uses a selection process that does not include peer review but is still not comparable to the purely plebiscitary US system. Candidates for party leadership must pay an entrance fee and, in some parties, collect the signatures of a specified number of party members. In the case of the Conservatives and the New Democratic Party, voting for party leaders is limited to party members, who number in the realm of 150,000 in a total eligible electorate of around 25 million.

Outside the United States, the first purely popular, open-primary selection process in an established democracy did not occur until 2005—in Italy.[26] Several Italian parties now use open primaries with large electorates to choose their leaders. In France, as well, several parties currently use open primaries comparable to those in the United States.

But even in these countries that use open primaries, parties wield greater control over leadership candidates than US parties do, thanks to additional features in the structure of European elections. For example, most public and private funding for primary (and general) elections in Europe is channeled through party organizations, inevitably enhancing party control of the process. In the United States, by contrast, a great deal of campaign funds are raised by candidates and controlled by them. In addition, in most countries, there is a fairly well-understood track, in terms of qualifications and experience, toward becoming the party's candidate for chief executive. This may include educational background, work in and for the party in various junior and then more senior capacities, and time spent as an elected representative or official. But since the shift to primaries in the 1970s, there is no similar track or set of qualifications and experiences broadly viewed as necessary to compete for party nominations in the United States.

For most of American history, peer review played an important role in determining which candidates would carry the major parties' banners into the general election. The mixed system of the modern convention era combined elements of popular input, through a select number of primaries, with a continuing role for elected party figures from around the country. The dramatic shift in the 1970s to a more voter-centered selection system that we now take for granted has increased the risk that more extremist and demagogic candidates can prevail in the nomination contests and in the presidential election.

Below, we offer thoughts for how a degree of peer review, or input from elected officials, might be built back into our nominations process without compromising the popular participation that is now the norm.

Contested Conventions

Perhaps the most straightforward way to reintroduce elected officials into the process would be for conventions to reclaim their role as places for deliberation and decisionmaking. A few small changes could bring back "contested" conventions: More proportional delegate-selection rules and a shorter calendar would send a more representative group of delegates to the convention. Those delegates, in turn, could be further empowered and prepared to deliberate. Such deliberation would reflect the views of the party's primary electorate, in much the same way that Congress represents the views of the national electorate, but the delegates could negotiate compromises, balance competing party constituencies, and perform the function of peer review.

As noted above, the McGovern-Fraser reforms were intended not to remove delegates from the selection process, only to make their role more transparent and democratic. The reformers' objection to Humphrey's nomination was not that he was selected at a convention but that he was selected by delegates who did not reflect the view of rank-and-file Democrats.[27] Reformers envisioned a convention in which underrepresented elements of the party's coalition (including the antiwar supporters of Humphrey's main rivals for the nomination) would have a voice in the selection of the eventual nominee. But conventions today have become only ceremonial, formally ratifying the results of primary elections.

Enabling conventions to again become decisionmakers when there is not a strong consensus choice within the parties would not require changing the basic structure of the nomination process. A few relatively simple changes could return delegates to their decisionmaking role. First, the parties could adjust their delegate-allocation rules and the primary calendar to eliminate the tendency for a single candidate, even one with only a plurality of support, to amass a majority of votes before the convention. Parties could improve the proportionality of their allocation rules and shorten the primary calendar to make it easier for candidates to stay in the contest until the end, thereby ensuring that convention delegates more accurately reflect the preferences of the voters across the entire country. In addition, parties could ensure that delegates selected to attend the convention are prepared and enabled to play a more active role in the nomination process. Candidates could do this by giving more attention to the kind of delegates selected when they win.

Proportional representation in the selection of delegates would make the convention more representative of the party's supporters. If a majority of delegates support the same candidate on the first ballot, there is currently no opportunity for further deliberation. If this majority reflects similar majority support among the primary electorate, then the favored candidate has a reasonable claim to be the nominee. More often, however, the process exaggerates the eventual winner's support in two ways.

First, on the Republican side, delegate-selection rules often give a bonus to first-place candidates. Some Republican primaries are winner-take-all, giving no delegates to second- or third-place finishers. Even in states with more proportional allocation formulas, this proportionality is imperfect. For instance, it is well known that smaller district magnitudes (the number of delegates available in the constituency) and high thresholds (the vote share needed to win any delegates) can undermine proportionality.[28]

States typically allocate delegates by congressional district, meaning that the number of delegates to be divided is relatively small. This requires candidates to win a high share of the vote to earn any delegates. In some states, parties raise the bar even further with a formal threshold of support, often 15 percent, to win delegates. In today's fairly large primary fields, many candidates with substantial national support might fail to win enough of the vote in state primaries to garner any delegates at all.

This advantage to the top few candidates then feeds into the second way that majorities are exaggerated, which is the winnowing of candidates over time. Running for the nomination is expensive and laborious. Candidates who do not perform well in early states often drop out. Their supporters either switch their support to candidates who remain in the race or else don't vote in the primary at all.[29] By the time the contest reaches the final states to hold primaries, often there is only one serious candidate still competing. That candidate picks up a lot of votes, but only after having effectively already won the nomination, exaggerating their support.[30] We never learn the true preferences of primary voters in those states. Because of this phenomenon, political scientist Caitlin Jewett has shown, a majority of voters never have the opportunity for what she calls "meaningful participation" in the nomination process.[31]

Because parties believe they need the process to end with one clear winner, the current rules are often designed to encourage the winnowing process. But the opposite could be done. Parties could try to make the conditions for a contested convention more likely. They could use more proportional delegate-allocation rules—eliminating winner-take-all or other top-finisher bonuses, lowering thresholds, and moving to statewide allocation of delegates. The parties could also arrange a shorter primary calendar, making it easier for candidates to survive until the end.

Currently, a contested convention—one in which the delegates deliberate and make a decision later than the first ballot—is a technical possibility. It is so unlikely, however, that many of the delegates might not be prepared to play that role. Parties should improve their selection rules to better prepare delegates to deliberate.

Delegate selection varies by state, and some states might need few formal changes to their rules to enable the best delegates to be selected. The key is that candidates for the nomination should invest more in their delegate selection. They should choose people with negotiating skills and a willingness to form coalitions with the delegates representing other candidates.

To make this proposal work, the way delegates are allocated would also have to change. Currently, both parties largely allocate delegates by district. On the Republican side, all districts award three delegates. On the Democratic side, the number per district ranges from three to nine. In large multicandidate fields, the current structure would not be capable of awarding delegates proportionately to a large number of candidates.

One solution to this problem would be for both parties to shift to awarding delegates on a statewide basis. Another possibility, if the current system of district-based allocation remained in place, would be to award delegates on a fractional basis or to expand significantly the number of delegates awarded per district.

However, it might not be adequate to leave the campaigns fully in charge of putting forward slates of delegates if brokered conventions become more of a possibility. Campaigns have incentives to nominate delegates who will be loyal to them. Thus, it might make sense to have at least one delegate from each state party be the highest-ranking elected official in that state from that party—the governor, for instance, or party leader in the state senate. Elected officials with strong statewide support would have the greatest legitimacy in brokering the outcome of a contested convention.

Such a convention would be comparable to a multiparty parliament charged with forming a government. Delegates pledged to different candidates can be thought of as analogous to parties, with the candidates as their effective leaders. Just as parties do when forming a coalition, the delegates would negotiate—over platform language, policy priorities, even the vice presidential slot. The presidential nominee would also be subject to that kind of negotiation.

If contested conventions become more likely, then politicians will adapt their strategies and choose delegations that are prepared to negotiate. Currently, delegates are not selected for their capacity to negotiate over such critical matters as the party's nominees; nor do they necessarily have the stature to play that role effectively. Delegates should be chosen not merely for their loyalty to their candidate but for their fidelity to the principles and priorities that their candidate campaigned on. Their voters favored a candidate who articulated a particular vision of the party and the presidency, so they should represent that vision. At the same time, the delegates should be prepared to negotiate and compromise with their fellow delegates to best achieve that vision, just as members of Congress negotiate and compromise with their fellow legislators.

Even if contested conventions were more likely, most cycles might still end with a clear winner, as was common even before the McGovern-Fraser reforms.[32] As the authors of *The Party Decides: Presidential Nominations Before and After Reform* argue, political leaders often throw their support behind a particular candidate, helping that candidate win.[33] But such informal support is a crude and imprecise tool, usually most effective when there is broad consensus within the party. When there is not, a contested convention could occur.

The most significant hurdle would be convincing the public that such an approach is legitimate. Since the 1980s, there has been little doubt about the identity of the eventual nominee, and so conventions have evolved into pageants. The idea that the nominee might not be chosen on the first ballot is treated as an unusual and even undemocratic technicality.

Parties and news media should do more to explain the history of conventions as decisionmaking institutions, as well as the benefits and costs of selecting nominees in this manner. Representative democracy is today's model of democracy in the United States and throughout the world. The current nomination system uses an unrepresentative aggregation of votes, dominated by those voting in the early primary states. A contested convention could be more representative and more democratic than our current system for selecting party nominees.

Acceptance of Superdelegates

The so-called superdelegates that the Democratic Party has used in every convention since 1984 (whose potential role has been a source of criticism since 2008, including from within the party) can provide an element of peer review in the nomination process. As it stands now in the Democratic Party, every member of Congress, governor, and national committeeperson is automatically a delegate to the nominating convention. In 2018, under pressure from the left wing of the Democratic Party, the rule was changed to allow the automatic delegates a vote only on the second ballot, if there was one. The rule was a compromise that kept the party leaders at the convention but kept them from using their numbers to overturn the will of primary voters—unless the will of these voters was unclear enough to mean there was no first-ballot winner.

But the core of the argument for automatic delegates is the element of peer review.[34] Presumably, members of Congress and party leaders, many of whom have worked with past presidents, would be sensitive to whether or not the presidential aspirant had the gravitas and the talent in areas like negotiation to actually do the job. No Republican member of Congress, for instance, would have taken seriously Trump's campaign pledge to make Mexico pay for his border wall. Likewise, no Democratic member of Congress would seriously believe that Marianne Williamson should be the leader of their party with a veto over legislation.

But in the modern nominating system, the most experienced members of the political class have been cut out of the nomination process by two new rules. The first is the requirement that delegates be pledged to a presidential candidate or uncommitted—and uncommitted never wins a delegate in state primaries. (Many members simply don't want to endorse in an intraparty contest.) The second is the adoption of open caucuses for the selection of delegates, which means that elected officials have to run against their constituents for delegate spots—so they stay home instead.

On the Republican side, members of the Republican National Committee (RNC), including the critically important state chairs and vice chairs, are automatic delegates and so don't have to run against their constituents. Still, they are bound to the candidate who wins their state.

Very few superdelegates in the current era see their role as upending the judgment of voters in primaries. Rather, they see it as preventing clearly unacceptable candidates from winning the nomination. Because the nomination race takes place over a period of more than six months—usually beginning with the Iowa caucuses in January and ending with the conventions in the summer—candidates who look good at the outset may turn out to have substantial problems by the end of the process. Imagine, for example, if North Carolina senator John Edwards had done well in the winter of 2008 and gone on to amass enough delegates to be the presumptive nominee that summer. News of his extramarital affair while his wife was dying of cancer and that his mistress was pregnant could have severely damaged his candidacy in this instance, potentially prompting the party's elected leaders to take up the task of finding a replacement and nominating him or her at the convention.[35]

Superdelegates might or might not have kept Republicans from nominating Trump in 2016. The base of the Republican Party was clearly very angry and rejected more traditional candidates in primary after primary.[36] But more formal engagement of party figures in the nomination process might have resulted in more support for the "Stop

Trump" movement. He went into the convention with 306 delegates more than he needed for the nomination—hardly an enormous margin.[37] And at the time of the convention, there were doubts about his electability. More than one Republican in Cleveland, the site of the convention, said they expected Hillary Clinton to win and saw Trump as "our McGovern"—a reference to Senator George McGovern, who won the Democratic nomination in 1972 against the judgment of party leaders and went down to a resounding defeat in November.[38] Republican senators, representatives, and governors might have resisted a Trump nomination, but they were not even in attendance.

Preprimary Endorsement

Another option for injecting an element of peer review into the current nomination process would be for each party to mandate a preprimary endorsement of one or more candidates.[39] In Massachusetts since the 1980s, Democrats have held an annual party convention, which, in election years, endorses candidates for statewide office. A candidate who does not receive at least 15 percent of the convention votes on the first ballot is not eligible for placement on the primary ballot. The candidate who wins the majority of votes is the endorsed candidate of the Democratic Party and has the first position on the primary ballot.[40] This process guarantees that candidates are at least minimally acceptable to the local party leadership, and newcomers are regularly kept off the ballot.[41] The Massachusetts state courts concluded that the state's primary laws would violate the party's constitutional rights unless this preprimary nomination convention were permitted; in a 6–3 vote, the Supreme Court dismissed the state's appeal for lack of jurisdiction.[42]

A national endorsing convention would give party officials and activists a significant role in determining who could run for president under the party's banner, since potential candidates would have to cross a threshold of support to be eligible for the ballot. As effective as this method is for establishing some peer review in Massachusetts, however, it would be extremely difficult to pull off on a national level. It would push the presidential race to start even earlier than it does now, since delegates would have to be elected in the year *before* the primaries were held.

Preprimary Vote of Confidence

A more feasible option, at least logistically, might be to have members of Congress and the parties' national committees give up their convention votes in exchange for a January session or sessions with the presidential candidates that would allow them to drill the candidates (in private) and then issue a vote of confidence or no confidence. Members could be allowed to vote for more than one candidate and their role would simply be to let primary voters know what people in government think of the capabilities of these candidates prior to the beginning of the nomination contests. As a further possibility for giving these endorsements more effect, candidates not receiving a minimum share of votes—say 15 percent—in these forums could be barred from at least the early televised primary debates, which have become such an important part of the primary process. But they could still get on ballots and try to compete in the nominating contests.

The political "elites" would not make any final decisions—the voters would still do that—but they would give voters answers to two important questions. First, are the candidates knowledgeable and experienced enough to have the judgment to do the job of president? Second, are they in line with the general philosophy of the Democratic or Republican Party?

A version of this process is already in place in California. There, the major parties adapted to the switch to a nonpartisan "top-two" election system by issuing preprimary endorsements to signal their preferred candidates to voters. This has been shown to have a real effect on voters, with endorsed candidates receiving a roughly ten-point advantage over nonendorsed candidates.[43] Partisan voters hear their party's signal and will respond to it.

While pizza executives with no government experience, reality television stars, and spiritual advisors may fulfill the ballot requirements to run in the primaries, the party electorate could at least be formally forewarned, and some people might vote accordingly. By forcing would-be presidents to appear before the people they would need to work with if elected, a preprimary vote of confidence could add some element of peer review to the process.

National Party Administration of Presidential Primary Debates

Historically, primary debates were organized and negotiated directly between media organizations and candidates' campaigns. Over time, however, the growing proliferation of unregulated debates proved unsustainable for candidates and their campaigns. The national parties recognized that they needed to regulate the primary debate process and, beginning with the 2016 presidential election cycle, have increasingly stood in to negotiate with media sponsors on behalf of their candidates.[44] Yet outsourcing to the media such key debate components as who will moderate, which candidates will participate (usually based on the media's small-sample polls), and the debate format has led to frustrations for candidates and voters alike. In addition, as media audiences have segmented and declined, the slice of the electorate reached by such debates has been limited to the media sponsor's audience.

At the same time, Democrats and Republicans have also had to devise approaches for managing large fields of candidates. Neither of these problems—excessive demand for debates and large fields of candidates—is likely to disappear.

In light of these developments, the national parties should directly host the primary debates. In other words, they should take full control of organizing, producing, and disseminating them. In so doing, the parties can act in the best interests of their candidates and voters to build a primary debate process that addresses concerns about timing, sequence, content, locations, and fair moderation, rather than relying on media and other organizations that often have different incentives than those of the candidates and parties in hosting these events.

What's Wrong with the Current System?

Under the current system, parties outsource to the media all facets of debates, from topics discussed, to polling that determines which candidates are allowed to participate, to the selection of moderators. Yet the primary incentive of media outlets is commercial, not improving the quality of the candidates or advancing their party.

A constant concern for primary campaigns and their parties has been the role of debate moderators. As part of the traditional bargain, the sponsoring media outlet gets to have its talent moderate the primary debate. The incentive for media is to create "buzz," which has often resulted in "gotcha questions" on subjects of little relevance to the parties' primary voters.[45] On occasion, moderators effectively serve as opposition researchers for the opposing party.[46]

Furthermore, the audience for primary debates is typically restricted to the sponsoring media entity's audience (and perhaps that of a partner or two), thereby limiting its reach. The current model of relying on one principal media outlet to run each debate thus misses an important opportunity for the political parties to help their candidates reach more people.

Primary debates are vitally important forums. In terms of informing voters and shaping their impressions, they matter much more than general election debates. Primary debates increase issue knowledge, influence perceptions of candidates' character, and can affect voter preferences.[47] Since parties remain neutral in open-seat presidential primaries, voters do not have the most important heuristic for determining their vote choice. So primary debates are an opportunity for voters to compare candidates, see what issues and stances they emphasize, and gauge whom they're comfortable with. A process this vital for parties, candidates, voters, and the political system as a whole should be handled directly by the parties, the entities with the strongest motivation to ensure that the process serves their candidates and voters.

An enhanced party role in the debates could help reverse the parties' loss of leverage in their historic role as candidate gatekeepers. With the current campaign finance system and online environment allowing for easy political organization, parties are weak, if not powerless, when it comes to deciding who becomes a presidential candidate. Unless and until they become strong enough to play a bigger role in this process, they should assume greater responsibility for managing primary debates.

Why Would Parties Do a Better Job?

Although national party organizations have seen their influence decline in the last twenty years, they maintain relevance through their role as rule setters for their presidential nominations processes. While no longer a force in shaping which and how many candidates can enter the field, the parties have assumed an increasingly central role, through their management of presidential primary debates. This is a positive development in that the parties should have stronger incentives than other actors to ensure that the nominating process serves the interests of their party's candidates, voters, and aligned constituencies.

The national parties are, at least in theory, the only organizations incentivized to ensure a debate process that is fair to their candidates and focused on the issues and concerns that their party's voters and aligned interests care about most. By contrast, media organizations, the current sponsors of the primary debates, naturally care primarily about their share in a fiercely competitive market for viewers and advertisers and are often perceived by party loyalists as having their own partisan agendas.[48]

Unlike for-profit media organizations, parties stand in a good position to ensure that the debates focus on issues relevant to primary voters and to what presidents actually do, rather than on hot-button issues designed to elicit controversy. It is problematic when primary debates focus on matters that are peripheral to the president's job description. Education, for example, is primarily a state and local responsibility, in which the federal government has only a relatively limited role. Meanwhile, foreign policy takes up a large share of a president's work every day.

To better inform voters, the issue agenda of primary debates should steer toward what presidents actually do and issues of concern to the party's primary voters. Party-organized primary debates can be conducted with more seriousness of purpose than debates held with an eye toward audience ratings, which may feature silly questions.[49]

There are clear precedents for the parties assuming a more central role in primary debates. Parties have been moving in that direction over the past decade. The Republican National Committee moved to assert greater control over primary debates after 2012, as part of its postelection "autopsy." The RNC's review found that the primary process before 2012 did not well serve the party's candidates or their campaigns because it featured too many debates, which hinged more on gaffes, one-liners, and "gotcha moments" than on discussion of issues.[50] Moreover, those debates, as well as forums sponsored by Republican-affiliated interest groups, were often announced on such short notice that preexisting campaign plans and strategies had to be interrupted.

Embracing an even stronger and more innovative role in managing primary debates would be one way for the parties to reverse their declining influence in the political process without becoming mired in populist controversies such as the one over superdelegates.

As a general matter, having the parties themselves in sole charge of the debates would enhance both the content of the debates and the strength of the parties. The debates would be run by organizations whose mission is the success of their candidates rather than by entities with different, sometimes contrary interests. Specifically, the parties' producing and disseminating the debates would mean the following:

- The potential for a vastly increased audience
- Moderators with an incentive to ask questions relevant to the party's voters rather than "gotcha" questions to enhance media moderators' ratings and reputations

- The ability to employ formats more conducive to meaningful and fair debate and to select locations that mirror the party's political priorities
- More control of the criteria used to determine which candidates can participate, rather than outsourcing such decisions to small-sample media organization polls
- Fund-raising opportunities to solicit contributions for putting on the debates

What Can the Parties Do?

Today's parties obviously need to be prepared for large fields of candidates, since there is every reason to expect large fields to remain the norm for presidential nomination contests not featuring an incumbent seeking renomination. Parties should embrace this reality and exercise a gatekeeping function through the use of debates to ensure a suitable but not overly inclusive process. By taking full control of administering the debates, the parties can enhance their own role, help their candidates reach more people, and provide better information to primary voters.

1. *Audience size:* Producing the primary debates would allow parties to take advantage of today's media technology, making the debates freely available on many more pathways than a lone major cable or broadcast network. Parties could stream the debates online directly and make the feed available at no cost to all interested national and local media organizations, issue organizations, and the public through a flat, universal, and open feed developed according to predefined, public technical standards. Giving access to all kinds of content providers in today's fragmented media landscape would allow the parties to reach much wider audiences than the current model of partnering with only one primary broadcast network or cable outlet.

2. *Moderators:* By organizing the debates themselves, parties would be empowered to select moderators who do not depend on ratings for their livelihoods. They could choose from a wider array of suitable moderators, including party leaders, retired judges or public officials, academics, or other subject matter experts, who could ask questions curated from supporters and reporters. Compared to networks' star journalists, such moderators would be likely to play a less domineering role in the debates, instead allowing for more direct exchanges between the candidates about subjects relevant to primary voters. Rather than taking responsibility for follow-ups, a moderator might ask an initial ques-

tion and then keep time while relying on other candidates to raise the issues of greatest relevance or highlight contrasts among the presidential aspirants. Parties are also better positioned to insist on impartiality when conducting debates, reducing the likelihood that candidates will be asked questions deliberately designed to embarrass (often referred to as "when did you stop beating your wife?" questions).

In addition, the parties will be able to demand that moderators reflect the concerns and priorities of the party's electorate as they pose questions. It is entirely appropriate to expect that moderators remember that they are conducting a debate for a party nomination, not a general election. Parties do not need to apologize for the fact that their voters have priorities and concerns that differ from those of the national media and the electorate at large, and it is appropriate for them to choose moderators accordingly.

3. *Selecting debate participants:* In addition to providing a stronger gatekeeping function in the debates, the parties should reassess their criteria for determining who gets on the debate stage. For instance, the Republican Party's two main criteria for joining the 2024 debates—media polls and number of donors—both have serious flaws as currently implemented.[51]

In regulating access to the debate stage, parties should be cautious about relying on small-donor counts. A growing body of research suggests that the techniques necessary to succeed in small-donor fund-raising encourage grandstanding and extreme rhetoric and behavior.[52] A long list of small donors is also obviously something that candidates with sufficient financial resources can purchase. Expenditures purely aimed at meeting a threshold number of donors from around the country for debate participation are counterproductive for campaigns' broader purposes of gaining votes in specific states to win primaries. Parties lose credibility by deliberately encouraging this kind of pointless gamesmanship.[53]

While polls are clearly relevant in ascertaining candidate viability, the current reliance on media polls presents some challenges. In effect, the parties are outsourcing the determination of which of their candidates are viable to entities they (especially Republicans) accuse of being biased against them. In addition, the number of people polled is so small that admission to the debate stage can hinge on whether or not a handful of people answer their phones or turn on their computers in states that will not be relevant to picking the nominee.

In an attempt to address this problem, the RNC in 2023 issued rules requiring that candidates show at least 1 percent support in polls that include at least 800 likely Republican primary voters or caucus-goers (up from 500-person samples in 2020).[54] But this still leaves three major problems. First, a 1 percent threshold falls well within the margin of error of any media poll, such that random sampling error will determine which of the candidates at very low levels of support meet the threshold. Second, exceedingly few media polls meet the requirement of including 800 likely Republican primary voters or caucus-goers.[55] Third, media polls do not release the states in which their respondents reside, meaning that in a nationwide poll, larger states, which may not be relevant to that party's primary, exert an outsize influence.[56]

At minimum, parties should consider doing their own polls with larger sample sizes instead of relying on media entities. Short of doing that, however, they will need to be realistic about the standards they set for polls conducted (and financed) by other organizations.

Numbers of donors and polling results are not the only indicators that can be used to assess candidate viability, moreover. Other indicators could include the number of states in which candidates have established working campaign headquarters and visible organizations, as well as the number of campaign staffers reported on their Federal Election Commission reports. In addition, it should not be off limits for parties to consider the total amount of campaign funds that candidates have raised, even though it would be inadvisable to set a firm benchmark. More controversial but highly relevant in today's campaigns would be taking into account the strength of third-party support for a candidate, such as supportive super political action committees and other aligned outside groups like 501(c)(4)s.

As they design their debate-inclusion criteria, parties should think long term by aiming to set up processes that can accumulate legitimacy over time. Obviously, no party organization can bind itself into the future. But parties should seek to develop primary debate rules that they can live with and that can accumulate legitimacy by enduring across multiple cycles.

4. *Fund-raising opportunity:* By putting on debates, parties would create an opportunity to solicit contributions for a "debate fund" to pay for the events. The current primary debate structure has not evolved from its concept of twenty-five years ago to take into account the changed fund-raising status of the political parties. In the 2019–2020 cycle, the RNC raised $890,495,917, and the Democratic National Convention raised $490,635,675, sufficient funds to cover the costs of the debates.

5. *Maximizing debate locations:* Debate locations and venues are now a matter of negotiation between the parties and the media sponsors.

By producing the debates themselves, the parties alone could decide the locations. As a lower-cost alternative to going to multiple states, the parties could rent out sound studios in central locations, use them for multiple primary debates with different signage and state party sponsors, and organize multiple watch parties in each of the "host" states. And, given the tradition of hosting debates in each of the pre-March states, the parties could hold debates in each of these early states and then use the central location for debates once multiple states start voting on the same days.

6. *Formats:* There is clearly a ceiling on the number of candidates who can meaningfully debate on a stage simultaneously. Parties should not hesitate, especially early in the primary process, to use multiple debate stages, even using random groupings of candidates rather than a "main stage" and an "undercard" one. Even so, there is a limit to the number of candidates a party can usefully and appropriately include.

By taking direct control of primary debates, parties can experiment with different formats. They can likewise regulate the terms of the debate, restricting audience participation and applause, so that the focus is on the candidates themselves rather than on the reaction of attendees who may or may not be representative of the party's broader electorate.

Conclusion

By managing the primary debates in a manner that voters and candidates respect as fair, appropriately inclusive, and focused on issues that matter to their voters, the parties can both enhance their relevance and shape one of the most important aspects of the primary nominating process. We encourage parties to build on the expanded role they have played in recent cycles to make this vital aspect of the presidential nominating process function better.

Notes

1. Nelson W. Polsby and Aaron B. Wildavsky, *Presidential Elections: Strategies of American Electoral Politics* (Chicago: University of Chicago Press, 1964), 230.

2. The first national conventions were held in 1831, by the Anti-Masons and the National Republicans (who soon became the Whigs). In 1832, another national convention adopted the Whig nominations. In 1836, the Jacksonian Democrats selected through a national convention, but their opponents did not. But by 1840, however, all significant parties had come to use the national convention system.

See, e.g., James S. Chase, *Emergence of the Presidential Nominating Convention, 1789–1832* (Urbana: University of Illinois Press, 1973), 294–295.

3. James W. Ceaser, *Presidential Selection: Theory and Development* (Princeton, NJ: Princeton University Press, 1979), 132, 136.

4. Here it is important to note that the party coordination project extended beyond the nomination process and that a significant organizing principle for national parties in this era was keeping slavery off the political agenda. See, e.g., Martin Van Buren's embrace of the "gag rule" petitions regarding slavery in the House of Representatives. Jeffery A. Jenkins and Charles Stewart III, "The Gag Rule, Congressional Politics, and the Growth of Anti-slavery Popular Politics," *Legislative Studies Quarterly* 32 (2007): 33–57.

5. One example of this is the 1844 Democratic nomination, in which the southern veto prevented Martin Van Buren's nomination because of his opposition to the annexation of Texas. The process led to the nomination of James K. Polk, a slave owner whose policies exacerbated conflict over the expansion of slavery.

6. The first caucus was in 1800, when Republicans were united behind Jefferson as their presidential candidate but were uncertain about their vice presidential candidate and so gathered in private to forge agreement on Aaron Burr. James Bryce, *The American Commonwealth*, vol. 2 (Carmel, IN: Liberty Fund, 1995 [1888]).

7. James W. Ceaser, *Presidential Selection: Theory and Development* (Princeton, NJ: Princeton University Press, 1979), 132, 136.

8. James W. Ceaser, *Presidential Selection: Theory and Development* (Princeton, NJ: Princeton University Press, 1979), 127.

9. For one description, see Leon Epstein, *Political Parties in the American Mold* (Madison: University of Wisconsin Press, 1986), 90.

10. Leon Epstein, *Political Parties in the American Mold* (Madison: University of Wisconsin Press, 1986), 90.

11. Leon Epstein, *Political Parties in the American Mold* (Madison: University of Wisconsin Press, 1986), 1.

12. In 1952, the American Political Science Association surveyed each state party organization in the country to find out how they selected delegates to the conventions and who effectively controlled that process. In carefully reviewing that survey data, the authors of *The Party Decides* concluded, "Most party organizations were sufficiently insulated from popular pressures that the selection of delegates to the party conventions—and hence the choice of party nominee—was dominated by insiders." Marty Cohen et al., *The Party Decides: Presidential Nominations Before and After Reform* (Chicago: University of Chicago Press, 2008), 118.

13. Leon Epstein, *Political Parties in the American Mold* (Madison: University of Wisconsin Press, 1986), 91.

14. Howard L. Reiter, *Selecting the President: The Nominating Process in Transition* (Philadelphia: University of Pennsylvania Press, 1985), 3. The one exception is the Democratic Party convention of 1956, when twenty states used primaries of some form.

15. Howard L. Reiter, *Selecting the President: The Nominating Process in Transition* (Philadelphia: University of Pennsylvania Press, 1985), 3 (Table 1.1). Again, there is also some discrepancy between the sources on exactly how many states used primaries. Some sources report sixteen or seventeen states as using primaries in 1968. See, e.g., Leon Epstein, *Political Parties in the American Mold* (Madison: University of Wisconsin Press, 1986), 91.

16. Marty Cohen et al., *The Party Decides: Presidential Nominations Before and After Reform* (Chicago: University of Chicago Press, 2008), 125–126.

17. Marty Cohen et al., *The Party Decides: Presidential Nominations Before and After Reform* (Chicago: University of Chicago Press, 2008), 142.

18. Marty Cohen et al., *The Party Decides: Presidential Nominations Before and After Reform* (Chicago: University of Chicago Press, 2008), 145.

19. Marty Cohen et al., *The Party Decides: Presidential Nominations Before and After Reform* (Chicago: University of Chicago Press, 2008), 145.

20. Byron E. Shafer, *Quiet Revolution: The Struggle for the Democratic Party and the Shaping of Post-Reform Politics* (New York: Russell Sage Foundation, 1983), 4.

21. Byron E. Shafer, *Quiet Revolution: The Struggle for the Democratic Party and the Shaping of Post-Reform Politics* (New York: Russell Sage Foundation, 1983), 6.

22. Marty Cohen et al., *The Party Decides: Presidential Nominations Before and After Reform* (Chicago: University of Chicago Press, 2008), 161; Elaine C. Kamarck, *Primary Politics: How Presidential Candidates Have Shaped the Modern Nominating System* (Lanham, MD: Rowman & Littlefield, 2009), 15; Byron E. Shafer, *Quiet Revolution: The Struggle for the Democratic Party and the Shaping of Post-Reform Politics* (New York: Russell Sage Foundation, 1983), 387.

23. Austin Ranney, *Curing the Mischiefs of Faction: Party Reform in America* (Berkeley: University of California Press, 1975), 203–209.

24. Anika Gauja, "Party Leaders in Australia," in *The Selection of Political Party Leaders in Contemporary Parliamentary Democracies: A Comparative Study*, edited by Jean-Benoît Pilet and William P. Cross (London: Routledge, 2014), 189, 204–205.

25. See, e.g., Tim Bale and Paul Webb, "The Selection of Party Leaders in the UK," in *The Selection of Political Party Leaders in Contemporary Parliamentary Democracies: A Comparative Study*, edited by Jean-Benoît Pilet and William P. Cross (London: Routledge, 2014), 12.

26. In 1995, during the country's period of democratization, the Taiwanese Democratic Progressive Party held an open primary for its candidate in the first direct presidential election, although it reverted to closed primaries of party members for subsequent ones.

27. Marty Cohen et al., *The Party Decides: Presidential Nominations Before and After Reform* (Chicago: University of Chicago Press, 2008).

28. Douglas W. Rae, *The Political Consequences of Electoral Laws*, 2nd ed. (New Haven, CT: Yale University Press, 1971); Arend Lijphart, "The Political Consequences of Electoral Laws, 1945–1985," *American Political Science Review* 84, no. 2 (1990): 481–496.

29. Voter turnout in earlier contests is often much higher than for those in later states. In 2020, average turnout in Democratic primary elections through March 3 (Super Tuesday) was 28.5 percent, including 42.4 percent in New Hampshire and the lowest turnout in South Carolina with 13 percent. Average turnout in primaries after Super Tuesday was 22.8 percent, with a minimum in North Dakota of 2.6 percent. Michael P. McDonald, "2020 Presidential Nomination Contest Turnout Rates," United States Elections Project.

30. From 1972 to 2016, the eventual nominee effectively locked up the nomination having won, on average, less than half the voters who had a chance to vote before the decision was effectively made. About half of the nominees had control of less than a majority of voters when they effectively eliminated their competition. Hans Hassell and Hans Noel, "Double Take: Party On, Rules," *New America Weekly*, August 11, 2016.

31. Caitlin Jewitt, *The Primary Rules: Parties, Voters, and Presidential Nominations* (Ann Arbor: University of Michigan Press, 2019).

32. Marty Cohen et al., *The Party Decides: Presidential Nominations Before and After Reform* (Chicago: University of Chicago Press, 2008), 97.

33. Marty Cohen et al., *The Party Decides: Presidential Nominations Before and After Reform* (Chicago: University of Chicago Press, 2008).

34. See Elaine C. Kamarck, *Primary Politics: Everything You Need to Know About How America Nominates Its Presidential Candidates* (Lanham, MD: Roman & Littlefield, 2023), chap. 7.

35. For a description of the scandal, see Andrew Young, *The Politician: An Insider's Account of John Edwards's Pursuit of the Presidency and the Scandal That Brought Him Down* (New York: St. Martin's Press, 2010).

36. See, e.g., Nicholas Confessore, "How the GOP Elite Lost Its Voters to Trump," *New York Times*, March 28, 2016.

37. See "Election 2016—Republican Delegate Count," RealClear Politics.

38. These comments were made to Elaine Kamark, one of this task force's members, who attended the Republican convention in Cleveland as part of her research into the presidential nomination system.

39. See Elaine C. Kamarck, *Primary Politics: Everything You Need to Know About How America Nominates Its Presidential Candidates* (Lanham, MD: Roman & Littlefield, 2023).

40. See 2024 Convention Rules of the Massachusetts Democratic Party, p. 3 Accessed at https://docs.google.com/document/d/1jjQ-n5VuSPh6mRSRPsWey-ZG ZYJcX1uV/edit.

41. For instance, at the 2014 Democratic convention, Juliette Kayyem, a former Obama administration official, failed to reach the 15 percent threshold at the convention and was not on the primary ballot.

42. *Bellotti v. Connolly*, 460 U.S. 1057 (1983).

43. Thad Kousser et al., "Kingmakers or Cheerleaders? Party Power and the Causal Effects of Endorsements," *Political Research Quarterly* 68, no. 3 (2015): 443–456.

44. Julia R. Azari and Seth Masket, "Intraparty Democracy and the 2016 Election," in *Conventional Wisdom, Parties, and Broken Barriers in the 2016 Election,* ed. Jennifer Lucas, Christopher Galdieri, and Tauna Starbuck Sisco (Lanham, MD: Lexington Books, 2017).

45. See, e.g., "Newt Gingrich Slams John King for Question on Ex-Wife," *Washington Post*, January 19, 2012.

46. Media moderators have also effectively served as opposition research agents for the other party. See George Stephanopoulos in Iowa 2012 in an ABC News primary debate, January 7, 2012, posing a question to Mitt Romney about banning contraception ("New Hampshire Republican Debate: Mitt Romney Says Contraception Is 'Working Just Fine,'" video posted to YouTube by ABC News, January 8, 2012) and Lis Smith, *Any Given Tuesday: A Political Love Story* (New York: Harper Collins, 2023), 105–109 (Kindle version, Chapter 6).

47. William L. Benoit, Glenn J. Hansen, and Rebecca M. Verser, "A Meta-analysis of the Effects of Viewing U.S. Presidential Debates," *Communication Monographs* 70, no. 4 (2003): 335–350.

48. For example, from the July 9, 2023, *Politico Playbook*: Florida governor Ron DeSantis on Fox News' *Sunday Morning Futures* says, "The media does not want me to be the nominee. I think that's very, very clear. Why? Because they know I will beat Biden."

49. Adam Nagourney, "2008 Republican Field Shuns the Snowman," *The Caucus* (blog), *New York Times*, July 30, 2007.

50. See, e.g., Kendra Marr, "Memorable Primary Debate Moments," *Politico*, September 7, 2011.

51. Democrats did not plan 2024 primary debates because their standard bearer was an incumbent president, but they used similar criteria in 2016 and 2020.

52. For a discussion of these issues, see Richard H. Pildes, "The Neglected Value of Effective Government," NYU School of Law, Public Law Research Paper No. 23-51, *University of Chicago Legal Forum* 2023, article 8 (2024): 185–210.

53. See Geoffrey Skelley, "The Creative Fundraising Tactics Some Republicans Are Using to Make the Debate Stage," *FiveThirtyEight*, July 17, 2023; Amy B. Wang, "GOP Candidates Scramble to Attract Donors to Qualify for First Debate," *Washington Post*, July 13, 2023; Anjali Huynh, "Desperate to Debate: Why a G.O.P. Candidate Is Offering $20 for $1 Donations," *New York Times*, July 10, 2023.

54. In an 800-person sample poll, 1 percent is 8 people. Yet if parties admit only a set number of candidates, then literally a handful of people determine whether one candidate makes the debate stage while another does not, with obvious deleterious effects on his or her candidacy. The media polls do not disclose the states of the poll respondents or how they "weight" their sample to, in their minds, reflect the actual electorate.

55. Steven Shepard, "The RNC's Debate Plans Have a Major, Largely Unnoticed Problem," *Politico*, July 1, 2023.

56. A nationwide sample is generally weighted by state, resulting in California and New York (not exactly typical Republican voters) being 18 percent of the respondents. Precious few poll respondents would be from the states that set the stage for the primary—Iowa has 0.96 percent of the US population (8 people in an 800-person sample); New Hampshire, 0.41 percent; South Carolina, 1.56 percent; and Nevada, 0.96 percent. See "U.S. State Population by Rank," *Infoplease*, June 13, 2023.

7

Campaign Finance

Ray La Raja

In this chapter we offer recommendations about how to attenuate political extremism by reforming the campaign financing system. We root our insights in scholarly research and an informed understanding of campaign dynamics in the United States. Yet we approach the question of reform with intellectual humility, because the campaign finance system interacts in complicated ways with the broader electoral and political systems. Moreover, regulating money in politics touches on core questions of free speech and association, which are essential to a vibrant democracy.

All these considerations elevate the challenge of trying to parse how specific reforms might affect politics. Campaign finance reform has a long history of unintended consequences. One does not need to be an expert to see that previous well-intentioned reforms have not kept "big money" out of politics but rather shifted where it flows. In various ways, these reforms have sometimes exacerbated problems of weak accountability, unfairness in access to campaign funds, and partisan polarization.[1]

Despite our caution, however, we understand the perils of not engaging in a clear-eyed assessment of pathologies in the campaign finance system and how we might mitigate them. We want to be clear that our focus here is on the relationship between political extremism and the campaign finance system, although we acknowledge there are broader issues involved with money in politics that we do not fully address.

Rob Boatright, Brandice Canes-Wrone, Lee Drutman, Erika Franklin Fowler, Ben Ginsberg, Jake Grumbach, Nolan McCarty, Rick Pildes, Lynda Powell, and Brad Smith contributed substantially to this chapter.

These include, among others, concerns that civic activity involving political contributions tends to bias participation toward wealthier citizens.

We make our appraisals at a time when the dynamics of campaign finance are in great flux. The intensity of partisanship, the legal landscape, and technologies have changed considerably in the past two decades. New internet platforms have lowered the barriers to entry for millions of small donors, while the changing legal environment makes it easier for a small group of wealthy Americans to donate large sums to organizations such as super political action committees (PACs), which played a minimal role in election campaigns less than two decades ago.

Fortunately, we have a foundation of research findings about campaign finance that helps us understand several dynamics related to political extremism. We review them here, connect them to our recommendations, and offer areas for continued research. As part of our effort, we also identify reforms we do not endorse because we believe they are unlikely to address the problems of political extremism and could quite possibly make them worse or create problems in other aspects of American democracy.

We address political extremism in two senses. In the first instance, we see extremism in the uncivil and illiberal behavior of candidates and other political actors who undermine the rule of law and democratic norms. As elaborated by scholars Steven Levitsky and Daniel Ziblatt, such norms include mutual toleration (when competing parties accept one another as legitimate rivals) and forbearance (when politicians exercise restraint in deploying their institutional prerogatives and avoid "constitutional hardball").[2] So, for example, claims by members of either party that the duly elected president of a rival party has been elected fraudulently and is illegitimate would violate a norm of mutual toleration.[3] In a similar way, efforts by either party to use the law or institutional prerogatives in ways that might be legal but violate their spirit, including attempting to "pack" the Supreme Court or refusing to approve a president's judicial or cabinet nominations, would flout a norm of forbearance.

In the second instance, we see extremism as the ideological distancing—often called polarization—between the two major parties, particularly among elected officials and activists. Our concern here is that the widening gap in preferences between the two parties may reduce the system's capacity for negotiation and compromise, with deleterious consequences for governance. A related aspect of polarization is affective—an intense dislike of the other side. We consider affective polarization under the domain of behavioral extremism when politicians encourage demonization or question the legitimacy of the rival party, which intensifies such attitudes among the electorate.

A third normative consideration is political representation. This includes a democratic goal of widespread and equal participation, with political inputs from a representative set of citizens, under the assumption that such inputs will lead to a fairer and more representative distribution of outputs. Some of our proposals address this important concern, but again, we focus primarily on the first two considerations of behavioral and ideological extremism.

Furthermore, our proposals lean toward reforms with a realistic prospect of adoption based on the views of the public and strategic considerations of partisan leaders. We feel the need to propose reforms that have a chance of passage rather than simply staking out bold positions. The public tends to want populist reforms, which appear to have the virtue of giving more power to average Americans. When closely scrutinized, however, such reforms sometimes have the potential to undermine key democratic values, institutions, and constitutional principles. Meanwhile, politicians and party leaders have their own strategic considerations, which make finding common ground exceedingly difficult. We therefore focus on proposals that could plausibly attract bipartisan support, which, at least at the national level, would be required for any successful legislation.

We also want to be clear that adjusting campaign finance laws is unlikely to have a major impact on mitigating the two kinds of extremism. The dynamics of extremism are complex, and campaign finance is but one structural element among many that could be contributing to them. Additionally, our recommendations are targeted at attenuating extremist sources of funding, but the causality of extremism may run as much from candidates to donors as from donors to candidates. Candidates mobilize extremist donors when the context incentivizes them to do so.[4] This means that our recommended changes to the campaign finance system should be considered as part of a package of reforms suggested by our task force in the other chapters of this book. Our goals in this chapter are to explain how the current system for financing politics may be supporting political extremism, offer recommendations to mitigate extremism through campaign finance reforms, and identify future research avenues that may help us better understand these dynamics.

General Trends

The amount of money in federal elections has risen steadily over the past two decades, spurred primarily by the activity of independent groups.[5]

In presidential elections, we have seen a rapid rise in fund-raising and spending, both by candidate campaigns and independent groups, which accompanied the demise of the public financing system. In congressional elections, candidate financing has shifted toward a reliance on individual ideological donors and super PACs relative to traditional PACs and political parties.[6] In the most competitive elections, a small number of wealthy individual donors have funneled large sums to independent spending organizations such as super PACs.[7]

Beyond super PACs, another set of groups, often organized as 501(c)(4)s, participates in elections without having to report the names of donors or file reports with the Federal Election Commission (FEC). Although public corporations did not appear to take advantage of a landmark judicial decision rendered in *Citizens United v. Federal Election Commission* to finance their own super PACs, it is unclear to what extent they might be donating to these kinds of organizations through intermediaries.[8] It appears that super PACs and 501(c)(4)s are funded primarily by individual wealthy ideologues and private corporations associated with them.[9] But we do not know the full extent of contributions or where they originate. Additionally, campaigns rely increasingly on the internet, especially social media, to raise money from intensely loyal and ideological partisans, particularly using platforms such as ActBlue for Democratic or liberal causes and WinRed for Republican or conservative causes.

Generally, we have observed a sharp increase in money from sources beyond the traditional gatekeepers: political parties, traditional PACs, and partisan bundlers of contributions. While such gatekeepers continue to play a key role, there has been a consequential shift toward super PACs, 501(c)(4)s, and individual donors (including small donors), many of whom are mobilized by media-savvy candidates and various ideological groups with support from the partisan media. These emergent funding sources are often allied with elements of the "old" system. Party leaders, for example, exploit the use of super PACs. Nonetheless, there is a scholarly consensus that politicians now rely more heavily on ideological sources of money than on the traditional PAC system of "access" givers.[10] Previous reforms aimed at limiting the influence of wealthy donors have shifted who donates money and engages in political organizing, restricting contributions from some kinds of actors and, in conjunction with technological and judicial changes, expanding contributions from others. Some believe these reforms have also risked imposing constitutional burdens on citizens' free speech and association.[11]

How the Campaign Finance System Contributes to Political Extremism

The money flowing into American politics likely contributes to political extremism because its sources are increasingly ideological and weakly mediated by long-standing institutions such as political parties and PACs. The reasons behind this are complex. One driver is certainly the design of campaign finance laws, which privilege private financing by individual donors, who tend to be highly ideological, over institutional donors like parties and business-oriented PACs that tend to seek pragmatic goals.[12] Additionally, new technologies—widespread cable television, the internet, social media, and associated fund-raising platforms—contribute to the nationalization of political financing by helping to channel money from ideological and even illiberal sources around the country. All of this fund-raising from ideologically extreme sources takes place in the wider ecosystem of US politics, which includes a highly polarized party system with unstable majorities, elevating the stakes significantly for partisan loyalists.[13]

The following dynamics appear to contribute to polarization and behavioral extremism.

Political donors tend to be more extreme than rank-and-file partisans. Research shows clearly that individual donors exist largely at the ideological poles of the electorate, favoring policies that are more extreme than rank-and-file partisans.[14] Figure 7.1 shows the percentage of partisans who consider themselves strongly ideological. It illustrates over several election cycles that donors are consistently more likely to say they are strongly liberal or strongly conservative than fellow partisans who do not make contributions. This dynamic holds true for both large and small donors.[15] Several studies also show that individual donors do not simply self-identify as more extreme but in fact hold more extreme and intense policy preferences than the typical voter who affiliates with either party.[16]

Additionally, individual donors tend to favor more ideologically extreme candidates when making contributions and to support candidates who share their policy positions.[17] Such findings are particularly salient for activists affiliated with advocacy groups.[18] At the same time, politicians are strategic in mobilizing the most ideologically extreme donors in different contexts.[19]

Donors are also less demographically diverse than the broader electorate. They are older, wealthier, and more educated than those who do not contribute.[20] Younger Americans and racial minorities are highly underrepresented in campaign finance,[21] as are women, although the gap appears to be closing.[22] It is possible that the polarizing dynamics of money, the inequalities it tends to support,[23] and the growing public cynicism about campaign finance fuel populism, setting the stage for the entry of norm-breaking candidates. When this dynamic is accompanied by a fragmentation of campaign actors and a weakening of traditional gatekeepers in financing politics, nonmainstream candidates, including norm-breaking ones, may find an even larger electoral opening.[24]

Figure 7.1   Strongly Ideological Donors

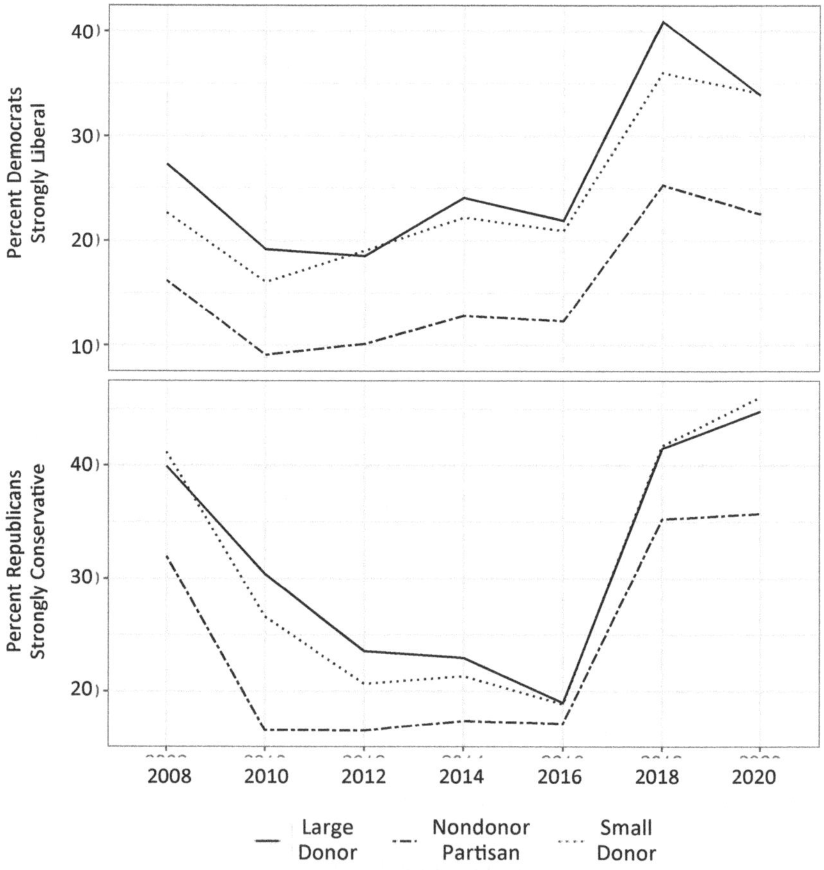

Source: Cooperative Election Survey, figure created by Zachary Albert, Brandeis University.

Political extremists have access to a national population of donors. American politics has become increasingly nationalized, with Americans more engaged with politics and issues in the nation's capital than in their states and localities.[25] This dynamic incentivizes candidates for Congress to market themselves nationally to donors, which in turn may reinforce nationalization. In the decade from 2012 to 2022, the average percentage of money coming from inside a congressional district declined from 37 to 26 percent.[26] As Figure 7.2 illustrates, the share of donations coming from within the state of House races also declined significantly, from 81 percent in 1998 to 62 percent in 2022. In the Senate, where out-of-state donations have generally been more common, the changes have been more variable, but the trend shows a clear decline of in-state contributions. These out-of-district and out-of-state donors benefit from a form of surrogate representation since they lack a geographic connection to a candidate.[27]

Research shows that out-of-district donors are motivated primarily by partisanship and ideology. Donors seek to influence close electoral

Figure 7.2   Percentage of Money In-State

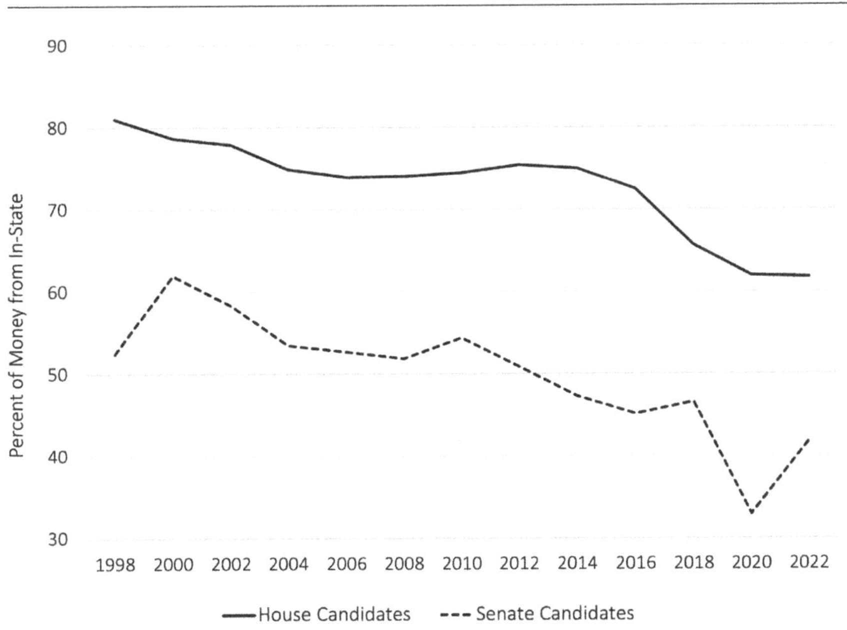

Source: OpenSecrets.

contests and tip the scales toward their favored candidate with funds.[28] The intense partisanship and strong ideology of many donors can pose challenges to democratic norms. More extreme partisans and ideologues, who are disproportionately reflected among donors, appear less supportive of constitutional protections when their party holds power.[29] The most extreme among them have rejected the legitimacy of their opponents and the outcome of elections.[30]

A relevant question is whether out-of-district donors influence representatives' policy decisions and other behaviors. Out-of-district donors are more ideologically extreme than legislators' constituents,[31] including in-district donors.[32] Even accounting for strong partisan voting in the House, members—particularly from safe districts—appear responsive to the preferences of the national donor base, and their responsiveness increases as they become more reliant on such donors.[33] These dynamics have important implications for American democracy: out-of-district contributions tend to reduce geographic representation, shifting candidates in the direction of the preferences of a national pool of donors.[34] It is not entirely clear whether these shifts result from a *selection* effect—when candidates emerge that reflect the views of donors—or an *adaptation* effect—when candidates alter their ideological positions to align with those of their benefactors. Recent research suggests both effects may be at play.[35] Regardless, the increasing nationalization of fund-raising potentially affects political representation, party polarization, and opportunities for norm-breaking candidates.[36]

While nationalized fund-raising is not new for members of Congress, it has been turbocharged by a changing media environment. The growth of partisan cable news, social media, and internet-based campaigning have provided abundant information for ardent partisans about congressional and statewide races, favoring norm-breaking extremists and ideologues.[37] At the same time, giving money has never been easier with new platforms, such as ActBlue and WinRed, enabling contributors to enter credit card information and make repeated donations. The urge to donate comes quickly to loyal partisans who follow politics like sports fans.[38] And politicians have learned that eliciting emotional responses through symbolic acts and statements can unleash a cascade of contributions from a national audience of ideological extremists and illiberal donors. Representative Ilhan Omar, a Democrat from Minnesota, raised $832,000 in the first quarter of 2019 after drawing fire for invoking anti-Semitic tropes about US politicians' support for Israel.[39] In 2009, Representative Joe Wilson, a Republican from South Carolina, shouted. "You lie!" during President Barack Obama's speech to a joint session of Congress. Wilson was formally rebuked by the House for his outburst, but he later netted more than \$2.7 million from donors around the country.[40]

Other politicians observe these dynamics and try to market themselves by getting national attention. Since the media have incentives to cover novelty and norm breaking—and evidence shows they do feature extremists in US House races—we are likely to see politicians engage in highly partisan and norm-breaking behaviors to raise money, especially from small donors whose contributions are less mediated by traditional party networks.[41]

To give a sense of who benefits most from small donations, Table 7.1 lists the top ten recipients in the 117th Congress (from January 2021 to January 2023). Ideology was not the only driver of contributions for this group, but it certainly appeared to be relevant. Except for the party leaders, these politicians tended to belong to caucuses that sparred with the establishment and centrist wings of their parties, often invoking populist, anti-institutionalist themes in their public statements and campaigns.

All of them had prominent national profiles based on being perceived as combative partisans or factional leaders. This included the party leaders at the time, Speaker Nancy Pelosi and Minority Leader Kevin McCarthy, although they both relied heavily on large contributions as well. There was also Representative Adam Schiff, who led impeachment investigations against President Donald Trump, and Representative Katie Porter, cofounder of the "End Corruption Caucus" (both are running as Democrats for the US Senate in California in 2024).[42]

Table 7.1   Top Small-Donor Fund-Raisers, US House Election, 2022

Rank	Candidate	Party	Total Small Donors (millions)	Percentage of Small Donors
1	Katie Porter	D	\$14.30	56
2	Adam Schiff	D	\$14.20	57
3	Marcus Flowers	D	\$13.30	80
4	Nancy Pelosi	D	\$12.30	49
5	Kevin McCarthy	R	\$10.30	38
6	Marjorie Taylor Greene	R	\$8.60	68
7	Alexandria Ocasio-Cortez	D	\$8.30	68
8	Jim Jordan	R	\$8.10	58
9	Dan Crenshaw	R	\$7.50	49
10	Matt Gaetz	R	\$4.00	62

Source: OpenSecrets.

Since entering office in 2019, Representative Alexandria Ocasio-Cortez, a Democrat from New York, has been an extraordinary small-donor fundraiser, relying on a massive social media following and adopting a public-facing activist approach to her role as legislator. Like Ocasio-Cortez, Representative Dan Crenshaw, a Republican former Navy SEAL from Texas, has attracted a younger following and been savvy in gaining a national audience by appearing on *Saturday Night Live* and building an enormous social media following.[43] Representatives Jim Jordan and Marjorie Taylor Greene are among the most conservative members of Congress. Along with Representative Matt Gaetz, they are viewed nationally as provocative factional leaders, often pursuing controversial tactics against the rival party, as well as members of their own party. And finally, there is Marcus Flowers, a relatively unknown figure until he chose to run against Greene in Georgia's 14th District, which helped him bring in more small donations than even Pelosi, thanks to Democratic ire toward the incumbent.

With a nationalized pool of donors easily accessible, candidates can gain attention by staking out polarizing, noncentrist positions to appeal to strong partisans who intensely dislike the rival party, as well as ideological donors who are well to the flanks of rank-and-file partisans on issues. It literally pays to differentiate oneself to gain attention and secure funds from interest groups and individual donors around the country.

Politicians rely increasingly on individual rather than institutional donors. Contributions from extreme donors have been increasing relative to contributions from donors who tend to give to less divisive (and generally more experienced) incumbents in Congress. This dynamic reflects a shift from more established institutional donors—political parties and traditional PACs—toward individual donors and independent spending organizations, which have mushroomed in the past two decades.

We believe these changes have implications for political extremism. As noted above, individual donors tend to be motivated by partisan loyalty and ideological commitments, benefiting the most combative, attention-seeking politicians. These donors constitute the most ideological sources of financing; the most extreme among them are open to supporting illiberal behaviors by officeholders to advance their partisan goals. By contrast, most institutional donors tend to direct money toward more pragmatic candidates and experienced legislators.[44] Traditional business-oriented PACs are most likely to back experienced legislators, although this means full-throated support for incumbents rather than challengers.[45]

There is an obvious trade-off between privileging individual donors over nonparty institutional donors. Individual donors, for example, are more inclined to support ideologues and challengers, including anti-establishment candidates, because they wish to move Congress closer into alignment with their views. In contrast, most traditional PACs tend to support incumbents in both parties, because they favor the status quo and having access to officeholders.[46] These PACs, most of which are oriented toward economic issues, are especially likely to support incumbents in key positions in Congress who are effective at achieving policy outcomes they favor.[47] This kind of access-oriented influence over economic issues can produce rents for donors and policy that is out step with the desires of the American public. However, access-oriented groups have generally not supported highly extreme or ideological candidates. Recent research shows that Republican members who relied more on business PACs than on individual donors were less likely than Republican members with the opposite funding breakdown to object to counting electors on January 6, 2021.[48] The reason for PAC support of institutionalists in Congress likely has less to do with being pro-democracy than with favoring access and stability over uncertainty.

Of all the groups supporting candidates, political parties are the best positioned to advance the prospects of relatively moderate politicians. Political parties seek majorities in Congress, which means they will want to contribute to those who have the highest odds of winning—the ones closest to the median voter rather than ideologues.[49] And unlike traditional PACs, political parties pursuing majorities in legislatures have strong incentives to support challengers to defeat incumbents from the other party and win more seats.[50] Moreover, research shows that the network of donors affiliated with political parties may boost the prospects of women candidates, as well as racial and ethnic minorities, since parties are likely to use their donor networks to support these candidates as much as white and male ones.[51] On balance, we believe party organizations play an important role in generating positive system outcomes, including by channeling donations to pragmatists, challengers, and women and minority candidates.

Disconcertingly, at the federal level, we see a clear shift toward ideological donors and away from traditional organizational donors. Figure 7.3 shows aggregate campaign contributions to congressional candidates between 1980 and 2020 from both individual and organizational sources. Since many proposed reforms seek to increase the importance of small donors (giving $200 or less to a candidate), we plot them separately from large donors. Since 2008, the amount of

Figure 7.3   Sources of Funding, 1980–2020

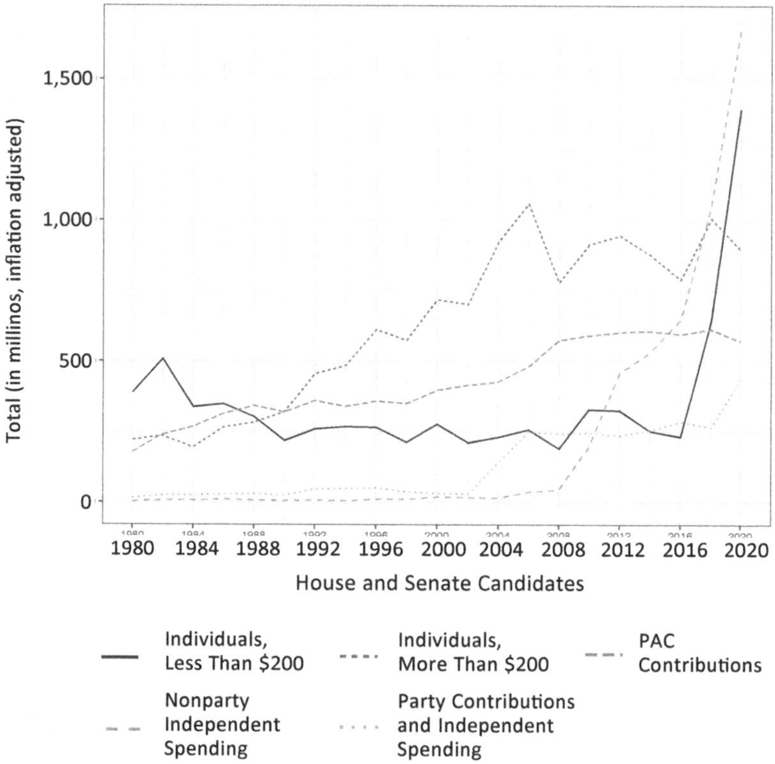

Source: Adam Bonica, *Database on Ideology, Money in Politics, and Elections: Public Version 3.0* (Stanford, CA: Stanford University Library, 2023), available at https://data.stanford.edu/dime. Figure created by Zachary Albert, Brandeis University.

money coming from small donors has risen slowly, before exploding in 2018 and again in 2020, when it reached more than $1.2 billion (figures are adjusted for 2020 dollars).[52]

Large donations to candidates had been increasing rapidly since the 1990s, during a lengthy period when majority control over Congress became highly contested and unstable, thereby raising the electoral stakes considerably. The incentives for partisans and ideologues to give money only increased as the parties became more distinctive and polarized with their policy agendas. Note the sharp increase in 2004, following the passage in 2002 of the Bipartisan Campaign Reform Act (BCRA), a major piece of reform legislation that doubled the amount individuals could give from \$1,000 to \$2,000 per election. It may appear surprising, given the stakes, that in the past four election cycles the contributions from large donors have remained relatively flat. One reason for this is that the very largest donors have been giving money to independent spending organizations, which have no limits on contributions.

Turning to organizational funding, party committee support for congressional candidates was relatively flat between 2006 and 2018, hovering under \$300 million and then increasing to \$435 million in 2020. When party organizations were banned from using soft money in 2002 (not shown in this figure), they turned to independent spending in 2004, which allowed them to increase their support for candidates. Parties also relied heavily on allied super PACs (see below), often managed by consultants who previously worked for the party or its candidates. The comparison between party support for candidates and individual donor support is critical for our analysis of extremism. Since parties are more likely than other funders to make contributions in ways that support moderation and electoral competitiveness,[53] it follows that reducing the role of political parties in financing elections means that money is less likely to flow toward pro-institution candidates and challengers seeking to hold incumbents accountable.

With respect to traditional PACs, Figure 7.3 shows that like parties, these entities have been falling behind large individual donors, and their contributions have reached a plateau at approximately \$500 million. Importantly, the sums given by large individual donors and traditional PACs started to diverge in the early 1990s, and PAC contributions have remained mostly flat since 2008. The passage of the BCRA in 2002 did not increase the size limit for PAC contributions, as it did for individual contributions, or allow for inflationary adjustments, so any increases in PAC contributions have taken place within the limits of the original 1974 laws. As a result, a PAC contribution limit of \$5,000 in 1976 would need to have been raised to \$22,743 to have the same value in the 2020 election. Put differently, the relative value of a maximum PAC donation today is less than one-fifth what it was when these limits were instituted.

In the years after the BCRA reforms to the campaign finance system, partisans experimented with new funding vehicles that would avoid the restrictions on PACs and political parties. Two judicial decisions clarified that groups could raise and spend independently without limits, paving the way for the rise of super PACs—so named because of their financing clout (see more details on super PACs and the court decisions below). Figure 7.3 shows the extraordinary spike in nonparty independent spending, mostly from super PACs. In 2008, the year before the two court decisions, independent spending amounted to just $47 million. By the 2020 election, it stood at almost $1.67 billion, a more than thirty-five-fold increase.

Unlike traditional PACs, super PACs cannot contribute directly to candidates. Rather than advancing an access-oriented strategy, super PACs appear to follow an electoral strategy: devoting resources to electing candidates in competitive races to influence the composition of government.[54] Some super PACs behave like political parties, supporting either a single candidate or a host of partisan candidates to assist one of the two major parties.[55] Nonetheless, many of these organizations, particularly on the Republican side, compete with official party organizations over resources and political talent. The sponsors of these organization may have different issue agendas and priorities than party officials and are not widely recognized by the American public.[56] Other super PACs and nonparty groups are highly ideological, pushing narrow agendas in support of their particular issues. In fact, party committees have become diminished actors in the campaign environment, competing with an array of lightly regulated single-issue groups that lack the accountability of parties because they are neither transparent nor rooted in institutions of government.[57]

Independent spending has become a routine part of campaign finance. Perhaps the most significant change in the fund-raising landscape is the increasing importance of independent spending committees. These committees can raise and spend unlimited sums so long as they do not coordinate directly with candidates or political parties. Surrogates for the candidates and various other supporters raise funds for these groups, typically from wealthy individuals and organizations. The use of independent spending committees has become a standard part of the campaign repertoire, and our task force has concerns about the increased flow of money into these kinds of nontraditional and opaque channels, which may undermine political accountability and weaken the gatekeepers who have traditionally made it more difficult for norm-breaking candidates to gain electoral traction.[58]

Independent campaigns have always existed in US elections, but their salience has increased considerably.[59] This is due to a combination of legal restrictions on the size of donations to candidates and political parties, including those enacted as part of the BCRA of 2002, and judicial decisions rooted in the First Amendment, starting with *Buckley v. Valeo* in 1976 and reinforced by *Citizens United v. Federal Election Commission* and *SpeechNow.org v. Federal Election Commission* in

2010.[60] The regulatory landscape means that while candidates and parties face limits on contributions, political committees that do not coordinate with them may raise and spend as much as they like. Problems that ensue from the institutionalization of independent expenditures include the following:

• *Funding arms races:* Research suggests that independent spending contributes to more spending and fund-raising by candidates. Independent spending is concentrated in the most competitive congressional races.[61] Multi-issue groups making independent expenditures tend to be loyal foot soldiers in support of party candidates,[62] but they increasingly attack opponents as well.[63] As a result, incumbent legislators perceive a growing threat of independent expenditures against them and respond by raising campaign funds from partisan and ideological donors outside their districts and traditional PACs, while keeping more cash on hand for themselves instead of distributing it to other candidates or party committees.[64] They also raise additional money for their leadership PACs, funds that cannot be used for their own campaigns but can be spent to help the party obtain majority status or to curry favor among colleagues by making contributions.[65]

• *Weakened accountability and transparency:* The contemporary campaign environment weakens accountability, since many independent spending groups lack recognizable labels and candidates can dissociate themselves from their advertising. Moreover, there is a wide range of organizational vehicles through which interest groups and candidate supporters may engage in political campaigns. To be sure, the ability of individuals and interest groups to conduct campaigns and disseminate information is vital for free speech.[66] But with numerous committees waging partisan battles, the campaign landscape fragments, making it more difficult for rival candidates to campaign around messages and agendas they believe will help them win votes. Additionally, the nebulous linkages between candidate campaigns and opaquely named independent committees enable the latter to focus heavily on negative advertising—and in some cases, disinformation—which potentially diminishes voter trust and knowledge.[67] Notably, 501(c)(4) groups appear to back more extremist candidates—especially during primary elections—than formal party organizations, allied super PACs, or traditional PACs.[68]

The challenge of accountability is made more acute by the fact that some organizations, specifically 501(c)(4)s, are not required to publicize their donors. In 2020, these groups spent roughly $80 million airing advertisements. More critically, they spent more than $723 million on contributions to super PACs, about ten times more than in the last presidential election cycle.[69] Although super PACs are required to report donors, it is nearly impossible to determine the original source of the money if the contribution to the super PAC is from a 501(c)(4) or a pass-through organization that funnels funds through a 501(c)(4) on their way to the super PAC.[70]

• *Undermining democratic norms:* 501(c)(3) and (4) organizations appeared central to the "Stop the Steal" movement that sought to delegitimize the 2020 presidential election. These nonprofit groups engaged in radical rhetoric and tactics to challenge the election results. On the other end of the political spectrum, a group called "Ruth Sent Us" distributed the addresses of conservative Supreme Court justices and organized protests outside their homes after a leaked draft of a majority opinion overturning *Roe v. Wade* was published.[71] Understanding the financial dynamics of these norm-breaking groups is beyond the scope of our task force, which focused on campaign activity. Nonetheless, 501(c) organizations may be funded by some of the same individuals and groups that engage in elections. It is also plausible that related groups finance disinformation campaigns, which may spread easily thanks to social media and artificial intelligence (AI) technology.[72]

• *Supporting extremists in primaries:* While in general elections many super PACs operate as extensions of political parties, a different dynamic may animate super PACs in primaries. In these contests, different factions of the party may compete to nominate their favored candidates.[73] In Republican primaries, for example, a small group of super PACs appear to defect from leadership choices and support candidates who are less experienced and more extreme.[74] The ease with which groups can form super PACs and less transparent committees presents a latent threat to the party's dominant coalition, since these groups can boost a favored candidate against one preferred by the broader party coalition.[75] In a fragmented campaign environment, the emergent campaign finance system may empower more extreme groups that spend in primary elections. The goal of such groups is not necessarily to win but to set an issue agenda and make officeholders attentive to more extremist positions.

Sometimes, factions intervene in the contests of the opposing party. In the 2022 midterms, for instance, Democrat-affiliated groups engaged strategically in Republican primaries to help boost extreme candidates they believed would fare less well in the general election.[76] Such partisan ploys increase the odds of an extremist candidate gaining office.

At the presidential level, super PACs funded by a few very wealthy individuals can boost the messages of divisive candidates. These groups may also prolong the nomination process and strengthen the campaigns of long-shot candidates.[77] The typical pattern in presidential nominations is for candidates to drop out as they lose contributions from rank-and-file donors. A few wealthy donors, however, can prevent the parties from winnowing candidates, which may increase the odds of highly polarized nominees winning nominations with small pluralities of delegates.

Expenditures on litigation have risen as partisans increasingly challenge electoral outcomes. Most research on political finance focuses on campaign expenditures. By comparison, little has been written about spending on election litigation. Some litigation is necessary to challenge threats to election integrity and uphold voting rights, but frequent litigation may intensify disputes about the electoral process and undermine its legitimacy. Institutions charged with rendering decisions—state election boards on voting procedures, for instance, or state legislatures on redistricting—find themselves with diminished authority as their rulings are challenged frequently by partisans on all sides. The public is left wondering about the finality of electoral decisions if they are always subject to court review.[78]

According to election law expert Richard Hasen, election litigation rates in the United States have been increasing rapidly, nearly tripling since the 2000 election. In 2020, the rate of election litigation was almost 26 percent higher than in the previous presidential year, 2016.[79] The attendant rise in legal expenses can be seen in Figure 7.4. Between 2003 and 2015, party committees' legal expenditures stayed constant at around $5 million, but in 2016 they ballooned to $15 million. By 2020, the parties had spent a total of $66 million.[80] Over time, the share of party resources devoted to election litigation has increased as well. In 2010, only about 1 percent of total expenditures were put toward election litigation. By 2020, that share had reached 4 percent. Much of the increase may be attributed to a rider to legislation passed by Congress in 2014 allowing parties to raise additional funds to defray legal costs.[81]

Dynamics That May Mitigate Extremism

Our discussion so far has underscored polarizing trends fueled by ideological donors who provide an increasing amount of campaign money. These trends likely cause politicians to adopt more extreme positions or

Figure 7.4   Partial FEC Legal Expenses, 2000–2023

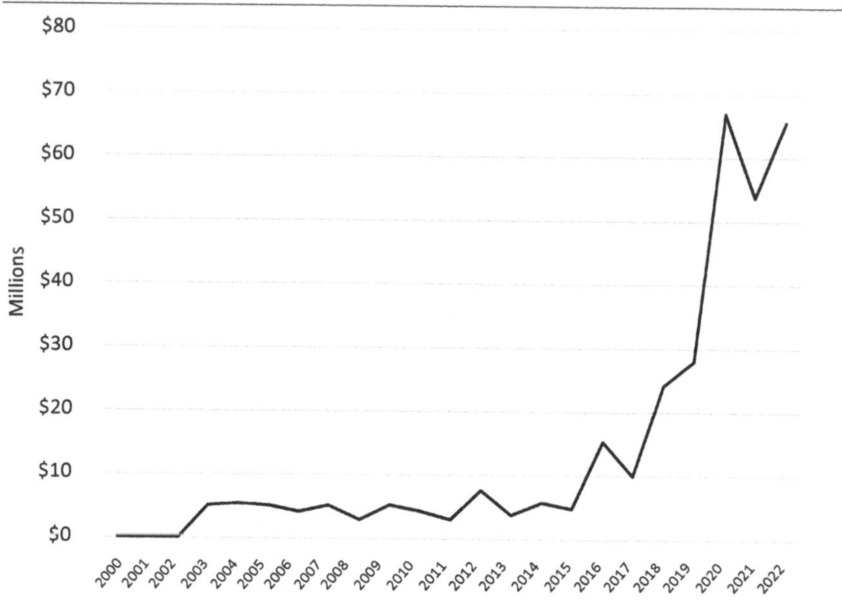

Source: Derek T. Muller, "Reducing Election Litigation," University of Iowa Legal Studies Research Paper No. 2021-49, *Fordham Law Review* 90, no. 2 (2021): 561–582.
Note: We thank Professor Muller for providing us with his data to replicate this figure.

entice more extreme candidates to run for office.[82] In addition to supporting ideologues, the national population of donors consistently funds norm-breaking candidates who attract media attention with uncivil statements and behaviors. The rise of such independent spending increases the odds that groups—financed by wealthy extremists—will air highly divisive advertisements that support politically extreme and norm-breaking candidates.

Of course, one cannot simply regulate these behaviors out of existence. Regulating political advertising raises serious First Amendment concerns and risks anticompetitive behavior by regulators. We believe, however, that a pragmatic shift in the design of the campaign finance system can attenuate these distortions. A revised campaign finance system should aim to accomplish two things: increase funding sources that are more broadly representative and incentivize the flow of money through transparent and accountable committees. Below, we explain these goals in greater detail.

Increasing Funding Sources That Are More Broadly Representative

To reduce the polarizing effects of campaign funding, candidates should become less reliant on contributions that come directly from individuals. With the sorting of partisans into ideological camps, the current campaign finance system has created a dynamic that reinforces polarization. As explained above, abundant research shows that individual donors are unrepresentative of the voting public, both in terms of demographics and ideology. Not only are they wealthier, whiter, older, and more likely to be male, but they are also more extreme.

Given the distorting effects of individual campaign contributions, several of our recommendations resist a common populist approach to campaign finance. For decades, political reforms have been designed to elevate the role of individual donors and minimize group-based donations. This may have been a mistake, especially without efforts to mobilize a broader set of individual donors, particularly those living in the same districts and states as the candidates, all of which is very difficult. Individual donors are often activists in the party driving it toward the extremes. In nationalized elections, the populist marketplace will be wide open to norm-breaking candidates who can raise millions from individual donors across the country within a few days via platforms like ActBlue and WinRed.

Group-based donations—those from parties and traditional PACs—are more likely to be mediated, enabling group representatives to allocate them based on the short- and long-term interests of group members. These groups are also capable of working with broader party coalitions to pursue majorities. Reforms, therefore, should focus on incentivizing the formation and strengthening of political committees that represent broad groups of Americans. The broadest such organization is the political party. More funds might also flow through other broad-based groups, including membership organizations and various groups with popular support, particularly centrist factions within each party and factions that pursue policy goals that cross partisan divisions.

Effective reforms to mitigate extremism will also aim to diversify the sources of financing. A basic principle of reform is to design a system that encourages pluralistic sources of funding to attenuate overreliance on any one set of donors, especially those outside the district or state where the candidate is running. That is effective policy for both dampening political extremism and enhancing the likelihood that politicians will be responsive to their constituents rather than to a national population of ideologues and wealthy interests.[83]

Incentivizing the Flow of Money Through Transparent and Accountable Committees

We believe that a healthy campaign finance system enables money to flow through committees that disclose donors and are accountable to the broader public.[84] The current system stimulates spending by independent groups with weak accountability. Voters do not know these independent groups; nor do they have a good idea of who funds them.[85] This opacity makes it easy for such groups to run negative ads and sometimes support extremists. The public has little capacity to evaluate the sources of information put out by independent groups or to hold them accountable because they are not directly tied to candidates or parties. These are often campaign committees set up tactically to pursue short-term goals. Like tents in a traveling carnival, they emerge to join in raucous campaigns, only to fold up and leave town the day after elections. This frees them to do the dirty work of political campaigns without being sanctioned by the public at the ballot box and without having to maintain a reputation that connects them with future voters.

One additional problem with institutionalizing independent spending by super PACs is that it creates opportunities for factional and extreme candidates that lack broad support. A few very wealthy individuals can finance favored candidates and set the political agenda. The ease with which these committees can arise (with the help of well-paid lawyers and consultants) increases the odds that a large and unwieldy number of candidates will pursue party nominations. And candidates backed by independent organizations need not win to gain benefits. They make other politicians talk about issues they care about, and they can play the spoiler in a context that fails to winnow the field to a manageable number of candidates.

Both of these reform goals—increasing the diversity of funding sources and pushing money through more transparent and accountable organizations—point in the direction of designing a system in which funds flow through regulated channels of candidate committees, broad-based PACs, and especially political parties.

What Is Unlikely to Work

Before we get into the details of our recommendations, we think it is important to highlight widely discussed reform proposals that may do little to mitigate problems and could even make them worse. These remedies appear popular with the public and many reform advocacy groups, even though they may be ill-advised. We collectively do not support them.

Tighter Limits on Financing Campaigns

A common strategy to keep money out of politics and limit corruption has been to lower contribution limits. The hope is that low limits on how much individuals and groups can give will compel candidates to seek financing from more donors who are representative of constituents. Some argue that low limits also help curtail the undue influence of big donors over politicians. However, abundant experience and research show that low limits do not keep money out of politics; nor do they prevent some of the largest donors from giving money. Limits can work to some degree, but if they are too low, they incentivize independent spending and other strategies to get around them.[86]

We believe that lowering contribution limits will achieve the opposite of what is intended. It will make politicians try even harder to get money from ideologically extreme donors, especially those who reside outside their districts or states. Relying on independent spending, which has few financial constraints, will become even more attractive.

Small-Donor Matching with Public Funds

We do not endorse small-donor matching programs in federal elections, as used in New York City, because of their potential to reinforce polarization by subsidizing extreme donors and candidates who rely on them. Small donors are as ideologically polarized as large donors. This reform would effectively subsidize an unrepresentative group of voters and incentivize politicians to pay a disproportionate amount of attention to them. We value participation from small donors as part of a mix of financing strategies for candidates, but we do not agree that they should be privileged in the campaign finance system, except insofar as we design programs that emphasize in-district donations (see recommendations).[87] There may be other reasons to promote public subsidies for small donors, but mitigating political extremism is not one of them.

Attempting to Overturn Citizens United v. Federal Election Commission

Members of our task force have different views on pursuing a strategy of overturning the Supreme Court's 2010 decision, but it is *Buckley v. Valeo*

(1976) that makes independent spending constitutionally protected. And most large contributions to super PACs come from individual donors. *Citizens United* held that corporations and unions, not just individuals, have constitutional rights to engage in unlimited independent spending. Thus, overruling *Citizens United* without also overruling *Buckley v. Valeo* would have more limited effects than many assume, since the latter is the foundation for unlimited individual contributions to super PACs. Even so, some task force members argued that large inflows of independent expenditures after the *Citizens United* ruling contributed to the decline of democratic norms and institutions at the state level and that preventing corporations and labor unions from spending sums without limit will push more financing into the traditionally regulated campaign finance system (candidate committees, conventional PACs, and party committees). Apart from these practical considerations, some task force members also believe *Citizens United* properly protects free speech rights.

Most importantly for our purposes, the political strategy of overturning *Citizens United* is fraught with challenges. It involves either building significant majorities in the states for an amendment to the US Constitution or generating a sustained set of court cases to test the long-standing jurisprudence on unrestricted political spending dating back at least to *Buckley v. Valeo*. Our approach has been a more pragmatic one. We focus on reforming the campaign finance system through the regulatory process rather than offering remedies of constitutional significance.

What Might Work

Based on our assessment of the underlying dynamics in campaign finance that help fuel political extremism, we focus our recommendations around the following principal strategies:

1. Increasing financing for political parties and other broad-based political entities
2. Improving disclosure
3. Increasing financing from multicandidate committees
4. Targeting public subsidies
5. Eliminating party litigation funds

Below, we discuss how each of these recommendations may diversify fund-raising and incentivize more campaign funds to go through transparent and accountable channels.

1. Increasing Financing for Political Parties

Political parties are the central actors in democracies. We believe previous campaign finance reforms have prevented them from playing a more robust and positive role in US elections. Parties meet all of our criteria for attenuating extremism. They are broad based; inclined to finance a range of candidates, including challengers and relative moderates; highly transparent with sources of money; and accountable because they are widely recognized with labels that voters use to make their choices. That is not to say that political parties are beyond criticism. Through their leaders and activists, they have contributed to intense partisanship and strategic maneuvering around the current campaign finance rules. Nonetheless, parties are core actors in all facets of democratic politics, and campaign finance rules need to reflect their centrality to our political system.[88] While party committees infrequently engage directly in primaries, in combination with other reforms recommended in this book, including to primary rules, we believe financially strong party committees could improve electoral politics and diminish extremism. Here are the specific changes we recommend:

Raise limits on individual contributions to political parties to reflect inflation since the 1974 amendments to the Federal Election Campaign Act (FECA). The limits on contributions to national political parties were not pegged to inflation when they were established in 1974. If we used that year as a baseline and adjusted the limits for inflation, the current ceiling on individual contributions to national parties would be over $130,000 per year. Today, it is only $41,000 due to the BCRA reforms of 2002. Those reforms also removed party soft money,[89] which had enabled the parties to control more campaign resources. We therefore recommend raising the contribution limits to at least reflect inflation since 1974.

We also recommend that state and local parties benefit from increased contribution limits. They are currently capped at $10,000 per year for federal accounts, which is a combined amount for both the state and local committees. These limits are not indexed for inflation. Again, we suggest using the 1974 contribution limit of $5,000 per year as a baseline to adjust the limit to at least $32,550. This cap should be adjusted again after every two-year cycle for inflation.

Such a change may strengthen healthy kinds of campaign coordination and accountability between the national and state committees. State parties were affected negatively by the BCRA reforms, which constrained their efforts to organize on behalf of the entire party ticket for candidates in federal, state, and local contests.[90] Figure 7.5 illustrates the inflation-adjusted limits for the national and state/local

Figure 7.5 Contribution Limits in 1974 Versus CPI-Adjusted 2023 Versus BCRA Limits

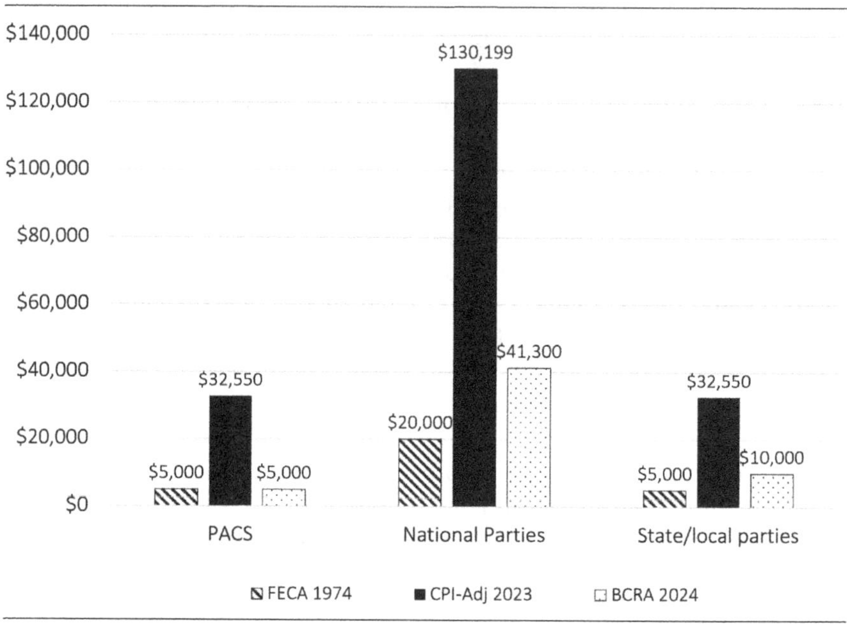

political parties. We also include adjustments for multicandidate PACs (more on PACs below).

Some members of our task force expressed concern about increasing the financial resources of some state parties, which have been taken over by their extremist wings. But where that has happened, funding appears to have dropped off significantly. Many donors do not appear interested in supporting such parties. Raising contribution limits to parties only matters if donors are willing to contribute. Moreover, when state parties are hollow shells because they have few resources and limited practical power, they become more vulnerable to capture by small groups of activists. If state parties are revitalized, in part by gaining more resources, they are likely to draw in a wider range of party members. Finally, strong parties, at both the national and state levels, are critical to the long-term health of American democracy. We should not be deterred from measures to help enable parties by fixating too much on short-term factors in a few states. We also believe that deregulating political parties financially may help the development of third parties, which may require significant infusions of resources to jumpstart operations and messaging. The arguments for expanding opportunities for third parties have been made in other parts of this book.

Remove or greatly increase the limits on party-coordinated expenditures. Under the 1974 reforms, parties can coordinate their spending with candidates up to specific amounts, adjusted for inflation. The amount in 2024 for the House will be $59,400. A significant majority of countries do not limit the ability of parties to support their own candidates.[91] We want to enable parties to work closely with candidates rather than spend independently, which undermines organizational cohesion and accountability. Congressional reforms, first implemented in the 1976 elections, aimed to prevent candidates from circumventing contribution limits by having earmarked funds available to them through the party. We think this concern is excessive. Rules exist against earmarking, which can be enforced. Moreover, with limits on party contributions, the parties are incentivized to use their funds efficiently in a range of contests rather than giving them to a single candidate simply because he or she raised them jointly with the party. Most members of our task force were in favor of removing all limits, while some members opposed removing some limits. Regardless, there was widespread recognition that the limits on coordinated expenditures are unreasonably low.

Experiment with providing public funds to political parties. Given our concerns about the financial health of political parties and their incentives to spin off independent entities, we discussed the possibility of subsidizing them, as almost all other advanced democracies do. Such subsidies are often accompanied by spending limits, which would not be workable in the United States, given current jurisprudence. Public funds might diversify the sources of income for parties and possibly attenuate the influence of private donors.[92] Six states already provide limited subsidies by allowing taxpayers to check a box on their returns indicating a desire to contribute to the state's political parties in amounts ranging from $1 to $25.[93] There was less consensus in our task force on the public-funding approach than on our other recommendations for political parties. (See recommendation 4 for a possible pilot using vouchers in US states, some of which might go to local political parties.)

2. Improving Disclosure

We are for both more and less disclosure at different ends of the donor spectrum. We want more transparency for the major donors who give to 501(c)(4)s and other groups that are not compelled to disclose donations. These funds often make their way into super PACs that account for most independent spending. We have practical and constitutional concerns about all-encompassing efforts to compel disclosure. But on balance, we think that greater transparency, properly designed, should strengthen accountability mechanisms,[94] including enforcement of rules against illegal foreign financing.[95]

At the same time, we seek less transparency for smaller donors to mitigate chilling effects that discourage participation. Citizens who experience conflicting pressures from different sources regarding their political beliefs—for example, if they are somewhat conservative but live in a neighborhood of mostly liberals—may refrain from giving when they know their donations might be made public.[96] Such cross-pressured citizens can feel that open expressions of political preferences could roil social relationships. For this reason, if we want greater ideological diversity among donors at the lower end, we might raise the disclosure threshold. We are also concerned about donors who may face retaliation from employers that disapprove of their political choices. As a society, we are greatly concerned about privacy in the voting booth for these reasons.[97] Somewhat oddly, we do not apply these concerns to other forms of political participation. Given that relatively small donations pose little risk of corruption, we see no compelling reason to divulge identifying information about them. Here are the specific changes we advocate:

Require meaningful disclosure of major donations to influence elections, regardless of the entity or medium used. Large donors have the capacity to shape elections in ways that other citizens do not. The arguments for anonymity are much weaker for major donors than for voters at the ballot box, where everyone has one vote, or even for small donors (see below). For this reason, there are fairness and informational arguments for publicly disclosing the major financiers from whom candidates draw significant support.

The exact wording of disclosure statutes would have to be narrowly tailored to address First Amendment issues. A thoughtful approach must balance the positive aspects of disclosure, especially providing helpful information for voters, with practical and constitutional concerns.[98] We feel the need to point out that anonymity in the public sphere is an underappreciated dynamic that potentially increases free speech, gives citizens space to act on their personal beliefs without coercive pressure, and sometimes enables arguments to be considered with less prejudice (on this last point, the anonymous writers of the Federalist Papers appeared to agree). For all these reasons, we do not take an absolutist approach to the question of disclosure, but most of our task force members support judicious efforts to provide voters with more information about the major funding sources of groups trying to influence elections.

Importantly, the Federal Election Commission has rules in place to consider disclosure exemptions for groups at risk of harassment, and these are supported by constitutional jurisprudence (see, for example, *Brown v. Socialist Workers '74 Campaign Committee*).[99] Nonetheless, there are practical realities that must be addressed in pursuing disclosure of donations by groups not currently regulated by the FEC.[100]

For example, not all donations given to 501(c)(4)s are necessarily made with the goal of influencing an election, which calls into doubt the quality of information that would be provided by disclosure and raises the possibility that "outed" donors could face negative consequences for election-oriented activities they did not intend to support. Our purpose in pointing out practical considerations is to suggest that sweeping calls for full disclosure have costs. They could plausibly impose both constitutional and administrative burdens that outweigh the benefits of disclosure in important instances. Therefore, we encourage thoughtful deliberation about how to implement better disclosure rules for donors trying to influence elections with committees not regulated by the FEC, while minimizing genuine burdens.

Raise the threshold for donor disclosure. We recommend raising the disclosure threshold to reflect inflation since the 1974 FECA amendments, from $200 to roughly $1,000. We also suggest experimenting with forms of semidisclosure that would give the public access to information about the kinds of interests donors represent but not their individual identities.[101] Semidisclosure may help avoid the problem of straw donors, since regulators would retain access to files that fully identify donors. One challenge is that online fund-raising platforms collect donor information. We recommend rules to require these platforms to keep donors' information private unless their contributions exceed the reportable threshold.

Pass antiretaliation legislation to protect workers from employers. Making donations is a form of free speech, since it reflects an endorsement of a political candidate or party. Citizens should not worry they will suffer professional consequences for engaging in political activity that does not present an obvious conflict of interest for their employer. According to legal scholar Eugene Volokh, about half of Americans live in jurisdictions that protect some private speech or political activity from employers. Three American states directly address protections for making political donations: Louisiana, Massachusetts, and Oregon.[102] These states forbid employers from threatening to discriminate against or in favor of an employee. We encourage the federal government to write into law such protections.

3. Increasing Financing from Multicandidate PACs

We recommend raising contribution limits for multicandidate PACs. These political committees appear to fulfill at least three criteria for attenuating extremism. First, most are inclined to finance moderates and incumbents with experience. Second, multicandidate PACs are highly transparent with respect to sources of money. And third, they tend to be oriented toward stability in government. A main concern we have with PACs is that they are not representative of the broader public. The current population of PACs overwhelmingly represents business and professional organizations.[103] As political insiders, PACs and lobbyists affiliated with them may use contributions to help shape the legislative agenda.[104] However, research suggests that the influence of business PACs stems less from their political contributions than from their capacity to finance policy information for legislators and executive agencies.[105]

Critically, we are not advocating for large increases but recommending that the contribution limits rise with inflation. The relative value of PAC contributions has plummeted, giving much more importance to ideologically oriented contributors who finance elections through independent spending groups. We recommend increasing the limit for contributions from PACs to candidates to roughly $32,000, accounting for inflation since the $5,000 limit was established in 1974. (See Figure 7.5, which shows adjustments for the Consumer Price Index (CPI)/inflation.) We do not believe that a $32,000 limit would risk inducing corruption, especially given the rising cost of elections, which require fund-raising from many donors. In our view, pushing more funds through PACs to candidates would reduce incentives for the sponsors of these committees to give money, without limits, to super PACs and other opaque organizations.

By design, multicandidate PACs are aggregators of contributions from many individuals, whereas super PACs rely on a few megadonors and nontransparent 501(c)(4)s. We believe the campaign finance system should encourage more aggregating organizations, which function as effective intermediaries for citizens to participate in elections. One challenge is to stimulate the formation of PACs that better represent the diversity of American voters. Policymakers might consider giving "connected" PACs—those that are linked to sponsoring organizations, such as labor unions and corporations, with *voluntary* members—even higher limits on contributions to candidates. Or they might consider doing the same for nonconnected PACs, which may solicit funds from any citizen or lawful permanent resident of the United States. However, we are divided on whether to pursue this strategy because donors to these PACs are unlikely to be representative of the American electorate. They are likely to be wealthier, more partisan, and more ideological than other voters—all characteristics that may contribute to the extremism we seek to attenuate. That said, funds from membership-based PACs will be more transparent and accountable because they flow directly to the campaign committees of candidates running for office.

Regardless, we urge civic leaders—including from local associations, foundations, and other institutions—to develop strategies for incentivizing membership groups to form PACs that represent a broader spectrum of Americans. Such PACs could focus on both mobilizing voters and contributing to candidates. It would be especially beneficial to the political system if such groups were not already aligned with one or the other major political party. This would not only broaden the sources of funds to candidates but also create the kind of cross-pressures to partisan alignments that might weaken the rigid orientations that have arisen in the past several decades.

4. Targeting Campaign Subsidies

We were divided over the use of subsidies as a method to limit extremism. Recent research suggests that public financing for campaigns may encourage greater polarization and degrade representation of constituents.[106] Some research on subsidy programs that stimulate small donors illustrates that such donors are closer to the typical American voter than larger donors, although they remain demographically unrepresentative of the electorate.[107] However, since small donors in general appear as polarized as large donors, it remains possible that new donors brought into the system by subsidy programs might also be highly polarized.[108] We would like to see more evidence that public subsidies would broaden and diversify the viewpoints of donors.

We encourage continued local experimentation with subsidies for small donors, as Seattle is doing with vouchers and New York City is doing with matching funds.[109] We can imagine experimentation with public subsidies for small donors in at least two scenarios at the state and local levels. First, given our concerns about the nationalization of fundraising from extreme donors, we could support subsidies that target donors within their legislative districts, as recommended by campaign finance expert Michael Malbin and implemented by New York State for its legislative elections.[110] Compared to a national donor base, in-district donors likely focus more on local issues and may have personal connections with candidates, which could moderate their ideological leanings.[111] Second, given our interest in seeing political parties play a larger role in public financing, we could conceive of a financing system where a portion of subsidies goes toward the parties.[112] For example, if a voucher system was in place, a portion of every voucher—say, $5 out of every $25—could go to the political party of the candidate. This might also incentivize local party organizing to raise voucher money on behalf of candidates, which may lead to stronger efforts by local committees to build grassroots operations. Mobilization would encourage parties to work closely with candidates not only to court voters but also to secure financial resources for both the candidate and party.[113] Research in a comparative, international context suggests public funding of parties increases confidence in the conduct of elections.[114]

Some members of our task force would also encourage eliminating voluntary limits on campaign spending for candidates who participate in public financing programs. These limits tend to be too low for the most competitive contests, which encourages nontransparent independent spending.

5. Eliminating Party Litigation Funds

The creation of separate party funds for legal expenses in 2014 (called recount funds) appears to have incentivized litigation. To be sure, there may be good reasons to litigate. However, having a pool of funds solely for legal expenses surely encourages litigation, perhaps even frivolous lawsuits. These cases undermine the integrity of election results and add to voter skepticism. Intense litigation may even radicalize voters when their candidates lose. We recommend eliminating party funds that allow donors to contribute up to $123,900 per year for legal fees, while simultaneously increasing the cap on contributions to general party funds.

Public Opinion

A key challenge to moving the campaign finance system in a more pluralistic direction is that the public tends to embrace populist reforms due to their apparent democratic design. For this reason, large majorities of Americans want more constraints on money in politics, more campaigns financed by small donors, and fewer PACs.[115] Moreover, they are not typically inclined to support a system that gives a stronger role to political parties. Nonetheless, voters favor imposing fewer restrictions on parties than on other groups and support allowing parties to give large or unlimited contributions to their own candidates.[116]

It is important to keep in mind as well that the reforms we suggest are hardly radical and fit within the architecture of designs approved by Congress during the post-Watergate era. A key theme of our recommendations is to adjust original contribution limits for inflation, a change that most Americans will readily understand. It is clear that the original 1974 limits, as well as those put in place by the BCRA in 2002, have not kept pace with the rising cost of goods and services. Nor have they matched well with the intense rise in partisanship and campaign organizing by partisan networks, leaving the formal party committees in a weakened state to mediate coalitions.[117]

A second key theme is making the system more transparent, which Americans wholeheartedly support. Our proposals call for the disclosure of major donors to all committees engaged in campaigns, with ample attention to the constitutional and practical burdens of designing and implementing such rules. In our deliberative poll, a supermajority endorsed a policy of requiring all organizations that make election campaign expenditures over a minimum level to disclose their donors.[118] This proposal had majority support across Republicans, Democrats, and Independents—even before we started the deliberative process. After conversations initiated among participants, support increased even more, from 71 to 81 percent in favor of greater transparency.

Support for public funds, either by using vouchers or matching small-donor contributions, is less widespread. In our deliberative poll, majorities agreed with the proposition that public funds should *not* be used to finance elections. However, the poll did not ask whether participants' views would change if the subsidies targeted only citizens residing in the district or state where the election was taking place. We recommend that a future survey include this kind of question.

Political Elites

Political actors, such as legislators, will be sensitive to partisan advantages that reforms could induce. The political parties also stand for distinctive approaches to government regulation, which could cause resistance to some of our proposals. However, there is mixed evidence that campaign finance reforms confer structural advantages on either party.[119] The intense rivalry between the two parties pushes them toward gathering sufficient resources to compete toe-to-toe in competitive contests. We also think our proposals would not put third parties at a disadvantage. In fact, increased contribution limits are arguably more supportive of third parties.

Importantly, we believe our recommendations contain elements of principles espoused by both major parties. In broad terms, the Democrats tend to favor egalitarian approaches while Republicans support those that enhance freedom. For Democrats, we emphasize additional disclosure of major donors and consider some form of targeted public financing. For Republicans, we propose higher contribution limits for political parties as well as for multicandidate PACs. Both parties should see reasons to support rules that give more privacy to small donors by increasing the threshold for disclosure and passing antiretaliation laws.

Future Research

Political parties: More work should investigate how political parties spend their funds on building their infrastructure and whether an infusion of resources in particular contexts might make them more vibrant as associational organizations.[120] We know that parties tend to allocate funds toward competitive contests, but does financial strength incentivize them to become more integrated with voters at the grass roots and responsive to local communities? And what happens when illiberal factions take over the party apparatus? Some members of our task force were concerned about empowering political parties at a time when several state party organizations have fallen under the control of factions pursuing illiberal policies. We noted, however, that several insurgent organizations have not been attracting contributions and face financial difficulties, even in highly competitive states and those with laws allowing unlimited contributions to political parties.[121] Additionally, we could use more research on what the public thinks about strengthening party organizations financially and making them more central to political campaigns.

Candidate gatekeepers: We need research on the role of potential gatekeepers who shape and winnow the field of candidates, especially those who donate early in campaigns.[122] We seek an understanding of who they are, what kinds of candidates they support, and how this may have changed over time. The ability to circumvent party leaders, PACs, and traditional money brokers means that more candidates can present themselves directly to the public with minimal filtering. It also raises the prospect that unfit candidates might break into politics and get elected to office. In the past, new candidates tended to rely on their personal social and professional networks.[123] Candidates emerging from some professions appear to have unique network structures that advantage them in fund-raising.[124] Additional research might explore whether other subgroups have unique advantages and how these may impact the quality of representation and governance. Research suggests that fewer moderates are running for office, in part because they lack financial support among partisan activists.[125] Distortions in the campaign finance system also have implications for candidate emergence in minority communities and among women.[126] Finally, we need an investigation of the incentive structures that might support the formation of broad-based PACs, which could play a larger role in financing campaigns of candidates who are less extreme and more representative of American voters.

Disclosure: We lack a firm grasp of who donates to nontransparent groups that spend significant sums on elections. Better disclosure of donors and their interests will help advance our understanding of how the campaign terrain may be changing and who benefits. Additionally, more work needs to be done on the trade-off between enhanced political accountability and the potentially chilling effects of transparency. We encourage additional research using field experiments to understand the pros and cons of transparency. We also encourage experimentation with semidisclosure of donors.

Small-donor programs: Several task force members want to know more about whether and how small-donor programs might broaden participation, particularly beyond voters who are highly ideological and partisan. We would like to see more experimentation with small-donor subsidies for small in-district donors to legislative candidates. Given our appreciation for mediating groups, we wonder what role interest groups and political parties might play in mobilizing the distribution, use, and collection of vouchers. This could include "bundling" or other methods of aggregating vouchers on behalf of candidates. Additional work should examine at what point public subsidies with voluntary spending limits substantially encourage independent expenditures. Finally, we want to understand public opinion, beyond our deliberative poll, about the use of vouchers in varying contexts.

Independent spending: Research is instructive but not conclusive about the impact of independent spending on political extremism. We believe that independent spending on political ads by interest groups, particularly in primaries, has the potential to boost the candidacies of norm-breaking candidates. We need more research on whether such spending is more likely to come from less-transparent 501(c)(4)s or from super PACs. Studies should be expanded to examine spending on social media advertising, grassroots mobilization, and contact campaigns for elected officials.

Much more work needs to be done on independent spending in primary elections, where interest groups or wealthy individuals can back their favored candidates without limit. In several states, a few wealthy individuals have been able to finance candidates, usually in Republican primaries, to challenges incumbents who compromise on issues.[127] Wealthy individuals may also finance parallel party structures that can undermine the work of traditional party committees.[128]

Disinformation: Research about online campaigning and how it may support extremism and disinformation is in the early stages of development.[129] In the near term, we recommend studies that collect data on the amount of advertising and sources of extremist campaigning, particularly when it reflects misinformation and disinformation. We recognize that evolving technologies such as AI make it cheaper and easier to create fake campaign ads.[130] We are reluctant to offer specific recommendations regarding regulation of AI-generated ads since applications of this technology are recent. However, we strongly encourage research experiments to understand how AI affects voter perceptions and how interventions like labeling ads "AI generated" and other strategies may affect voter decisionmaking.

Election litigation: We would like to see robust scholarly examination of data and messaging to understand the degree to which postelection activities are linked to electioneering groups. The goal might be to understand how strategists potentially exploit fund-raising vehicles to contest or relitigate elections after the fact. We encourage examining party committee litigation efforts, as well as the incentives for parties to devote larger shares of their expenditures to election litigation. Research might explore public attitudes when electoral decisions move to the courts and how this affects citizens' faith in election outcomes.

Conclusion

In this chapter, we have offered several strategies to counter the campaign finance dynamics that undergird political extremism. The prevailing campaign finance regime tends to rely heavily on ideological funding sources, while fueling fragmentation and opaqueness across political campaigns. These dynamics stimulate the polarization of politics and improve the odds of success for ideological and illiberal candidates. This gives rise to fragmentation and dysfunction within parties, making it more difficult to build governing coalitions.[131]

We emphasize the importance of attracting funding sources that are more broadly representative. This includes incentivizing more funds to flow through political parties, which perform a central function as broad-based coalition builders. Reformers might also focus on innovations making it easier for a representative group of Americans to make contributions through multicandidate PACs, which would mediate interests that are not adequately reflected among contemporary donor groups. We also advocate experimentation in the states using vouchers to encourage small donors who reside in the legislative districts of candidates. This would help make candidates more attentive to local constituents than to a national population of ideologues. While this chapter on campaign finance focuses on extremism, we cannot ignore the fact that political participation through making campaign contributions favors wealthier Americans, even more so than other forms of participation where socioeconomic status predicts participation. There are no simple remedies to this challenge that do not impose significant burdens on freedom of speech and association.

We also emphasize a system that incentivizes the flow of campaign money through transparent and accountable committees. This would mean pushing more money through identifiable groups, including parties and multicandidate PACs, particularly those that represent large groups of voters. It would also mean disclosure of all major donors to any entity involved in elections, including but not limited to 501(c)(4)s. Greater disclosure would give the public additional information about campaigns that support political extremists. At the same time, we believe that individuals who give smaller sums should have more privacy. Raising the threshold at which identities are made public (or semidisclosed) would stimulate more donations, including from citizens who tend to avoid giving because they fear reprisals in their social and occupational networks. All donors should also be protected through antiretaliation laws.

Notes

1. Nolan McCarty, *Polarization: What Everyone Needs to Know* (New York: Oxford University Press, 2019).

2. Steven Levitsky and Daniel Ziblatt, *How Democracies Die*, Reprint ed. (New York: Crown, 2018).

3. In 2021, 147 Republican lawmakers raised objections to the official certification of electoral votes. This effort was an unprecedented example of breaking norms of mutual toleration and forbearance by using electoral rules to challenge the legitimacy of election results. However, it must be said that in previous elections, Democrats contested the election results. This includes 2001, 2005 (when thirty-one Democratic members of the House and Senator Barbara Boxer voted to reject Ohio's electoral votes), and 2017, with the election of Donald Trump, when several Democrats claimed that Russian interference in the election affected the outcome. Derek T. Muller, "Democrats Have Been Shameless About Your Presidential Vote Too," *New York Times*, January 6, 2021. We say this not to imply that the Republican and Democratic behaviors have been equally harmful—they have not been—but to point out that both parties have engaged in norm breaking around election results, which increases the odds that others in either party may do so in the future.

4. Tyler Culberson, Michael P. McDonald, and Suzanne M. Robbins, "Small Donors in Congressional Elections," *American Politics Research* 47, no. 5 (2019): 970–999.

5. Nathaniel Persily, Robert F. Bauer, and Benjamin L. Ginsberg, "The State of Campaign Finance in the U.S.," Bipartisan Policy Center, January 19, 2018.

6. Michael Barber, "Donation Motivations: Testing Theories of Access and Ideology," *Political Research Quarterly* 69, no. 1 (2016): 148–159.

7. Diana Dwyre, "The Origin and Evolution of Super PACs: A Darwinian Examination of a Campaign Finance Species," *Society* 57, no. 5 (October 1, 2020): 511–519; Raymond J. La Raja, "Money in the 2014 Congressional Elections: Institutionalizing a Broken Regulatory System," *The Forum* 12, no. 4 (December 1, 2014): 713–727.

8. Wendy L. Hansen, Michael S. Rocca, and Brittany Leigh Ortiz, "The Effects of Citizens United on Corporate Spending in the 2012 Presidential Election," *Journal of Politics* 77, no. 2 (April 2015): 535–545. The Supreme Court in *Citizens United v. FEC*, 558 U.S. 310 (2010), ruled that aspects of federal campaign finance laws violated free speech under the First Amendment. The court held that the government could not prohibit independent expenditures for political campaigns by corporations, labor unions, or any form of association.

9. Kenneth P. Vogel and Shane Goldmacher, "Democrats Decried Dark Money. Then They Won with It in 2020," *New York Times*, January 29, 2022.

10. Michael Barber and Nolan McCarty, "Causes and Consequences of Polarization," in *Task Force Report: Negotiating Agreement in Politics*, ed. Jane Mansbridge and Cathie Jo Martin (Washington, DC: American Political Science Association, 2013), 19–53; Raymond J. La Raja and Brian F. Schaffner, *Campaign Finance and Political Polarization: When Purists Prevail* (Ann Arbor: University of Michigan Press, 2015).

11. John Curtis Samples, *The Fallacy of Campaign Finance Reform* (Chicago: University of Chicago Press, 2006); Bradley A. Smith, *Unfree Speech: The Folly of Campaign Finance Reform* (Princeton, NJ: Princeton University Press, 2009).

12. Michael J. Barber, "Ideological Donors, Contribution Limits, and the Polarization of American Legislatures," *Journal of Politics* 78, no. 1 (2016): 296–310; Michael Barber, "Donation Motivations: Testing Theories of Access and Ideology," *Political Research Quarterly* 69, no. 1 (2016): 148–159.

13. Frances E. Lee, *Insecure Majorities: Congress and the Perpetual Campaign* (Chicago: University of Chicago Press, 2016); Morris P. Fiorina, *Unstable Majorities: Polarization, Party Sorting, and Political Stalemate* (Stanford, CA: Hoover Institution Press, 2017).

14. Joseph Bafumi and Michael C. Herron, "Leapfrog Representation and Extremism: A Study of American Voters and Their Members in Congress," *Ameri-

can Political Science Review 104, no. 3 (2010): 519–542; Michael J. Barber, "Ideological Donors, Contribution Limits, and the Polarization of American Legislatures," *Journal of Politics* 78, no. 1 (2016): 296–310; David E. Broockman and Neil Malhotra, "What Do Partisan Donors Want?," *Public Opinion Quarterly* 84, no. 1 (March 1, 2020): 104–118; Brandice Canes-Wrone and Kenneth M. Miller, "Out-of-District Donors and Representation in the US House," *Legislative Studies Quarterly* 47, no. 2 (2022): 361–395.

15. Tyler Culberson, Michael P. McDonald, and Suzanne M. Robbins, "Small Donors in Congressional Elections," *American Politics Research* 47, no. 5 (2019): 970–999; Richard H. Pildes, "Small-Donor-Based Campaign-Finance Reform and Political Polarization," *Yale Law Journal Forum* 129 (2019): 22; Zachary Albert and Raymond La Raja, "Small Donors in US Elections," *Politique américaine* 35, no. 2 (2020): 15–45; Raymond J. La Raja and Brian F. Schaffner, *Campaign Finance and Political Polarization: When Purists Prevail* (Ann Arbor: University of Michigan Press, 2015).

16. Brandice Canes-Wrone and Kenneth M. Miller, "Out-of-District Donors and Representation in the US House," *Legislative Studies Quarterly* 47, no. 2 (2022): 361–395; Michael J. Barber, "Representing the Preferences of Donors, Partisans, and Voters in the US Senate," *Public Opinion Quarterly* 80, no. S1 (January 1, 2016): 225–249.

17. Michael J. Barber, Brandice Canes-Wrone, and Sharece Thrower, "Ideologically Sophisticated Donors: Which Candidates Do Individual Contributors Finance?," *American Journal of Political Science* 61, no. 2 (2017): 271–288; Seth J. Hill and Gregory A. Huber, "Representativeness and Motivations of the Contemporary Donorate: Results from Merged Survey and Administrative Records," *Political Behavior* 39, no. 1 (March 2017): 3–29.

18. Jacob M. Grumbach and Alexander Sahn, "Race and Representation in Campaign Finance," *American Political Science Review* 114, no. 1 (February 2020): 206–221.

19. Tyler Culberson, Michael P. McDonald, and Suzanne M. Robbins, "Small Donors in Congressional Elections," *American Politics Research* 47, no. 5 (2019): 970–999; Alex Keena and Misty Knight-Finley, "Are Small Donors Polarizing? A Longitudinal Study of the Senate," *Election Law Journal: Rules, Politics, and Policy* 18, no. 2 (June 2019): 132–144; Raymond J. La Raja and David L. Wiltse, "Don't Blame Donors for Ideological Polarization of Political Parties," *American Politics Research* 40, no. 3 (May 1, 2012): 501–530.

20. Sidney Verba, Kay Lehman Schlozman, and Henry E. Brady, *Voice and Equality: Civic Voluntarism in American Politics* (Cambridge, MA: Harvard University Press, 1995); Seth J. Hill and Gregory A. Huber, "Representativeness and Motivations of the Contemporary Donorate: Results from Merged Survey and Administrative Records," *Political Behavior* 39, no. 1 (March 2017): 3–29. Donors are also a highly concentrated group of individuals. Specifically, the top 0.01 percent of earners hold a share of around 5 percent of the nation's total income, yet account for nearly 40 percent of the total share of individual campaign contributions. See Adam Bonica et al., "Why Hasn't Democracy Slowed Rising Inequality?," *Journal of Economic Perspectives* 27, no. 3 (September 2013): 103–124.

21. Jacob M. Grumbach and Alexander Sahn, "Race and Representation in Campaign Finance," *American Political Science Review* 114, no. 1 (February 2020): 206–221.

22. Zachary Albert and Raymond La Raja, "Small Donors and the Evolving Democratic Party" (conference paper for the Southern Political Science Association Annual Meeting, New Orleans, Louisiana, January 10–13, 2020).

23. Nolan McCarty, Keith T. Poole, and Howard Rosenthal, *Polarized America: The Dance of Ideology and Unequal Riches* (Cambridge, MA: MIT Press, 2006).

24. See, e.g., Richard H. Pildes, "Small-Donor-Based Campaign-Finance Reform and Political Polarization," *Yale Law Journal Forum* 129 (2019).

25. Daniel J. Hopkins, *The Increasingly United States: How and Why American Political Behavior Nationalized* (Chicago: University of Chicago Press, 2018).

26. The percentages are roughly similar for incumbents, challengers, and open-seat candidates. See Sarah Bryner, "The Nationalization of Political Contributions and the Rising Role of Out-of-State Donations," Open Secrets, June 1, 2023.

27. Jane Mansbridge, "Rethinking Representation," *American Political Science Review* 97, no. 4 (November 2003): 515–528; Anne E. Baker, "The Partisan and Policy Motivations of Political Donors Seeking Surrogate Representation in House Elections," *Political Behavior* 42, no. 4 (December 1, 2020): 1035–1054.

28. James G. Gimpel, Frances E. Lee, and Shanna Pearson-Merkowitz, "The Check Is in the Mail: Interdistrict Funding Flows in Congressional Elections," *American Journal of Political Science* 52, no. 2 (2008): 373–394; Alex Keena and Misty Knight-Finley, "Are Small Donors Polarizing? A Longitudinal Study of the Senate," *Election Law Journal: Rules, Politics, and Policy* 18, no. 2 (June 2019): 132–144.

29. Jon Kingzette et al., "How Affective Polarization Undermines Support for Democratic Norms," *Public Opinion Quarterly* 85, no. 2 (October 1, 2021): 663–677.

30. Nathan P. Kalmoe and Lilliana Mason, *Radical American Partisanship: Mapping Violent Hostility, Its Causes, and the Consequences for Democracy*, 1st ed. (Chicago: University of Chicago Press, 2022).

31. Joseph Bafumi and Michael C. Herron, "Leapfrog Representation and Extremism: A Study of American Voters and Their Members in Congress," *American Political Science Review* 104, no. 3 (2010): 519–542; Michael J. Barber, "Representing the Preferences of Donors, Partisans, and Voters in the US Senate," *Public Opinion Quarterly* 80, no. S1 (January 1, 2016): 225–249.

32. Anne E. Baker, "Getting Short-Changed? The Impact of Outside Money on District Representation," *Social Science Quarterly* 97, no. 5 (2016): 1096–1107; Michael J. Barber, Brandice Canes-Wrone, and Sharece Thrower, "Ideologically Sophisticated Donors: Which Candidates Do Individual Contributors Finance?," *American Journal of Political Science* 61, no. 2 (2017): 271–288; Brandice Canes-Wrone and Kenneth M. Miller, "Out-of-District Donors and Representation in the US House," *Legislative Studies Quarterly* 47, no. 2 (2022): 361–395.

33. Anne E. Baker, "Getting Short-Changed? The Impact of Outside Money on District Representation," *Social Science Quarterly* 97, no. 5 (2016): 1096–1107; Brandice Canes-Wrone and Kenneth M. Miller, "Out-of-District Donors and Representation in the US House," *Legislative Studies Quarterly* 47, no. 2 (2022): 361–395.

34. Brandice Canes-Wrone and Nathan Gibson, "Does Money Buy Congressional Love? Individual Donors and Legislative Voting," *Congress & the Presidency* 46, no. 1 (January 2019): 1–27.

35. Mitchell Kilborn and Arjun Vishwanath, "Public Money Talks Too: How Public Campaign Financing Degrades Representation," *American Journal of Political Science* 66, no. 3 (2022): 730–744.

36. Both parties appear to rely on spatially and socioeconomically similar contributors. The financial bases of support for candidates reside primarily in densely populated, affluent, well-connected communities. Indeed, Democrats and Republicans appear to raise funds from the same precincts and city blocks, with little semblance to the geographic distribution of electoral votes. See, e.g., Wendy K. Tam Cho and James G. Gimpel, "Prospecting for (Campaign) Gold," *American Journal*

of Political Science 51, no. 2 (2007): 255–268; Brittany Bramlett, James Gimpel, and Frances Lee, "The Political Ecology of Opinion in Big-Donor Neighborhoods," *Political Behavior* 33, no. 4 (2010): 1–36. This research on geospatial fund-raising needs to be updated. There has been significant sorting geographically since these papers were published.

37. Jeremy Padgett, Johanna L. Dunaway, and Joshua P. Darr, "As Seen on TV? How Gatekeeping Makes the U.S. House Seem More Extreme," *Journal of Communication* 69, no. 6 (December 31, 2019): 696–719; Michael W. Wagner and Mike Gruszczynski, "Who Gets Covered? Ideological Extremity and News Coverage of Members of the U.S. Congress, 1993 to 2013," *Journalism & Mass Communication Quarterly* 95, no. 3 (September 1, 2018): 670–690.

38. Eitan Hersh, *Politics Is for Power: How to Move Beyond Political Hobbyism, Take Action, and Make Real Change* (New York: Scribner, 2020).

39. Steven Shepard and Sarah Ferris, "Omar Rakes in Cash Online as Controversies Pile Up," *Politico*, April 15, 2019.

40. Jonathan Allen, "'You Lie!' Worth $2.7 Million for Wilson," *Politico*, October 10, 2009.

41. Jeremy Padgett, Johanna L. Dunaway, and Joshua P. Darr, "As Seen on TV? How Gatekeeping Makes the U.S. House Seem More Extreme," *Journal of Communication* 69, no. 6 (December 31, 2019): 696–719; Michael W. Wagner and Mike Gruszczynski, "Who Gets Covered? Ideological Extremity and News Coverage of Members of the U.S. Congress, 1993 to 2013," *Journalism & Mass Communication Quarterly* 95, no. 3 (September 1, 2018): 670–690.

42. Taylor Giorno, "Rep. Kattie Porter Raised More Money Than Other House Democrats During the 2022 Election—Without Contributions from Corporate PACs or Lobbyists," OpenSecrets, January 12, 2023.

43. Hailey Fuchs, "Dan Crenshaw Is Building a Young Activist Army, One Summit at a Time," *Politico*, September 16, 2021.

44. Alexander Fouirnaies and Andrew B. Hall, "The Financial Incumbency Advantage: Causes and Consequences," *Journal of Politics* 76, no. 3 (2014): 711–724; Justin Grimmer and Eleanor Neff Powell, "Congressmen in Exile: The Politics and Consequences of Involuntary Committee Removal," *Journal of Politics* 75, no. 4 (October 2013): 907–920. Labor PACs tend to contribute to left-of-center and progressive candidates, while corporate and trade PACs tend to favor right-of-center and conservative candidates. See Keith T. Poole and Thomas Romer, "Patterns of Political Action Committee Contributions to the 1980 Campaigns for the United States House of Representatives," *Public Choice* 47, no. 1 (January 1, 1985): 63–111.

45. Raymond J. La Raja and Brian F. Schaffner, *Campaign Finance and Political Polarization: When Purists Prevail* (Ann Arbor: University of Michigan Press, 2015).

46. Alexander Fouirnaies and Andrew B. Hall, "The Financial Incumbency Advantage: Causes and Consequences," *Journal of Politics* 76, no. 3 (2014): 711–724; Alexander Fouirnaies and Andrew B. Hall, "How Do Interest Groups Seek Access to Committees?," *American Journal of Political Science* 62, no. 1 (2018): 132–147; Paul S. Herrnson, Costas Panagopoulos, and Kendall L. Bailey, *Congressional Elections: Campaigning at Home and in Washington* (Thousand Oaks, CA: CQ Press, 2019); Janet Grenzke, "Candidate Attributes and PAC Contributions," *Western Political Quarterly* 42, no. 2 (1989): 245–264.

47. Lee Drutman, *The Business of America Is Lobbying: How Corporations Became Politicized and Politics Became More Corporate*, Reprint ed. (New York: Oxford University Press, 2017); Eric S. Heberlig and Bruce A. Larson, "The Strategic

Allocation of PAC Funds to Effective Legislators," *Interest Groups & Advocacy* 11, no. 4 (December 2022): 466–492.

48. Kenneth M. Miller and Tanner Bates, "PACs and January 6th: Campaign Finance and Objections to the Electoral College Vote Count," *Research & Politics* 10, no. 3 (July 1, 2023): 1–10.

49. At the local level, there is evidence that even leaders in the formal party are more likely to favor the nomination of more extreme candidates over moderates. See David Broockman et al., "Why Local Party Leaders Don't Support Nominating Centrists," *British Journal of Political Science* 51, no. 2 (April 2021): 724–749. Their survey research indicates that Democratic leaders prefer more extreme candidates over moderate ones by a margin of two to one, and Republicans by ten to one. However, see Hans J. G. Hassell, "Principled Moderation: Understanding Parties' Support of Moderate Candidates," *Legislative Studies Quarterly* 43, no. 2 (2018): 343–369, which finds that party leadership prefers moderate over more extreme candidates and that they do so for ideological rather than strategic purposes.

50. On the behavior of political parties with respect to political contributions, see Raymond J. La Raja and Brian F. Schaffner, *Campaign Finance and Political Polarization: When Purists Prevail* (Ann Arbor: University of Michigan Press, 2015). On how more extreme candidates pay an electoral price, see Andrew B. Hall, "What Happens When Extremists Win Primaries?," *American Political Science Review* 109, no. 1 (2015): 18–42.

51. Bernard L. Fraga and Hans J. G. Hassell, "Are Minority and Women Candidates Penalized by Party Politics? Race, Gender, and Access to Party Support," *Political Research Quarterly* 74, no. 3 (September 1, 2021): 540–555.

52. At the federal level, the conventional definition of small donors is that they are the unitemized donations that are $200 or less. However, this implies that the value of a small donation has been decreasing over time due to inflation. This may account, in part, for the fact that small donations were not increasing over time until relatively recently, possibly due to the intensified stakes of elections and fund-raising platforms like ActBlue, started in 2004, and WinRed, started in 2020.

53. Raymond J. La Raja and Brian F. Schaffner, *Campaign Finance and Political Polarization: When Purists Prevail* (Ann Arbor: University of Michigan Press, 2015).

54. Samuel Issacharoff and Jeremy Peterman, "Special Interests After Citizens United: Access, Replacement, and Interest Group Response to Legal Change," *Annual Review of Law and Social Science* 9, no. 1 (2013): 185–205.

55. Diana Dwyre and Evelyn Braz, "Super PAC Spending Strategies and Goals," *The Forum* 13, no. 2 (July 1, 2015): 245–267; Michael S. Rocca and Jared W. Clay, "Allocating Unlimited Money: What Explains Super PAC Spending in Congressional Elections?," *The Forum* 19, no. 2 (September 1, 2021): 229–252.

56. Travis N. Ridout, Michael M. Franz, and Erika Franklin Fowler, "Sponsorship, Disclosure, and Donors: Limiting the Impact of Outside Group Ads," *Political Research Quarterly* 68, no. 1 (March 1, 2015): 154–166.

57. See Samuel Issacharoff, "Outsourcing Politics: The Hostile Takeover of Our Hollowed-Out Political Parties," *Houston Law Review* 54, no. 4 (2017): 845–880; Raymond J. La Raja and Brian F. Schaffner, *Campaign Finance and Political Polarization: When Purists Prevail* (Ann Arbor: University of Michigan Press, 2015); Cory Manento, "Party Crashers: Interest Groups as a Latent Threat to Party Networks in Congressional Primaries," *Party Politics* 27 (2021): 137–148; Stan Oklobdzija, "Dark Parties: Unveiling Nonparty Communities in American Political Campaigns," *American Political Science Review* 1 (April 5, 2023): 1–22.

58. See, e.g., Anne E. Baker, "Do Interest Group Endorsements Cue Individual Contributions to House Candidates?," *Political Behavior* 44 (2015): 759–784; Bruce E. Cain, *Democracy More or Less: America's Political Reform Quandary*, Cambridge Studies in Election Law and Democracy (Cambridge: Cambridge University Press, 2014); Michael Franz, "Campaign Finance Law: The Changing Role of Parties and Interest Groups," in *Rethinking American Electoral Democracy*, ed. Matthew Streb, 2nd ed. (New York: Routledge, 2012), 69–86; Heather K. Gerken and Alex Tausanovitch, "A Public Finance Model for Lobbying: Lobbying, Campaign Finance, and the Privatization of Democracy," *Election Law Journal: Rules, Politics, and Policy* 13, no. 1 (March 1, 2014): 75–90; Richard L. Hasen, *Money, Politics, and the Decline of American Democracy* (New Haven, CT: Yale University Press, 2016); Samuel Issacharoff and Jeremy Peterman, "Special Interests After Citizens United: Access, Replacement, and Interest Group Response to Legal Change," *Annual Review of Law and Social Science* 9, no. 1 (2013): 185–205; Raymond J. La Raja and Brian F. Schaffner, *Campaign Finance and Political Polarization: When Purists Prevail* (Ann Arbor: University of Michigan Press, 2015); Nolan McCarty, "Reducing Polarization by Making Parties Stronger," Hewlett Foundation Workshop on Solutions to Political Polarization in the US, October 17, 2013; Travis N. Ridout, Michael M. Franz, and Erika Franklin Fowler, "Sponsorship, Disclosure, and Donors: Limiting the Impact of Outside Group Ads," *Political Research Quarterly* 68, no. 1 (March 1, 2015): 154–166.

59. Robert G. Boatright, *Interest Groups and Campaign Finance Reform in the United States and Canada* (Ann Arbor: University of Michigan Press, 2011); Richard L. Hasen, *Plutocrats United: Campaign Money, the Supreme Court, and the Distortion of American Elections*, 1st ed. (New Haven, CT: Yale University Press, 2016); Raymond J. La Raja, *Small Change: Money, Political Parties, and Campaign Finance Reform* (Ann Arbor: University of Michigan Press, 2008).

60. In *SpeechNow.org v. FEC*, the DC Circuit Court ruled for the plaintiffs that limiting the size of political contributions to independent spending committees burdened free speech rights. The decision argued that states do not have a compelling anticorruption interest to regulate such limits because these expenditures are not coordinated with the candidates or a political party.

61. Erika Franklin Fowler, Travis N. Ridout, and Michael M. Franz, "Political Advertising in 2016: The Presidential Election as Outlier?," *The Forum* 14, no. 4 (2016): 445–469; Dante J Scala, "Are Super PACs Super-Efficient?" (paper delivered at the State of the Parties: 2020 and Beyond Virtual Conference, Akron, Ohio, November 4–5, 2021).

62. Erika Franklin Fowler, Michael M. Franz, and Travis N. Ridout, *Political Advertising in the United States*, 2nd ed. (New York: Routledge, 2022); Michael M. Franz, Erika Franklin Fowler, and Travis N. Ridout, "Loose Cannons or Loyal Foot Soldiers? Toward a More Complex Theory of Interest Group Advertising Strategies," *American Journal of Political Science* 60, no. 3 (2016): 738–751.

63. Karen Sebold and Andrew Dowdle, "The Evolution of Independent Expenditures in U.S. Federal Elections Before and After Citizens United," *Politique américaine* 35, no. 2 (2020): 47–66.

64. Daniel P. Tokaji and Renata E. B. Strause, *The New Soft Money: Outside Spending in Congressional Elections* (Columbus: Ohio State University Michael E. Moritz College of Law, 2014); Eric S. Heberlig and Bruce A. Larson, "U.S. House Incumbent Fundraising and Spending in a Post–Citizens United and Post-McCutcheon World," *Political Science Quarterly* 129, no. 4 (December 1, 2014): 613–642.

65. Eric S. Heberlig and Bruce A. Larson, *Congressional Parties, Institutional Ambition, and the Financing of Majority Control* (Ann Arbor: University of Michigan Press, 2012).

66. Joel M. Gora, "In Defense of Super PACs and of the First Amendment," *Seton Hall Law Review* 43 (2013): 1185.

67. Erika Franklin Fowler and Travis N. Ridout, "Negative, Angry, and Ubiquitous: Political Advertising in 2012," *The Forum* 10, no. 4 (February 9, 2013): 51–61; Travis N. Ridout, Michael M. Franz, and Erika Franklin Fowler, "Sponsorship, Disclosure, and Donors: Limiting the Impact of Outside Group Ads," *Political Research Quarterly* 68, no. 1 (March 1, 2015): 154–166; Erika Franklin Fowler, Travis N. Ridout, and Michael M. Franz, "Political Advertising in 2016: The Presidential Election as Outlier?," *The Forum* 14, no. 4 (2016): 445–469; Deborah Jordan Brooks and Michael Murov, "Assessing Accountability in a Post–Citizens United Era: The Effects of Attack Ad Sponsorship by Unknown Independent Groups," *American Politics Research* 40, no. 3 (May 1, 2012): 383–418; Conor M. Dowling and Amber Wichowsky, "Does It Matter Who's Behind the Curtain? Anonymity in Political Advertising and the Effects of Campaign Finance Disclosure," *American Politics Research* 41, no. 6 (November 1, 2013): 965–996.

68. Stan Oklobdzija, "Dark Parties: Unveiling Nonparty Communities in American Political Campaigns," *American Political Science Review* 1 (April 5, 2023): 1–22.

69. Anna Massoglia, "Dark Money Gets Darker with Less Disclosure in the 2022 Election," Open Secrets, May 19, 2022.

70. Lee Drutman, "The Rise of Dark Money," in *Interest Group Politics*, ed. Allan J. Cigler, Burdett A. Loomis, and Anthony Nownes, 9th ed. (Thousand Oaks, CA: London: CQ Press, 2015).

71. Lexi Lonas, "Abortion Rights Activists Plan Protests Outside of Supreme Court Justices' Homes," *The Hill* (blog), May 7, 2022.

72. Richard L. Hasen, *Cheap Speech: How Disinformation Poisons Our Politics—and How to Cure It* (New Haven, CT: Yale University Press, 2022).

73. Paul Herrnson and Justin Kirkland, "Political Parties and Campaign Finance Networks," in *Oxford Handbook of Political Networks*, ed. Jennifer Victor, Alexander Montgomery, and Mark Lubell (Oxford: Oxford University Press, 2017), 407–432; Raymond J. La Raja and Brian F. Schaffner, *Campaign Finance and Political Polarization: When Purists Prevail* (Ann Arbor: University of Michigan Press, 2015).

74. Cory Manento, "Party Crashers: Interest Groups as a Latent Threat to Party Networks in Congressional Primaries," *Party Politics* 27 (2021): 137–148.

75. Stan Oklobdzija, "Dark Parties: Unveiling Nonparty Communities in American Political Campaigns," *American Political Science Review* 1 (April 5, 2023): 1–22.

76. Dario McCarty, "Democrats Spend Millions on Republican Primaries," OpenSecrets, July 15, 2022.

77. Dino P. Christenson and Corwin D. Smidt, "Following the Money: Super PACs and the 2012 Presidential Nomination," *Presidential Studies Quarterly* 44, no. 3 (2014): 410–430.

78. Richard L. Hasen, "Research Note: Record Election Litigation Rates in the 2020 Election: An Aberration or a Sign of Things to Come?," *Election Law Journal: Rules, Politics, and Policy* 21, no. 2 (June 1, 2022): 150–154.

79. Richard L. Hasen, "Research Note: Record Election Litigation Rates in the 2020 Election: An Aberration or a Sign of Things to Come?," *Election Law Journal: Rules, Politics, and Policy* 21, no. 2 (June 1, 2022): 150–154.

80. Derek Muller, "Reducing Election Litigation," *Fordham Law Review* 90, no. 2 (2021): 561.

81. Nicholas Confessore, "G.O.P. Angst over 2016 Led to Provision on Funding," *New York Times*, December 13, 2014.

82. Mitchell Kilborn and Arjun Vishwanath, "Public Money Talks Too: How Public Campaign Financing Degrades Representation," *American Journal of Political Science* 66, no. 3 (2022): 730–744; Brandice Canes-Wrone and Nathan Gibson, "Does Money Buy Congressional Love? Individual Donors and Legislative Voting," *Congress & the Presidency* 46, no. 1 (January 2019): 1–27.

83. Brandice Canes-Wrone and Kenneth M. Miller, "Out-of-District Donors and Representation in the US House," *Legislative Studies Quarterly* 47, no. 2 (2022): 361–395.

84. Abby K. Wood, "Voters Use Campaign Finance Transparency and Compliance Information," *Political Behavior* 45, no. 4 (December 1, 2023): 1553–1579; Conor M. Dowling and Amber Wichowsky, "Attacks Without Consequence? Candidates, Parties, Groups, and the Changing Face of Negative Advertising," *American Journal of Political Science* 59, no. 1 (2015): 19–36.

85. Travis N. Ridout, Michael M. Franz, and Erika Franklin Fowler, "Sponsorship, Disclosure, and Donors: Limiting the Impact of Outside Group Ads," *Political Research Quarterly* 68, no. 1 (March 1, 2015): 154–166.

86. Raymond J. La Raja and Brian F. Schaffner, *Campaign Finance and Political Polarization: When Purists Prevail* (Ann Arbor: University of Michigan Press, 2015).

87. Michael J. Malbin, "A Neo-Madisonian Perspective on Campaign Finance Reform, Institutions, Pluralism, and Small Donors," *University of Pennsylvania Journal of Constitutional Law* 23 (2021): 907.

88. Michael S. Kang, "Hyperpartisan Campaign Finance," *Emory Law Journal* 70 (2021): 1171.

89. Soft money consisted of funds that parties could raise without limit (based on election laws in states that allowed higher limits or no limits) so long as they were used for party-building activities such as voter identification and get-out-the-vote. The parties expanded that definition by running campaign ads in support of candidates, which made them seek ever more amounts of soft money. BCRA's primary purpose was to put an end to party soft money.

90. Raymond J. La Raja, *Small Change: Money, Political Parties, and Campaign Finance Reform* (Ann Arbor: University of Michigan Press, 2008).

91. In the most recent analysis of 180 countries, 70 percent do not limit the amounts that political parties may spend in support of candidates. See Elin Falguera, Samuel Jones, and Magnus Ohman, *Funding of Political Parties and Election Campaigns: A Handbook on Political Finance* (Stockholm: International Institute for Democracy and Electoral Assistance, 2014), 27.

92. Conversely, political parties are heavily regulated in the United States, and providing them with public funds may blur too much the distinction between their private and public roles. Vibrant political parties emerge from civil society, and scholars have argued that having them too reliant on public funds may make them less adaptive and responsive to diverse constituencies. See, e.g., Richard S. Katz and Peter Mair, "Changing Models of Party Organization and Party Democracy: The Emergence of the Cartel Party," *Party Politics* 1, no. 1 (January 1995): 5–28; Richard S. Katz and Peter Mair, "The Cartel Party Thesis: A Restatement," *Perspectives on Politics* 7, no. 4 (2009): 753–766.

93. "Public Financing of Campaigns: Overview" National Conference of State Legislatures, updated February 6, 2003.

94. Abby K. Wood and Christian R. Grose, "Campaign Finance Transparency Affects Legislators' Election Outcomes and Behavior," *American Journal of Political Science* 66, no. 2 (2022): 516–534; Abby K. Wood, "Voters Use Campaign Finance Transparency and Compliance Information," *Political Behavior* 45, no. 4 (December 1, 2023): 1553–1579.

95. Richard L. Hasen, "'Citizens United' and the Illusion of Coherence," *Michigan Law Review* 109, no. 4 (2011): 581–623.

96. Raymond J. La Raja, "Political Participation and Civic Courage: The Negative Effect of Transparency on Making Small Campaign Contributions," *Political Behavior* 36, no. 4 (December 1, 2014): 753–776; Diana Carole Mutz, *Hearing the Other Side: Deliberative Versus Participatory Democracy* (Cambridge: Cambridge University Press, 2006).

97. Bruce E. Cain, *Democracy More or Less: America's Political Reform Quandary*, Cambridge Studies in Election Law and Democracy (Cambridge: Cambridge University Press, 2014).

98. Bradley Smith, "Disclosure in a Post–Citizens United Real World," *University of St. Thomas Journal of Law and Public Policy* 6, no. 2 (May 31, 2016): 257.

99. This is the leading case on exemptions for groups facing harassment. See *Brown v. Socialist Workers '74 Campaign Comm.*, 459 U.S. 87 (1982). The Federal Election Commission has long determined when groups are entitled to such an exemption. See, e.g., Federal Election Commission, Advisory Op. 2016-23 (granting renewed partial disclosure exemption for Socialist Workers Party).

100. Bradley Smith, "Disclosure in a Post–Citizens United Real World," *University of St. Thomas Journal of Law and Public Policy* 6, no. 2 (May 31, 2016).

101. Bruce E. Cain, *Democracy More or Less: America's Political Reform Quandary*, Cambridge Studies in Election Law and Democracy (Cambridge: Cambridge University Press, 2014).

102. Eugene Volokh, "Private Employees' Speech and Political Activity: Statutory Protection Against Employer Retaliation," *Texas Review of Law & Politics* 16, no. 2 (spring 2012): 295–338.

103. Lee Drutman, *The Business of America Is Lobbying: How Corporations Became Politicized and Politics Became More Corporate*, Reprint ed. (New York: Oxford University Press, 2017).

104. Lynda W. Powell, *The Influence of Campaign Contributions in State Legislatures: The Effects of Institutions and Politics*, Illustrated ed. (Ann Arbor: University of Michigan Press, 2012).

105. Frank R. Baumgartner, *Lobbying and Policy Change : Who Wins, Who Loses, and Why* (Chicago: University of Chicago Press, 2009); Richard L. Hall and Alan V. Deardorff, "Lobbying as Legislative Subsidy," *American Political Science Review* 100, no. 1 (February 2006): 69–84.

106. Andrew B. Hall, "How the Public Funding of Elections Increases Candidate Polarization" (working paper, Stanford Democracy and Polarization Lab, August 2014); Mitchell Kilborn, "Public Campaign Financing, Candidate Socioeconomic Diversity, and Representational Inequality at the U.S. State Level: Evidence from Connecticut," *State Politics & Policy Quarterly* 18, no. 3 (2018): 296–323; Mitchell Kilborn and Arjun Vishwanath, "Public Money Talks Too: How Public Campaign Financing Degrades Representation," *American Journal of Political Science* 66, no. 3 (2022): 730–744.

107. Cites Yorgason, Geoffrey Henderson, and Hahrie Han, "If We Build It, Only Some Will Come: An Experimental Study of Mobilization for Seattle's Democracy

Voucher Program," *Journal of Experimental Political Science* 9, no. 1 (2022): 131–146; Brian J. McCabe and Jennifer A. Heerwig, "Diversifying the Donor Pool: How Did Seattle's Democracy Voucher Program Reshape Participation in Municipal Campaign Finance?," *Election Law Journal: Rules, Politics, and Policy* 18, no. 4 (September 24, 2019): 323–341; Laurent Bouton, Shana E. Gadarian, and David L. Leal, "Small Campaign Donors," SSRN Scholarly Paper, December 6, 2021.

108. Adam Bonica, "Small Donors and Polarization," *Boston Review*, July 26, 2011.

109. See "Democracy Voucher Program," Seattle.gov; "Matching Funds Program," New York City Campaign Finance Board.

110. Michael J. Malbin, "A Neo-Madisonian Perspective on Campaign Finance Reform, Institutions, Pluralism, and Small Donors," *University of Pennsylvania Journal of Constitutional Law* 23 (2021): 907. For a description of the New York State program, see "Program Overview," New York State Public Campaign Finance Board.

111. Brandice Canes-Wrone and Kenneth M. Miller, "Out-of-District Donors and Representation in the US House," *Legislative Studies Quarterly* 47, no. 2 (2022): 361–395.

112. Political parties are subsidized in several American states already. Alabama, Arizona, Minnesota, New Mexico, Rhode Island, and Utah allow taxpayers to check a box on their return indicating a desire to contribute to the state's political parties. The amounts range from $1 to $25. Florida and Iowa also provide subsidies in other forms. See "Public Financing of Campaigns: Overview," National Conference of State Legislatures, updated February 6, 2023.

113. The group was largely split on whether to recommend large public grants to qualifying candidates. Some view positively the system used in Connecticut and Arizona, which provide candidates a lump sum grant.

114. Sarah Birch, "Electoral Institutions and Popular Confidence in Electoral Processes: A Cross-National Analysis," *Electoral Studies* 27, no. 2 (June 1, 2008): 305–320.

115. See, e.g., David M. Primo and Jeffrey D. Milyo, *Campaign Finance and American Democracy: What the Public Really Thinks and Why It Matters*, 1st ed. (Chicago: University of Chicago Press, 2020).

116. See Raymond J. La Raja and Brian F. Schaffner, *Campaign Finance and Political Polarization: When Purists Prevail* (Ann Arbor: University of Michigan Press, 2015), 158 (with figures).

117. Michael S. Kang, "Hyperpartisan Campaign Finance," *Emory Law Journal* 70, no. 5 (2021): 1171–1208; Raymond J. La Raja, *Small Change: Money, Political Parties, and Campaign Finance Reform* (Ann Arbor: University of Michigan Press, 2008).

118. See also Abby K. Wood, "Voters Use Campaign Finance Transparency and Compliance Information," *Political Behavior* 45, no. 4 (December 1, 2023): 1553–1579.

119. For studies showing a conservative or Republican bias, see Anna Harvey and Taylor Mattia, "Does Money Have a Conservative Bias? Estimating the Causal Impact of Citizens United on State Legislative Preferences," *Public Choice*, October 9, 2019; Andrew B. Hall, "Systemic Effects of Campaign Spending: Evidence from Corporate Contribution Bans in US State Legislatures," *Political Science Research and Methods* 4, no. 2 (May 2016): 343–359. For minimal effects, see Raymond J. La Raja and Brian F. Schaffner, "The Effects of Campaign Finance Spending Bans on Electoral Outcomes: Evidence from the States About the Potential Impact of Citizens United v. FEC," *Electoral Studies* 33 (March 1, 2014): 102–114.

120. Tabatha Abu El-Haj and Didi Kuo, "Associational Party-Building: A Path to Rebuilding Democracy," *Columbia Law Review Forum* 122, no. 7 (November 21, 2022): 127–176.

121. Jim Geraghty, "The Quiet Collapse of Four Key State Republican Parties," *National Review*, July 24, 2023.

122. Early donations have a positive impact on future fund-raising capabilities. See Robert Biersack, Paul S. Herrnson, and Clyde Wilcox, "Seeds for Success: Early Money in Congressional Elections," *Legislative Studies Quarterly* 18, no. 4 (1993): 535–551; Adam Bonica, "Professional Networks, Early Fundraising, and Electoral Success," *Election Law Journal: Rules, Politics, and Policy* 16, no. 1 (March 2017): 153–171; Jonathan S. Krasno, Donald Philip Green, and Jonathan A. Cowden, "The Dynamics of Campaign Fundraising in House Elections," *Journal of Politics* 56, no. 2 (May 1994): 459–474; David L. Leal, "Early Money and Senate Primary Elections," *American Politics Research* 31, no. 1 (January 1, 2003): 93–104; Corwin Smidt and Dino Christenson, "More Bang for the Buck: Campaign Spending and Fundraising Success," *American Politics Research* 40, no. 6 (November 1, 2012): 949–975.

123. Peter L. Francia et al., *The Financiers of Congressional Elections: Investors, Ideologues, and Intimates.* Power, Conflict, and Democracy: American Politics into the 21st Century (New York: Columbia University Press, 2003).

124. Adam Bonica, "Professional Networks, Early Fundraising, and Electoral Success," *Election Law Journal: Rules, Politics, and Policy* 16, no. 1 (March 2017): 153–171.

125. Danielle M. Thomsen, *Opting Out of Congress: Partisan Polarization and the Decline of Moderate Candidates* (Cambridge: Cambridge University Press, 2017).

126. Jacob M. Grumbach and Alexander Sahn, "Race and Representation in Campaign Finance," *American Political Science Review* 114, no. 1 (February 2020): 206–221; Danielle M. Thomsen and Michele L. Swers, "Which Women Can Run? Gender, Partisanship, and Candidate Donor Networks," *Political Research Quarterly* 70, no. 2 (June 1, 2017): 449–463.

127. Alan Greenblatt, "Rex Sinquefield: The Tyrannosaurus Rex of State Politics," *Governing*, May 20, 2015; Theda Skocpol and Caroline Tervo, *Upending American Politics: Polarizing Parties, Ideological Elites, and Citizen Activists from the Tea Party to the Anti-Trump Resistance* (Oxford: Oxford University Press, 2019).

128. Raymond J. La Raja and Jonathan Rauch, "The State of State Parties—and How Strengthening Them Can Improve Our Politics" (Washington, DC: Brookings, March 2016); Vanessa Williamson, Theda Skocpol, and John Coggin, "The Tea Party and the Remaking of Republican Conservatism," *Perspectives on Politics* 9, no. 1 (2011): 25–43.

129. See, e.g., Richard L. Hasen, *Cheap Speech: How Disinformation Poisons Our Politics—and How to Cure It* (New Haven, CT: Yale University Press, 2022).

130. Oma Seddiq and Amelia Davidson, "AI Disinformation Drives Lawmakers Fears About 2024 'Wild West,'" *Bloomberg Government*, July 20, 2023.

131. Mike Norton and Richard H. Pildes, "How Outside Money Makes Governing More Difficult," *Election Law Journal: Rules, Politics, and Policy* 19, no. 4 (December 1, 2020): 486–502.

8

Conclusion

Richard H. Pildes, Larry Diamond,
and Edward B. Foley

Addressing the toxic tribalism and political extremism that has arisen in recent decades requires action along many fronts. One of these is the institutional framework within which democratic politics and elections take place. This volume has brought together a highly distinguished group of academics from several disciplines who have spent much of their careers studying how the design of democratic processes shapes politics and the political culture more generally. Our task force also includes lawyers and others with substantial experience with the political process.

We do not believe there is a single institutional-design reform, or even a series of reforms, that could magically transform our political culture. But institutional reforms can matter at the margins in combatting political extremism, and those margins can make a significant difference in the kind of politics we experience and the larger political culture we inhabit. The institutional framework within which politics and elections take place creates incentive structures that shape which candidates decide to run, which are likely to win, and the relationship between political parties, candidates, officeholders, interest groups, and the general public. Moreover, because many citizens take political cues from those who hold public office, particularly the most visible public officials, the types of candidates who succeed also shape the larger political culture.

In this book, we have brought to bear the best current empirical knowledge on a variety of institutional reforms that have been offered to combat extremism. We believe it is critical to test reform proposals against the best data available, and, indeed, one aim of this book is to

297

show which reform proposals are *unlikely* to achieve their goals—or could even make things worse by fueling extremism. There can be a great deal of herding behavior within reform circles, as well as a reluctance to deviate from conventional wisdom. As academics, we have striven to marshal the current state of knowledge about various proposals and to highlight the lines along which future empirical work would be desirable.

We have explored reform proposals addressing the structure of primary elections, the types of voting rules, the potential use of proportional representation for legislative elections, the system of campaign finance, the presidential nomination process, and the presidential primary debate process. On some issues, we achieved substantial consensus regarding directions to take or to avoid. On others, we had significant disagreements, which we discussed. In some areas, we endorsed specific recommendations for reforms. In others, we offered what we characterize as suggestions—that is, proposals on which we hope to begin discussions, with less firm convictions about where those discussions should end up. A common theme across many of the proposals is that our politics has become too captured by factions and that we should aim for reforms that will help make the system more responsive to political majorities.

Most of the reforms we discuss can be undertaken at the state level. Indeed, some are on the ballot in several states in the fall 2024 election, as this volume goes to press. We believe the most significant political reform these days is much more likely to take place at the state level than the national level. The political process at the national level is too polarized over election-related issues to be a likely source of innovation. Even at the state level, prospects for reform on many of these issues are best in states where voters have the power to make changes through direct democratic processes, such as voter initiatives. Incumbent officeholders and political parties are often reluctant to make any changes to the rules under which they have been elected. If some of these changes are implemented and prove popular and successful at the state level, this can build momentum for eventually adopting such changes at the national level. Much of the history of political reform in the United States has followed this path.

There is currently much cynicism and despair about deepening political polarization and extremism in the United States. But such conditions can serve as catalysts for political reform, and, indeed, a great deal of successful reform has taken place in recent years. More states have adopted independent redistricting commissions, often led by citizens' groups that push to get such measures on the ballot. A number of states have adopted automatic voter registration to shift the burden of registration from voters to the government.

In terms of specific reforms discussed in this volume, we believe the Alaska model of a single, all-candidate primary, with the top four or five candidates going on to a general election in which ranked-choice voting (RCV) determines the winner, offers a promising template for the type of reform capable of ensuring that candidates with the broadest support among the general electorate are able to get elected. Voters in other states will soon be deciding whether to adopt this model or variations of it. In 2022, voters in Nevada voted to amend their state constitution to adopt the Alaska model, modified slightly to allow the top five candidates to advance to the general election. The Nevada constitution requires that an amendment be adopted by voters in two consecutive elections, and so the amendment will be voted on a second time in November 2024. In those elections, voters in Idaho will vote on an initiative that would implement the Alaska system of a nonpartisan primary and a "top-four" general election with RCV. A similar measure is headed for the November 2024 ballot in Colorado.

Related reform measures include a proposed initiative in Arizona that would mandate an Alaska-style all-candidate primary while leaving to the legislature the choice of whether the general election should advance only two candidates, as in California, or more than two, in which case ranked-choice ballots will be required. The Arizona proposal is especially innovative insofar as it also leaves to the legislature the choice of which tabulation method to employ if ranked-choice ballots are used. This flexibility could serve the state well, given the findings in Chapter 2 of this volume. Arizona is a highly polarized state, and alternative forms of RCV are most likely to provide extra benefits in counteracting polarization and extremism under such conditions. Montana, too, is pursuing a similar constitutional reform that would give the state great flexibility in tailoring its electoral system to reduce polarization: a requirement that candidates win office with a majority, not just a plurality, of votes. This simple requirement tends to induce the adoption of electoral innovation that is less likely to cause polarized outcomes.

Ranked-choice voting is also being adopted in more jurisdictions. In a ballot measure, Maine became the first state to adopt it statewide; Maine now uses RCV for federal elections and for state primary elections. In 2019, New York City's voters adopted an amendment to the city charter to use RCV in primary elections for the city council and executive offices, including mayor. Since the Democratic primary often determines the race for mayor of New York City, this was a significant development. A growing number of smaller American cities have also adopted RCV over the past decade. A ballot measure referred by the state legislature in Oregon for voter approval in the fall of 2024 would implement RCV in all state primary and general elections for executive offices at the state and federal levels, as well as for the US House and Senate. But RCV has recently come to be seen as a partisan issue, even though there is no reason it ought to favor one party or the other. As a result, several states have enacted laws prohibiting its use. (As noted in Chapter 2, there are ways to achieve the depolarizing benefits sought from Alaska-style reforms without the use of ranked-choice ballots.)

Many Americans are deeply troubled by our current political culture. But we need not passively accept this state of affairs as our inevitable fate. A variety of institutional reforms to various aspects of our political process and electoral system can help combat the political extremism and toxic tribalism that has arisen in recent years. This volume draws on the best knowledge we currently possess to suggest the most promising directions for institutional changes that would push back against political extremism.

Acronyms

AfD	Alternative for Germany
AI	artificial intelligence
BCRA	Bipartisan Campaign Reform Act
BTR	bottom-two runoff
CES	Cooperative Election Study
FEC	Federal Election Commission
FECA	Federal Election Campaign Act
FPTP	first-past-the-post
GDP	gross domestic product
IRV	instant-runoff voting
LPR	lowest-plurality runoff
MMD	multimember district
MPV	most-preferred voting
OECD	Organization for Economic Cooperation and Development
PAC	political action committee
PR	proportional representation
RCV	ranked-choice voting
RNC	Republican National Committee
SMD	single member district
SMDP	single-member-district, plurality
STV	single-transferable vote
V-Dem	V-Dem Institute

Bibliography

Abu El-Haj, Tabatha, and Didi Kuo. "Associational Party-Building: A Path to Rebuilding Democracy." *Columbia Law Review Forum* 122, no. 7 (November 21, 2022): 127–176.

Adam, James, and Samuel Merrill III. "Candidate and Party Strategies in Two-Stage Elections Beginning with a Primary." *American Journal of Political Science* 52 (2008): 344–359.

Adams, James, Jane Green, and Caitlin Milazzo. "Has the British Public Depolarized Along with Political Elites." *Comparative Political Studies* 4, no. 4 (2012): 507–538.

Adams, James, and Zeynep Somer-Topcu. "Moderate Now, Win Votes Later: The Electoral Consequences of Parties' Policy Shifts in 25 Postwar Democracies." *Journal of Politics* 71, no. 2 (April 2009): 678–692. https://doi.org /10.1017/S0022381609090537.

Albala, Adrián, André Borges, and Lucas Couto. "Pre-electoral Coalitions and Cabinet Stability in Presidential Systems." *British Journal of Politics and International Relations* 25, no. 1 (February 2023): 64–82. https://doi.org/10 .1177/13691481211056852.

Albarracín, Juan, Laura Gamboa, and Scott Mainwaring. "Deinstitutionalization Without Collapse: Colombia's Party System." In *Party Systems in Latin America*, edited by Scott Mainwaring, 227–254. 1st ed. Cambridge: Cambridge University Press.

Albert, Zachary, and Raymond J. La Raja. "Who Should Decide the Party's Nominee? Understanding Public Attitudes Toward Primary Elections." *Party Politics* 27, no. 5 (September 1, 2021): 928–941.

Allen, Jonathan. "'You Lie!' Worth $2.7 Million for Wilson." *Politico.* October 10, 2009.

Amengay, Abdelkarim, and Daniel Stockemer. "The Radical Right in Western Europe: A Meta-analysis of Structural Factors." *Political Studies Review* 17, no. 1 (2019): 30–40. https://doi.org/10.1177/1478929918777975.

Anderson, Christopher J. "Parties, Party Systems, and Satisfaction with Democratic Performance in the New Europe." *Political Studies* 46, no. 3 (August 1, 1998): 572–588. https://doi.org/10.1111/1467-9248.00155.

Anderson, Christopher J., André Blais, Shaun Bowler, Todd Donovan, and Ola Listhaug. *Losers' Consent: Elections and Democratic Legitimacy.* Oxford: Oxford University Press, 2005.

Anderson, Sarah E., Daniel M. Butler, and Laurel Harbridge-Yong. *Rejecting Compromise: Legislators' Fear of Primary Voters.* New York: Cambridge University Press, 2020.

Anderson, Sarah E., Daniel M. Butler, Laurel Harbridge-Yong, and Renae Marshall. "Top-4 Primaries Help Moderate Candidates via Crossover Voting: The Case of the 2022 Alaska Election Reforms." *The Forum* 21 (2023): 123–136.

André, Audrey, and Sam Depauw. "District Magnitude and Home Styles of Representation in European Democracies." *West European Politics* 36, no. 5 (September 2013): 986–1006. https://doi.org/10.1080/01402382.2013.796183.

Andrews, Josephine T., and Jeannette Money. "The Spatial Structure of Party Competition: Party Dispersion Within a Finite Policy Space." *British Journal of Political Science* 39, no. 4 (October 2009): 805–824. https://doi.org/10.1017/S0007123409990172.

Arnold, Christian, David Doyle, and Nina Wiesehomeier. "Presidents, Policy Compromise, and Legislative Success." *Journal of Politics* 79, no. 2 (April 2017): 383–395.

Arzheimer, Kai, and Carl C. Berning. "How the Alternative for Germany (AfD) and Their Voters Veered to the Radical Right, 2013–2017." *Electoral Studies* 60 (August 2019): 102040. https://doi.org/10.1016/j.electstud.2019.04.004.

Atkinson, Nathan, Edward B. Foley, and Scott Ganz. "Beyond the Spoiler Effect: Can Ranked Choice Voting Solve the Problem of Political Polarization?" Georgetown McDonough School of Business Research Paper No. 4411173. *Illinois Law Review* (forthcoming October 2024). http://dx.doi.org/10.2139/ssrn.4411173.

Atkinson, Nathan, and Scott Ganz. "Robust Electoral Competition: Rethinking Electoral Systems to Encourage Representative Outcomes." Georgetown McDonough School of Business Research Paper No. 4728225. *Maryland Law Review* (forthcoming 2024). http://dx.doi.org/10.2139/ssrn.4728225.

Atkinson, Nathan, Scott Ganz, and John Mantus. "A Simple Agent-Based Model for Simulating Single Winner Elections." SSRN. July 31, 2024.

Bafumi, Joseph, and Michael C. Herron. "Leapfrog Representation and Extremism: A Study of American Voters and Their Members in Congress." *American Political Science Review* 104, no. 3 (2010): 519–542.

Baker, Anne E. "Do Interest Group Endorsements Cue Individual Contributions to House Candidates?" *Political Behavior* 44 (2015): 759–784.

———. "Getting Short-Changed? The Impact of Outside Money on District Representation." *Social Science Quarterly* 97, no. 5 (2016): 1096–1107.

———. "The Partisan and Policy Motivations of Political Donors Seeking Surrogate Representation in House Elections." *Political Behavior* 42, no. 4 (December 1, 2020): 1035–1054.

Baldassarri, Delia, and Scott E. Page. "The Emergence and Perils of Polarization." *Proceedings of the National Academy of Sciences* 118, no. 50 (December 14, 2021). https://doi.org/10.1073/pnas.2116863118.

Balz, Dan, and Clara Ence Morse. "American Democracy Is Cracking. These Forces Help Explain Why." *Washington Post*. August 18, 2023.

Barber, Michael J. "Donation Motivations: Testing Theories of Access and Ideology." *Political Research Quarterly* 69, no. 1 (2016): 148–159.

———. "Ideological Donors, Contribution Limits, and the Polarization of American Legislatures." *Journal of Politics* 78, no. 1 (2016): 296–310.

Barber, Michael J., Brandice Canes-Wrone, and Sharece Thrower. "Ideologically Sophisticated Donors: Which Candidates Do Individual Contributors Finance?" *American Journal of Political Science* 61, no. 2 (2017): 271–288.

Bartels, Larry M. *Democracy Erodes from the Top: Leaders, Citizens, and the Challenge of Populism in Europe*. Princeton, NJ: Princeton University Press, 2023.

Benoit, William L., Glenn J. Hansen, and Rebecca M. Verser. "A Meta-analysis of the Effects of Viewing U.S. Presidential Debates." *Communication Monographs* 70, no. 4 (2003): 335–350.

Berger, J. M. *Extremism*. Cambridge, MA: MIT Press, 2018.

Berman, Sheri. "Taming Extremist Parties: Lessons from Europe." *Journal of Democracy* 19, no. 1 (2008): 5–18.

Bernauer, Julian, and Adrian Vatter. "Can't Get No Satisfaction with the Westminster Model? Winners, Losers and the Effects of Consensual and Direct Democratic Institutions on Satisfaction with Democracy." *European Journal of Political Research* 51, no. 4 (2012): 435–468. https://doi.org/10.1111/j.1475-6765.2011.02007.x.

Biersack, Robert, Paul S. Herrnson, and Clyde Wilcox. "Seeds for Success: Early Money in Congressional Elections." *Legislative Studies Quarterly* 18, no. 4 (1993): 535–551.

Binder, Sarah. "The Dysfunctional Congress." *Annual Review of Political Science* 18, no. 1 (2015): 85–101.

Birch, Sarah. "Electoral Institutions and Popular Confidence in Electoral Processes: A Cross-National Analysis." *Electoral Studies* 27, no. 2 (June 1, 2008): 305–320.

Bishop, Bill, and Robert Cushing. *The Big Sort: Why the Clustering of Like-Minded America Is Tearing Us Apart*. New York: Houghton Mifflin, 2008.

Black, Duncan. *The Theory of Committees and Elections*. New York: Cambridge University Press, 1958.

Blum, Rachel. *How the Tea Party Captured the GOP: Insurgent Factions in American Politics*. Chicago: University of Chicago Press, 2020.

Boatright, Robert G. "Congressional Primary Challenges and the Health of the Parties." In *The State of the Parties*, edited by John C. Green, 59–74. 9th ed. Lanham, MD: Rowman & Littlefield, 2022.

———. *Congressional Primary Elections*. New York: Routledge, 2014.

———. *Getting Primaried*. Ann Arbor: University of Michigan Press, 2013.

———. *Interest Groups and Campaign Finance Reform in the United States and Canada*. Ann Arbor: University of Michigan Press, 2011.

———. *Reform and Retrenchment: A Century of Efforts to Fix Primary Elections*. New York: Oxford University Press, 2024.

Boatright, Robert G., and Zachary Albert. "Factional Conflict and Independent Expenditures in the 2018 Democratic House Primaries." *Congress & the Presidency* 48 (2021): 50–77.

Boatright, Robert G., Vincent G. Moscardelli, and Clifford Vickrey. "Primary Election Timing and Voter Turnout." *Election Law Journal* 19 (2020): 472–485.

Bogaards, Matthijs. "De-democratization in Hungary: Diffusely Defective Democracy." *Democratization* 25, no. 8 (November 17, 2018): 1481–1499. https://doi.org/10.1080/13510347.2018.1485015.

Bonica, Adam. Database on Ideology, Money in Politics, and Elections: Public Version 3.0 [Computer file]. Stanford, CA: Stanford University Libraries, 2023.

―――. "Professional Networks, Early Fundraising, and Electoral Success." *Election Law Journal: Rules, Politics, and Policy* 16, no. 1 (March 2017): 153–171.

Bonica, Adam, Nolan McCarty, Keith T. Poole, and Howard Rosenthal. "Why Hasn't Democracy Slowed Rising Inequality?" *Journal of Economic Perspectives* 27, no. 3 (September 2013): 103–124.

Borges, André, Mathieu Turgeon, and Adrián Albala. "Electoral Incentives to Coalition Formation in Multiparty Presidential Systems." *Party Politics* 27, no. 6 (November 2021): 1279–1289. https://doi.org/10.1177/1354068820953527.

Boris, Shor, and Nolan McCarty. "Two Decades of Polarization in American State Legislatures." *Journal of Political Institutions and Political Economy* 3 (2022): 343–370.

Bouton, Laurent, Julia Cage, Edgard Dewitte, and Vincent Pons. "Small Campaign Donors." NBER Working Paper No. 30050 (May 2022).Boxell, Levi, Matthew Gentzkow, and Jesse M. Shapiro. "Cross-Country Trends in Affective Polarization." *Review of Economics and Statistics* 106, no. 2 (2024): 557–565.

Broockman, David, Nicholas Carnes, Melody Crowder-Meyer, and Chris Skovron. "Why Local Party Leaders Don't Support Nominating Centrists." *British Journal of Political Science* 51, no. 2 (2021): 724–749.

Broockman, David E., and Neil Malhotra. "What Do Partisan Donors Want?" *Public Opinion Quarterly* 84, no. 1 (March 1, 2020): 104–118.

Brookes, R. H. "The Analysis of Distorted Representation in Two-Party Single-Member Elections." *Political Science* 12, no. 2 (September 1960): 158–167. https://doi.org/10.1177/003231876001200204.

Brooks, Deborah Jordan, and Michael Murov. "Assessing Accountability in a Post–Citizens United Era: The Effects of Attack Ad Sponsorship by Unknown Independent Groups." *American Politics Research* 40, no. 3 (May 1, 2012): 383–418.

Broz, J. Lawrence, Jeffry Frieden, and Stephen Weymouth. "Populism in Place: The Economic Geography of the Globalization Backlash." *International Organization* 75, no. 2 (2021): 464–494.

Bryce, James. *The American Commonwealth*. 2 vols. Carmel, IN: Liberty Fund, 1995 [1888].

Burden, Barry C., Bradley M. Jones, and Michael S. Kang. "Sore Loser Laws and Congressional Polarization." *Legislative Studies Quarterly* 39, no. 3 (August 2014): 299–305.

Butler, Daniel M. *Representing the Advantaged: How Politicians Reinforce Inequality*. Cambridge: Cambridge University Press, 2014. https://doi.org/10.1017/CBO9781139871969.

Cain, Bruce E. *Democracy More or Less: America's Political Reform Quandary.* Cambridge Studies in Election Law and Democracy. Cambridge: Cambridge University Press, 2014.

Calvo, Ernesto, and Timothy Hellwig. "Centripetal and Centrifugal Incentives Under Different Electoral Systems." *American Journal of Political Science* 55, no. 1 (2011): 27–41.

Canes-Wrone, Brandice, and Nathan Gibson. "Does Money Buy Congressional Love? Individual Donors and Legislative Voting." *Congress & the Presidency* 46, no. 1 (January 2019): 1–27.

Canes-Wrone, Brandice, and Kenneth M. Miller. "Out-of-District Donors and Representation in the US House." *Legislative Studies Quarterly* 47, no. 2 (2022): 361–395.

Carole Mutz, Diana. *Hearing the Other Side: Deliberative Versus Participatory Democracy.* Cambridge: Cambridge University Press, 2006.

Carter, Elisabeth. "Does PR Promote Political Extremism? A Rejoinder." *Representation* 41, no. 1 (January 2004): 63–66.

———. "Does PR Promote Political Extremism? Evidence from the West European Parties of the Extreme Right." *Representation* 40, no. 2 (January 2004): 82–100. https://doi.org/10.1080/00344890408523290.

Chaisty, Paul, Nic Cheeseman, and Timothy Power. "Rethinking the 'Presidentialism Debate': Conceptualizing Coalitional Politics in Cross-Regional Perspective." *Democratization* 21, no. 1 (January 2, 2014): 72–94. https://doi.org/10.1080/13510347.2012.710604.

Chase, James S. *Emergence of the Presidential Nominating Convention, 1789–1832.* Urbana: University of Illinois Press, 1973.

Cheibub, José Antonio, Adam Przeworski, and Sebastian M. Saiegh. "Government Coalitions and Legislative Success Under Presidentialism and Parliamentarism." *British Journal of Political Science* 34, no. 4 (October 2004): 565–587.

Cheney, Liz. *Oath and Honor: A Memoir and a Warning.* New York: Little, Brown & Co., 2023.

Christenson, Dino P., and Corwin D. Smidt. "Following the Money: Super PACs and the 2012 Presidential Nomination." *Presidential Studies Quarterly* 44, no. 3 (2014): 410–430.

Claassen, Christopher, and Pedro C. Magalhães. "Public Support for Democracy in the United States Has Declined Generationally." *Public Opinion Quarterly* 87, no. 3 (fall 2023): 719–732. https://doi.org/10.1093/poq/nfad039.

Cohen, Marty, David Karol, Hans Noel, and John Zaller. *The Party Decides: Presidential Nominations Before and After Reform.* Chicago: University of Chicago Press, 2008.

Coll, Joseph, Caroline J. Tolbert, and Michael Ritter. "Understanding Preferences for Comprehensive Electoral Reform in the United States." *Social Science Quarterly* 103 (2022): 1523–1538.

Confessore, Nicholas. "G.O.P. Angst over 2016 Led to Provision on Funding." *New York Times.* December 13, 2014.

———. "How the GOP Elite Lost Its Voters to Trump." *New York Times.* March 28, 2016.

Cramer, Katherine J. *The Politics of Resentment: Rural Consciousness in Wisconsin and the Rise of Scott Walker.* Chicago: University of Chicago Press, 2016.

Crisp, Brian F., and Scott W. Desposato. "Constituency Building in Multimember Districts: Collusion or Conflict?" *Journal of Politics* 66, no. 1 (February 2004): 136–156. https://doi.org/10.1046/j.1468-2508.2004.00145.x.

Crisp, Brian F., and Patrick Cunha Silva. "The Role of District Magnitude in When Women Represent Women." *British Journal of Political Science* 53, no. 3 (July 2023): 1061–1069. https://doi.org/10.1017/S0007123422000576.

Culberson, Tyler, Michael P. McDonald, and Suzanne M. Robbins. "Small Donors in Congressional Elections." *American Politics Research* 47, no. 5 (2019): 970–999.

Curtis Samples, John. *The Fallacy of Campaign Finance Reform.* Chicago: University of Chicago Press, 2006.

Dahl, Robert A. *Polyarchy: Participation and Opposition.* New Haven, CT: Yale University Press, 1971.

———. *A Preface to Democratic Theory.* Chicago: University of Chicago Press, 2006.

Dahlberg, Stefan, and Jonas Linde. "Losing Happily? The Mitigating Effect of Democracy and Quality of Government on the Winner-Loser Gap in Political Support." *International Journal of Public Administration* 39, no. 9 (July 28, 2016): 652–664. https://doi.org/10.1080/01900692.2016.1177831.

de Weck, Joseph. "Germany Is No Longer Exceptional." *Atlantic.* July 22, 2023.

Diamond, Larry. *Developing Democracy: Towards Consolidation.* Baltimore: Johns Hopkins University Press, 1999.

Dinas, Elias, Konstantinos Matakos, Dimitrios Xefteris, and Dominik Hangartner. "Waking Up the Golden Dawn: Does Exposure to the Refugee Crisis Increase Support for Extreme-Right Parties?" *Political Analysis* 27, no. 2 (2019): 244–254. https://doi.org/10.1017/pan.2018.48.

Doherty, David, Conor M. Dowling, and Michael G. Miller. *Small Power: How Local Parties Shape Elections.* New York: Oxford University Press, 2022.

Doherty, Erin. "Romney's Third-Party Dance with Manchin Spills into View." *Axios.* September 13, 2023.

Donovan, Todd. "The Top Two Primary: What Can California Learn from Washington?" *California Journal of Politics and Policy* 4 (2012): 1–22.

Dow, Jay K. "Party-System Extremism in Majoritarian and Proportional Electoral Systems." *British Journal of Political Science* 41, no. 2 (April 2011): 341–361. https://doi.org/10.1017/S0007123410000360.

Dowling, Conor M., and Amber Wichowsky. "Attacks Without Consequence? Candidates, Parties, Groups, and the Changing Face of Negative Advertising." *American Journal of Political Science* 59, no. 1 (2015): 19–36.

———. "Does It Matter Who's Behind the Curtain? Anonymity in Political Advertising and the Effects of Campaign Finance Disclosure." *American Politics Research* 41, no. 6 (November 1, 2013): 965–996.

Downs, Anthony. *An Economic Theory of Democracy.* New York: Harper & Bros., 1957.

Drutman, Lee. *The Business of America Is Lobbying: How Corporations Became Politicized and Politics Became More Corporate.* Reprint ed. New York: Oxford University Press, 2017.

———. "Elections, Political Parties, and Multiracial, Multiethnic Democracy: How the United States Gets It Wrong." *New York University Law Review* 96 (2021): 36.

————. "The Rise of Dark Money." In *Interest Group Politics*, edited by Allan J. Cigler, Burdett A. Loomis, and Anthony Nownes, 135–154 9th ed. Thousand Oaks, CA: CQ Press, 2015.

————. "What We Know About Congressional Primaries and Congressional Primary Reform." *New America*. Last updated July 1, 2021.

Dwyre, Diana. "The Origin and Evolution of Super PACs: A Darwinian Examination of a Campaign Finance Species." *Society* 57, no. 5 (October 1, 2020): 511–519.

Dwyre, Diana, and Evelyn Braz. "Super PAC Spending Strategies and Goals." *The Forum* 13, no. 2 (July 1, 2015): 245–267.

Easton, David. *Systems Analysis of Political Life*. New York: John Wiley & Sons, 1965.

Ecker, Alejandro, and Thomas M. Meyer. "Coalition Bargaining Duration in Multiparty Democracies." *British Journal of Political Science* 50, no. 1 (January 2020): 261–280. https://doi.org/10.1017/S0007123417000539.

————. "The Duration of Government Formation Processes in Europe." *Research & Politics* 2, no. 4 (October 1, 2015): 2053168015622796. https://doi.org/10.1177/2053168015622796.

Elazar, Daniel J. *American Federalism: A View from the States*. 2nd ed. New York: Thomas Y. Crowell, 1972.

Elmelund-Praestekaer, Christian. "Beyond American Negativity: Toward a General Understanding of the Determinants of Negative Campaigning." *European Political Science Review* 2, no. 1 (March 2010): 137–156. https://doi.org/10.1017/S1755773909990269.

————. "Negative Campaigning in a Multiparty System." *Representation* 44, no. 1 (April 1, 2008): 27–39.

Epstein, Leon. *Political Parties in the American Mold*. Madison: University of Wisconsin Press, 1986.

Erikson, Robert S., Karl Sigman, and Linan Yao. "Electoral College Bias and the 2020 Presidential Election." *Proceedings of the National Academy of Sciences* 117, no. 45 (November 10, 2020): 27940–27944. https://doi.org/10.1073/pnas.2013581117.

Ezrow, Lawrence. "Are Moderate Parties Rewarded in Multiparty Systems? A Pooled Analysis of Western European Elections, 1984–1998." *European Journal of Political Research* 44, no. 6 (2005): 881–898. https://doi.org/10.1111/j.1475-6765.2005.00251.x.

————. "Parties' Policy Programmes and the Dog That Didn't Bark: No Evidence That Proportional Systems Promote Extreme Party Positioning." *British Journal of Political Science* 38, no. 3 (July 2008): 479–497.

————. "The Variance Matters: How Party Systems Represent the Preferences of Voters." *Journal of Politics* 69, no. 1 (2007): 182–192. https://doi.org/10.1111/j.1468-2508.2007.00503.x.

Falguera, Elin, Samuel Jones, and Magnus Ohman. *Funding of Political Parties and Election Campaigns: A Handbook on Political Finance*. Stockholm: International Institute for Democracy and Electoral Assistance, 2014.

Figueiredo, Argelina Cheibub, and Fernando Limongi. "Presidential Power, Legislative Organization, and Party Behavior in Brazil." *Comparative Politics* 32, no. 2 (2000): 151–170. https://doi.org/10.2307/422395.

Finkel, Eli J., Christopher A. Bail, Mina Cikara, Peter H. Ditto, Shanto Iyengar, Samara Klar, Lilliana Mason, et al. "Political Sectarianism in America." *Science* 370, no. 6516 (October 30, 2020): 533–536.

Fiorina, Morris P. *Unstable Majorities: Polarization, Party Sorting, and Political Stalemate.* Stanford, CA: Hoover Institution Press, 2017.

Fishkin, James. *Democracy When the People Are Thinking: Revitalizing Our Politics Through Public Deliberations.* Oxford: Oxford University Press, 2018.

Foley, Edward B. "The Nomination and Election of Statewide Candidates." *Illinois Law Review* (forthcoming October 2024).

———. "Self-Districting: The Ultimate Antidote to Gerrymandering." *Kentucky Law Journal* 111 (2023): 693.

———. "Total Vote Runoff: A Majority-Maximizing Form of Ranked Choice Voting." *New Hampshire Law Review* 21, no. 2 (2023): 323.

Foley, Edward B., and Eric Maskin. "Alaska's Ranked Choice Voting Is Flawed. But There's an Easy Fix." *Washington Post.* November 1, 2022.

Ford, Henry Jones. "The Direct Primary." *North American Review* 190, no. 644 (1909): 1–14.

Fortunato, David, and Randolph T. Stevenson. "Perceptions of Partisan Ideologies: The Effect of Coalition Participation." *American Journal of Political Science* 57, no. 2 (2013): 459–477. https://doi.org/10.1111/j.1540-5907.2012.00623.x.

Fouirnaies, Alexander, and Andrew B. Hall. "How Do Interest Groups Seek Access to Committees?" *American Journal of Political Science* 62, no. 1 (2018): 132–147.

Fowler, Anthony, Seth J. Hill, Jeffrey B. Lewis, Chris Tausanovitch, Lynn Vavreck, and Christopher Warshaw. "Moderates." *American Political Science Review* 117, no. 2 (2023).

Fowler, Erika Franklin, Michael M. Franz, and Travis N. Ridout. "Political Advertising in 2016: The Presidential Election as Outlier?" *The Forum* 14, no. 4 (2016): 445–469.

Fraga, Bernard L., and Hans J. G. Hassell. "Are Minority and Women Candidates Penalized by Party Politics? Race, Gender, and Access to Party Support." *Political Research Quarterly* 74, no. 3 (September 1, 2021): 540–555.

Francia, Peter L., Paul S. Herrnson, Richard G. Niemi, and John C. Green. *The Financiers of Congressional Elections: Investors, Ideologues, and Intimates.* Power, Conflict, and Democracy: American Politics into the 21st Century. New York: Columbia University Press, 2003.

Franz, Michael. "Campaign Finance Law: The Changing Role of Parties and Interest Groups." In *Rethinking American Electoral Democracy*, edited by Matthew Streb, 69–86. 2nd ed. New York: Routledge, 2012.

Franz, Michael M., Erika Franklin Fowler, and Travis N. Ridout. "Loose Cannons or Loyal Foot Soldiers? Toward a More Complex Theory of Interest Group Advertising Strategies." *American Journal of Political Science* 60, no. 3 (2016): 738–751.

Freudenreich, Johannes. "The Formation of Cabinet Coalitions in Presidential Systems." *Latin American Politics and Society* 58, no. 4 (2016): 80–102. https://doi.org/10.1111/laps.12003.

Fuchs, Hailey. "Dan Crenshaw Is Building a Young Activist Army, One Summit at a Time." *Politico.* September 16, 2021.

Gallagher, Michael. "Proportionality, Disproportionality and Electoral Systems." *Electoral Studies* 10, no. 1 (1991): 33–51.

Ganesh, Janan. "Britain Is Europe's Haven from the Hard Right." *Financial Times*. October 3, 2023.

García, Diego, and Frederico Ferreira da Silva. "The Electoral Consequences of Affective Polarization? Negative Voting in the 2020 US Presidential Election." *American Politics Research* 50, no. 3 (May 1, 2022): 303–311. https://doi.org/10.1177/1532673X221074633.

García, Diego, Frederico Ferreira da Silva, and Simon Maye. "Affective Polarization in Comparative and Longitudinal Perspective." *Public Opinion Quarterly* 87, no. 1 (spring 2023): 219–231. https://doi.org/10.1093/poq/nfad004.

Gauja, Anika. "Party Leaders in Australia." In *The Selection of Political Party Leaders in Contemporary Parliamentary Democracies: A Comparative Study*, edited by Jean-Benoît Pilet and William P. Cross, 189–204. London: Routledge, 2014.

Gelman, Jeremy, Evan Pristos, and Benjamin Reilly. "The Consequences of a Top-5/RCV System in Nevada: Advantaging Moderates but Sidelining Third Parties?" SSRN. Last revised April 27, 2024.

Geraghty, Jim. "The Quiet Collapse of Four Key State Republican Parties." *National Review*. July 24, 2023.

Gerken, Heather K., and Alex Tausanovitch. "A Public Finance Model for Lobbying: Lobbying, Campaign Finance, and the Privatization of Democracy." *Election Law Journal: Rules, Politics, and Policy* 13, no. 1 (March 1, 2014): 75–90.

Germer, Matthew. "Restoring Losers' Consent: A Necessary Step to Stabilizing Our Democracy." *R Street Institute*. September 2021.

Gidron, Noam, James Adams, and Will Horne. *American Affective Polarization in Comparative Perspective*. Cambridge: Cambridge University Press, 2020.

———. "Who Dislikes Whom? Affective Polarization Between Pairs of Parties in Western Democracies." *British Journal of Political Science* 53, no. 3 (July 2023): 997–1015. https://doi.org/10.1017/S0007123422000394.

Gimpel, James G., Frances E. Lee, and Shanna Pearson-Merkowitz. "The Check Is in the Mail: Interdistrict Funding Flows in Congressional Elections." *American Journal of Political Science* 52, no. 2 (2008): 373–394.

Golder, Sona N. "Bargaining Delays in the Government Formation Process." *Comparative Political Studies* 43, no. 1 (January 2010): 3–32. https://doi.org/10.1177/0010414009341714.

Golder, Sona Nadenichek. "Pre-electoral Coalition Formation in Parliamentary Democracies." *British Journal of Political Science* 36, no. 2 (April 2006): 193–212. https://doi.org/10.1017/S0007123406000123.

Goodwin, Matthew. "Extreme Politics: The Four Waves of National Populism in the West." In *Extremes*, edited by Duncan Needham and Julius Weitzdörfer, 104–123. 1st ed. Cambridge: Cambridge University Press, 2019. https://doi.org/10.1017/9781108654722.007.

Gora, Joel M. "In Defense of Super PACs and of the First Amendment." *Seton Hall Law Review* 43 (2013): 1185.

Graham, Matthew H., and Milan W. Svolik. "Democracy in America? Partisanship, Polarization, and the Robustness of Support for Democracy in the

United States." *American Political Science Review* 114, no. 2 (May 2020): 392–409. https://doi.org/10.1017/S0003055420000052.

Green, John C., and Paul S. Herrnson, eds. *Responsible Partisanship: The Evolution of American Political Parties Since 1950*. Lawrence: University Press of Kansas, 2003.

Grenzke, Janet. "Candidate Attributes and PAC Contributions." *Western Political Quarterly* 42, no. 2 (1989): 245–264.

Groenendyk, Eric. "Competing Motives in a Polarized Electorate: Political Responsiveness, Identity Defensiveness, and the Rise of Partisan Antipathy." *Political Psychology* 39 (February 2018): 159–171.

———. "Justifying Party Identification: A Case of Identifying with the 'Lesser of Two Evils.'" *Political Behavior* 34, no. 3 (September 2012): 453–475.

Grofman, Bernard, and Scott L. Feld. "If You Like the Alternative Vote (a.k.a. the Instant Runoff), Then You Ought to Know About the Coombs Rule." *Electoral Studies* 23 (2004): 641.

Grose, Christian R. "Reducing Legislative Polarization: Top-Two and Open Primaries Are Associated with More Moderate Legislators." *Journal of Political Institutions and Political Economy* 1 (2020): 267–287.

Grumbach, Jacob M., and Alexander Sahn. "Race and Representation in Campaign Finance." *American Political Science Review* 114, no. 1 (February 2020): 206–221.

Gudgin, Graham, and Peter J. Taylor. *Seats, Votes, and the Spatial Organisation of Elections*. Colchester, UK: ECPR Press, 2012.

Hahm, Hyeonho, David Hilpert, and Thomas König. "Divided We Unite: The Nature of Partyism and the Role of Coalition Partnership in Europe." *American Political Science Review* 118, no. 1 (February 2024): 69–87. https://doi.org/10.1017/S0003055423000266.

Hajnal, Zoltan, and Jessica Trounstine. "Where Turnout Matters: The Consequences of Uneven Turnout in City Politics." *Journal of Politics* 67, no. 2 (2005): 515–535.

Hall, Andrew B. "How the Public Funding of Elections Increases Candidate Polarization." Working Paper. Stanford Democracy and Polarization Lab. August 2014.

———. "What Happens When Extremists Win Primaries?" *American Political Science Review* 109, no. 1 (2015): 18–42.

Hall, Andrew B., and Daniel M. Thompson. "Who Punishes Extremist Nominees? Candidate Ideology and Turning Out the Base in US Elections." *American Political Science Review* 112, no. 3 (2018): 509–524.

Handley, Lisa, and Bernard Grofman. *Redistricting in Comparative Perspective*. Oxford: Oxford University Press, 2008.

Hansen, Wendy L., Michael S. Rocca, and Brittany Leigh Ortiz. "The Effects of Citizens United on Corporate Spending in the 2012 Presidential Election." *Journal of Politics* 77, no. 2 (April 2015): 535–545.

Harteveld, Eelco. "Ticking All the Boxes? A Comparative Study of Social Sorting and Affective Polarization." *Electoral Studies* 72 (August 1, 2021): 102337. https://doi.org/10.1016/j.electstud.2021.102337.

Harteveld, Eelco, Lars Erik Berntzen, Andrej Kokkonen, Haylee Kelsall, Jonas Linde, and Stefan Dahlberg. "The (Alleged) Consequences of Affective Polarization: Individual-Level Evidence and a Survey Experiment in 9 Countries." OSF Preprints. October 1, 2022.

Harvey, Anna, and Taylor Mattia. "Does Money Have a Conservative Bias? Estimating the Causal Impact of Citizens United on State Legislative Preferences." *Public Choice*. October 9, 2019.

Hasen, Richard L. *Cheap Speech: How Disinformation Poisons Our Politics—and How to Cure It.* New Haven, CT: Yale University Press, 2022.

———. *Money, Politics, and the Decline of American Democracy.* New Haven, CT: Yale University Press, 2016.

———. *Plutocrats United: Campaign Money, the Supreme Court, and the Distortion of American Elections.* 1st ed. New Haven, CT: Yale University Press, 2016.

Hassell, Hans J. G. *The Party's Primary: Control of Congressional Nominations.* New York: Cambridge University Press, 2018.

———. "Principled Moderation: Understanding Parties' Support of Moderate Candidates." *Legislative Studies Quarterly* 43, no. 2 (2018): 343–369.

Heberlig, Eric S., and Bruce A. Larson. *Congressional Parties, Institutional Ambition, and the Financing of Majority Control.* Ann Arbor: University of Michigan Press, 2012.

———. "The Strategic Allocation of PAC Funds to Effective Legislators." *Interest Groups & Advocacy* 11, no. 4 (December 2022): 466–492.

———. "U.S. House Incumbent Fundraising and Spending in a Post–Citizens United and Post-McCutcheon World." *Political Science Quarterly* 129, no. 4 (December 1, 2014): 613–642.

Hernández, Enrique, Eva Anduiza, and Guillem Rico. "Affective Polarization and the Salience of Elections." *Electoral Studies* 69 (February 1, 2021): 102203. https://doi.org/10.1016/j.electstud.2020.102203.

Herrnson, Paul S., Costas Panagopoulos, and Kendall L. Bailey. *Congressional Elections: Campaigning at Home and in Washington.* Thousand Oaks, CA: CQ Press, 2019.

Hersh, Eitan. *Politics Is for Power: How to Move Beyond Political Hobbyism, Take Action, and Make Real Change.* New York: Scribner, 2020.

Hill, Seth J. "Sidestepping Primary Reform: Political Action in Response to Institutional Change." *Political Science Research and Methods* 10 (2022): 391–407.

Hill, Seth J., and Gregory A. Huber. "Representativeness and Motivations of the Contemporary Donorate: Results from Merged Survey and Administrative Records." *Political Behavior* 39, no. 1 (March 2017): 3–29.

Hill, Seth J., and Chris Tausanovitch. "A Disconnect in Representation? Comparison of Trends in Congressional and Public Polarization." *Journal of Politics* 77 (2015): 1058–1075.

Hobolt, Sara B., Thomas J. Leeper, and James Tilley. "Divided by the Vote: Affective Polarization in the Wake of the Brexit Referendum." *British Journal of Political Science* 51, no. 4 (October 2021): 1476–1493. https://doi.org/10.1017/S0007123420000125.

Hopkin, Jonathan. *Anti-system Politics.* Cambridge: Cambridge University Press, 2022.

Hopkins, Daniel J. *The Increasingly United States: How and Why American Political Behavior Nationalized.* Chicago: University of Chicago Press, 2018.

Horne, Will, James Adams, and Noam Gidron. "The Way We Were: How Histories of Co-governance Alleviate Partisan Hostility." *Comparative Political Studies* 56, no. 3 (2023): 299–325. https://doi.org/10.1177/00104140221100197.

Horowitz, Donald L. "Electoral Systems: A Primer for Decision Makers." *Journal of Democracy* 14 (October 2003): 115.

"How Democrats and Republicans See Each Other." *The Economist*. August 17, 2022.

Huber, John D. "Measuring Ethnic Voting: Do Proportional Electoral Laws Politicize Ethnicity?" *American Journal of Political Science* 56, no. 4 (2012): 986–1001.

Issacharoff, Samuel, and Jeremy Peterman. "Special Interests After Citizens United: Access, Replacement, and Interest Group Response to Legal Change." *Annual Review of Law and Social Science* 9, no. 1 (2013): 185–205.

Jacobs, Lawrence. *Democracy Under Fire*. New York: Oxford University Press, 2022.

Jenkins, Jeffery A., and Charles Stewart III. "The Gag Rule, Congressional Politics, and the Growth of Anti-slavery Popular Politics." *Legislative Studies Quarterly* 32 (2007): 33–57.

Jensen, Christian B., and Daniel J. Lee. "Potential Centrifugal Effects of Majoritarian Features in Proportional Electoral Systems." *Journal of Contemporary Central and Eastern Europe* 29, no. 1 (January 2, 2021): 1–21. https://doi.org/10.1080/25739638.2021.1928879.

Jewitt, Caitlin. *The Primary Rules: Parties, Voters, and Presidential Nominations*. Ann Arbor: University of Michigan Press, 2019.

Johnson, Gregg B., Meredith-Joy Petersheim, and Jesse T. Wasson. "Divisive Primaries and Incumbent General Election Performance: Prospects and Costs in U. S. House Races." *American Politics Research* 38, no. 5 (2010): 931–955.

Jones, Jeffery M. "Support for Third U.S. Political Party Up to 63%." Gallup. October 4, 2023.

Kalmoe, Nathan P., and Lilliana Mason. *Radical American Partisanship: Mapping Violent Hostility, Its Causes, and the Consequences for Democracy.* 1st ed. Chicago: University of Chicago Press, 2022.

Kamarck, Elaine C. *Primary Politics: How Presidential Candidates Have Shaped the Modern Nominating System*. Lanham, MD: Rowman & Littlefield, 2009.

Kang, Michael S. "Hyperpartisan Campaign Finance." *Emory Law Journal* 70, no. 5 (2021): 1171–1208.

———. "Voting as Veto." *Michigan Law Review* 108 (2009): 1221.

Kang, Michael S., and Barry C. Burden. "Sore Loser Laws in Presidential and Congressional Elections." In *Handbook of Primary Elections*, edited by Robert G. Boatright, 456–466. New York: Routledge, 2018.

Katz, Richard S., and Peter Mair. "The Cartel Party Thesis: A Restatement." *Perspectives on Politics* 7, no. 4 (2009): 753–766.

———. "Changing Models of Party Organization and Party Democracy: The Emergence of the Cartel Party." *Party Politics* 1, no. 1 (January 1995): 5–28.

Keena, Alex, and Misty Knight-Finley. "Are Small Donors Polarizing? A Longitudinal Study of the Senate." *Election Law Journal: Rules, Politics, and Policy* 18, no. 2 (June 2019): 132–144.

Kevins, Anthony, and Stuart N. Soroka. "Growing Apart? Partisan Sorting in Canada, 1992–2015." *Canadian Journal of Political Science/Revue canadienne de science politique* 51, no. 1 (March 2018): 103–133. https://doi.org/10.1017/S0008423917000713.

Kilborn, Mitchell. "Public Campaign Financing, Candidate Socioeconomic Diversity, and Representational Inequality at the U.S. State Level: Evidence from Connecticut." *State Politics & Policy Quarterly* 18, no. 3 (2018): 296–323.

Kilborn, Mitchell, and Arjun Vishwanath. "Public Money Talks Too: How Public Campaign Financing Degrades Representation." *American Journal of Political Science* 66, no. 3 (2022): 730–744.

Kirkland, Justin H. "Multi-member Districts' Effect on Collaboration Between U.S. State Legislators." *Legislative Studies Quarterly* 37, no. 3 (2012): 329–353. https://doi.org/10.1111/j.1939-9162.2012.00050.x.

Kleinfeld, Rachel. *Polarization, Democracy, and Political Violence in the United States: What the Research Says*. Washington, DC: Carnegie Endowment for International Peace, 2023.

Klüver, Heike, Hanna Bäck, and Svenja Krauss. *Coalition Agreements as Control Devices: Coalition Governance in Western and Eastern Europe*. Oxford: Oxford University Press, 2023.

Kosar, Kevin R. "Conservatives Should Look More Closely at Systemic Election Reforms." American Enterprise Institute. October 3, 2023.

Kousser, Thad, Scott Lucas, Seth Masket, and Eric McGhee. "Kingmakers or Cheerleaders? Party Power and the Causal Effects of Endorsements." *Political Research Quarterly* 68, no. 3 (2015): 443–456.

Krishnarajan, Suthan. "Rationalizing Democracy: The Perceptual Bias and (Un)Democratic Behavior." *American Political Science Review* 117, no. 2 (2023): 474–496. https://doi.org/10.1017/S0003055422000806.

Kurlowski, Drew. *Election Law Revealed*. St. Paul, MN: West Academic, 2019.

La Raja, Raymond J. "Political Participation and Civic Courage: The Negative Effect of Transparency on Making Small Campaign Contributions." *Political Behavior* 36, no. 4 (December 1, 2014): 753–776.

———. *Small Change: Money, Political Parties, and Campaign Finance Reform*. Ann Arbor: University of Michigan Press, 2008.

La Raja, Raymond J., and Alexander Theodoridis. "How Ranked-Choice Voting Saved the Virginia GOP from Itself." *Washington Post*. November 5, 2021.

La Raja, Raymond J., and David L. Wiltse. "Don't Blame Donors for Ideological Polarization of Political Parties." *American Politics Research* 40, no. 3 (May 1, 2012): 501–530.

Laakso, Markku, and Rein Taagepera. "'Effective' Number of Parties: A Measure with Application to West Europe." *Comparative Political Studies* 12, no. 1 (April 1, 1979): 3–27. https://doi.org/10.1177/001041407901200101.

Laver, Michael, and Norman Schofield. *Multiparty Government: The Politics of Coalition in Europe*. Oxford: Oxford University Press, 1990.

Laver, Michael, and Ernest Sergenti. *Party Competition: An Agent-Based Model*. Princeton, NJ: Princeton University Press, 2011.

Lawrence, Eric, Todd Donovan, and Shaun Bowler. "The Adoption of Direct Primaries in the United States." *Party Politics* 19, no. 1 (2013): 3–18.

Lazarus, Jeffrey. "Unintended Consequences: Anticipation of General Election Outcomes and Primary Election Divisiveness." *Legislative Studies Quarterly* 30 (2005): 435–461.

Lee, Frances E. *Insecure Majorities: Congress and the Perpetual Campaign*. Chicago: University of Chicago Press, 2016.

Levendusky, Matthew. *The Partisan Sort: How Liberals Became Democrats and Conservatives Became Republicans*. Chicago: University of Chicago Press, 2009.

Levitsky, Steven, and Daniel Ziblatt. *How Democracies Die*. Reprint ed. New York: Crown, 2018.

Lijphart, Arend. "Negotiation Democracy Versus Consensus Democracy: Parallel Conclusions and Recommendations." *European Journal of Political Research* 41, no. 1 (2002): 107–113. https://doi.org/10.1111/1475-6765.00005.

Lipset, Seymour Martin. *Political Man: The Social Bases of Politics*. New York: Doubleday, 1960.

Lipset, Seymour Martin, and Earl Rabb. *The Politics of Unreason: Right-Wing Extremism in America, 1790–1977*. 2nd ed. Chicago: University of Chicago Press, 1970.

Loepp, Eric, and Benjamin Melusky. "Why Is This Candidate Listed Twice? The Behavioral and Electoral Consequences of Fusion Voting." *Election Law Journal* 21 (2022): 105–123.

Lublin, David, and Shaun Bowler. "Electoral Systems and Ethnic Minority Representation." In *The Oxford Handbook of Electoral Systems*, edited by Erik S. Herron, Robert J. Pekkanen, and Matthew S. Shugart, 158–174. Oxford: Oxford University Press, 2018. https://doi.org/10.1093/oxfordhb/9780190258658.013.26.

Mainwaring, Scott. "Presidentialism, Multipartism, and Democracy: The Difficult Combination." *Comparative Political Studies* 26, no. 2 (July 1, 1993): 198–228.

Mair, Peter. *Ruling the Void: The Hollowing of Western Democracy*. New York: Verso Books, 2013.

Maisel, L. Sandy. *From Obscurity to Oblivion*. Knoxville: University of Tennessee Press, 1982.

Malbin, Michael J. "A Neo-Madisonian Perspective on Campaign Finance Reform, Institutions, Pluralism, and Small Donors." *University of Pennsylvania Journal of Constitutional Law* 23 (2021): 907.

Manento, Cory. "Party Crashers: Interest Groups as a Latent Threat to Party Networks in Congressional Primaries." *Party Politics* 27 (2021): 137–148.

Mansbridge, Jane. "Rethinking Representation." *American Political Science Review* 97, no. 4 (November 2003): 515–528.

Marchal, Nahema, and David Watson. "The Rise of Partisan Affective Polarization in the British Public." SSRN Scholarly Paper. October 25, 2019. https://doi.org/10.2139/ssrn.3477404.

Marsh, Sarah. "German Coalition, Beset by Crises, Could Get More Fractious After Vote." *Reuters*. October 10, 2022.

Martin, Lanny W., and Georg Vanberg. "Parties and Policymaking in Multiparty Governments: The Legislative Median, Ministerial Autonomy, and the Coalition Compromise." *American Journal of Political Science* 58, no. 4 (2014): 979–996. https://doi.org/10.1111/ajps.12099.

———. "Wasting Time? The Impact of Ideology and Size on Delay in Coalition Formation." *British Journal of Political Science* 33, no. 2 (April 2003): 323–332. https://doi.org/10.1017/S0007123403000140.

Martini, Sergio, and Mario Quaranta. "Political Support Among Winners and Losers: Within- and Between-Country Effects of Structure, Process and Performance in Europe." *European Journal of Political Research* 58, no. 1 (2019): 341–361. https://doi.org/10.1111/1475-6765.12284.

Masket, Seth. "The Surprising Takeaway from My Survey on How Trump Got a Grip on the GOP Grassroots." *Politico*. March 4, 2024.

Mason, Lilliana. "A Cross-Cutting Calm: How Social Sorting Drives [US] Affective Polarization." *Public Opinion Quarterly* 80, no. S1 (2016): 351–377.

Mason, Lilliana, and Julie Wronski. "One Tribe to Bind Them All: How Our Social Group Attachments Strengthen Partisanship." *Political Psychology* 39 (February 1, 2018): 257–277.

Matakos, Konstantinos, Orestis Troumpounis, and Dimitrios Xefteris. "Electoral Rule Disproportionality and Platform Polarization." *American Journal of Political Science* 60, no. 4 (2016): 1026–1043. https://doi.org/10.1111/ajps.12235.

Mayhew, David R. *Placing Parties in American Politics*. Princeton, NJ: Princeton University Press, 1986.

McBeath, Gerald A. "Alaska Electoral Reform: The Top 4 Primary and Ranked Choice Voting." *California Journal of Politics and Policy* 15, no. 1 (2023).

McBeath, Gerald A., and Thomas A. Morehouse. *Alaska Politics and Government*. Lincoln: University of Nebraska Press, 1994.

McCabe, Brian J., and Jennifer A. Heerwig. "Diversifying the Donor Pool: How Did Seattle's Democracy Voucher Program Reshape Participation in Municipal Campaign Finance?" *Election Law Journal: Rules, Politics, and Policy* 18, no. 4 (September 24, 2019): 323–341.

McCarty, Nolan. *Polarization: What Everyone Needs to Know*. New York: Oxford University Press, 2019.

———. "What We Know and Don't Know About Our Polarized Politics." *Washington Post*. January 8, 2014.

McCarty, Nolan, Keith T. Poole, and Howard Rosenthal. *Polarized America: The Dance of Ideology and Unequal Riches*. Cambridge, MA: MIT Press, 2006.

McCarty, Nolan, Jonathan Rodden, Boris Shor, Chris Tausanovitch, and Christopher Warshaw. "Geography, Uncertainty, and Polarization." *Political Science Research and Methods* 7, no. 4 (October 2019): 775–794. https://doi.org/10.1017/psrm.2018.12.

McCoy, Jennifer, and Murat Somer. "Toward a Theory of Pernicious Polarization and How It Harms Democracies: Comparative Evidence and Possible Remedies." *ANNALS of the American Academy of Political and Social Science* 681, no. 1 (2019): 234–271. https://doi.org/10.1177/0002716218818782.

McDonald, Michael D., and Ian Budge. *Elections, Parties, Democracy: Conferring the Median Mandate*. Oxford: Oxford University Press, 2005.

McGann, Anthony J., and Michael Latner. "The Calculus of Consensus Democracy: Rethinking Patterns of Democracy Without Veto Players." *Comparative Political Studies* 46, no. 7 (July 2013): 823–850.

McLean, Iain, and Fiona Hewitt. *Condorcet: Foundations of Social Choice and Political Theory*. Brookfield, VT: Edward Elgar, 1994.

McNitt, Andrew D. "The Effect of Preprimary Endorsement on Competition for Nominations: An Examination of Different Nominating Systems." *Journal of Politics* 42 (1980): 257–266.

Merriam, Charles, and Louise Overacker. *Primary Elections*. Chicago: University of Chicago Press, 1928.

Miller, Gary, and Norman Schofield. "Activists and Partisan Realignment in the United States." *American Political Science Review* 97, no. 2 (2003): 245–260.

Miller, Kenneth M., and Tanner Bates. "PACs and January 6th: Campaign Finance and Objections to the Electoral College Vote Count." *Research & Politics* 10, no. 3 (July 1, 2023): 1–10.

Miller-Idriss, Cynthia. *Hate in the Homeland*. Princeton, NJ: Princeton University Press, 2022.

Mudde, Cas. "The Far-Right Threat in the United States: A European Perspective." *ANNALS of the American Academy of Political and Social Science* 699, no. 1 (2022): 101–115.

———. "Three Decades of Populist Radical Right Parties in Western Europe: So What?" *European Journal of Political Research* 52, no. 1 (2013): 1–19. https://doi.org/10.1111/j.1475-6765.2012.02065.x.

Muller, Derek. "Reducing Election Litigation." *Fordham Law Review* 90, no. 2 (2021): 561.

Muller, Derek T. "Democrats Have Been Shameless About Your Presidential Vote Too." *New York Times*. January 6, 2021.

Mussel, Johanan D., and Henry Schlechta. "Australia: No Party Convergence Where We Would Most Expect It." *Party Politics* (July 21, 2023). https://doi.org/10.1177/13540688231189363.

Mutz, Diana C. "Cross-Cutting Social Networks: Testing Democratic Theory in Practice." *American Political Science Review* 96, no. 1 (2002): 122.

Nadeau, Richard, and Andre Blais. "Accepting the Election Outcome: The Effect of Participation on Losers' Consent." *British Journal of Political Science* 23, no. 4 (1993): 553–563.

Nadeau, Richard, Jean-François Daoust, and Ruth Dassonneville. "Winning, Losing, and the Quality of Democracy." *Political Studies* 71, no. 2 (May 1, 2023): 483–500. https://doi.org/10.1177/00323217211026189.

Nagourney, Adam. "2008 Republican Field Shuns the Snowman." *The Caucus* (blog), *New York Times*. July 30, 2007.

National Municipal League. *A Model Direct Primary Election System: Report of the Committee on the Direct Primary*. New York: National Municipal League, 1951.

Nordlinger, Eric A. *Conflict Regulation in Divided Societies*. Washington, DC: University Press of America, 1984.

Norrander, Barbara, and Jay Wendland. "Open Versus Closed Primaries and the Ideological Composition of Presidential Primary Electorates." *Electoral Studies* 42 (2016): 229–236.

Norris, Pippa. "'Things Fall Apart, the Center Cannot Hold': Fractionalized and Polarized Party Systems in Western Democracies." *European Political Science* (January 31, 2024). https://doi.org/10.1057/s41304-023-00467-0.

Norton, Mike, and Richard H. Pildes. "How Outside Money Makes Governing More Difficult." *Election Law Journal: Rules, Politics, and Policy* 19, no. 4 (December 1, 2020): 486–502.

Oklobdzija, Stan. "Dark Parties: Unveiling Nonparty Communities in American Political Campaigns." *American Political Science Review* 1 (April 5, 2023): 1–22.

Orhan, Yunus Emre. "The Relationship Between Affective Polarization and Democratic Backsliding: Comparative Evidence." *Democratization* 29, no. 4 (May 19, 2022).

Padgett, Jeremy, Johanna L. Dunaway, and Joshua P. Darr. "As Seen on TV? How Gatekeeping Makes the U.S. House Seem More Extreme." *Journal of Communication* 69, no. 6 (December 31, 2019): 696–719.

Pereira, Carlos, and Marcus André Melo. "The Surprising Success of Multiparty Presidentialism." *Journal of Democracy* 23, no. 3 (July 2012): 156–170. https://doi.org/10.1353/jod.2012.0041.

Pildes, Richard H. "Democracies in the Age of Fragmentation." *California Law Review* 110 (2022): 2051–2092.

———. "The Neglected Value of Effective Government." NYU School of Law, Public Law Research Paper No. 23-51. *University of Chicago Legal Forum* 2023, article 8 (2024): 185–210.

———. "Political Fragmentation in the Democracies of the West." *Brigham Young University Journal of Public Law* 37 (2023): 209–245.

———. "Political Reforms to Combat Extremism." In *Our Nation at Risk: Election Integrity as a National Security Issue*, edited by Karen J. Greenberg and Julian E. Zelizer, 70–92. New York: NYU Press, 2014.

———. "Skepticism About Proportional Representation for Congress." *Illinois Law Review* (forthcoming 2024).

———. "Small-Donor-Based Campaign-Finance Reform and Political Polarization." *Yale Law Journal Forum* 129 (2019): 22.

Pinner, Frank A. "Cross-Pressure." In *International Encyclopedia of the Social Sciences*, edited by David L. Sills, 3:116–118. New York: Macmillan, 1968.

Polsby, Nelson W., and Aaron B. Wildavsky. *Presidential Elections: Strategies of American Electoral Politics*. Chicago: University of Chicago Press, 1964.

Poole, Keith T., and Thomas Romer. "Patterns of Political Action Committee Contributions to the 1980 Campaigns for the United States House of Representatives." *Public Choice* 47, no. 1 (January 1, 1985): 63–111.

Powell, G. Bingham. "Election Laws and Representative Governments: Beyond Votes and Seats." *British Journal of Political Science* 36, no. 2 (2006): 291–315.

———. "Ideological Trends and Changing Party System Polarization in Western Democracies." In *Politics in South Asia: Culture, Rationality and Conceptual Flow*, edited by Siegfried O. Wolf, Jivanta Schöttli, Dominik Frommherz, Kai Fürstenberg, Marian Gallenkamp, Lion König, and Markus Pauli, 17–30. Cham: Springer International Publishing, 2015. https://doi.org/10.1007/978-3-319-09087-0_2.

Powell, G. Bingham, and Georg S. Vanberg. "Election Laws, Disproportionality and Median Correspondence: Implications for Two Visions of Democracy." *British Journal of Political Science* 30, no. 3 (2000): 383–411.

Powell, G. Bingham, Jr. "Extremist Parties and Political Turmoil: Two Puzzles." *American Journal of Political Science* 30, no. 2 (1986): 357–378.

Powell, Lynda W. *The Influence of Campaign Contributions in State Legislatures: The Effects of Institutions and Politics*. Illustrated ed. Ann Arbor: University of Michigan Press, 2012.

Primo, David M., and Jeffrey D. Milyo. *Campaign Finance and American Democracy: What the Public Really Thinks and Why It Matters*. 1st ed. Chicago: University of Chicago Press, 2020.

Rae, Douglas. "A Note on the Fractionalization of Some European Party Systems." *Comparative Political Studies* 1, no. 3 (October 1, 1968): 413–418. https://doi.org/10.1177/001041406800100305.

Rae, Douglas W. *The Political Consequences of Electoral Laws*. 2nd ed. New Haven, CT: Yale University Press, 1971.

Ramírez González, Victoriano, Blanca Luisa Delgado Márquez, and Adolfo López Carmona. "Electoral System in Poland: Revision and Proposal of Modification Based on Biproportionality." *Representation* 51, no. 2 (April 3, 2015): 187–204. https://doi.org/10.1080/00344893.2015.1056217.

Rawls, John. *Political Liberalism*. New York: Columbia University Press, 2025.

Reiljan, Andres. "'Fear and Loathing Across Party Lines' (Also) in Europe: Affective Polarisation in European Party Systems." *European Journal of Political Research* 59, no. 2 (2020): 376–396. https://doi.org/10.1111/1475-6765.12353.

Reiljan, Andres, Diego Garzia, Frederico Ferreira Da Silva, and Alexander H. Trechsel. "Patterns Of Affective Polarization Toward Parties And Leaders Across the Democratic World." *American Political Science Review* (June 29, 2023): 1–17.

Reilly, Benjamin. "Centripetalism and Electoral Moderation in Established Democracies." *Nationalism and Ethnic Politics* 24, no. 2 (2018): 201–221.

Reilly, Benjamin, David Lublin, and Glenn Wright. "Alaska's New Electoral System: Countering Polarization or 'Crooked as Hell'?" *California Journal of Politics and Policy* 15 (2023).

Reilly, Briana. "Johnson Calls Senate Border Deal 'Dead on Arrival' in House." *Roll Call*. January 26, 2024.

Reiter, Howard L. *Selecting the President: The Nominating Process in Transition*. Philadelphia: University of Pennsylvania Press, 1985.

Ridout, Travis N., Michael M. Franz, and Erika Franklin Fowler. "Sponsorship, Disclosure, and Donors: Limiting the Impact of Outside Group Ads." *Political Research Quarterly* 68, no. 1 (March 1, 2015): 154–166.

Riera, Pedro, and Marco Pastor. "Cordons Sanitaires or Tainted Coalitions? The Electoral Consequences of Populist Participation in Government." *Party Politics* 28, no. 5 (September 2022): 889–902. https://doi.org/10.1177/13540688211026526.

Rocca, Michael S., and Jared W. Clay. "Allocating Unlimited Money: What Explains Super PAC Spending in Congressional Elections?" *The Forum* 19, no. 2 (September 1, 2021): 229–252.

Rogers, Steven. *Accountability in State Legislatures*. Chicago: University of Chicago Press, 2023.

Rogowski, Jon, and Joseph Sutherland. "How Ideology Fuels Affective Polarization." *Political Behavior* 38, no. 2 (2016): 485–508. https://doi.org/10.1007/s11109-015-9323-7.

Rosenblum, Nancy. "'Extremism' and Anti-extremism in American Party Politics." *Journal of Contemporary Legal Issues* 12 (2002): 843–886.

Samples, John Curtis. *The Fallacy of Campaign Finance Reform*. Chicago: University of Chicago Press, 2006.

Sandbu, Martin. "Europe's Cordon Sanitaire Against the Far Right May Not Work." *Financial Times*. June 30, 2024.

Santucci, Jack. *More Parties or No Parties*. New York: Oxford University Press, 2022.

Sartori, Giovanni. *Parties and Party Systems: A Framework for Analysis*. Cambridge: Cambridge University Press, 1976.

Schaffner, Brian F., and Raymond J. La Raja. *Campaign Finance and Political Polarization: When Purists Prevail.* Ann Arbor: University of Michigan Press, 2015.

Scheppele, Kim Lane. "The Party's Over." In *Constitutional Democracy in Crisis?*, edited by Mark Graber, Sanford Levinson, and Mark Tushnet, 1:495–515. Oxford University Press, 2018. https://doi.org/10.1093/law/9780190888985.003.0028.

Schiller, Wendy J. *Partners and Rivals: Representation in US Senate Delegations.* Princeton, NJ: Princeton University Press, 2000.

Schlesinger, Joseph. *Ambition and Politics: Political Careers in the United States.* Chicago: Rand McNally and Co., 1966.

Schneider, Gerald, and Nina Wiesehomeier. "Rules That Matter: Political Institutions and the Diversity—Conflict Nexus." *Journal of Peace Research* 45, no. 2 (March 2008): 183–203. https://doi.org/10.1177/0022343307087176.

Schofield, Norman, ed. *Collective Decision-Making: Social Choice and Political Economy.* Recent Economic Thought 50. Berlin: Springer Science & Business Media, 2013.

Sebold, Karen, and Andrew Dowdle. "The Evolution of Independent Expenditures in U.S. Federal Elections Before and After Citizens United." *Politique américaine* 35, no. 2 (2020): 47–66.

Seddiq, Oma, and Amelia Davidson. "AI Disinformation Drives Lawmakers Fears About 2024 'Wild West.'" *Bloomberg Government.* July 20, 2023.

Selway, Joel, and Kharis Templeman. "The Myth of Consociationalism? Conflict Reduction in Divided Societies." *Comparative Political Studies* 45, no. 12 (December 2012): 1542–1571. https://doi.org/10.1177/0010414011425341.

Shafer, Byron E., and Regina L. Wagner. *The Long War over Party Structure.* New York: Cambridge University Press, 2019.

Shapiro, Ian, and Frances Rosenbluth. *Responsible Parties: Saving Democracy from Itself.* New Haven, CT: Yale University Press, 2018.

Shehaj, Albana, Adrian J. Shin, and Ronald Inglehart. "Immigration and Right-Wing Populism: An Origin Story." *Party Politics* 27, no. 2 (2021): 282–293. https://doi.org/10.1177/1354068819849888.

Shepard, Steven. "The RNC's Debate Plans Have a Major, Largely Unnoticed Problem." *Politico.* July 1, 2023.

Shepard, Steven, and Sarah Ferris. "Omar Rakes in Cash Online as Controversies Pile Up." *Politico.* April 15, 2019.

Shor, Boris, and Nolan McCarty. "Two Decades of Polarization in American State Legislatures." *Journal of Political Institutions and Political Economy* 3 (2022): 343–370.

Shugart, Matthew S., Erika Moreno, and Luis E. Fajardo. "Deepening Democracy by Renovating Political Practices: The Struggle for Electoral Reform in Colombia." In *Electoral Systems and Political Transformation in South America*, edited by Scott Mainwaring and Timothy R. Scully, 80–108. Cambridge University Press, 2004.

Siaroff, Alan. "Two-and-a-Half-Party Systems and the Comparative Role of the 'Half.'" *Party Politics* 9, no. 3 (2003): 267–290.

Sides, John, Chris Tausanovitch, Lynn Vavreck, and Christopher Warshaw. "On the Representativeness of Primary Electorates." *British Journal of Political Science* 50, no. 3 (2018): 677–685.

Simonovits, Gabor, Jennifer McCoy, and Levente Littvay. "Democratic Hypocrisy and Out-Group Threat: Explaining Citizen Support for Democratic Erosion." *Journal of Politics* 84, no. 3 (2022): 1806–1811.

Skelley, Geoffrey. "The Creative Fundraising Tactics Some Republicans Are Using to Make the Debate Stage." *FiveThirtyEight*. July 17, 2023.

Smirnov, Oleg, and James H. Fowler. "Policy-Motivated Parties in Dynamic Political Competition." *Journal of Theoretical Politics* 19, no. 1 (January 2007): 9–31. https://doi.org/10.1177/0951629807071014.

Smith, Bradley. "Disclosure in a Post–Citizens United Real World." *University of St. Thomas Journal of Law and Public Policy* 6, no. 2 (May 31, 2016): 257.

Smith, Bradley A. *Unfree Speech: The Folly of Campaign Finance Reform.* Princeton, NJ: Princeton University Press, 2009.

Sniderman, Paul M., and Edward H. Stiglitz. *The Reputational Premium: A Theory of Party Identification and Policy Reasoning.* Princeton, NJ: Princeton University Press, 2012.

Spicer, Jason S. "Electoral Systems, Regional Resentment and the Surprising Success of Anglo-American Populism." *Cambridge Journal of Regions, Economy and Society* 11, no. 1 (March 10, 2018): 115–141. https://doi.org/10.1093/cjres/rsx029.

Stanovich, Keith E., Richard F. West, and Maggie E. Toplak. "Myside Bias, Rational Thinking, and Intelligence." *Current Directions in Psychological Science* 22, no. 4 (August 2013): 259–264. https://doi.org/10.1177/0963721413480174.

Staudenmaier, Rebecca, and Sabine Kinkartz. "Satisfaction in German Government Plummets." *DW*. September 1, 2023.

Stephanopoulos, Nicholas. "Finding Condorcet." *Washington and Lee Law Review* (forthcoming).

Stephanopoulos, Nicholas O. *Aligning Election Law.* New York: Oxford University Press, 2024.

Tam Cho, Wendy K., and James G. Gimpel. "Prospecting for (Campaign) Gold." *American Journal of Political Science* 51, no. 2 (2007): 255–268.

Thomsen, Danielle M. "Competition in Congressional Elections: Money Versus Votes." *American Political Science Review* 117, no. 2 (2023): 675–691.

———. *Opting Out of Congress: Partisan Polarization and the Decline of Moderate Candidates.* Cambridge: Cambridge University Press, 2017.

Thomsen, Danielle M., and Michele L. Swers. "Which Women Can Run? Gender, Partisanship, and Candidate Donor Networks." *Political Research Quarterly* 70, no. 2 (June 1, 2017): 449–463.

Tokaji, Daniel P., and Renata E. B. Strause. *The New Soft Money: Outside Spending in Congressional Elections.* Columbus: Ohio State University Michael E. Moritz College of Law, 2014.

Van Der Brug, Wouter, Meindert Fennema, and Jean Tillie. "Why Some Anti-immigrant Parties Fail and Others Succeed: A Two-Step Model of Aggregate Electoral Support." *Comparative Political Studies* 38, no. 5 (June 2005): 537–573. https://doi.org/10.1177/0010414004273928.

Van Spanje, Joost, and Wouter Van Der Brug. "The Party as Pariah: The Exclusion of Anti-immigration Parties and Its Effect on Their Ideological Positions." *West European Politics* 30, no. 5 (November 2007): 1022–1040. https://doi.org/10.1080/01402380701617431.

Vegetti, Federico. "The Political Nature of Ideological Polarization: The Case of Hungary." *ANNALS of the American Academy of Political and Social Science* 681, no. 1 (January 1, 2019): 78–96. https://doi.org/10.1177 /0002716218813895.

Verba, Sidney, Kay Lehman Schlozman, and Henry E. Brady. *Voice and Equality: Civic Voluntarism in American Politics.* Cambridge, MA: Harvard University Press, 1995.

Vogel, Kenneth P., and Shane Goldmacher. "Democrats Decried Dark Money. Then They Won with It in 2020." *New York Times.* January 29, 2022.

Wagner, Aiko. "Party System Change in Eastern and Western Germany Between Convergence and Dissimilarity." *German Politics* 32 (2023).

Wagner, Michael W., and Mike Gruszczynski. "Who Gets Covered? Ideological Extremity and News Coverage of Members of the U.S. Congress, 1993 to 2013." *Journalism & Mass Communication Quarterly* 95, no. 3 (September 1, 2018): 670–690.

Ward, Dalston G., and Margit Tavits. "How Partisan Affect Shapes Citizens' Perception of the Political World." *Electoral Studies* 60 (August 1, 2019).

Ware, Alan. *The American Direct Primary.* New York: Oxford University Press, 2002.

Wittman, Donald. "Candidate Motivation: A Synthesis of Alternative Theories." *American Political Science Review* 77, no. 1 (March 1983): 142–157. https://doi.org/10.2307/1956016.

Wolak, Jennifer. *Compromise in an Age of Party Polarization.* New York: Oxford University Press, 2020.

Wood, Abby K. "Voters Use Campaign Finance Transparency and Compliance Information." *Political Behavior* 45, no. 4 (December 1, 2023): 1553–1579.

Wood, Abby K., and Christian R. Grose. "Campaign Finance Transparency Affects Legislators' Election Outcomes and Behavior." *American Journal of Political Science* 66, no. 2 (2022): 516–534.

Wunsch, Natasha, and Theresa Gessler. "Who Tolerates Democratic Backsliding? A Mosaic Approach to Voters' Responses to Authoritarian Leadership in Hungary." *Democratization* 30, no. 5 (July 4, 2023): 914–937. https:// doi.org/10.1080/13510347.2023.2203918.

Young, Andrew. *The Politician: An Insider's Account of John Edwards's Pursuit of the Presidency and the Scandal That Brought Him Down.* New York: St. Martin's Press, 2010.

Contributors

Robert G. Boatright is professor of political Science at Clark University, and director of research at the National Institute for Civil Discourse, University of Arizona.

Larry Diamond is senior fellow at the Hoover Institution, and Mosbacher Senior Fellow at the Freeman Spogli Institute for International Studies, Stanford University.

Lee Drutman is senior fellow in the political reform program at New America.

Edward B. Foley is Charles W. Ebersold and Florence Whitcomb Ebersold Chair in Constitutional Law and director of election law at Moritz College of Law, Ohio State University.

Ray La Raja is professor of political science and codirector of UMass Poll, University of Massachusetts Amherst.

Frances Lee is professor of politics and public affairs at Princeton University.

Richard H. Pildes is Sudler Family Professor of Constitutional Law at New York University School of Law.

Index

About the Book

In the midst of the political ugliness that has become part of our everyday reality, are there steps that can be taken to counter polarization and extremism—practical steps that are acceptable across the political spectrum? To answer that question, starting from the premise that the way our political processes are designed inevitably creates incentives for certain styles of politics and candidates, the Task Force on American Electoral Reform spent two years exploring alternative ideas for reforming key aspects of the US electoral process. The results of their work are presented in this essential book.

Larry Diamond is Mosbacher Senior Fellow at the Freeman Spogli Institute and William L. Clayton Senior Fellow at the Hoover Institution, Stanford University. **Edward B. Foley** is Ebersold Chair in Constitutional Law and director of Election Law program in the Moritz College of Law, Ohio State University. **Richard H. Pildes** is Sudler Family Professor of Constitutional Law in the School of Law, New York University.